OSHO, India and Me

A Tale of Sexual and Spiritual Transformation

OSHO, India and Me

A Tale of Sexual and Spiritual Transformation

Jack Allanach
Swami Krishna Prem

NIYOGI BOOKS

in collaboration with

OSHO World Foundation

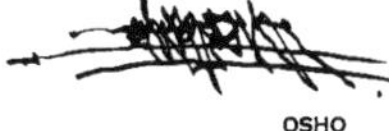

OSHO

Published by

NIYOGI BOOKS

D-78, Okhla Industrial Area, Phase-I
New Delhi-110 020, INDIA
Tel: 91-11-26816301, 49327000
Fax: 91-11-26810483, 26813830
email: niyogibooks@gmail.com
website: www.niyogibooks.com

In collaboration with

OSHO

Osho World Foundation,
C-5/44, Safdarjung Development Area,
New Delhi-110016
Phone: 91-11-26862898, 26964533
Email: contact@oshoworld.com
Website: www.oshoworld.com

ISBN: 978-93-81523-58-2
Publication: 2013

Author's note:
To protect the privacy of certain individuals, at their request some names in this book have been changed. The names marked with an asterisk (*) have also been changed and are fictional.

Printed at: Niyogi Offset Pvt. Ltd., New Delhi, India

To the legacy of Osho

The master follows you even in your nights and in your dreams. He is like a shadow constantly watching what is happening, whether you are aware of his watching or not. And you will not be aware, because it is such a subtle thing.

Osho

My Way: The Way of the White Clouds

Contents

Foreword

MA DHYAN SOURABH

The book you are about to read has its own interesting story. Thirty years ago Jack, then known as Krishna Prem, lived in India, at the commune of the enlightened mystic Osho, where he was head of the press office. In 1980 Osho asked him to write "a little book" about his experience in Pune.

Reliving his search that would lead him to India and the challenges of embarking on the spiritual path, the excitement of discovering meditation and the early years with Osho—all became part of a growing manuscript that was typed on a red Olivetti Valentine.

When the Osho commune moved to the USA, the manuscript was left behind and forgotten. During a visit to Pune in the early nineties Divyananda, by serendipity, came across the "forgotten" work and returned it to Krishna Prem.

Several years later while preparing *Osho, India and Me* for publication he scanned the text page by page into the computer and started his edit, finishing three weeks before his death in September 2007.

To bring his work to completion we finished the edit and many friends have helped us along the way with their expertise and support. Our warmest thanks go to Pratima, Pramod, Sangeet, Dhanyam, John, Paul Allanach and Michael Mann.

When finalizing the manuscript, Krishna Prem's voice, his incredibly acute observations and his humour, his ability for poetry and his unique storytelling gift have led us, time and time again, in waves of laughter, tears, and delight. And for me, Sourabh, the pangs of missing him.

In this timeless account set in India, Krishna Prem tells the story of a Master at work with a willing disciple.

I come not to teach but to awaken.
Surrender and I will transform you.
This is my promise.

Osho

Text of a banner hanging above Osho's chair at the last meditation camp he conducted in person at the Bikaner Palace Hotel in Mount Abu, Rajasthan in January 1974.

Chapter One: 1973-1974

BOMBAY

The first time I see him he is reading *Zorba the Greek.*

He sits in an orange armchair in the far corner of the room, legs crossed, the novel resting lightly on one knee. Apart from the single chair, a shelf of books, and a wide bed that lies close to the floor like a futon, the room is empty.

At the sound of the door closing behind me, he looks up, setting the book aside. A smile of welcome lights his face. He motions me to a spot on the floor beside him.

Crossing to him I am surprised—he doesn't appear Indian at all. His complexion is pale, almost European, as if he never sees the sun. He is bald; his forehead high and smooth, without lines or wrinkles. From his temples a circle of hair begins, black laced with silver, falling in wispy, curling tendrils to his broad shoulders, mingling with his beard and the fine mat of dark hair that coats his bare, athletic chest. Around his waist, a lunghi of white cotton is knotted; across his shoulders a cream towel lays, protection against the draft of the air conditioner that hums hoarsely behind his head.

Dropping awkwardly to the floor, I am surprised. This is not the frail ascetic I'd expected. This man's body is stocky, compact. It gives the impression of power, of virility, of strength. But at the same time there is a softness, a serenity about him.

He reaches down to take my hand in his, his eyes never leaving my face. Long, elegant fingers enfold mine in a clasp that is at once infinitely gentle and inescapably firm. I feel nervous, uncomfortable; all I want is for him to let my hand go. Then he asks me something.

But I cannot hear the question. The second our eyes met I'd exploded inside, my ears filling with an all-consuming roar. And then, like a far off sound cutting through the crashing waves of emotion, a distant voice had repeated a single word over and over again: Superman! Superman! Superman!

As the storm abates I realize with a new clarity that I am sitting in front of a being unlike any I have ever encountered before. He simply watches me, smiling, his eyebrows arching.

"Osho," I manage at last, my voice strangely thick and unfamiliar, "I couldn't believe anyone like you really existed."

He chuckles, a deep rumble that seems to bubble up from his very toes. "What I am, you also are," he says quietly, leaning towards me, his eyes holding mine. "The only difference between you and me is that I have recognized it. If you allow me, I will help you recognize it too."

Yes. My head nods yes.

"Have you tried my Dynamic Meditation?" he asks, settling back in his chair.

No. My head shakes no.

"A group of people do it every morning at five-thirty on Chowpatty Beach. Just nearby," he adds, waving towards the street. "You do it for seven days and then come back and tell me what happens."

Yes. My head is nodding yes.

"And tonight I am giving a discourse here. In English. Be sure to come."

It is early November 1973. Osho lives in a single room in a three-bedroom flat in Woodlands, a luxury-apartment complex off Peddar Road in the affluent Malabar Hill section of Bombay, just alongside the Hanging Gardens and the Parsi Towers of Silence.

What brought me here, to Woodlands, was the transformation I'd seen in a friend who'd become Osho's disciple—a sannyasin he called himself. I'd known Alex for thirteen years and, on his return to Montreal from India, had been floored by the change in him. It was so impossibly great I decided, then and there, that I had to see this man for myself. My boyfriend Michael, at first reluctant, at last agreed to accompany me.

Anything I knew about Osho was sketchy. What really intrigued me was Alex's claim that Osho had become enlightened—under a tree on March 21, 1953—and that his effort, ever since, was to trigger the same phenomenon in others.

For the last five years, Alex told me, Osho had been sitting in his room, available. His thirteen years as a university professor—summer holidays and countless weekends spent wandering India, challenging, provoking—were over. And his huge outdoor lectures to tens of thousands were, I was also told, things of the past. Now, three or four times a year, usually at a hill-station within easy access from Bombay, he conducts a ten-day meditation camp and, once a month, gives a series of discourses, alternating English with Hindi, in the flat's spacious, book-lined living room.

There's a meditation camp in January and, as far as the English talks are concerned, our timing's been good—tonight's the last in the current series.

Michael and I arrive at the flat around seven to find thirty or more people already there, cross-legged on the carpeted floor, awaiting Osho's arrival. Everyone is silent; many have their eyes closed. Somewhat self-consciously we join them, neither of us fully recovered from our afternoon meetings with him. Where I'd exploded, Michael told me his entire face had become a single, spasmodic, uncontrollable tic. And, as I'd been instructed, he was also told to do the Dynamic Meditation for a week before returning to see Osho.

There are very few Westerners in the room. Except for a couple of white-haired ladies I'd seen earlier that day, I can only pick out three or four foreigners whose ages approximate ours, their blond and brown mops standing out amidst the sea of sleek black heads that fill the air with the heavy sweetness of coconut oil. Many of the Indians are in ordinary clothes, but most wear orange and a mala, the string of wooden beads ending in a tiny oval locket that carries a photo of Osho.

A tremor of excitement sweeps the audience and, suddenly, he is there, his face radiant, his palms meeting in namaste, in the Indian greeting. He moves noiselessly across the room to the space in the centre where a chair awaits. Crossing his legs, he leaves one sandal behind him on the floor. An Indian lady leans forward to touch it, bringing her cupped hand, as if it carried something of him, first to her forehead, then to her heart. Laxmi, his secretary, breaks the silence with the mechanical click of a cassette recorder. Someone starts to sing, a verse from the *Upanishads*. When the voice stops, Osho begins to speak.

To listen to the words is impossible. The presence transfixes me, holds me rapt. He is electric, kinetic. The sense of light is extraordinary. From some deep inner source it seems to come, surfacing through translucent flesh that appears to be fashioned from the finest, palest porcelain. His hands are never still. Pointing, punctuating, they weave mystery in the air.

A superman. A new kind of being. Unexpected. Inexplicable.

And then words begin to form, to take shape. "You never set out to discover who you are until you realize you are not who you thought you were," I hear him saying. "This realization is a kind of awakening. You awaken to the fact that what you really are is different from what you always thought yourself to be. And this moment of awakening often comes in times of crisis..."

There is the slightest pause as his eyes scan the audience and find mine.

"...like in a car accident."

And suddenly it all disappears—him, the room, Bombay, everything—and I am there again, in the middle of a spinning mass of twisting metal, smashing over and over again into a steel guard-rail on the rain-soaked New York State Thruway.

One April afternoon, a few hours after announcing to my partner in the public relations firm we owned that I wanted out of the company and out of the whole superficial industry, I set out from Montreal in my MG for a long weekend in New York. Just over a hundred miles short of Manhattan, skimming along at eighty-five despite the darkness and the spring downpour, a front tire blew.

The force of the blow-out sent the car into a spin, and throwing my weight to the other side was all that had kept it from rolling over onto the soft canvas roof. And like a rubber ball tied to a wooden paddle, the little white roadster rammed the rail again and again, the momentum of each collision whirling it back for more.

Aloud, I heard my voice say in wonder, "So this is how I die!" I'd always been curious—now I knew. And exactly as they tell it in novels, my life passed before me like a speeded-up strip of film—episode upon episode, scene after scene.

I knew there was nothing to be done. There was no one to hear my scream; there was no one to reverse the inevitable. I knew no great hand was going to scoop down from the sky and lift me aloft to safety. And with that understanding came a great acceptance. I simply surrendered. I said okay, relaxed, and waited for death.

Then my mind stopped. And all that remained was silence. The word "silence" had always meant the absence of sound to me, but this was different. This silence was full and rich and literally pulsating with unmanifest life. And there was nothing else. There was no mind, no body, just a tiny point of light, and that point of light was *me*. And the light! Light enveloped me like a protective shield. I sat there, still and peaceful at the centre of a raging storm. I sat there, filled with a silence of a depth and profundity I had never imagined. I sat there, bliss bubbling up in me from the inner silence, surrounded and sheltered by a column of dancing, sparkling light.

After a while I became aware that the car had come to rest. And then I knew, for the very first time, that there was more to life than I had known.

"...like in a car accident," Osho is saying, his gaze fixed on me.

And now, almost two years later, I realize that finally and at long last I have come home.

At five o'clock on a Bombay morning, nothing much is stirring but the rats. They scurry here and there over mounds of rubble, back and forth across the empty streets, breakfasting on shreds of chappati and bits of fruit skins tossed into the gutters from the cafés the night before. The taxi drivers are still asleep in the backs of their cabs, feet tangled in steering wheels or dangling, bare and callused, from open windows. Smothered in ragged blankets, row upon row like sailors awaiting burial at sea, beggars line the silent sidewalks. No breeze carries freshness into the slumbering city.

The air is rank, stale with yesterday's sweat and petrol fumes. From the temple at the corner come the sound of clanging bells and the pungent smell of burning sandalwood.

We rouse a Sikh driver and tell him we want to go to Chowpatty Beach. Striking a match, he checks his watch in disbelief: "Chowpatty going?"

"Chowpatty," Michael verifies.

Smoothing the sleep from his beard and straightening his turban in the mirror, he finally manages to turn the engine over. And shaking and sputtering, with windows rattling, handles clacking and the seat slipping forward at every stop and start, we ricochet out of Colaba, turning onto the sweep of Marine Drive towards Chowpatty.

The air from the sea is a gift: it pours through the open window in great gulping gusts, heavy with salt. The arc of Marine Drive is in virtual darkness, the occasional light giving no indication of the spectacular night-time display, of what Bombay calls the Queen's Necklace, of that dazzling chain of electric jewels that rings the seafront after sundown, sparkling in reflection on the moonlit waves.

By five-twenty we jerk to a halt at Chowpatty. Gasping, the engine coughs itself to silence. Mid-way between the street and the sea, on a stretch of brown sand just beyond a line of grey stone benches, I can make out a group of people, the orange of their clothing luminous in the half-light. Off to one side, huddled around a tiny fire, a few Indian sadhus squat. Thin ochre lunghis partly cover their bony bodies; long, matted snakes of dirty hair fall about their shoulders; streaks of pigment, deep red and bright yellow, are smeared in Hindu symbols across their foreheads. Beside one, a Vishnu trident stands, speared into the sand. They call out, laughing, as we head towards the sea.

"Ten minutes of deep, fast, chaotic breathing through the nose," a lilting Indian voice explains out of the semi-darkness. "Then, explode into ten minutes of catharsis. Scream, cry, laugh—let whatever arises in body be expressed. For ten minutes, shout the sound 'Hoo!', letting it hammer above sex centre. And when I call 'Stop!' stop. Just freeze in whatever posture you are in and let energy move within; let energy carry you into meditation. Now," the voice drops, instructions complete, "everyone should be wearing blindfold."

Suddenly the beach is alive with gyrating bodies, filled with the rasping sound of breathing—in and out through the nose, in and out, in and out, like a thousand saws felling a forest. *This is insane,* I tell myself. *What am I doing here on this filthy Bombay beach in the middle of the night with a bunch of loonies in orange robes? They're all quite crazy!*

"...like in a car accident," I hear Osho say once again.

"Aw, what the hell!" I shout into the faintly reddening sky. And, donning my blindfold with the rest of them, I dive into the madness too.

"Good catharsis happen?" Laxmi inquires, grinning broadly behind her little secretarial desk as we walk into Woodlands that afternoon. I mutter something inaudible; I haven't a clue what she means—the word "catharsis" might as well be Hindi to me. "Sit," she invites, pointing to the sofa beside her, and sends the Gurkha servant, Gaghan Singh, to bring tea. By the time the steaming, all-milk chai arrives, spiced with ginger and cloves and cardamom and generously laced with sugar, she's introduced us to a few of the Westerners we'd seen at the discourse the evening before.

Mostly they're older and, to my mind, a bit weird. There's a pear-shaped Swiss-Italian with hips like the Matterhorn, and her snow-haired mother. The mother speaks no English; the daughter is simply rude. There's a swarthy American lady whose face resembles a prune, a spacey young blonde sitting in the corner giggling, and a lanky black lady who waves at us from the midst of a dance she's doing, like a Jules Feiffer cartoon, to the bookshelves. Michael and I exchange glances, wondering what we're doing here.

Down the hall, carrying a tea tray towards Osho's room, is a slim young woman I'd seen taking a stack of books to him yesterday. She'd intrigued me. She was somewhere in her mid-twenties, I'd judged, with fine English-schoolgirl features softly framed by deep bangs of light-brown hair that, in the back, fall straight past her shoulders. But it had been her face that had captured my attention. She radiated a mysterious, enigmatic beauty, giving at one and the same time a feeling of fragility and strength. Clad in a dark orange shift, the mala about her neck, she moves back and forth from Osho's room to another, hidden part of the flat, soundlessly, eyes downcast, intent on something that has only to do with her. Apart from Laxmi and a few Indian men bent over manuscripts, she appears to be the only other permanent member of the household. "Who's that?" I ask.

"Ma Vivek," Laxmi replies. "From England. Her work is to look after his body." Whatever that entails remains unsaid.

"Ah! Ma Mukta!" Laxmi calls, turning towards the doorway. Michael and I stand to greet her. We'd met Mukta the day before and liked her immediately. Both she and Laxmi have a soft spot for my friend Alex, and they are warm and friendly, making us feel welcome and at ease.

Mukta, approaching fifty, her mane of salt-and-pepper hair, deep-throated "h" and olive skin betraying her Greek origins, has just moved from New York to Bombay. She's worldly, sophisticated and easy to talk to. Laxmi, on the other hand, is a bit more difficult. Her English is fine, but she has the most disconcerting habit of referring to herself in the third person singular.

And totally ignoring any idea of doing, she also tends to look upon every action as a "happening", as some sort of unmotivated cosmic occurrence.

"And when is sannyas going to happen?" she asks cheerfully, retying her orange headscarf for the umpteenth time. I look at her blankly, not knowing what to reply. She laughs, smoothing the ankle-length skirt that, combined with the bandana and loose over-shirt, makes her look like a little Indian schoolgirl on her way to a costume party disguised as an English hospital matron. "Sannyas is love affair," she says, her brown eyes twinkling. "Sannyas is love affair with Master. And sannyas is trapless trap. And Laxmi can tell," she guffaws, slapping my knee with gusto, "trapping has already happened!"

"She can go on like this for hours," Mukta laughs, standing. "I'm going into the city to do some shopping. Can I drop you somewhere, or do you want to stay here and let Laxmi practice her missionary work on you?"

We opt for the drive downtown.

And so the week passes. Every morning it's up at five and out to Chowpatty.

By the third day the Sikh driver is waiting for us when we step into the street. After the Dynamic, we invariably breakfast at the New York Café near the beach. A sign above the cash register advises us it's a Grade Two eatery, but it's passably clean, and what's more important after an hour cavorting on the sand, it's close.

We begin to learn the vagaries of Indian restaurants. The first and cardinal rule is that any deviation from the menu card is unheard of and any attempt thereat, a grave and unforgivable insult. We learn that "ek plate fried egg" is considered acceptable Marathi, that "single fry" means sunny-side-up and that "double fry" is the signal to turn them over and let them sizzle until the yolks solidify. We learn that "toast-butter" means dry toast with butter on the side—the way I like it—but that "toast-butter-jam" brings soggy little fingers of toasted bread dripping with a fake strawberry preserve, horrific in its sweetness.

And we learn to be very specific ordering tea. There's "half-cup" and there's "full-cup", where they fill the saucer too, but if I don't want it sweet and spicy and all pre-mixed, if I want to put my own milk and sugar in like a grownup, I learn to ask for "tea on tray". We learn, too, to pronounce Nescafe as "Ness-coffee" and discover its availability is a source of such national pride that it comes as a haughty brown raft on a lake of hot milk—a guarantee of its authenticity, proof one isn't taken for a ride.

And I begin to enjoy Bombay and her people. The Westernised Indians, the types that staff the shops around the Gateway to India and pose as puffed-up maître d's in the Grade One restaurants are, frankly, in their fifties' fashions gleaned from the films, pains in the ass. But beyond the façade of Gothic office buildings, Victorian emporiums, Edwardian townhouses and deco apartment blocks, in the teeming maze of unnumbered, unlimited laneways fanning out behind the English legacy, we find the real Indians, fresh and friendly, amazingly open and insatiably curious—and I delight in them.

Michael has agreed to buy fabrics for a friend with a shop in Madrid and we spend our mornings in Chor Bazaar, Bhindi Bazaar and the maze of Crawford Market, sitting cross-legged on white cushions, sipping spicy chai, watching meter after meter of silk and satin and cotton sent fluttering across the floor with a flourished flick of a practiced wrist to land, unfurled, at our feet.

Poring over lengths of hand-embroidered braid; waving wads of cotton-soaked scent, of patchouli and myrrh and attar of roses, under his nose; gleaning the best from a sidewalk pile of second-hand silk saris; testing the nap of Kashmiri and Tibetan carpets; walking away from the Rajasthani gypsies and their multi-coloured mirrored panels only to turn back at the shout of a better price, I watch Michael at play. And I watch the people he is playing with.

The Indians love to bargain; I see the disappointment on their faces when a tourist pays the first price asked. Business is a game. Buy, don't buy—it appears to make little difference. A game is not to be taken seriously; a game is to be enjoyed. Tossing prices back and forth, Michael's in his element. "I love this," he glows, adding another package to my already overfull arms. "I am half-Jewish after all. Never really got into it before." He spies a peddler with a mound of Kutchi wall-hangings and with a lip-smacking "Yum!" is off again across the street, the bumper-to-bumper traffic ignored at the prospect of yet another find.

Following, taking my own time, I remember people I'd met in Montreal who'd hung out in India. I'd been impressed with their lack of speediness, with how laid-back they were. And I'm beginning to understand. The average Westerner could easily go berserk in India—three hours to cash a traveller's check, a day of countless forms to make a train reservation or post a parcel, hotel clerks who insist on finishing their tea in peace before acknowledging one's presence, and queue upon queue upon endless queue. To accept it, to relax into it, is the only way.

And with this newfound looseness, my eyes begin to open. As a city, Bombay pulls no punches. The whole spectrum is blatantly here. Wealth and poverty, joy and misery, health and sickness, cleanliness and filth, fat and emaciation, life and death—all rub shoulders in her steaming streets. In the West we hide our feeble and deformed in institutions, herd our aged into homes, paint our dead to resemble the living—trying to create a make-believe world where age and disease and death do not exist. And when nature finally has her way, we weep and wail, helpless in our frustration. In Bombay, for the first time, I am in a society where life is accepted as it is—death along with birth, famine along with feast, pleasure along with pain. I am in a land where the human condition is on parade, as it is, no holds barred; where man's puny judgments—right and wrong, good and bad, ugly and beautiful—pale in the presence of a greater reality.

And I am grateful. After all, I have come to India to find the real.

About Osho, there is a little anxiousness—anxiousness to see him, anxiousness at the prospect. We've met a few people, but apart from afternoon chats with Laxmi and Mukta, we keep pretty much to ourselves. With no more discourses at Woodlands, evenings are spent quietly, sampling Punjabi, Gujarati and South Indian foods, inventing new fruit-drink combinations at Dipti's juice bar—Michael's pièce de résistance is apple, grape and pomegranate—and taking long walks along the seawall in front of the Taj Mahal Hotel. And, suddenly, lying in bed one night, it strikes me that the week is over. It hits Michael at the same time. "Tomorrow's the seventh day," I hear from across the room.

"Yes, I know," I reply. "I know."

"Tell me what's been happening in the meditation," he says, almost before we position ourselves on the floor in front of him. I mutter a few inanities about seeing blue lights and viewing things differently than before. Michael is equally vague.

"Mmm," Osho murmurs. "And how about sannyas?"

I can't. I just can't, I think. *Whether he knew about the car accident or not, I can't wear one of those stupid orange robes with that tacky plastic picture. I absolutely cannot!* Aloud I say, "But I don't understand what it means"—evasion seeming the tactic best suited to the difficult situation.

"And how about you?" he asks, turning to Michael, ignoring me for the moment.

There is a moment of deep, almost tangible silence as Michael's gaze meets Osho's. And, beginning to laugh quietly, never taking his eyes from his, Michael simply shrugs his shoulders. "Why not?" he answers.

Leaning back in his chair, Osho picks up a felt-tip pen and a clipboard and begins to write on a sheet of paper. When he is finished, he calls Michael closer, places a mala about his neck and the paper in his hand. Craning forward, I can make out some Hindi lettering with Roman characters underneath, and across the bottom, those electrocardiogram-like lines Osho uses as a signature.

"This will be your new name," he says with such love in his voice I think I may cry. "Swami Divyananda. Divya means divine; ananda means bliss. Divyananda: divine bliss."

Then he swings back to me again. "And now, how about you?"

Trapless trap, Laxmi had said. There is no way out. I want what Osho has, and if the robe and the mala are the price, then the price has to be paid. I give up. "Why not?" I reply, echoing Michael.

Once again, the pen, the clipboard, the total absorption as he forms the letters on the page—and I am completely blank. I seem to be floating will-less, in some kind of in-between place. And then, suddenly, there's a mala about my neck as well.

"This will be your new name: Swami Krishna Prem. The love of Krishna."

Krishna! Krishna? Visions of clanging bells and cymbals and whirling orange bands of shaven-headed freaks on Canadian street corners immediately fill my head. Krishna? And Prem? It reminds me of canned meat.

"Krishna Prem," he repeats. "Will it be easy to pronounce?"

Forget pronouncing: looking is all I can get together. The Hare Krishnas have gone and everything's blank again.

"Good," he says, settling back in his chair, the formalities concluded, "now we can get to work. Tell me, what are you doing in Bombay?"

"Nothing really," Michael—Divyananda—answers, seeing that I'm useless for the time being. "I'd very much like to go to the country."

"Good," Osho replies. "We have friends in the country with an ashram where you can stay. It's in Lonavla—Laxmi will give you a letter—and it's only two hours by train from Bombay so you can come and see me easily if you need to. And stay at least three weeks; there's a meditation camp in Mount Abu in January and I want to prepare you for it. If you're ready I can teach you in eight days what would otherwise take eight years."

Now he is talking my language! I want knowledge, wisdom, secrets. I am all ears.

"In the morning, do the Dynamic Meditation, and in the afternoon, just lie on the ground and talk gibberish into the sky. Just let the sounds come; don't bother whether they are words or not. Do this for twenty minutes; the second twenty minutes, watch the sky within."

Sky within? What sky within?

"And then," he continues—and I'm sure I spy a twinkle at my reaction—"in the evening, just before you go to bed, put my picture in front of you and gaze at it without blinking for at least forty minutes." He raises his hand to arrest the protest I feel starting up in me. "Tears will come, but don't stop; don't close the eyes. The tears are an automatic mechanism to keep the eyes moist. Then, close the eyes and watch the energy moving inside."

He seems to be finished. I have to get away to digest all of this. I stand to leave.

"And one more thing," he says, motioning me back to the floor. "While you're there, during the three weeks, don't read."

Fine.

"And don't write. Not even letters."

After a moment's hesitation, I concede that this is also fine.

"And don't talk," he concludes, chuckling.

Don't talk! For three weeks! But at this point it isn't really a problem anyway. I couldn't speak right now even if I wanted to. I am totally and utterly speechless.

The next morning the Sikh is also speechless. He takes in the stiff, new orange robes in silent amazement and swings wordlessly into the street.

"V.T." I say. "Victoria Terminus."

"No Chowpatty going?" he asks, looking over his shoulder.

"No, V.T." I reply. "Lonavla going."

Lonavla

A tonga is at best a curious conveyance, particularly if one prefers to face what's coming rather than what one is leaving behind. But it's what's available. At our request for transport to Tulsi Sadhana Kutir, our destination for three wordless weeks, the driver of the single taxi at the Lonavla station jerks a dismissing thumb towards his only colleague in the compound. And despite my conviction the archaic springs will never hold, we find ourselves lurching along at a steady clip and a somewhat erratic clop—the pony has a penchant for veering to the right—the vista of Lonavla unfolding at our feet.

Nestling as she does on the edge of the Western Ghat, just before it begins its steep descent from the Deccan Plateau to sea level, a rich monsoon leaves Lonavla lush for months after the rainy season has come and gone. Her warm days and cool nights are a welcome relief from the sweltering coastal metropolis, and Lonavla is a favourite weekend and vacation spot for affluent Bombayites. And up sloping hills and down gentle valleys, shaded by ancient banyans and flanked by banks of cascading ferns, we amble past rose-covered cottages, mansions festooned with twisted knots of flowering vines, veranda-wrapped villas trellised with waving fronds of bougainvillea in red and purple and gold—the cluck, cluck, cluck of the driver at our backs.

Then, rounding a corner and rocking across the railroad tracks, the scene abruptly changes. I turn to see, beyond the driver, sparse brown fields stretching wide on either side, falling here and there in sudden sharp slashes into the dark mouths of hidden crevasses only to rise again, further on, climbing upwards to merge with the cliffs and boulders of the tabletop sierra that rings the valley through which we ride.

"Tulsi Sadhana Kutir," the driver says, pointing ahead, speaking for the first time. "This last hill."

"From 'Ingaland' coming?" he inquires over his shoulder.

"No," I reply. "Canada."

"No British?" He sounds disappointed.

I shake my head.

"India better when British here," he confides. "Not so good now."

Cresting the hill and dipping downwards, we see a man, tall and lean, standing by the roadside, silhouetted in the afternoon sun. One foot rests, flamingo-like, on the calf of the other leg. His white dhoti sways gently in the warm November breeze.

"Guruji," the driver calls to him. "Sadhus! Foreign-side! From 'Ingaland' coming!" And he looks back at me, grinning, making me part of his secret, trusting me with his prestige.

Sparse, wood-slatted beds stand on either side of the rectangular room, a stuffed cotton mattress rolled at the foot of each. The floor is cement, grooved in squares and painted brick red in that odd Indian attempt to simulate tiles. The walls are also cement, covered with the criss-cross cracks of faded lime wash.

The back wall is high and empty. It supports, on giant pine beams, a roof of corrugated tin that slopes downward, ending outside, covering a narrow porch that runs the length of the cottage. A ceiling fan hangs from the central beam.

A single naked bulb, like a solitary sentinel, is suspended above the door. The sidewalls each have a window, a protective grill of connecting swastikas bolted to the frame.

In front is a small yard enclosed by a shoulder-high hedge of cedar. A few scraggly crotons and spindly geraniums dot the grass. A worn path of packed earth leads from the steps of the porch under an arbour of white-throated morning glories, their bright blue funnels pinching in the afternoon sun, into the compound beyond. From the doorway I can see several other huts, each with the same cement walls, the same sloping roofs. Clustered together, they lie in the shade of the big main house. It stands high to the right, a stone wall setting it apart from the cottages below.

"Harikishandas Agrawal," Guruji says, indicating the house. "Businessman. Bombay living. Ashram built for wife." He points to a marble bust of an Indian matron, her stone sari demurely shading her downcast eyes.

To the left, the property ends sharply, dropping into a shallow riverbed, dry now except for a trickle meandering down its centre. Past the gully the land rises again towards the distant hills.

"Take tea now," Guruji insists, stuffing Laxmi's letter into his shirt and shouting "Chai lao!" down the path. From the hut below I hear a kerosene stove whoosh into instantaneous action. A few moments later a woman of indeterminate age places a tray on the floor before us and backs quickly away, as if afraid to linger any longer than absolutely necessary. "My wife," Guruji mutters apologetically.

Over tea, he explains the daily drill. Two meals per day will be provided, one at noon and one at six. The room is free, compliments of the absent Harikishandas Agrawal; the meals, three rupees each a day. His wife will make us tea twice a day if we wish, he adds, or he can lend us a kerosene stove to make our own. An inveterate consumer of liquids, I choose the stove.

"Chillies?" he inquires.

"A little," Divyananda replies, well aware of the Indians' delight in tongue scorching peppers.

"Okay," he says. "Thora, thora. Little, little."

As well as being Tulsi Sadhana Kutir's caretaker, he tells us in halting English, he's the village schoolmaster. Like us, he meditates daily, but in the tradition of his Brahman caste, he won't become a sannyasin until the last years of his life. "Then," he explains, "saffron clothing and begging bowl." He waves a lean arm towards the hills. "And wandering." He falls silent for a moment, as if considering something. "Evening-times I come?" he asks after a bit. "For talking?"

I sense his loneliness, but I also sense a not-always-welcome regular visitor. Slowly I explain why Osho sent us here and what he wants us to do. "No talking. Silence."

"Ha," he says, wobbling his head from side to side in the Indian version of the Western yes-signal, indicating he understands. "Maun. Silence." He wobbles his head a little more and, with a look of resigned disappointment on his face, collects the tea things and leaves us on our own.

With Divyananda stretched out on his bed and me on mine, we talk late into the evening—about Montreal, about friends there, about Osho, about the weeks to come. And when we settle down for the night it's with the idea that after the Dynamic tomorrow morning we'll venture into Lonavla to stock up on tea, Nescafe, milk powder, sugar, candles, bidis and the like.

"We can start our silence in the afternoon," I say, drifting into sleep.

The Lonavla bazaar is, literally, on the other side of the tracks, the farthest possible cry from the stately Raj-style bungalows the tonga had drawn us past the afternoon before. We reach Lonavla by following the railway line, stepping on tie after tie, carefully avoiding the grey beds of glass-sharp stones that separate them. At one point, heeding the warning whistle, we step aside quickly to let the Deccan Queen whiz by on her way to Pune.

One long street—the buildings facing an untended bank of scraggly shrubs and bushes that hide the track—houses the Lonavla bazaar. It is a panoply of shops. Some are Western in flavour, with shelves and counters and smiling shop assistants; others are Indian, with white cotton sitting-cushions and clusters of shoes and sandals left behind at the door. Others are not really shops at all, but, suspended above the earthen street, resemble hanging steamer trunks, their doors swung open to reveal chubby little men dispensing treasures from a thousand tiny drawers.

There are tailors everywhere. They perch on ledges in front of shops, pumping ancient treadle Singers, transforming bolts of blue-white hand loomed khadi cotton into starch-stiff pyjama pants and kurtahs. In the back of other establishments, high on raised platforms with no room to stand, I spy more tailors, cross-legged, bending over machines like upscaled toys, feeding khadi into them, free hands turning the wheel that drives the needle up and down.

The street is a cacophony of noise. The sound of bleating goats, braying donkeys, tapping cobblers, mewling beggars, squalling children and fretting mothers is just the undercurrent. High above it all are the cries of scores of vendors, each with his own grating pitch, barking and bellowing, calling and cooing, extolling and entreating: buy, buy, buy.

And yet a strange harmony emerges from the apparent dissonance. A new and unfamiliar beauty surfaces through the chaos and confusion of the street. It is the beauty of contrast, the beauty of India. The yellow and blue and green of the women's saris are brighter for the dark dust underfoot; the rows of coloured tassels richer, more inviting for the grimy, blackening wall on which they hang; the panwallah's brass tray, shinier, more dazzling, more gleaming for the faded, greying cottons of the bidi-smoking, pan-chewing, spitting customers that surround him; the rasping, nasal whine of the complaining haggler making tastier, more delicious, the song of sweet mangoes the pushcart vendor sings.

That afternoon, riddled with indigestion from the flaming Lonavla lunch of pakoras and samosas deep-fried in enormous woks of bubbling peanut oil—and still recovering from the sight of a man at our table spraying a noseful of snot straight onto the floor—I get down to the serious business of meditating. I remove myself from the cottage, leaving Divy, already having begun his silence, on the porch. He is quite content with the bits of thread and cloth he is sorting for a patchwork vest he has decided to make by hand. Crossing the dry riverbed, I lie down on the grass to begin my twenty minutes of gibberish into the sky—a prelude, I expect, to a spectacular view of that unknown but promised sky within.

First an ant bites me, so I move. Then the grass is too prickly, so I move again. Finally, a half-dozen attempts later, I find a comfortable spot and, setting my watch beside me for easy checking, I begin. I had no idea just how long twenty minutes could be—it was interminable, unending—nor had I realized how difficult it could be, even for a big-mouth like me, to talk non-stop for that length of time. And there is no inner sky. When I close my eyes at last it is just black—plain, ordinary, unrelieved black. I am not at all pleased.

Divy has disappeared when I get back. Later, when he returns from doing his own gibberish meditation, he looks light and rested and that makes my mood even worse. And, ignoring my attempt to indicate my willingness to talk if he will, he goes back to his vest. For the rest of the evening I glower while he sews.

The night-time meditation, the tratak, the gazing into the eyes in Osho's picture, isn't much of a success either. I am tense, straining, fighting against my smarting eyes, my mind screaming at me to close them, simply to forget all this nonsense and shut them tight.

The first week is hell. But I can be tenacious and, somewhere inside, there is a trust in Osho that makes me persevere. And despite the rationalizations and pressures of my Western mind, I stick it out—Dynamic, gibberish, tratak, day after day. The times between meditation techniques are filled with sunrises and sunsets, with climbing the hills and wandering in the valleys, with shopping expeditions into Lonavla, pen and paper in hand like an itinerant mute, and fuelled by chai and coffee and bidi-smoking on the porch, with hour after hour spent watching the fluffy white clouds drifting by.

From deep inside things are beginning to surface—forgotten childhood incidents, adolescent events long set aside, adult experiences that have all contributed to moulding my life, to the formation of me as I know myself. And, slowly slowly, at the same time, I become aware of another presence arising in me. It's as if some interior one is watching the familiar me, simply observing, unmoved by the constant stream of thoughts and memories, of anxieties and arguments. It is faint, distant, yet undeniably there.

Then, one morning, I notice that something has changed. To say I have moved in, behind my face, is the only way I can express it. And my face becomes a mask, a set arrangement of skin and muscles grouped together into a certain topography, reflecting an inner concept I have of me for presentation to the world. A mask. A persona. A personality. "But it's not me," I see with wonder. "I am something else." I know not what or who, nor do I care. I am filled with the joy of something new. I have left the surface. There's a gap now. Inside there's this unchanging presence, and outside there's me. My inner journey has finally begun.

For the first time I also begin to see the life around me. I see it in the blades of grass, in the silent stones, in the wildflowers, heavy with blossoms, waving beside the stream. I begin to discern it in the trees as well. I can almost see the sap pulsating from hidden roots into upturned leaves, opening, like offering hands, into the unclouded azure expanse of the Indian sky. Life. It is everywhere. The same life that beats in me, fed by the same source. It's always been there, around me—but I've never seen it, never felt it before. And a kind of veil begins to lift; a new and unknown vision of reality begins to dawn in me. Watching the sun sink behind the horizon one evening, I realize that the sun isn't setting, the earth is turning. I see the trap of words. I see the snare of concepts. I see how we perpetuate the illusion that hides the real each and every day, in a thousand tiny ways. And I resolve to remember. Each time I see a sunset, I resolve to remember.

Yet the sunset has lost none of its beauty. On the contrary, it is magnified, intensified. It's as if there is nothing between us now but the communion, the fellowship of reality. The sun hangs in space, its last spreading rays bathing my body. I sit on my hill, the earth beneath me turning me slowly away, and we are brothers.

It is not all blissful in Lonavla; it is not week after week of cosmic revelations. There are some very heavy periods—the silence terminated and re-started dozens of times. And there is a great deal of pain. The cathartic stage of the Dynamic begins to release a well of emotion in me that is, at times, almost unbearable in its intensity. There is rage at my mother for dying when I was two months old, anger at my second mother for dying when I was eight, bitterness at my father for his inability to love—every unexpressed tear begging to be shed, every pent-up feeling aching to be unburdened. Day after day the flood is newly released, deep and hurting.

It is obvious it all has to be faced, purged, released, but the worst is sex, my sexuality, my going from a woman to a man, from a man to another woman, until, tired of it all, my life and career in Canada abandoned, I find myself in London with Michael.

But I look around me and it all seems so wrong, so out of tune. The boy-birds and the girl-birds, the erect stamen emerging from the soft pink petals of the hibiscus, the tall trees throwing their seeds onto the warm earth—the dance of male and female surrounds me and I am out of step. I sit in silent condemnation, impotent in my frustration, blaming my mother, blaming my father—blaming, blaming, blaming.

One morning I awaken and, silence-be-damned, announce to Divy that I am going to Bombay to see Osho. An hour later I am on the train. Three more hours and I am in his room in Woodlands, sitting on the floor in front of him. He doesn't seem surprised to see me at all. I have the distinct feeling he's been expecting me.

I get right to the point. "I don't really know why I'm here, Osho," I say, surprised at the forcefulness of my own voice. "But I had to come. I had to see you. I had to tell you that homosexuality is of the past for me and that heterosexuality is of the future. I don't know why, but I had to come to tell you that."

"That is true for you," he says, with a chuckle. "And I knew you would see it. But be patient. And don't create any conflict about it. Homosexuality is just a by-product of a society that represses sex. And your Christian and Jewish societies *do* repress sex. But don't worry. It's just a getting stuck. I'll help you to get unstuck!"

And, as if it had all been a dream, I am suddenly back in Lonavla, back in the hut with the swastikas on the window, telling Divy what has happened, telling him how I feel.

He is beautiful. "Look," he says, "it's not a problem for me. I've tried to tell you what our relationship is for me, how something happens in my heart just by being with you, just by sitting together in a room like we are now. I've tried to explain, but you've never understood. Maybe now you'll be able to.

"For me, the heart connection's always been the real thing," he continues.

"I have a really deep love for you and I want you to be happy. And the way you're moving feels good to me. Something new is happening to me too. Don't worry about me. I'm fine. Just be true to yourself."

As we sit together on the floor that evening, scooping rice and dhal from our thali plates with bits of chappati, I see what's been happening to Divy while we've been in Lonavla. I've been so preoccupied with myself I haven't noticed what's been going on with him at all.

"Ecstasy," he says, his blue eyes shining. "Ecstasy. That's all I can say. I've been in ecstasy here. Some nights I just lie on the bed writhing from it, from wave after wave of bliss. Sometimes it's so much it hurts. There's been lots of shit too, all kinds of old garbage coming up in the meditations, but the ecstasy..."

His face, glowing in the candlelight, picks up where words fail and tells me everything I need to know.

The tratak that night is easier, more relaxed, and I find myself moving way back inside, tears washing the windows that are my eyes like sporadic bursts of rain on the windscreen of a car. Osho's face, the face in the picture, is in motion tonight, changing, undulating, surging into new and unfamiliar forms and features.

Suddenly he isn't there any more and I am looking at the face of a woman. The shock is such my eyes almost close, but somehow I am able to pull back inside, to hold the vision. My heart is racing; my chest can barely contain it.

I know she is Spanish and I know it's Madrid. I've no idea how, yet I know. Her hair is black, oiled, pulled-back. Her eyes are dark, ringed with kohl; her lips, scarlet. There is torment on her face, rage and helplessness in her eyes.

And again I know. There's been too much time spent with the men from the cabaret in which she dances. There's been too little caring for her infant son. And the women of the neighbourhood, staunch Catholic matrons, have judged her unfit and taken her child away. The conflict of lust and love, of animal and spiritual, are etched in the confusion and anguish of her face.

This was *me*! Or this *is* me. I don't know how to formulate it—but I know I am seeing myself in another time. And the child I also know. Divy.

And then I am aware of other eyes. I turn. Divy is watching me.

"I remember too," he says quietly. "I could feel them taking me away. All I could see was a white wall, but I knew you were inside, on the steps. I knew they were taking me away from you."

We fall back into silence, looking at each other, simply looking. So much is clear now, so very much. But there is nothing more that can, or need, be said.

Mount Abu, Rajasthan

Nothing prepares me for the cold of Mount Abu in January. It is an insidious, all-pervading, inescapable presence. Almost tangible, it hovers in the mountain air, biting and snapping at toes and fingers and unprotected noses. It creeps into the walls, settling there in laughing derision of the weak winter sun. It lies in wait for me like some chilling torturer, stabbing at my very bones from bed sheets and stone bathroom floors. It even turns the morning tea tepid as it cascades from spout to cup. I decide to wear the wool blanket from my bed everywhere I go, promising the clerk faithfully to bring it back to the hotel at night. On that score, he needn't worry at all.

The lengthening sun begins to warm me to the beauty of Mount Abu. It rises high out of the Rajasthani desert, at its topmost point a famous Jain temple, hand-carved from white marble over the centuries. They dot the barren peaks that ring the desert, these Jain temples. Like lofty white-spired aeries to the gods, they jut into the sky, beckoning to pilgrims from the dusty plains. But Mount Abu has a second distinction. It is Rajasthan's only hill-station, the state's only refuge from the brutal sun that scorches the arid land in summer. This is not a problem at present—far from it—and so Mount Abu is ours. Here and there, orange clothes peeking out from under more hotel blankets are other sannyasins who have come a few days early, just to relax a little before beginning the ten-day meditation camp with Osho. Among the first arrivals are Prageet and Virag, a Canadian couple we'd met in Bombay, and, in the hotel room next to ours, Rani, Divy's ex-wife.

Rani and I first met in London in 1971, a couple of weeks after I'd given up my company, done my disappearing act from Montreal and found myself plunked down, futureless for the first time in my life, at Heathrow. I stayed with friends of my former secretary at a Toronto ad agency for a while and then met Divy through a mutual friend. The second time we saw each other he invited me home. On the way up in the lift he told me he was married. He'd been born in London but raised in Sweden and he and his wife, Ulla, had been friends since childhood. She had a lover, he told me, and wouldn't mind my staying there at all. I liked Ulla immediately and so, after an hour of filtered coffee and creamy cakes, I went back to the friends I'd been bunking with, collected my things and moved in.

The flat was large and airy, a kitchen, bedroom, bath and sitting room on the third floor of a Victorian brownstone on Beaufort Street, steps away from the King's Road, near where Chelsea winds into World's End. There was plenty of room in the flat, and nobody got into anyone else's hair, but after a time the strain on Ulla began to show.

At first it wasn't apparent, but it slowly began to sink in that the liberal, emancipated young Ulla was as much a façade as the streaked hair, shaved eyebrows and colour-coded Biba fashions. Underneath, she was very much in love with Michael. The longer I was there the more frequent her evening sorties to the bottle shop at the corner became, and as each new morning dawned we seemed to be putting more and more empty barley wine and sherry bottles out into the trash. And as her drinking grew, so did the number of telltale giveaways. And, ever so tentatively, emboldened by the bottle, she started to show her claws.

"Surely you know Ulla is in love with you?" I ask Michael one morning after she'd left for the office of the magazine where she works. "You must have known you couldn't give her what she wants. So why did you marry her?"

"Guilt."

"Guilt?"

"I've told you how much I dislike Sweden," he says. "I've always hated it. It's so narrow and hypocritical and dull. Ever since we were kids I had a great influence over Ulla, and I ended up turning her against Sweden and the Swedes. But it wasn't until I came to England that I saw what I'd done. At art college in Plymouth I'd get these terrible, unhappy letters from her. When I went back to Stockholm after my last semester and said I was moving to London for good, she fell apart. She begged me to take her with me. I couldn't leave her behind, in a country I'd made her hate, so I married her. It was all out of guilt."

"You knew she was in love with you?"

He runs his hands through his tousled blond hair, as if to clear his thoughts. "Yeah, I guess so. But I was straight with her. She knew I wasn't available, and it's been pretty much okay."

"But it's not okay any more, is it?"

"No," he replies quickly, his brows furrowing. "It isn't okay any more." He spreads his hands in confusion. "But what can we do?"

"Let's get out of here," I say, giving voice to a feeling that's been growing in me for days. "I need the sun and the sand and the sea. I need a beach in Spain."

And our plan to go to Ibiza was born.

We'd thrown ourselves into the project, checking fares, contacting Michael's friend Gustavo in Madrid, arranging for him to meet us in Ibiza.

We were both relieved at the prospect of getting out of London, of being by ourselves, of putting the situation in the flat behind us. A $900 income tax rebate was coming my way within the next month, and so, to tide us over and to cut his ties, Michael decided to burn his bridges behind him and liquidate the flat. The evening we told Ulla of our plans she was fine. She assured us she understood, agreeing it was best for all of us. The next morning she left for work as usual, but that night a lady from her office telephoned to say she'd freaked out at work, thrown her typewriter across the room, locked herself in the toilet and threatened to hang herself with the pull-chain. A girlfriend, knowing the scene at home, called Ulla's mother in Stockholm. She'd flown to London and taken her back to Sweden that very afternoon.

One evening, weeks later, lying on the terrace of the house we'd found in San Rafael, the Mediterranean stars twinkling brightly above us, Michael brings her up. "Ulla's been very much on my mind of late," he says. "I feel I have to write to her." And within a week or so comes her reply, warm and friendly, devoid of any hint of a grudge. The rest of our three months in Ibiza, we exchanged letters regularly.

We saw her for the first time after London when we were en route to Canada via Barcelona and Stockholm. And it had been fine.

A year later we saw her again, when we stopped off in Sweden to visit Michael's parents before travelling to India to meet Osho. She'd been fascinated by what we could tell her and, while we were in Lonavla, had written to ask if we'd meet her in New Delhi and bring her to Bombay. We'd done as she'd asked, taking the overnight train to Delhi, collecting her at Palam Airport and flying back with her to Bombay. Her first meeting with Osho, she'd taken sannyas. He named her Ma Satya Rani, the empress of truth.

Except for the cold, the three of us fall in love with Mount Abu instantly. The bus ride up the mountain—hour after hour of grinding gears and hairpin curves, of seemingly impossible inclines, of sparse vegetation and massive grey cliffs—held no promise. But all at once there'd been pines and cedars and gnarled, tangled vines, and big silver baboons lining the narrow road, jumping and barking in welcome, leaping in invitation from rock to rock as the bus continued its climb. And then, without warning, we were suddenly in a secluded tabletop paradise where groves of swaying palms bent graciously over romantic lagoons edged with pale purple lichen and cool green moss. The sense of stone was overwhelming. Primitive, primeval, it thrust through the shallow soil everywhere—dominating, asserting.

They are a rock and desert people, the Rajasthanis, given to roaming their stony hills and dusty lowlands with sheep and goats and camels, grazing them wherever their sun-bleached land yields up her rough grasses. And the town of Mount Abu, white and sparkling, hugging the mountainside in the distance, also seems to have been yielded up, as if some giant sculptor, loving his children, has carved them a tiny village from a massive block of stone.

There is a festive feeling in the town. The shopkeepers are thrilled at the off-season bonanza of Osho's sannyasins, and the tailors are beside themselves as we order this and that made up as quickly as possible to protect ourselves against the morning chill and the night-time cold. Bearers rush up and down the cobbled streets between the restaurants and the bus depot, carrying fresh produce from the markets of the plains, knees bending and turbans crushing under the weight of enormous baskets overflowing with cabbage and potatoes, spinach and cauliflower, bright red tomatoes and crimson beets. Strings of onions and wreaths of garlic are prematurely summoned from winter cellars. Withering herbs and spices and chillies are summarily thrust outside to hurry their drying in the glare of the afternoon sun.

The smell of fires fills the air—coke and wood, charcoal and cow-dung. Everything is aboil. Vats of orange dye bubble with offerings fresh from the tailors. Woks of groundnut oil sizzle and spit as each new dough-wrapped samosa drops into their churning depths. Steaming cauldrons of buffalo milk boil down, preparing for transformation into rich, sugary sweets, into balls of puffed-rice ladoo and squares of milk-fudge barfi, each royally covered with edible silver paper that evaporates like mist on the tongue.

An orange circus has come to town and, from the hills, the villagers have come: many to sell their wares; many just to look. And they are spectacular, these Rajasthani peasants. In a land devoid of colour, in a land where the hues of sand and stone predominate, they have become rainbows unto themselves.

The women, in particular, are amazing. They are skirted, layer upon layer, in reds of every conceivable shade—ruby and garnet, carmine and vermilion, cherry and tomato. Strange, armour-like constructions cover their breasts, multi-coloured boleros in intricate appliqué designs encrusted with tiny circlets of mirrored glass. Ankles are encircled in great rings of soldered silver, and their arms, first from wrist to elbow, then from elbow to shoulder, are encased in graduating bands of ivory, yellow with age. Ears and noses are pierced in several places, hole after hole dripping with silver. Jet-black hair is gathered into braids, interwoven with heavy silver pendants that hang, low, framing their faces. And they are openly curious. They look us straight in the eye, their gazes direct, assessing. There is no blushing femininity. They are pure female—raw, fiery, rooted. Rani adores them. By the second day she's pierced her ears and her nose, and bought more baubles and bangles than any woman could ever hope to wear.

The men, by contrast, are tall and lean, and they look down on us with a lofty, sharp-featured disdain as if to remind us they are descended from the great Rajput warriors. They wear white, short midriff jackets that tie in front, a parade of stiff pleats flaring down the back. Their legs are tightly wrapped in dhotis of puckered cotton, gathered at the top into taut, bulging pouches, exaggerating their maleness. On their feet are tooled leather shoes with high curling toes. But it is in their turbans they declare their supremacy, outshining even their women, with yard upon yard of the finest, sheerest cotton, wound and looped and spiralled into enormous kingly crowns of the most vivid reds and the sharpest yellows.

And the Westerners pouring into Mount Abu are as great a surprise. I had only encountered a handful in Bombay, mostly older ladies apart from Prageet and Virag, the Canadian couple we'd befriended. I had no idea of the variety of people who, like us, had joined Osho's orange family. From England and America, Scotland and Ireland, Australia and New Zealand, there are young housewives and middle-aged milkmen, porky doctors and wiry construction workers, prim nurses and loosening librarians, keen students and greying professors, tense therapists and speedy psychiatrists, and a mob of long-haired freaks of every manner and description. Here and there I hear a smattering of other accents, of French and Spanish, Dutch and German, Italian and Portuguese.

We meet in the tea stalls and the restaurants, talking, sharing stories. The lack of interest in one's personal history is remarkable. No one seems to care about the past. The sun and the tea and the food and the smiling faces are enough. And we get together in the evenings, making music, dancing, singing—each night the crowd getting greater, the energy higher, ages and creeds and nationalities drowning, disappearing into the orange river that connects us all to Osho. And suddenly, he arrives. Someone breaks into the party, calls for silence, and tells us that Osho is in Mount Abu, that he will be sleeping here tonight as well. And, as if by some unspoken yet unanimous consent, the music and the dancing are simply unresumed. Quietly, we go our separate ways, as if the inner work we have come here to do has, by his very presence among us, already begun.

The meditation camp is being held in the ballroom of the Bikaner Palace Hotel. Once a maharajah's residence, it sits high above the town, its faded grandeur overlooking the winding path that leads upwards to the Jain temple. Osho is to give a discourse on Vedanta in the mornings and respond to written questions in the evening. Two meditations are to be held in his presence each day: the Dynamic following the morning talk, a new technique after the evening session.

The first morning the ballroom fills quickly. Groups of Westerners, newfound friends, arrange themselves awkwardly on the parquet floor, tousled bushes of blond and brown and red among the black forest of sleek, oiled Indian heads. At the front is a dais for Osho. Before it, a section has been roped off—a makeshift orchestra pit for the musicians who will play for the meditations. Above Osho's armchair, suspended from the ceiling, a huge banner reads, "I come not to teach but to awaken. Surrender and I will transform you. This is my promise." The words move me deeply.

But a moment later, when Osho himself is there, under the banner, speaking, his words do not move me, but throw me into panic. They are too much, too fast. There is no space to grasp them, no time to weigh, to ponder. To digest one sentence means to miss the next. And how to choose? How to select? I am in terror of missing, and in the terror, doing just that.

Before him I am inadequate. I cannot even understand what he is saying and yet I have the temerity to aspire to be like him. The immensity of my audacity shames me to the core.

But the admission brings a kind of peace with it. There is a settling, as if a great wave has risen out of the ocean and, breaking upon the sand, leaves it smooth again, refreshed and clean. And I raise my head to him with a humility that is new to me, with the openness and willingness of one who has seen he does not know and is willing to learn.

And then his words begin to penetrate and I see that now I am truly listening—not with the mind, not worrying the words like a dog at a bone, but rather drinking them, letting them pour into me, heedless of meaning. And I feel them filling me, nourishing me in some deep and intimate inner place. I realize he is singing his song and, relaxing, I simply listen.

His words waft over me, reaching down to me, touching me, caressing me, carrying with them the perfume of his promise. "I will transform you," the banner says. And I feel my heart opening to him, like hands extended, asking him to give me what it is he knows.

A sudden flurry of movement calls me back from some inner place and only then do I notice he's stopped speaking. All around me the crowd is dispersing and people are moving towards the walls of the ballroom, dropping robes and socks and shawls and cushions into neat little orange piles, stripping themselves down to essentials for the Dynamic. In the orchestra pit, tablas tap tap tap into tautness and a violin scratches and squeaks itself into tune.

"Everyone should be blindfolded," I hear Osho say from the podium. "No one should be without blindfold."

Standing between Divy and Rani, making sure we each have enough room, I cover my eyes. There is a moment's pause, that delicious pre-Dynamic moment of expectation, and then Osho shouts, "Now! Deep, fast, chaotic breathing!" And to a burst of music that begins—not builds, but begins—at a crescendo, I am gone into the breathing.

"Deeper. Faster. Deeper. Faster," I hear Osho exhorting, his words urging us on. And I respond, throwing myself completely into it for him. Then the most extraordinary thing happens. A fragrance suddenly fills the room, as if it has been whooshed over us from some great cosmic atomizer. It is at once sweet and sharp, soft and biting, but most of all it is cool, exhilaratingly and invigoratingly cool.

I gulp it in, knowing, somehow, that it comes from him. In the back of my mind a memory stirs, something about Padmagandha, the fragrance of the lotus, the otherworldly perfume supposed to emanate from the enlightened ones. But before my head can grab onto the thought and, with its hows and whys, destroy the magic, I fill my lungs with it and keep on breathing. Deeper and faster, deeper and faster I breathe. And then a point comes where I cannot find myself any more, where the breathing is all that is happening, all that I am.

When Osho calls, "Now, explode into the second stage," I immediately begin to cry. My body falls to the floor, great sobs gurgling up, tears coursing down my cheeks from under the blindfold. Strangely, there is no identification with the crying. The tears are totally unrelated to anything; the breathing has simply released a flood. But it feels so tremendously good, just to cry. It feels so incredibly cleansing, so unburdening.

When the third stage begins, still sobbing, I pull myself to my feet with difficulty. "Hoo! Hoo!" we shout, the ballroom floor shaking under our feet. I try to let the sound hit just above the sex centre, at a point in my belly just above my genitals. I experiment a bit, move my pelvis this way and that, until all at once I find the spot. There is no mistaking: I have hit the target. And I'm off. On and on and on: "Hoo! Hoo! Hoo!" I can feel the energy mounting, moving up and up, higher and higher, becoming more and more volatile, more and more explosive.

And then, from the platform, a single command: "Stop!" And, as if a kite string has abruptly been cut, there is suddenly no movement, no sound, no nothing. Inside, the energy courses upwards for a few seconds and then it too dissolves, absorbed. And then there is only the vastness of space, and in that space, a watching.

When I finally remove the blindfold, he has gone. But, remembering his perfume, I carry him with me out of the hotel ballroom and into the bright morning sun.

The afternoon meditation we've been told to do during the ten-day camp poses no problem. It's my old friend from Lonavla, the gibberish technique. But, despite the crisp, clear, cloudless Mount Abu blue, there's still no sky within. Will there ever be? I find myself wondering.

There's another technique to be done before going to sleep. We're to fill our lungs with air, empty them to the accompaniment of the sound "O", refill, empty, refill, empty and so on for twenty minutes.

But about the new meditation no one seems to know anything except that it's to be held after the evening session, in Osho's presence. When it's explained to us I am aghast. It sounds not only impossible but also completely mad. We're to jump up and down, arms in the air, shouting the sound "Hoo!" while we look Osho in the eyes without blinking for forty minutes.

Forty minutes! Apart from a few nervous yet incredulous giggles from a handful of old-timers, the rest of us are silent, stunned in our amazement.

And when it happens that night, I am literally stunned. I raise my arms, find Osho's eyes across the sea of heads, and when the music starts, begin to jump. Two or three jumps, and a pain, paralysing in its suddenness and intensity, flashes through my head, knocking me to the floor. I remain there, writhing in agony for a period of time I am incapable of judging until, finally, I manage to get to my feet and begin once more. But the lightning strikes again, sharper, more fiercely than before. This time I stay on the floor—standing, even standing, an impossibility.

Lying there, huddled in pain, rocking my hurting head in my hands, avoiding the feet pounding down again and again around me, there is that same sense of inadequacy felt in the morning, that same monstrous fear of missing—and, coupled with the torture in my brain, it becomes a blind, searing panic. I want to rush from the room into the night, away from all this frenzy, away from all this noise. But standing is out of the question. Flailing arms send me crashing twice more to the floor. On all fours, as if crawling through the churning pistons of a racing engine, I make it to the door. But I cannot leave. Through the open doorway lies the Rajasthani night, dark and desolate. Behind me there is vitality; there is life. I feel the coldness on my face, the fire at my back and I turn. Through the tangled mass of jumping, gyrating bodies, through the snaking mêlée of japing, thrusting, upraised arms, I see Osho, white and shining, standing at the platform's edge, his arms lifted in the air. His head is tilted back, his eyes are closed, and framing his face is a shimmering gold light that I have seen before. It is the light from the New York State Thruway. It is the light that came in the crashing car. Yet it is coming from within him, from some inner source. Leave? I laugh at my own stupidity and, dropping to the floor again, lean against the wall. And once more the tears come. They are not tears of pain this time, but tears of wonder released by a heart that can neither comprehend nor contain it all.

The next morning dawns inauspiciously, to say the least. The dhobi hasn't come and there's nothing clean to wear, and the hotel bearer can't get a bucket of hot bathing water together in time. A perfunctory splash in icy water and a cup of lukewarm tea with lumps of boiled milk-skin floating in it does nothing to brighten my rapidly blackening mood. Wisely, Divy and Rani ignore me.

The discourse is simply irritating. He's on about the transition from the second body to the third or some such thing. I haven't a clue what he's talking about. Finally he finishes. And the Dynamic's an equal bust. I hate the bloody thing today. By noon, after an over-spiced lunch, which I also hate, I decide I'd better see Osho.

But he's too busy, I'm told. By mid-afternoon I've managed to get through the phalanx of women guarding his door. "And what's happening with you?" he asks.

As I talk, explaining what happened, he closes his eyes. My feeling is he's not really listening to me, that he's not paying much heed to my words, but that there's a kind of penetration going on, a kind of inner exploration. He suddenly holds up his hand, stopping me in mid-sentence. "Just sit at the back with closed eyes tonight," he says, "and feel the energy within. You do this for the rest of the camp."

"But what's going on?" I insist. "I don't understand what..."

Up goes the hand again. "I want to take you beyond the mind," he says in a tone that precludes further questioning. "No need to know. No need to feed the mind. No need to throw more fuel on a burning fire. Don't you be concerned. When you surrender to a Master, he assumes responsibility for your spiritual growth. All you have to do is stay out of the way.

"Good, Krishna Prem," he adds, smiling in dismissal.

The down-space continues. Nothing seems able to dispel it. And for the next few days I tromp the town and stomp the hills in a shroud of deepening gloom. It's not that I don't do what I can to shake it. I throw myself totally into the meditations. I listen to the discourses with an attentiveness that borders on the desperate. But nothing helps. The cloud simply swells and darkens. I know I am missing some kind of point—and the most maddening thing is my awareness that it's something I already know. But it eludes me. It lurks somewhere inside, mocking, teasing, playing a devilish game of hide-and-seek.

Among the other sannyasins, Kailash and the touring kirtan group are the major topics. Many Westerners have simply come to India with no specific plans for going anywhere else, and it appears Osho doesn't want us just hanging about in Bombay, so two proposals are in the Mount Abu air.

The kirtan group holds no attraction for Divy or for me. Neither of us can carry a tune, and the idea of singing and dancing, albeit in praise of Osho, through a series of smelly Indian cities like a bunch of southern Baptists turns us both right off. Kailash, on the other hand, holds a certain appeal, and is not quite as unknown a quantity. Late one night in Lonavla a young Englishwoman named Paras had arrived. From Kailash. Her story was that Osho's mother from a past life—"Osho stood up and touched *her* feet when she became a disciple!" Paras had told us, her eyes ablaze with esoteric delight—was the wife of a rich landowner in central India and had donated a farm where a few Westerners were already living. Osho had named the farm Kailash after Lord Vishnu's mythological mountain abode.

"It's so beautiful there," she'd said, sitting on the porch of our hut in the moonlight. "It's so calm and peaceful."

"But what do you do there?" I'd asked.

"We've planted a huge garden," she'd replied, rhyming off a list of succulent taste-treats that had made me push my thali of rice and soggy veggies aside in disgust. And on and on she'd gone, far into the night, painting an idyllic, pastoral picture of down-home grassroots farm life.

So, when it's announced one afternoon that Osho wants thirty sannyasins to go to Kailash, Divy and I sign up, along with Prageet and Virag. Rani has to go back to Sweden to settle a few things, but says she'll join us later.

The majority of the volunteers are strangers to me, mostly English, all friends from London. There's a smattering of Americans, including Jagruti, the giggling blond from Woodlands, a couple of Germans and South Africans, and a fair representation from the former colonies, from Australia, New Zealand and Canada.

The thirty of us see Osho the next day, and it is both beautiful and inspiring. He talks to us about openness and honesty with each other and about working and living together in love and harmony. He talks to us as pioneers in a new experiment in consciousness, and about how he's looking to us to lay the foundations for a new ashram to which, he says, thousands will come. He outlines the meditation and work schedules he wants us to follow. Then he tells us we're on our own. Veda, a one-time South African jet pilot, has been at Kailash for a while already and Osho says it's fine for Veda to continue to be in charge.

"I want you all to commit yourself to stay at least six months," he says in conclusion. "And don't write to me with your complaints if things aren't going according to your wishes," he adds, the underlying chuckle in no way negating the admonition. "My whole effort is to make you free, not dependent on anything or on anyone—especially not me. But I'll be with you. Go with my blessings. And enjoy!"

Despite the excitement about Kailash and the various preparatory get-togethers, including one with an Indian doctor who freaks us all out with his graphic and terrifying descriptions of typhoid, cholera, dysentery, dengue fever, snake and scorpion bites, the space I'm in refuses to lighten. And that hidden understanding sitting on the tip of my tongue still refuses to surface.

An afternoon of quiet pondering seems in order and I set out by myself, climbing the hill behind the hotel in search of a solitary spot. Spying a large flat stone on the crest of a rise just above me, and sitting down to smoke a bidi when I reach it, I see that I'm on one of the foundation stones of what must once have been a small cottage. And there must also have been a garden when the house still stood, because I suddenly find myself facing a single, splendid, blood red rose. How it has survived on this parched Rajasthani hilltop is a mystery. But there it is.

And it brings back something Osho once said. "Labels are man-made things," he'd pointed out. "And they are destructive. When you look at a rose-flower, the mind immediately says 'rose' and then you think you know what the rose is. The rose has no name. The rose simply *is*. The next time you encounter a rose-flower, just look at it. Don't let the mind come in with its labels and destroy everything. Just meet the rose, being to being, in a wordless communion."

Looking at the rose, just looking at it, I see that I've been trying to do the same thing about my mood, about the space I've been in. I've been trying to figure it out, wanting to put a label to it, labouring under the illusion that pinpointing it would dispel it.

"I'll see Osho about it in Bombay," I tell myself once more as I pull the blankets over me that night.

This morning's discourse is the camp's last. I arrive at the Bikaner Palace early, installing myself on the ballroom floor near the front, close to the dais. Things are a bit better, but that sense of something having gone wrong, that feeling that I should be up and not down, lingers. My reverie is broken by Osho's entry. He mounts the platform, namastes, sits down and begins to speak. I close my eyes.

All at once there's the oddest sensation in my gut, hot and compelling, as if a blazing spotlight has just been turned on me. My eyes open to meet Osho's. His gaze is direct. There's no mistaking he is fixed on me.

"Go to the sea and meditate on the waves," he is saying. "The wave rises high, but just behind it there is a gap, a valley... The higher the wave, the deeper will be the valley just following it. This is what happiness and unhappiness are—waves. Whenever you reach a high peak of happiness, immediately unhappiness will follow. You have to accept that this is how life is."[1]

And the penny drops. The key sticking on the tip of my tongue has been "acceptance". I *had* known it! I'd known I had! Saying "okay" in that car accident, simply accepting what was happening had been the key that had unlocked the door to the other dimension, that had triggered that thrust to the core of my being, that had thrown me straight into the arms of the divine. I had forgotten. But now I am reminded. And I am listening.

"The real thing is to learn acceptance. And if you accept the valley, then the valley is also very mysterious and beautiful. It has its own splendour. Even anguish has its own beauty if you accept it. Even sadness has its own depth. Not only laughter is beautiful, sadness has its own beauty, a depth which no laughter can carry. Sadness has its own poetry, its own rhythm. If you allow me the expression, sadness has its own ecstasy. But one has to accept. Then one will be able to know.

"If you accept both, you transcend. Then neither misery can make you miserable, nor happiness can make you happy—you remain the same. Misery comes and goes, happiness comes and goes, you remain untouched. Until this is achieved your bliss is just a deception... Only that bliss is called bliss, ananda, which doesn't exist against misery, which transcends happiness and unhappiness, both.

"So," he is saying, looking once more at me, "when the peak has gone and the valley has come, accept it... Feel it. Be sensitive to it. Allow it to happen and you are changing its quality. And you

---

1 *Vedanta: Seven Steps to Samadhi*

are changing yourself also through it. And don't divide. Don't say 'happiness', 'unhappiness'. These are two aspects of the same coin. Accept both or reject both. Only then tranquillity, calmness, peace become possible."

As I walk through the streets of the town, back towards the hotel to begin packing for the return to Bombay, the inner clouds are clearing. The sun is high in the sky, warm and nourishing, and I can feel a light beginning to surface in me as well. But I am newly aware of one thing: this up that's coming will be followed by a down. This peak will be followed by a valley and the valley by a peak and that peak by yet another valley, in the continuing rhythm of life, until, one day, I move beyond it all. And it's fine. It's the way life is. It's the way life really is.

And everything is just fine.

Where a problem filled me yesterday, a sense of wonder has taken its place.

He answered me! I had a question, but I didn't even have to ask it. Somehow he heard it anyway. And he gave me my answer. He gave me what I needed to hear.

Rounding the last corner before the hotel, my steps quicken. Divy is on the balcony, drinking tea with Prageet and Virag. "Have you packed yet?" I shout. Suddenly I want to get to Kailash as quickly as I can.

Kailash

The road to Kailash is paved with good intentions. And with Indians. Out of a population of more than seven hundred million, it's calculated at least one per cent is on the trains at any given time, day or night. That's seven million people. When we arrive at V.T. in Bombay to begin the trip to Kailash—having chucked the idea of a week of queuing for berths and deciding to take our chances in the unreserved cars of third class—I am convinced that the totality of India's train travellers, day-trippers and night-riders alike, have reached a collective decision to celebrate the joys of locomotion-living in one great, steam-powered festival. And with a sinking feeling in the pit of my stomach, I know it's all going to happen on our train.

One of our band, Kaveeta, a therapist from England, has done the trek to Kailash once before. She arms a bearer with twenty rupees—ten for him and ten for one of the station cops—and sends him up the track that leads into the terminus. There, as the train slows for its approach, he'll hop aboard and find the space we need before it pulls to a halt in the station.

"When train coming," he warns, tucking the rupees under his porter's turban, "men watching for me in doorway. Then jumping on. But fast, sahibs!" he insists in a no kidding tone. "Very fast. And you ladies, you throwing baggage in through windows." And with a further, "Fast, sahibs. Very fast!" over his shoulder, he's off down the tracks.

There's a mounting tension in the crowd around us, and the sixteen of us on the station platform, bunched together in an orange barricade encircling our belongings, are picking up on it. I find myself wishing I'd gone straight from Mount Abu with the others. As each moment ticks by, the atmosphere gets more and more edgy. But it's only when I turn to see twelve red-turbaned luggage-bearers down on one knee, poised in a perfect sprinter's line, ready to spring forward into action, do I get a glimmer of the stampede that's going to start the second the train rolls in.

Our bearer has positioned us perfectly. We spy him hanging out the doorway of one of the unreserved coaches, signalling for our attention. The train stops exactly in front of us and, propelled by the haste in the air and the swell of the crowd behind us, we eight men are through the narrow entrance in a flash. Inside the carriage, with lightning speed, the bearer arranges us into a human grill, arms spread and legs astride, limbs interlocking in whatever combinations they can, defending two of the three-tier compartments against the onslaught of Indian passengers pouring into the car from both ends. At our backs, straining and shoving, the eight women squeeze our bags in through the windows and crawl in behind them, tripping over each other as, one by one, they tumble into a heap on the grimy floor.

"Close windows, memsahibs!" the bearer shouts above the din. And down come the glass windows.

"No, memsahibs, no! Shutters! Shutters also!"

Up go the windows again and the outer steel blinds are pulled down, plunging the compartment into semi-darkness. Without warning the train suddenly jerks into motion and the bearer, a few more notes shoved into his hand, touches his forehead in thanks and jumps from the slowly accelerating train onto the platform. One of the girls raises a steel shutter to wave goodbye.

Within seconds all hell breaks loose. The train stops again and when the mob on the platform finds the doors to our unreserved car closed and barred—it's already packed to overflowing—they make for the windows. We can't slam down the shutter in time, and, pushing a man's head back out through the window, all we can manage is to close the glass. All along the car, angry fists pound on the sides, beating a steady, furious tattoo, voices exploding in rage and indignation. Through the glass I see a couple of men clearing a tiny space. One of them pulls back and, raising his valise like a battering ram, begins a head-on charge for our window. A split second before our compartment would have filled with shattered glass the train lurches forward and I hear the suitcase smash into the steel shutter protecting the neighbouring window. Slowly gathering momentum, we pull out of the station, the sound of hammering fists, of shouts and curses disappearing down the track. No one speaks. We are mute, stricken dumb with shock. Mob violence is something new to all of us. But it is over. And soon we're all laughing and joking at our adventure.

"Boy, are they ever lucky they didn't break through the window!" Kaveeta says with the bravado of a Harlem street-fighter. "I always travel armed."

"With what?" one of the English girls asks. "Surely not a knife?"

"I'm not out to kill," Kaveeta laughs, "just to discourage." She reaches into her handbag. "And this always works," she says, brandishing a kitchen fork. "Works every time," she announces proudly, counting off the tines. "Guess it's the fear of four little holes instead of one."

Growing up in a Canadian railroad family left me with a fondness for train travel, for the ever-changing reel of images that unfolds in the frame of an open train window. And, as we move deep into Maharashtra towards Chandrapur, our destination, I lean back on the hard wooden seat and, gone from my companions, watch the movie of India passing before me.

The scenes are abundant. Women stand ankle-deep in mud, bright-coloured saris hoisted to their brown thighs, bending over to embed acid-green shoots of rice, one by one, in the sodden earth of square, sunken paddies. Young shepherds, boys and girls, laze in the shade of spreading trees, tracking, with half-open eyes, groups of grazing goats and sheep and water buffalo. Pairs of yoked bullocks strain up and down steep inclines raising hide-bags of cool, underground water from cavernous wells for spilling onto thirsty fields of wheat and corn and barley. Rajasthani women, laden with silver and layered in skirts, snake up and down the bamboo ladders of construction sites, carrying on their heads, in a continuous, revolving chain, neatly-piled stacks of dust red bricks. Ageless old men squat in the dust of the passing train, puffing bidis under the tents of big black umbrellas balanced across lean shoulders. Every once in a while the eye of the watched meets the eye of the watcher and a smile and a wave are exchanged.

In the background, the rolling hills stretch as far as I can see. Gentle and undulating, eroded to a round smoothness by eons of monsoon rains and a merciless sun, they remind me of the bodies of women—soft, receptive, curving.

At the station stops, by contrast, the window teems with activity. Into my view pours a stream of vendors, scrawny brown hands jutting into the carriage, offering tiny clay cups of steaming grey tea and cold drinks—pink lemon Limcas, deep yellow Mangolas, fizzy Fanta sodas, creamy soy milks and sweet black colas carried in sloshing, spilling buckets of quickly-melting ice. From over-laden baskets, oranges and bananas and floury-textured apples are thrust through the window; chikkus, papayas, jackfruit and white-fleshed custard-apples following. Woven straw tripods suddenly appear, bearing mountains of roasted nuts, salted-and-spiced or plain, and mounds of crunchy chickpeas, bursting hot from their skins. And even a bookshop on-wheels rolls by, sporting a staggering variety of novels and magazines—splashy, lurid covers in English and Hindi, in Marathi and Gujarati and Tamil.

And then moist banana leaves poke through the window and none of us can resist the treat they carry. Razor-thin slices of tart guava and juicy tomato are neatly stacked in alternating rows, pink and red, pink and red, and dusted with spices, with saffron and turmeric and salt and ground peppers of red and black and green.

A blind gypsy appears and begins to sing. Her voice is rich and full, the melody haunting. And there is a quality to her face that moves us all to silence. We sit, attentive, listening, and I sense that this blind woman, gnarled and worn with years, the outer denied her, has found that inner something that pulls us all. She suddenly stops her song, her nostrils flaring like an animal that has picked up a familiar scent, and she begins to laugh. And the laugh is joyous. It is the laugh of fellowship, of camaraderie, and it calls out to be shared. And we join her.

When the train pulls out again we leave her standing on the platform, still laughing. We leave her to her search, the train pulling us onwards towards ours.

When night falls and my window darkens, I turn my attention back to the others and to the sleeping arrangements. There are really far too many of us for the space available, but we manage. We double up on all three wooden tiers and on the floor, spreading sleeping bags and folded blankets between the seats. As I did on the trip from Mount Abu to Bombay, I somehow end up sharing the luggage rack again. But a sleeping pill, stashed with just this possibility in mind, serves me well. Within moments I am asleep.

Over morning chai we pull into Wardha, where we change trains. It's the home of Mahatma Gandhi's ashram and precious little else. By evening we arrive in Chandrapur.

Our final destination is a village called Saoli, and when we arrive at the State Transport depot the next day I am utterly and inalterably convinced that everyone from our train has ended up in Chandrapur and that they all intend getting on the same bus. The trip lasts four hours and they are four of the most agonizing hours of my life, four hours of the most intense physical discomfort and incredible heat I have ever known. When we finally pull into Saoli, my gratitude is unbounded. When I step off that torturous conveyance, a huge wet cow turd smack in front of me is the only thing that keeps me from falling to my knees and kissing the ground.

Saoli is basically a general store, a couple of other ramshackle buildings, a lot of dust and nothing much else. One road leads in and out. One end points towards civilization, from whence we have come; the other, towards the jungle, where we are going. Pressed by the rapidly setting sun and preceded by a pair of bullock carts piled high with our possessions, we set out on foot, a long erratic column of orange-clad city slickers picking its way gingerly along the rough and rocky footpath the road has quickly become. At the head of this sannyasin safari, Veda and Kaveeta pause frequently, casting nervous glances over their shoulders at the speed of the setting sun. Indian sunsets are dramatically sudden and extremely short-lived—and there is no moon tonight. They urge us on, hoping to cover as much ground as possible before the blackness envelops us. But we've made little progress before everything around us is suddenly bathed in that particular evening light that is unique to this country. It doesn't seem to come from above at all, but rather to skim along the surface of the ground itself, igniting everything it touches, setting trees and rocks and soil aflame, imparting to each leaf and pebble and grain of dust a fiery flush, a glowing luminosity. The spreading rays appear at once absorbed and reflected by everything they light upon, with no gap between, as if earth and sky have come together, consummating, in this brief, climactic union, the separation they have endured during the day. Ten, fifteen minutes and it is over. Then it is black.

For the next hour or so we stumble along by torchlight, tiny, insignificant shafts of light, weak and ineffectual in the all-consuming darkness. There is only a narrow strip of elevated earth flanked by flooded rice paddies and, from up and down the line, occasional curses in a variety of languages as one of us stubs a toe, slides sideways into a paddy, trips into a hole, slips on a dollop of buffalo dung or tramps on a neighbour's heel. When my sandal breaks, strap and sole irreparably separating, it is the last straw for me. But what to do? No cobbler, no Bata shoe shop, nothing. And so, mud squishing between my toes, my mind tripping out on the snakes and scorpions described by the Indian doctor at Mount Abu, I stagger on, tired and thirsty and totally fed up, furious with Osho for letting me get myself into this and furious with me for ever having volunteered for Kailash in the first place.

"A fire!" someone shouts, and there, just ahead of us, silhouetted against the amber glow, is a series of mounds that, at first glance, looks like the nesting place of a colony of giant ants. But as we move closer, the shapes, emerging from the darkness, reveal themselves as huts, crude constructions of mud and dung, capped with crowns of rough weeds and grasses. Backlit by cooking fires, the villagers crowd their doorways to watch us pass. A few children shout, "Hoo! Hoo! Hoo!" Kaveeta laughs. "They hear us do the Dynamic," she explains. But from the adults there is no word, no sign of welcome or rejection, but simply a silence as dark as the night, as primitive as the village itself.

Once through Usagow, we stop for a bidi and a rest. "Kailash is just over there," Kaveeta says, pointing ahead into the blackness. "It's just across these fields. Only twenty minutes more."

"God, I'm so incredibly tired," an American accent moans somewhere in back of me. "Let's just keep going and get it over with!"

As one, we lurch to our feet and set out across the stony fields, once more in single file behind Kaveeta and Veda who, in spite of the darkness, seem able to pick out and manoeuvre some hidden path that is imperceptible to the rest of us. Personally, I have simply given up caring. One bare foot in front of the other is all I can manage, and I just keep repeating the same process over and over until, finally, everything around me comes to a halt—people, movement, time, everything.

"We're here!" Kaveeta calls triumphantly.

We have arrived at the farm. At the legendary, long-awaited Kailash. In front of me is a building, but I cannot tell whether it's large or small. On the porch, through a hazy blur, I can make out a figure spreading mattresses. As I step onto the porch a cup of tea is put into my hands, but before I can raise it to my lips I have handed it back, dropped to a mattress and am sound asleep.

I am snapped awake in the morning by an explosion of coughing and hawking, by a blast of spitting and snorting that is staggering in its volume and intensity. There, not ten feet away, perched on a bench like a bald eagle in an epileptic fit is Parakh the landowner, spewing the sputum from his lungs and spraying the snot from his nose all over the earth before me. And beside him on the bench, stained bright betel red, grinning a ghoulish good-morning, is his set of store-bought teeth.

I make for the river, uncertain, when I get there, whether to have a swim or simply let myself drown.

The one thing about Kailash that fills me with deep and abiding gratitude is that, in India, cow-shitting is considered women's work. Anything else to do with building our sleeping hut is fine with me. Hot and dusty as it is, I'm okay with cutting and gathering reeds from the river bank, chopping sugar cane stocks and carrying them in from the fields, splitting bamboo poles and lashing them together, digging holes, whatever. But every morning, when I check the day's roster of jobs, there is a warm rush of joy in my heart that even our overseer, our very own Simon Legree, dare not break an age-old Indian tradition. Gathering cow shit, mixing it with water and spreading it on the earth to harden into smooth, cement-like flooring is, unquestionably, women's work.

After a few days the hut is ready. Considering the fact most of us have never done anything more manual than push a pencil or pound a typewriter, it's surprisingly well put together. It stands on a rise just above the river, kitty-corner to the tiny farmhouse with the porch where we've been spending the nights. It's a long, L-shaped construction, with half-walls of river reeds woven onto split-bamboo frames and secured to thick poles dug deeply into the ground.

A sloping roof of sugar cane sheaves, braided tightly together, is our protection from the sun. The floor is smooth and level, the swirling hand-strokes of the sannyasin women, like the footprints of Hollywood starlets, immortalized in cow shit—at least until the rains.

And we move in—a long line of red-and-cream stuffed cotton mattresses and white mosquito nets, possessions neatly stacked at the head of each bed on a rope-and-bamboo shelf that runs the length of the structure. We're told to choose spaces by sex, alternately: man, woman; man, woman, and to sleep facing east. There's a great discussion as to whether this means the top of one's head should be towards the east—"But then my *face* will be pointing west," someone complains in confusion—or whether it should be the other way around. I've nothing to contribute: it's all esoteric crap to me. I make for the river. Like an untethered water buffalo, I wallow in the water, letting the heaviness of the yoke I am beginning to feel dissolve in the freedom of the current. It lifts me, turns me, caresses me, carrying the caged feeling away. Finally, refreshed and unencumbered, I begin the climb back up the bank. As I mount the hill, the heat of the morning sun dries the river from my body and the sounds of the others' voices do the same to my heart. When I arrive at the hut the argument is over. "Facing east," has been resolved. And I lay my things out accordingly. Once again I am fettered. Once again I am part of the herd.

Food is the biggest hassle. There is simply not enough to eat. Not that there isn't ample money. We've all contributed to the Kailash affair, paying for mattresses and nets, for cooking and eating utensils, and we've thrown more than enough rupees into the communal pot to feed ourselves well until the crops come up. Primarily, it's that Veda is a first-class prick. Daily I find myself more and more fascinated by what I see unfolding before my eyes: a classic power-trip, with a nice Jewish boy from Johannesburg turning into a mini-Mussolini in the middle of Maharashtra. I cannot help but feel that somewhere along the line Veda is missing a pretty important point. He's about as communally minded as Joseph Stalin. And about as friendly. He sets himself apart from the rest of us, appearing only to issue orders or to stalk the work sites in supervisory superiority, his hairy chest puffed up like a strutting, self-important buck. His little private hut becomes his little private world.

It's a world no one wants to enter, a world no one wants to share. And yet Osho has said Veda should remain in charge. So we all continue to play the game. But the game is loveless. And the players are getting hungrier and hungrier with each passing day.

For some reason Veda is obsessed with the idea we should live like Indians. And in many ways we're into it. We paddle about barefoot, the occasional band-aid testifying to our Western soft-footedness. We work naked except for bright orange lunghis tied about our waists, and squat on our haunches to chat things over, calves and thighs stretching at the unaccustomed effort. It's all rather fun, this going native. But when it comes to mealtimes, Veda's meanness and obstinacy is maddening.

As it is anywhere in the world the first meal of the day is breakfast. The only difference at Kailash is that it's served after we've been up for almost three hours. At five a gong awakens us and we scurry to the river for a quick wash and a tooth scrub. Some of us have gone so native that even toothbrushes have been scrapped for neem twigs or for wet fingers dipped into foul-tasting Monkey-brand charcoal powder. After the fifteen minutes Veda has allotted us for ablutions, there's a cup of watery chai before we gather on the flat rice-cleaning field for Dynamic. And the intensity of the cathartic stage is amazing, the usual wailing over childhood traumas giving way to piercing, heart-rending cries to the heavens for "bacon and eggs" and "toast and jam".

When the breakfast call finally comes, we have at least an hour and a half of work under our lunghis, and precious little else. And what is dished out is, in a single word, disgusting. As a child I recall endless winter-morning fights over Cream of Wheat. I hated it with a passion. And here in India, thirty years later, it's Cream of Wheat again—except now they call it suji. It lays there, a heavy white lump in the middle of my metal thali, nuzzling a cup of boiled buffalo milk that tastes like chalk. And running down its sides in nasty brown rivulets is a stream of melting jaggery, the raw cane sugar that reminds me of blackstrap molasses that's been around so long it's given up going off and has simply passed away.

I think it's worse for Divy than for anyone else. Sweden may be boring but the food's remarkable, and Divy's never eaten anything he doesn't like in his entire life. But, along with the rest of us, famine overcoming aesthetics, he wolfs down his suji. But it won't stay down. He throws up moments later.

"I figure if it's in there for five or ten minutes," he says with resignation, "I must be getting some kind of nourishment from it."

Lunch makes me angry. It's supposedly the big meal of the day, but the only thing big about it is the mound of soggy white rice. The few cauliflower stems, the carefully-counted-out handful of peas, the half-potato and the sprigs of clover from the nearby field are simply a joke. And dinner? Dinner just makes me sad. There's one bowl of watery soup, the bouquet of wild clover predominating, and a single chappati. An ache in my heart and a growl in my stomach, I watch Virag, getting a little thinner with each passing day, tear her chappati in half and pass it to her husband. Even tall, strapping Prageet is beginning to look a little wan.

For a while now it's been obvious Veda is finding his position quite difficult. But any approach to him is met with rejection; any attempt at reason is met with resentment. More and more he is retreating into his self-imposed isolation. And it's painful to watch. He stalks the property like a hurt little boy, a pout on his lips, convinced of the rightness of what he's doing and angry at us for not understanding, for not accepting and appreciating him and his ways. He's very much the jetliner captain once more, apart, aloof, weighed down by the loneliness and responsibility of command.

On this particular morning we awaken to find that Veda is nowhere to be found. Also absent is the Land Rover that travelled all the way from England with the ITV film editor Anup and his Danish wife Pathika only to become the object of a swift expropriation by our resident tyrant. By nightfall, as we're tucking into our evening clover, the sound of an approaching engine heralds Veda's return.

"Where have you been?" a chorus of curious voices asks.

"I have a surprise for you," is all Veda will say. "You'll see what it is tomorrow."

There's something about him that looks suspiciously well fed to me, as if his stomach has received a royal pampering wherever he's been. That pisses me off more than the fact he's bothered to come back at all.

The next day, after lunch, Veda announces he's opening a sweets shop. "You all complain you're so hungry all the time," he says with unconcealed bitterness. "Now you can stuff yourselves to your hearts' content."

When the shop opens in the afternoon we're all there, like first-nighters at a long-awaited première. I can hardly believe what Veda has done. He's stocked the shop on our money and now he's selling the stuff back to us at a fifty per cent mark-up!

We're no longer a group of surrendered sannyasins. We've the makings of a mob. But when we turn en masse from the counter, Veda, again, is nowhere to be found.

The next morning Vishnu has disappeared. We scout the place—his things are still on the shelf above his mattress—but to no avail. We send people up and down the river; we dispatch a search party to the nearby fields. We even send a few people into the gully where we shit, into what we've christened "The Valley of the Flies", but that distinctive mop of carrot red hair remains unsighted.

But when I open my eyes after an afternoon nap there he is, sitting cross-legged on his bed, a naughty grin on his freckled face and a mischievous twinkle sparkling in his cobalt blue eyes. And before him, spread out on a bright orange lunghi, are mounds of Indian sweets, of barfi, peanut-brittle chikki and ladoo.

"Cost price, laddie," Vishnu says, uttering the first sounds I've heard in ages. "Cost price."

"Jesus, Vishnu," I laugh. "You're too much! You're a sneaky little bugger. Not a word for a week and now this—our very own black market!"

"It's a long walk to Saoli," he says, "but I'll go again tomorrow. And the next day. I'll keep going until that man sees some sense. By the way," he adds, turning to Veena, a friend from London, "here's a letter for you. They gave it to me in Saoli."

"It's from Laxmi in Bombay," Veena announces, examining the envelope.

"I wrote to her and told her to ask Osho about the food situation here. I somehow couldn't quite accept the fact that he wants us to go so native we'd starve to death."

Hardly a breath is drawn while Veena reads the letter. Word spread quickly that Laxmi had written and almost everyone's gathered in the hut. At last Veena looks up from the page. She's smiling. "He says to stop all this nonsense and give us what we want to eat."

When the hugging and kissing and general rolling about in ecstatic relief subside, Kaveeta speaks up. "Veena," she suggests, "you go and tell Veda."

As Veena sets out to locate our leader, clutching Laxmi's letter like a papal bull, a sudden feeling of understanding and compassion for Veda seems to fill the air. We all pick up on it at one and the same time. Our sharing of it is silent, no one saying anything—but finally the spell needs breaking and Kaveeta says, to no one in particular and yet to us all, "Let bygones be bygones?"

It is beautiful. The murmur of assent is unanimous. The way Osho would want it to be. Hallelujah! We eat again!

For me, the days begin to be virtually nothing more than spaces between one morning's Dynamic and the next. Whatever's happening to me through Dynamic is thanks to Veena.

Born in England and raised in South Africa, she had met Osho passing through Bombay one day. "I used to wear rings on all my fingers," she once told me. "For some reason I took them all off before meeting him for the first time. But the moment I walked in, Osho looked up from his chair and said, 'Ah, the lady with the rings has come!'"

She'd taken sannyas and had been named Prema Veena, instrument of love. And, armed with malas and a score of new names, she'd returned to London and opened Nirvana, Europe's first Osho meditation centre. She'd played tapes of Osho's discourses and given classes in Dynamic Meditation. Well over half the people at Kailash have taken sannyas from Veena.

On the way to Kailash one morning, as we began our meditation, Veena stopped me. "Look," she said, "if you breathe like that, nothing's ever going to happen."

I was a bit taken aback. I thought I was becoming quite good at it.

"Watch me," she said. All of us had gathered around her by this point.

Planting her feet firmly apart, standing loose at the knees, arms folded into wings—"Like a chicken"—Veena jutted her elbows sharply into the sky, level with her shoulders. She breathed in deeply, her bosom rising, and then down came the elbows and out flew the air in one single, powerful thrust. Up went the elbows again, and down they came, with a force that bent her double.

"Pump," she said. "Pump the air out. Don't worry about breathing in. Osho says nature fills a vacuum automatically. Just pay attention to pumping the air out, deeply and totally. First, get this technique down pat. And then go for speed. Like this."

I had never seen anything like it. We were all agape. Within seconds Veena was pumping away, up and down, in and out, a human piston travelling at an impossible speed. There wasn't one of her any more. She was moving so fast I saw dozens of Veenas, now in this posture, now in that, as if a strobe had been attached to my eyeballs, breaking movement down into its component parts.

"There," she said, gasping. "Do it like that. It'll take a week or so to build up the speed. Then things will really start to happen."

She had been right. With Veena's continuing help my proficiency increases. Two stages, the first and the third, the breathing and the "Hoo!" are pure technique. The second and fourth, the cathartic phase and the final stage, where meditation happens, are starting to show results.

The deeper the breathing goes, the faster and more chaotic it becomes, the more amazing is the stuff that begins to surface in the catharsis. The sensation of what's going on is strange and new to me. It's as if "I", whoever that is, simply sits there, perched on some inner peak, watching all the pain and sadness, anger and frustration bubbling up from some deep, churning volcano that is also me. I cannot explain any of it to myself. Yet it is happening. And I allow it. I put no obstacle in its way. It keeps surfacing and I keep expressing it, throwing whatsoever comes up in me out into the air, back into existence itself. The feeling I have is one of re-experiencing, of going through incomplete things all over again. But there is one great difference. This time it is all happening without identification. Now there's a gap between me and the experience being relived. I feel as if the recesses of my being, all the dark and musty corners, are being cleansed.

When it comes to the "Hoo!" I throw myself into it as totally as into the breathing, again using Veena's chicken-wing approach, aiming each explosion of sound deep into my gut, aiming at the sex centre. And it seems to be working. During the ten-minute stage I can feel the energy mounting, mounting, the pressure building, building—and then comes "Stop!" and, like a diver off a springboard, I am plummeted into space. It is curious, this sense of space, of vastness. It is at once empty and full. The body is gone, boundaries dissolved; the mind, a far off thought-producing mechanism to become involved in or simply to be observed. But what is most intriguing, most puzzling and infinitely mysterious is the presence growing way back inside my head. I can feel it in there, burning, and I know its nature is light. When the mind stops, for no matter how infinitesimal a fraction of time, it illuminates me. And something in me knows, with no shadow of doubt remaining, that this is the presence Osho calls "the witness", the presence that, he says, is the real, authentic me.

But despite the magic of the meditations and the virgin territories I am entering, some kind of spirit, some kind of individuality seems to be dying in me as well. The monotony of the work, the rigidity of the regime, the absolute uncreativity of it all is beginning to get me down. The food crisis had kept us all at a certain pitch. With that resolved, I find it more and more difficult to muster any enthusiasm about anything. Divy is in a similar space. So are most of us. I just avoid social contact, taking to the peace and soothing solitude of the river as often as I can.

One morning, beside my name on the work-sheet, I see the word "bricks". Bricks? I check with Veda and am told we're now going to build from bricks: the monsoon will be here in less than three months. Mrs Parakh or Ma Anandmai as we call her is brick mistress. She squats on a mound of earth, a big black umbrella for shade, and issues instructions. "Dig down," she tells me over and over again.

I keep digging, sweat pouring down my back in waterfalls, my hands beginning to bubble into blisters.

"Now right colour," she grunts at last, indicating a reddish layer of soil I've struck about a foot beneath the surface. "Now make bricks," she says, lurching to her feet to show me how. She mixes the earth with a little water, to the consistency of cement, packs it into a wooden mould and then, after a bit, turns it out on the flat ground to dry.

"Bas," she says, signalling the end of the lesson and, folding her umbrella under her arm, waddles back to the house where she plops down on the veranda in the shade.

Veda has set a quota of a thousand bricks a day per man. That day, six of us manage thirty-four.

As we move into the pre-monsoon heat, the temperatures are becoming harder and harder to bear. Even with heads covered at work and longer mid-day rest periods, the Indian climate is beginning to take its toll. In spite of the fact we're now well fed, the average weight loss is startling and, more and more, stomach cramps and dysentery are common complaints.

Ma, my brick-making master, is reported to be a qualified Ayurvedic doctor. On our Western bodies, Ma's home brews, her barks and her berries, are useless. All the sick seem able to do is ride illness out. And when all else fails she falls back on the age-old Hindu cure-all, cow urine. Applied externally or taken internally, as the ailment indicates, she stands by it. Lacking her faith in the sanctity and efficacy of bovine excreta, and buoyed by Teertha's refusal even to consider a glass of cow piss, our rejection of her ace remedy is unanimous.

The increase in our general vulnerability, both physical and mental, sparks a new wave of assertiveness in Veda. We are suddenly inundated with a flood of new rules—no talking here, no smoking there, no doing this, no doing that. Monitors are appointed. Their responsibility is, on pain of what I never quite figure out, to report any infringement of the rules to him personally. Divy, Prageet and several others refuse the proffered espionage assignment. Me, Veda doesn't even ask.

But there are those who accept the task gleefully. "It's sad," Kaveeta says, "it just creates a split among us. I don't understand that man at all."

Frankly, I'm simply not interested in Veda's latest game. And whenever Kunji, a dry English girl he's appointed as smoking spy tells me to put out my bidi, I tell her to fuck off. "Fuck off, Kunji," I must say a dozen times a day. And the threatened retribution, I come to see, is as empty as the rules are ridiculous. But when he sends Virag and Pratima, a young Australian woman who's become a really close friend, on a five-mile trek to a neighbouring field to pin numbers on papayas, I begin to think Veda's losing his marbles.

"But why?" Pratima asked, all blue-eyed innocence.

"Just do what you're told," Veda snarled in reply.

"But why?" she insisted, her eyes instantly steeling to a no-nonsense gaze of disarming directness.

"Well if you must know," he answered, "so no one can steal them."

"You're nuts, Veda," she informed him. "Quite, quite nuts."

Despite the insanity of his papaya-numbering burglar-protection scheme and the annoyance of Kunji's constant nagging about my bidi smoking, there's one thing I observe that doesn't strike me as ridiculous. On the contrary, it infuriates me. One afternoon, carrying one end of a plank, I stop and look about me as if I've just awakened from a deep sleep. The sensation is odd. It's as if I have suddenly been propelled from where I am into some far-off-yet-still-here netherworld from where I am watching the moving tableau that is being performed around me. There is Veda, the absolute monarch, Pyari at his side, and around him, the lords and ladies of his court—all his old pals from London. To my utter amazement, I see for the first time what has happened. The English are all lolling about, doing a little light easy work or directing others, while we, the Canadians and the Australians and the New Zealanders and the Americans—the Colonials—are doing all the toting of barges and lifting of bales.

"Shit!" I say to Prageet at the other end of the plank. "An English ruling-class!"

That night in Dynamic—we change it to twilight because of the heat—I carry my anger with me, moving into the breathing like one possessed. When we explode into the catharsis, my body falls abruptly to the ground, and from inside I watch myself, legs kicking in the air, arms flailing, hands clutching for the mother's breasts that are no longer there. I am two months old again, wailing for the mother who has gone.

As soon as I lie down in bed that night the coughing begins. And it continues whenever I lie down, night after night after endless night.

Intellectually, there's an understanding of what is happening. My father told me that after my mother's death I had whooping cough quite badly for a long time, and that he spent many nights walking me up and down in his arms, trying to soothe me to sleep. I'd heard Osho say that most illnesses, ninety-nine per cent, had psychosomatic origins. And somehow I can see where the childhood whooping cough began. I can see how the crying for my mother, so long unanswered, settled in and became a physical illness. I know the Dynamic has thrown me back into that infant space and that, now, a re-experiencing is happening. There's nothing to do but wait it out.

The people in the hut are beautiful, poking lozenges and syrups under my mosquito net at night, but the coughing doesn't abate. They're all very kind and understanding, but I'm aware no one's able to sleep, so I take to night-time wanderings. When I'm up and moving about, I don't cough.

And then, one night, in the brickfield, I come across Anup and Veeten, the ITV film editor and the former Irish burglar, stoned out of their cookies.

Needless to say, and understandably so, hashish is verboten at Kailash. But Anup, along with his Land Rover, nylon tent, cameras, binoculars, shooting stick, orange parasol and glamorous Danish wife, had come prepared for all eventualities—and a good, escape-from-it-all smoke was obviously one of them.

I take to joining them at night, spinning yarns, sharing stories, bad-mouthing Veda and thoroughly enjoying the rebelliousness. Anything's better than the coughing. But the dope begins to affect me and I find myself less and less accepting of the whole situation and, more and more, just not wanting to live like this. I mention how I'm feeling to Divy, but Veda has him embroiled in plans for the ashram he dreams of building here, and so I keep what I'm thinking pretty much to myself. But the Night of the Spring Onions I have a premonition I'm nearing the end.

"After supper tonight," Veda announces just before we begin one evening's Dynamic, "rest for an hour and then meet again here. We're planting spring onions."

The night is exquisite. The moon is high and full; the air, cool and caressing. Parakh is waiting for us by the road that leads from Usagow into the farm, at his feet scores of little bundles, bright green onion seedlings tied together like miniature sheaves of wheat. He indicates four sunken paddies just off the road and tells us to stand in them, spacing ourselves a few feet from each other. Novices at the intricacies of Indian farming, we follow his instructions, especially since, in Parakh's usual charming fashion, whatever questions we've asked so far have been ignored.

He picks up a spade-like tool and begins hacking away at the earth beside him. Suddenly I find I am standing ankle-deep in water. He hops from mound to mound, hacking here and there, and within moments the other three paddies are flooded as well.

"Mud!" he shouts. "Make mud!" And marching in place like he's out to rout the British, he sets us stomping—up and down; left, right; squish, squish; robots on parade.

I freeze in my sodden tracks in amazement, not so much at Parakh but at me, at what I am doing, at the mindless slave I am becoming.

Parakh spies me and, jumping up and down, his arms waving in frenzy, his stained blood-red teeth clacking, he begins to scream at me, "Dance! Dance! Dance!" Over and over again he points at me and shrieks, scarlet betel juice drooling off his chin to form violent red patches on his white cotton vest: "Dance! Dance! Dance!"

It is so unreal, so grotesque and macabre, that I simply cannot move any more. I fall to my knees in the mud, laughing and crying at the same time, laughing so uproariously and crying so profoundly that a point comes where I have no idea which I'm doing, no idea at all.

The next day I'm in a kind of shock. There's a deadness in me that would freak me out if I felt alive enough to care. And even that evening's Dynamic doesn't help. My efforts are less than half-hearted. I just can't muster any energy or enthusiasm.

Then, in the middle of the "Hoo!" I hear someone behind me—"Hoo! Hoo! Who? Who? Who gives a shit?" And then the voice is silent. But I'd recognized it as Veeten's. After the meditation I seek him out.

"You know, boyo, I've had it," he says with absolute certainty. "Tonight I saw I don't really give a shit who I am. Fuck all this. I want to die with one arm around a tart and the other around a bottle of good Irish whisky! This boy's getting out of here!"

The following afternoon we leave. Veeten's girlfriend Suresha goes with him and Divy comes with me.

The next day, on the bus from Saoli, I see I've missed. Despite what was apparent on the surface, I now see that something else was happening to me at Kailash—something inner, something hidden. I could have stayed but I didn't. I could have taken Veda and the rest of it but I wouldn't. In my heart it hurts. I've betrayed myself. I've betrayed Osho. All the way to Bombay I act the big phoney, the happiness at my liberation a pure pretence, a heavy, almost unbearable mask.

The third day in Bombay I simply cannot put off seeing Osho any longer.

Divy's already been to see him and he's inquired about me.

"Where have you come from?" he asks as I walk into his room.

"Downtown," I reply curtly, revealing nothing.

He motions me to sit beside him on the floor. "Tell me what happened," he says, leaning back in his chair and crossing his legs. "Why did you leave?"

I talk about the food, the rules, the spies and Parakh, letting it all spill out, but my pain at the feeling of having missed and my shame at the feeling of having betrayed him go unmentioned. I talk about finding Western society reconstructed in the middle of India and about the English ruling-class at the farm, but my own cry for help remains unuttered. When I tell him about the coughing he finally speaks. "Look, Krishna Prem," he says with such love and compassion I think my heart will burst, "there's a deep reservoir of repressed emotions in there. And they all have to come out." He spreads his hands, as if to tell me that this is just how it is.

I can feel myself getting angry. He won't help me or he can't. It all amounts to the same thing. But I hide my anger. At least I think I do. But, somewhere inside, a nagging feeling begins that things are happening on two levels here. One thing is going on, on the surface—this conversation—but I sense that something else, something I can't quite put my finger on, is transpiring underneath.

For a while now I've simply been looking at him, at a loss, not knowing what to say. He suddenly stands. I'm obviously being dismissed. "And what are you going to do now?" he asks, starting across the room. I get up to go and we walk across the room together. I am in complete confusion.

Where are we going? Where is he taking me? He pauses at the bathroom door and I realize he's simply going to the toilet!

"What are you going to do now?" he asks again, his hand on the doorknob.

It's my last chance. "Back to Kailash" is on the tip of my tongue, but with a burst of independence, with an urge to take my life into my own hands, I blurt, "I think I'll go to Goa." Then it's too late. The die is cast.

He looks intently at me for a few seconds. He smiles. "I'll be with you in Goa," he says, closing the bathroom door behind him.

Outside his room I cannot move for a couple of minutes. My legs simply will not carry me. Whatever's been happening with him on that unseen level has turned my knees to jelly. From down the hall Laxmi is watching me. I cannot face her. I rush past, mumbling something, heading for the exit, avoiding her eyes.

Twenty minutes later I am back in Colaba, in the sleazy room at the Rex Hotel, sitting on the hard bed staring at the filthy walls.

And then I am on the street. I buy a razor and a tola of hashish. Back in the room I smoke a joint and then I shave off my beard. I look into the mirror and the shock rocks me to my foundations—I have never seen that face before!

And ringing in my ears is the sound of Kailash: "Hoo! Hoo! Hoo!"

I join the noise in my head. "Hoo! Hoo!" I call to the stranger in the mirror. "Hoo! Hoo!" Then there are tears on the cheeks in the mirror and my own voice is sobbing, "Who? Who?"

The door opens and Divy is standing there. "Who? Divy. Who?" I say. "Who gives a shit, Divy? Who gives a shit?"

And I roll another joint.

Goa

"I've died and gone to heaven," Divy keeps saying, wide-eyed at the beauty that surrounds us. "I've died and gone to heaven."

We are lying, naked, on a stretch of pearl-white sand that rises out of the rolling green surf of the Arabian Sea. A swaying chorus of long-legged, high-hatted coconut palms dances behind us, hiding the brown sandy bluffs that slope upwards and inwards, ever so gently, to the tiny village that nestles above Anjuna Beach.

Everything is perfect, paradisal. The golden sunlight pours from the cloudless azure sky, the rows of sudsy white caps bubble along on the tips of the waves, and the sand beneath us is warm and welcoming and feather-bed delicious.

Divy rolls lazily over onto his stomach, looking at me through hooded lids, heavy with the sensuality of it all. "I've died and gone to heaven, you know. I've died and gone to heaven."

From Panjim, the capital, in a garland of glistening white crescents, separated one from the other by sudden outbursts of jagged black rock studded with phosphorescent mother-of-pearl, the beaches of Goa fan out along the coast: Calangute, Baga, Vagator, Anjuna, Chapora—names bespeaking the four hundred and fifty years of Portuguese rule India abruptly ended in 1962. And yet nothing could be less Indian than this minute speck on the map of the subcontinent, wedged between Maharashtra to the north and Karnataka to the south. Here, Krishna and the gopis give way to Christ on the cross; temples and mosques to churches and cathedrals; stone Vishnu-lingams to wooden statues of the Virgin Mary, and off to the market in printed cotton shifts instead of saris, their brown faces open and smiling instead of closed and reserved, are Mrs Rodriguez and Mrs Fernandez, Mrs DeSouza and Mrs D'Sa.

They are beautiful hybrids, the Goans, this mingling of Portuguese with Konkanese, of sea-faring Europeans with native women and they seem blessed with the best strains of both. There's a blending of the civilized and the primitive, of the sophisticated and the innocent that I have never encountered before. There is friendliness without pretension, generosity without expectation, work without tension and, as a visitor, something I appreciate tremendously after the rest of India: business without bargaining and service with a genuine, warm, unobsequious smile.

They love the food from the sea, the Goans—shark and swordfish, lobster and prawn—and they've also a lusty taste for the grape. But Portugal's wines have not transplanted as well as her seamen's seed. The white wines are too tart, too acid; the reds, too thick, too sweet. They demand a palate that's anxious rather than discerning. The Goan boozer, in any case, prefers his glass of cashew feni, the local brew that smells like coal oil mixed with honey and packs a punch like a mule.

There's a life in the air I didn't find in India. There's a kind of buoyancy and delight, a kind of infectious friskiness that thrills me just because I'm here. Nothing seems required of me: no action, no reaction. The headiness is simply there, available, exhilarating me anew with every breath.

I felt it as soon as we stepped out of the taxi, just off the main road that leads from Panjim, through the town of Mapuca, to the coast. The driver stopped at the edge of a pair of broad fields, a long causeway running between them, and pointed towards a cluster of palms on the other side. "Anjuna," he said.

I breathed out deeply, relaxing, grateful to be out of the steamy car, and what rushed in stoned me totally. Mixed together, in one bracing blast, filling my nostrils and filling my heart, was the salty smell of the sand and the sea, the sweetness of the wind in the palms and, coursing straight to my head, the invigorating and exquisite perfume of my own freedom.

The village of Anjuna is no more than a score of houses, squat, comfortable matrons, some in plain grey boulder, some in porous brown stone, some smartly dressed in brand new coats of dazzling whitewash. A few houses dot the hill that rises to the left, but for the most part they cluster around a pair of circular stone wells, cavernous affairs dug deep into the earth and ringed, on the surface, by fat, wide lips of worn rock. There are no lights, and so no wires. There are no telephones, and so no poles. All that connects the ladies of Anjuna is a narrow, well-trodden footpath that touches first one stoop and then another as it cuts through the village on its way to the sea.

Divy spies the house we're looking for first. "Shanti Niketan Meditation Centre" is written in faded blue paint above an open doorway in which a young woman and a small child are sitting. We introduce ourselves, saying we'd heard of the centre in Mount Abu and have just come from Bombay. Her name is Anasha, and her little girl, naked except for a mala, is Aneesha.

"Well, I guess I'm in charge with Ramesh away," she says in a north-country English accent, "and you're welcome to stay. Not many sannyasins are in Anjuna right now, so there's plenty of room. I'll show you where you can put your things," she adds, standing.

"I'd like a swim first," I say.

"Sure," Anasha replies. "Just leave your stuff with me. And follow the path. I'll have some chai ready when you get back."

Down the lane we go, through the long grasses, under the palms and up a gentle slope until, all at once, the earth beneath our feet ends. Straight down, several yards below, is sand, startling in its whiteness. Beyond, as far as the eye can see, is the green expanse of ocean. And she is breathing. I can hear her, deep and gurgling: out and in, out and in; blowing her emerald breakers onto the sands, then drawing them back. Out and in, out and in, depositing and reclaiming, emptying and regenerating, out and in, out and in.

I stand there, spellbound, transfixed by the majesty and simplicity, my belly rising and falling in tune with hers, in harmony, together, great and small—out and in, out and in, breathing, simply breathing with the sea.

And then an arm is laid across my shoulders. "Krishna," Divy says, his eyes shining, mirroring it all, "I think I've died and gone to heaven!"

We settle easily into Shanti Niketan, an afternoon at the Mapuca bazaar providing essentials: two straw mats, a pair of cotton mattresses and a couple of new lunghis each. By arrangement with the locals, Westerners live naked in Anjuna, and the lunghi is de rigueur for transit from one house to another or for passage along the footpath to the beach.

The nudity at first is odd. It shows me how many trips people have about their bodies, me included. But I see here, with six naked people sipping chai together on someone's porch or with a hundred bouncing bodies cavorting on the sand, how we're conditioned to reject our own flesh, how we've listened to the perfection-peddlers for so long—to Miss America and Mr. Universe, to the Playtex Living Bra and Charles Atlas's ninety-seven pound weakling—that we've come to hate our own bodies.

And sex? I am amazed to see that nothing is less sexy than the naked human body in the full light of day. I see here, so clearly, that the pull of sex lies in the suggestion, in the promise, in the imagined mystery hidden in the beautiful package. Au naturel, a body is a body. Some stomachs are flat and others are fat. Some breasts are big and others are small. Some dicks are short and others are long. It's that simple. That's the way we are.

The relationship between Anasha and Aneesha intrigues me and, for the first few days, I spend a great deal of time observing them, watching their interaction. Losing my own mother as a baby left a certain vacuum in me and I find that what goes on between them is nourishing me in a quiet and fulfilling way. Their love for each other is evident. What are not evident though are the over protectiveness of the average Western mother and the neediness of the normal Western child. There's a matter-of-factness between them, a security, an ease, a sense of rightness that delights me.

Anasha tells me she'd been a nurse in England. "I used to do private nursing," she explains, "and I was hired to look after this guy who was trying to quit junk. Didn't work though," she chuckles wryly. "He ended up turning me on instead."

She shakes her head at the memory: "When I think of it now! Crashing in parked cabs. Queuing at Boots in Piccadilly for my nightly, government-issue fix. But then I discovered Osho, and no more smack. It dropped away just like that.

"And then I came to India. It must be almost three years ago now. And after I was here for a while I began to want a baby. It was very, very strong. I just couldn't think about anything else for the longest time. I didn't want a husband, just a baby. So I waited until a really beautiful man came along, a man with a beautiful soul. He was Norwegian. He gave me Aneesha. She was born here, in Anjuna, in the stone house at the top of the hill."

Aneesha, one and a half, snuggles into her mother's lap. "Teat, mommy," she says, taking a nipple into her mouth and beginning to pull at it.

"The only word she knows," Anasha says, laughing, her hand patting Aneesha's brown little bum.

Aneesha drops the nipple and points to a line moving across the cow shit floor. "Ants."

"Oh yes, 'ants'. She knows 'ants' too. She blames everything on them."

Aneesha looks up at me, her cornflower-blue eyes connecting with mine. She touches a scratch on my leg. "Ants," she says, nodding knowingly like a wise old woman.

"Ants," I agree. And, patting the scratch gently, as if to help it heal, she turns back to her mother's breast.

Ants are the scourge of Anjuna. Never in my life have I seen so many. Everything chewable or climbable, table legs included, sits in a little tray of water—and let drop one single, careless crumb and, from a corner, crack or crevice, as straight as an arrow to the bull's eye, an ant armada sails forth to shanghai the booty and haul it back home. But if ants are the scourge, the pigs are the plague, the pandemic, the pestilence.

It's all a question of natural economics, I tell myself. It's just recycling at the elemental level, I say. But no matter the mental rationalizations, the prospect of my morning shit traumatizes me anew each day. I stand in the doorway, can of washing-water at the ready, eyes peeled and ears perked, prepared to retreat at the first sign of them, quite willing to hold on a bit longer, to wait just a little more. When I am convinced beyond doubt that they aren't around I venture forth. But it never fails. No sooner do I squat and my bowels begin to rumble than, crashing through the underbrush, noses twitching at the aroma and lips smacking in delight, come mama pig and her herd of nasty, bristly, squealing porkers, heading in a bee line right for my ass.

The first couple of occasions I am so freaked out I can't even bring myself to mention it. But on the third morning, Anasha, reading the consternation etched in the pallor of my face when I return to the house, and aware of the peculiar difficulty facing newcomers to Anjuna, offers the benefit of her experience. "They're absolute cowards, these pigs," she says. "Just take a handful of stones with you and they'll leave you alone."

So, the next morning, armed with a fistful of pebbles and a stick for good measure, I set out, necessity overcoming trepidation. Sure enough, the second I find a spot and my knees start to bend I can hear them coming. And Anasha, bless her, had been right. A few well-aimed hits and I'm left to finish my business in peace.

Still, raised as I was on Western sanitation, it's a shock to walk away from my morning toilet to the sounds of slurping and smacking, and then to watch a pack of piglets streaking past, snorting and shrieking at the sight of another victim, the steam of my faeces rising from their whiskers, traces of it dripping from their chops.

"Did you know," Anasha asks, "that Goan pork sausages are considered a great delicacy in Bombay?" and then collapses in laughter at the look of horror on my face.

One afternoon I return from the beach to find Anasha with a brawny, mustached man in his early thirties, his thinning salt-and-pepper hair pulled back into a single braid, Osho's mala about his neck. There is a bubbling boyishness about him, a catching enthusiasm as he extracts one item after another from the half dozen suitcases that surround him, holding each one out to Anasha proudly.

"This is Ramesh," she says, introducing us. "And this," she adds with a sweeping gesture embracing the goods that litter the floor, "is for his summer trip to Mykonos. Beach selling. It's how he takes care of us." She crushes him in a bear hug. "It's how he pays the rent."

I like him immediately. His heart is obviously big and warm. And he wears it openly and honestly on his sleeve.

I put water on for chai and join them, intrigued by the array spread out before me. Ramesh has been up north, to Gujarat and Rajasthan and Delhi and beyond, up into the foothills of the Himalayas to buy from the Tibetans settled in Dalhousie and Dharamsala and McLeod Ganj. He's returned with temple bells and prayer wheels, felt boots and appliquéd bonnets, silver belts and baubles, ivory carvings and bracelets. He's amassed hangings and batiks and quilted shawls and pouch after pouch of semi-precious stones to be fashioned, on languid Goa evenings, into chokers and pendants and earrings, all in readiness for when he leaves.

"It's so good to be home again," he says, stretching lazily for the glass of spicy chai I've placed before him. "Besides, I couldn't very well miss the last full-moon party of the season, could I?"

There's a noticeable buzz in the air of late, a kind of building exhilaration that mounts night by night, tantalizing and ripe with promise, keeping pace with the filling moon. All at once Anjuna is bursting at the seams. Shanti Niketan is suddenly overflowing with sannyasins, and the loads of freaks pouring into the village snap up every spare pallet they can find. The beach itself becomes a crash pad, a roll-up mat and a lunghi sufficing under the stars.

They come on foot from the nearby beaches and from the fresh water lake beyond Chapora. They come by bus from Kerala to the south, by train from Kathmandu and by boat from Bombay. But what floors me completely is that a group has flown in from San Francisco just for the weekend bash!

Never in my life have I seen so much dope. Everywhere I turn someone's holding something out to me—even at seven in the morning on Joe Banana's porch.

"Toke on a joint?"

"Hit on a chillum?"

"Line of coke?"

"Acid?"

"Mescaline?"

"Magic mushroom?"

"Jesus, Anasha," I ask the night before the party, "does everyone get ripped tomorrow night?"

"Yup," she replies. "And you may as well too. Besides, you can't really help it. There's acid in everything you touch—in the food, in the drinks, in the whole shebang."

Divy and I talk it over and decide to join in, to get stoned too. But, following Anasha's advice about relying on potluck, we seek out Tabitha the Acid Lady who, we're told, has some fine fresh windowpane-acid from the States, little see-through stowaways on the weekend charter from sunny California.

"What must she think?" I wonder, my head thrown back, gazing up at the rising moon, my ears throbbing to the grinding beat of the Rolling Stones. I had expected it to be fun, but it's not.

I wander through the mêlée once. And that's enough. A curving inlet, where I often sun, is tramped flat. Two-to-three hundred pairs of frenetic feet have stomped it down again and again, and a brace of blaring, kerosene-generated loudspeakers blast cacophony into the night, drowning out the waves.

And ringing the makeshift disco, passing from hand to hand, are fiery, fuming chillums, stoked with "the finest Afghani" and "the best Nepali", with fuel for the fantastic, the tokers huffing and puffing away, rising on pungent clouds of smoke, upwards, into the land of dreams.

I notice the sannyasins withdrawing bit by bit, wandering off by themselves, alone and in twos and threes, strolling up the beach or down to the sea. I do the same, pissed at myself for having dropped acid, for having been caught up in the whirl. But as Divy puts it when we cross paths on the sand, "What's done is done. You might as well enjoy it."

I'd first taken acid in 1968. A successful young PR exec who reached the target he'd been raised on and aimed at, only to find it empty and meaningless, I found the happiness I'd been promised nowhere in sight. Feeling cheated and desperate, and determined to get some sort of fulfilment out of my life, I'd gone for help to a doctor-friend of mine. I had some idea analysis might be the answer.

"Look, Jack," he said, having heard me out, "there's just nothing you can do. We're all in the same boat. And forget about psychiatrists. I won't recommend you to one. The ones I know are all birdier than you're ever going to be. I'm really sorry. I wish I could help. But that's the way life is, and you're just going to have to accept it."

I left Ted's chic little office in my trendy Hardy Amies suit and walked down the smart Toronto street, rejecting his advice to just resign myself to live like this, determined to find a way out. As I started the engine of my Buick convertible a light lit up in my head. "LSD," it flashed. "LSD!"

Driving back to my office I pondered my inspiration. I knew precious little about LSD, except that it had been developed initially to treat people with problems. The ensuing bad publicity I simply chose to ignore.

I made a few phone calls and that night dropped my first cap of acid, chasing it down with a glass of chilled chardonnay.

We became good friends, LSD and me. We went pretty well steady for a year or so, but after that night on the New York State Thruway, when something so real happened that LSD paled in comparison, we bade each other a friendly and grateful farewell.

And now, tonight, two years later, sitting under the Goan moon, a hit of acid again coursing through my being, I see, for the first time really, just what India has freed in me, just how much garbage the Dynamic has cleansed. Before, the drug released madness, pains and agonies that were embellished by the chemical but nonetheless real. Now nothing is coming up at all. No demons surface, no nightmares erupt, no wounds weep. There is only laughter and delight at where I am and at what I see before me.

Osho. That man in Bombay. I suddenly remember him and close my eyes, savouring his image. I left him in anger and confusion, but now I know, without a doubt, and accept without reservation, that I am irrevocably linked to him.

I also know I'm not ready, not quite yet, to face him again.

I walk slowly down the beach, away from the music and the noise. Laying my lunghi down, I stretch out naked on the sand. The moon is still climbing, sending lengthening palm-shadows over me. She dominates the night, erasing the distant stars. She has a presence, this cool, faraway globe ablaze with the sun's reflected glory. She has a presence and an intensity that pulls at me, calling me, striking some ancient chord that somehow still vibrates between us. I lay there watching: feeling, but not comprehending; sensing, but devoid of any understanding of her at all.

When she begins to peak, alone and supreme, ringed by her own brilliance, my attention is drawn to the sea. It is in a frenzy. Raised in towns and cities, in a world where light comes from switches and water from taps, I have never witnessed this interplay before, this desperate dance between the ocean and the full moon. It is as if the sea is in orgasm, driven by a churning, all-consuming passion to couple water with light, to breed breakers with moonbeams.

The waves are higher than I have ever seen, crashing and pounding against each other in frantic abandon, roaring and exploding into the night. Spume and spray and bursting white caps soar upwards, reaching, stretching, striving for the moon. And from way out, almost at the horizon, I see the combers begin. I watch them coming. Row upon rolling row of deep-green water advances, billowing and cascading, chute upon chute growing in size and speed, building up momentum, surging towards the shore as if, when they finally reach, the earth itself will springboard them, spiralling, straight up to the moon.

All at once a group of people breaks away from the party. They plant huge rockets in the sand in front of me and begin shooting streaming flares up into the sky, fireballs and sparklers and pinwheels bombarding the night. Soon they are surrounded by others, by a grotesque host of leaping, gyrating bodies, turning and twisting, howling and barking, braying and caterwauling at the moon.

The scene is not for me and, gathering my lunghi about my waist, I move farther away, down towards the swirling sea, to a natural quay. A ledge of smooth black rock juts outward, suspending me just above the water. There, until just before dawn, I wait out the drug, my eyes feasting on the visuals, my body sprayed by the brine and showered by the flying moonlit mist.

Two days later the hordes have gone, half Shanti Niketan is down for the count with hepatitis, and existence drops a beautiful gift right into our laps. An American sannyasin and his French girlfriend are heading north and offer their house to Divy and me. It's big and rambling, built from great blocks of petrified volcanic ash. Here and there a stone has been left out, creating a wind-hole to welcome the ocean breezes that filter through the palms. There is an enormous main room, spacious and airy, with a high vaulted ceiling of bare teak beams and baked red tiles. Three bedrooms adjoin. Across the front stretches a wide veranda, and in the back a long low kitchen leads to a private covered well. It's furnished, Goa style: mattresses and cushions and bolsters galore, dishes and pots and two kerosene stoves, and a maid, Mary, who comes every day.

"It's two hundred rupees a month," Nando, the American, tells us, "about twenty-three dollars. And Mary gets twenty rupees a week. Pay the rent to Mrs Rodriguez at the restaurant in back. And when you go, Mary will pack everything up and leave it at Joe Banana's store. Enjoy it!" There's nothing to do but walk up the hill, and Divy and I move in that very afternoon.

I love the new house, the peacefulness, the airiness, the remoteness of it. It stands alone on a slight rise, screened from the rest of the village by a thick bank of trees, a wild and unruly potpourri of bamboo and palm, hibiscus and banana, bougainvillea and lantana. A grove of ancient mango trees, gnarled and weathered with tiny green fruit beginning to appear, encloses the property in front.

The closest market is in Mapuca, a morning there and back. The vendors that come to the door stick to fruit, and Joe Banana never seems to stock anything more than wrinkled potatoes and wizened carrots, so we chuck our plans for cooking in favour of Mrs Rodriguez and her Lucky Star Restaurant.

Al Capp would have adored Mrs Rodriguez. The Lucky Star is Dogpatch come home to roost. In her tiny little yard, smack dab in the middle of the goats and the cows and the chickens—not to mention the dogs and the cats and the East African parrot that can only whistle the first eight bars of The Colonel Bogey March—Mrs Rodriguez, with the help of a few nails and some bits of string, has fashioned herself a straw and bamboo roof, suspended it above three wobbly tables and a handful of rickety chairs, and hung out her hand-lettered shingle. Her four front teeth stashed safely away in her apron pocket, but smiling nonetheless, Mrs Rodriguez ambles back and forth between the tables and her open fire, shooing her barnyard brood out from beneath her feet, cooking and serving some of the freshest and most delicious food I've eaten anywhere.

A routine settles in, a kind of set pattern to the days, but it is never boring. I awaken early, long before Divy, usually with the dawn, and await the sound of the milkman's daughter dropping our three daily litres of buffalo milk at the back door on her way to school. Boiling the milk on one stove and a pot of water on the other, I make my first glass of Ness-coffee and take it with me out onto the porch where I sit, smoking a bidi and watching the morning come alive. After a second coffee I stroll down the hill towards Shanti Niketan. Little Aneesha has taken to waiting for me on the stoop. I scoop her onto my shoulders and we head for the sea.

The morning is spent in and out of the water, Aneesha flopping about the edge, me venturing out a bit further. And I develop a taste for riding the waves, for hopping a breaker as it rolls in and letting it carry me, tossing and turning me, until it tumbles me headlong onto the shore—Aneesha cheering me on all the while. It's beautiful, our friendship, Aneesha's and mine—and pretty well wordless. Our communion exists in little unspoken things, in her hand tucking into mine, in my brushing sand from her golden hair, in a shared laugh at something silly, in a look that passes between us when we come across a strangely-shaped seashell we've never seen before.

By mid-morning the beach is filling and we're usually joined by Anasha and Divy. At the first sight of Anasha, Aneesha's gone, calling, "Teat, mommy," as she toddles away, her early-morning friend forgotten.

Afternoons and evenings are invariably quiet, given over to Mrs Rodriguez' cuisine, to long naps, to my sitting on the porch while Divy draws or sews. Visitors are rare, and this suits me fine.

More and more, the porch becomes my world. Except for eating, sleeping, and my seaside mornings with Aneesha, I seldom leave it. Goa has the most amazing sunsets, vivid, breathtaking extravaganzas that send kaleidoscopes of colour splashing across the sky, but even this interests me no longer. I sit on the porch hour after hour, drinking coffee or tea, smoking, sometimes a bidi, sometimes a joint, watching the empty mango grove before me.

A few days back I'd been thinking about Mount Abu and remembered a question Osho had answered. Someone had asked, "Does a buddha ever get bored?" and part of Osho's reply had stayed with me.

He'd spoken of how he lives in one room, never going out. "Life is so rich, even in an empty room," he said. "And every moment the room is changing, it is not the same. Nothing can be the same. Even the emptiness goes on changing. It has its own moods."

The mango grove becomes my empty room. And what was once a static scene, a motionless mural reflected in an unseeing eye, slowly comes to life for me.

I begin to see animation, a subtle vitality, where before I saw nothing. A branch sways languidly in the breeze. A loosened leaf floats to the ground. A lone gull swoops low, then swings high again, back out to sea. A grazing bull scratches himself against a crooked trunk, shaking two unripe mangoes down. A brown hare, ears flattened, shoots across my vision, and stopping once in mid-flight, sniffs, verifying his safety. The grove begins to enthrall me, to excite me. And I go to bed anxious for tomorrow, like a child who cannot wait to see if the seeds he has planted have already begun to grow.

It's changing me, this sitting, this grove watching: there's a quiet inside once more. And there's an appreciation of existence and an interest in life that hasn't been there for a very long while. And the joints drop. There's no effort involved; there's just no need.

The next thing I know, collecting Aneesha one morning, I want to do the Dynamic again. We do it together, Aneesha and me—she's picked it up from her mother. And there we are, thirty-six and almost-two, carrying on like crazy people, starkers on the beach. For the first time in months, I feel like a sannyasin again.

Over the last week or so, rumours have been reaching us that Osho is leaving Woodlands in Bombay, and the most talked-about destination is Pune, a place none of us know anything about, except that it's a big city some four hours inland from Bombay. And the news keeps changing. First it's yes, he's moving; then it's no, he's not; then it's yes again. Finally it's confirmed. On March 21, the anniversary of his enlightenment, he moves to Pune with Laxmi, Mukta, Vivek and a handful of others. The new address is 33 Koregaon Park.

But for me, at this point, Pune might as well be the moon. Something else is going on that requires my attention. For the past several days, it's seemed to me that Divy is looking unwell. He's appeared strained, a bit peaked, and has mentioned feeling tired. But when I awaken one morning to the sound of him vomiting out back, I know something is wrong. He comes in, ashen, clutching his right side, just below the ribs. The liver. I pull one lower eyelid down slightly and, sure enough, there's a yellow cast to the white of his eye, the telltale trace of bile. "Divy, you've got hepatitis."

When Divy is ill, he reverts. His animal nature springs to the fore. Not that he turns wild or runs amok or anything like that. He simply curls up, silent and uncomplaining, and withdraws from the world—from his body too I often feel, as if the occupant has vacated the house while it's being repaired. And so, for the next few days, I do what I can, bringing him what he wants when he surfaces to ask for things, getting him juices to drink and plain, boiled vegetables from the Lucky Star.

By the sixth day I am beginning to worry. He's now refusing food completely and his body, lean to begin with, is becoming thinner and thinner, more and more wasted. By the tenth day I realize he's dying. I'm not over-reacting; I'm not indulging in drama—it's just painfully, painfully obvious that he has no strength, no resistance left and that the life in him is slowly but certainly ebbing away.

And I don't know what to do. My mind throws up all sorts of ideas—a litter to Mapuca, calling the police—but the logistics of each seems more impractical than the next. Suddenly I just grab my mala. "Osho, help him!" I plead. "He's dying!"

Minutes later Anasha is standing in the doorway. "I had a feeling I should come," she says, "a feeling that you needed me." She walks past me, over to the bed, and looks down at Divy for a while.

"Go to Mapuca right now," she instructs, turning back to me, "and get me a couple of good syringes, some alcohol, and a half dozen vials of Vitamin B 12. Hurry. I'll stay with him."

Within three hours I'm back and the first injection has been administered.

"I'll give him another tonight," Anasha reassures me. "I'll give him a couple more tomorrow and then one a day for two or three more days, depending on how he is. I've got to go now, time for the teat, but you know where I am if you need me."

To my surprise, no more than a half hour after the shot, Divy's sitting up in bed, laughing, albeit feebly, and at long last, eating. All I can do is sit there, watching him, holding my mala in my hand, grateful the tide has turned, thankful he's not going to die after all.

His eyes suddenly widen. He utters a single word—"Rani"—and then he crashes, instantly asleep. At first I am confused. But then I turn and there, framed in the entrance, wearing a big straw hat, sweat and mascara pouring down her cheeks, her linen dress streaked and stained, is Rani!

"Obviously," she says, leaning breathlessly against the doorway, her tone dripping with understatement, "you didn't get my telegram. The driver let me out at the other end of the beach. Have you ever tried to carry two suitcases along a beach in high heels?" She notices Divy. "Is he sick?" she asks, suddenly concerned.

A brief explanation of the situation and Rani takes over, shooing me back out onto the porch. She loves Divy and is an amazing nurse. She cooks him the things he likes best, brings him fresh bouquets of flowers to arrange, paints and draws and sews and strings shells with him, the pair of them nattering all the while in Swedish.

I'm grateful to Rani. And I'm glad she's come. I don't feel left out for a second. Actually, with Divy in good hands, sitting on the porch again suits me just fine.

One evening, after Rani has been here for several days, I have been lying on the porch since dinner when, all of a sudden, I'm in some kind of gap, as if I've fallen into a tear in space. And, all at once, it hits me like a thunderbolt—time doesn't exist!

Time is an illusion, like the sunset is an illusion. Months and years, weeks and days, minutes and hours—none of them are real. They're utilitarian, man-made points of reference, but they're not really real. All that's real, authentic, is now, this very moment. And I see clearly that this is what life is, a succession of this-very-moments. The past is dead, memory; the future, projected dreams. All that's real is now.

And then I find I'm looking at a bright blue cloudless sky. I figure it's morning, that I've fallen asleep and spent the night out here on the porch. But then I realize my eyes are closed. I open them. It's pitch black all around me.

"The sky within!" I say aloud. "My God. There is a sky within!" And then, as clear as a bell, I hear a voice: "Come to Pune."

Two days later, with Divy and Rani to follow within a week, an auto rickshaw ferries me down a tree-lined street in Koregaon Park, Pune, past stately, faded mansions. It deposits me in front of number 33, where a group of sannyasins are standing at the gate. Mukta is there. Taking my hand, she leads me down a gravel drive. There, reclining in an armchair on the lawn, Vivek beside him, is Osho. He watches me as I walk across the lawn. "Ah, Krishna Prem," he says with a low chuckle, "I was with you in Goa."

Chapter Two: 1974

LONAVLA & PUNE

Unblinking, I sit by candlelight before the mirror, my reflected face undulating, changing, revealing facets, facades.

And suddenly the mirror is blank! The face I've been watching is gone. I am staring into emptiness! I hold my eyes open by sheer will. My body begins to shake, my heart races; the sweat streams from my brow, mingling with the tears from my smarting eyes. But somewhere inside a memory stirs, and I recall Osho, when he described this tratak technique, speaking about the mirror eventually going blank. He said that when this happened just to stay with it, to keep watching. Then, he said, faces from other lives would begin to come.

All at once it happens. There is a face in the mirror once again. It is not me, yet it is me. The features are different—the shape of the eyes, the cut of the jaw—but there is an unmistakable quality of me in it as well. Then it is gone, only to be replaced by another. And the reel begins. A face appears, filling the mirror for a moment, and then it fades, dissolving into another. Eyebrows thin and arch, then thicken, heavy on the brow. Hairlines advance and recede. Beards shorten and lengthen. Eyes open wide, then narrow into tiny slits. Finally, only one face remains, constant, watching me from the mirror. It is oval, older than mine, with high cheekbones and a smooth, flat brow. The beard is scraggly, greying, hiding the mouth; the eyes, a deep, liquid, oriental brown. Tibetan. For some reason the face looks Tibetan. Motionless, we reflect each other, our gazes locked.

And then, again, for the briefest fraction of a second, the mirror is blank once more. And then I am looking straight into the eyes of a snarling wolf! My eyes snap shut. And I sit there in my inner darkness, trembling.

As dawn creeps slowly across the stone floor the next morning, my fourteenth in silence in Lonavla, at Tulsi Sadhana Kutir once again, I am already awake, staring at the ceiling. Last night's experience has shaken me, stirring something ancient and forgotten. The slumber of some bygone memory has been disturbed, and it nags at me—but pointlessly, because I have no skill to engineer its recall. The empty mirror, my mind grasps, is the gap, like the jump between water and ice, between the chrysalis and the butterfly. Somehow, through the tratak, I fell into it, deep into the recesses of a me that goes beyond the me I know. As I pack to catch the seven o'clock train to Pune, I ponder what has happened. I cannot understand it, yet I cannot deny the experience. Last night I witnessed other incarnations. Of that, there is no question. I can see that there is a thread, a continuum that runs from life to life. Something continues, linking here and there, then and now, hidden by the bonds of flesh and what we grasp as time.

Divy and Rani, newly arrived from Goa, are standing at the gate when the rickshaw I've taken from the station drops me at number 33. They both look tremendous. Rani is tanned and relaxed, the remnants of the months in the West shed on the sands of Anjuna. Divy is healthy again, completely recovered, all traces of yellow gone. Four loving arms enfold me.

"You look fabulous!" Rani shrieks, overdoing it as usual. Divy just hugs me tightly, laughing into my shoulder. I'd written them that, arriving in Pune, I wanted to do another twenty-one days of silence and that Osho had agreed, but told me to come to Pune on Sundays for a shaktipat meditation he would conduct himself. Today is Sunday. They've timed their arrival specifically to meet me.

It's obvious from the two dozen or so sannyasins clustered at the gate this bright April morning that the population of Kailash has diminished drastically.

Teertha and Vishnu, Prageet and Virag and a host of others greet me. Like reunited, repatriated prisoners-of-war, like survivors of the Siberian labour camps, we hug each other, liberated, happy to be together again. Veda, I'm told, is still at the farm with Pyari, Veena and a few others.

"Come along. Osho's ready," a voice behind me announces. Unmistakably Mediterranean. Mukta.

She leads us down the gravelled drive and around the back of the house to a small, semi-circular mosaic patio. An empty armchair stands in the centre, just out from the wall. To the right is a door, closed now, leading into the house. After a few moments the door opens and Osho is standing there, palms meeting in namaste. He does not look well at all. There is an underlying frailty and pallor even his slight tan cannot mask. His body seems somewhat stooped as he moves slowly towards his chair; that it requires effort is painfully obvious. Laxmi and Vivek follow, sitting, as usual, on the floor beside him. They both watch him anxiously. The strain of shaktipat can be devastating. Last Sunday he'd needed help to make it back into the house.

At the morning darshan on the lawn two weeks back, when I told him of the pull to move into silence and he said to come to Pune on Sundays for shaktipat, he explained the technique. "Whenever a Master wants to help you," he said, "to cleanse your energy channel, your passage, if it is blocked, he simply possesses you. He simply descends into you, and his energy, which is of a higher quality, purer, unbounded, moves in your energy channels. They become open. Then your energy can move in them easily. This is the whole art of shaktipat."

He leans back in his chair and, folding his hands in his lap, watches us for a moment. "Everyone stand and raise your arms in the air."

Instructed to bring a flower with us, we've all done so and we stand, arms extended, a single blossom cupped in our hands.

"Now," he says, "project your ego into the flower."

I try to throw me into the flower, to focus my mind, my personality, my ego, everything I know as me, into the marigold I am holding on high. And suddenly, the second Osho's eyes close, a great shudder possesses me and my body begins to shake uncontrollably. A current courses through me, moving upwards to settle in my arms. My palms are burning; the tiny flower quivers between them.

"Drop it!" Osho calls. As the flower-egos hit the patio floor, the air fills with the cries and screams of catharsis, as deafening as the morning meditations in front of him at Mount Abu. At Kailash and in Goa, I'd forgotten the difference his presence could make. This shaktipat, this cleansing, is a bath of fire. It goes on and on, growing louder and louder, more and more intense, yet almost unbearably, never quite peaking.

"Stop!" Osho's voice cuts through the chaos like a sword. As one, we freeze. And there is innerness. And there is silence. And there is the purity and mystery of space.

Back at the room they've taken at the Green Hotel, Rani natters on about Divy's recuperation, the end-of-season Anjuna parties, the closing of the house, the boat to Bombay, the taxi ride to Pune and delivers love and affection from Mrs Rodriguez, Joe Banana, Mescaline Bobby, Eight-Finger Eddie, Mucous Mike and assorted other Goa characters. Divy doesn't say much. He seems to be watching me, weighing something in his mind. As for me, my silence is unbroken. The sensation is odd and at the same time agreeable—just to be able to sit and listen with no response expected, with nothing to do but enjoy Rani and her stories.

"Silence agrees with you," Divy says finally. "I think I'll ask Osho if I can do twenty-one days in Lonavla as well. I haven't been meditating since the hep and didn't realize until today just how much I've missed it."

My train to Lonavla leaves at three, and as I stretch across the bed to retrieve my bag from the bureau I am stopped in mid-motion by the most excruciating pain in my groin. It is so sharp and unexpected it takes my breath away. I try to reach for the bag again, but the pain is so bad I can't get off the bed.

"Krishna!" Divy says, seeing me hurting. "What's wrong?"

I have no idea, but then, on examination, nestled behind a testicle, right where the leg joins the torso, I discover an enormous boil, glowing like the fiery end of a burning cigar.

"You didn't know it was there?" Divy asks, surmising this from the look of surprise on my face.

I shake my head. It wasn't there when I left Lonavla, of that I'm certain. The shaktipat? Is it possible? Has the shaktipat brought this horrible thing out in me?

"Divy, see if the hotel knows how we can get a doctor," Rani instructs.

"And you," she adds, turning to me, "just forget about Lonavla and lie down. Mama's going to order more tea!"

Dr Tavildar's office, buried in the bowels of the poorest section of Pune, far from the princely mansions of Koregaon Park, is dark and dingy. The dusty certificate on the damp-stained wall testifies to his authenticity, to his graduation from a Bombay medical school. and he, at least, is clean. I have the feeling he's had little contact with foreigners—there's a nervousness in the way he's preparing his instruments—but he's very gentle with me.

"I'm sorry, but I can't use an anaesthetic, swamiji," he says apologetically, adding the honorific "ji", the sign of respect. He explains that the administration of a local injection in that particular area could be dangerous. My immediate reaction is one of panic: pain has always freaked me out. But what to do? I grit my teeth, realizing there's nothing to be done but to bear it in stoic silence. As the doctor advances towards me, the scalpel glinting in his hand, Divy moves in front to block my view. But it's too late. I've already seen it.

"This won't hurt too much," Dr Tavildar promises. And as the knife descends towards my groin, Divy takes my hand in his: "Squeeze."

One sharp stab and it's over. To my surprise there's no pain. There was just one quick twinge and then the most delicious relief. And I start to laugh. It's so apparent that the terror of pain exists in the tension of anticipation. And I am freed from an old fear. As I shake Dr Tavildar's hand, I am still laughing at myself. He doesn't see what's so funny. I'm sure he thinks I'm mad.

We take a room for three at the Green, and the next few days are spent recuperating, broken only by agonizing afternoon rickshaw rides over the potted streets to Dr Tavildar's office. There, with long steel pincers, he digs hard little lumps of pus out of the cavernous hole in my groin. In many ways, the cleanings are worse than the actual operation, but I've been in silence for almost three weeks now. It's so quiet inside nothing seems to shake me at all.

I begin to think about going back to Lonavla, feeling something has been left incomplete. But, through Mukta, a message comes from Osho. The silence has done its work, he says. There's no need to return to Lonavla. I should stay in Pune and become involved in the activities here. It's fine if I want to continue the silence, to complete the twenty-one days. I decide to see it through. The space is beautiful.

Osho's body still isn't well. The morning darshans on the lawn continue, but there are no more shaktipats. And no sign of any discourses. But he wants us to keep meditating. There's no room at 33, so Laxmi arranges with the city fathers for us to use Empress Botanical Gardens at the edge of the cantonment. We make the twenty-minute run by cycle at six in the morning for Dynamic and again at six in the evening for Sufi whirling.

One night there's a message from Osho. He is going to begin a series of eight discourses, in Hindi, on *Bhagavad Gita*, and we Westerners should also attend the discourses. We should sit at the back, eyes closed, and meditate on the sound of his voice. The first morning's turnout is disappointing—only a handful of Indians. Pune, it appears, isn't yet interested in its new godman. But Osho is in rare form. He looks fit and hearty again.

At this point, Divy leaves for three weeks of silence in Lonavla, and Rani and I separate, moving into single rooms in the Green. Prageet and Virag are down the hall.

Looking for matches one afternoon, I drop in on Prageet while Virag and Rani are shopping down Mahatma Gandhi Road. He's lying spread-eagled on the bed under the fan, a cup of tea perched precariously on the pillow beside him.

"Have you read this?" he asks, holding up a copy of *Sannyas* magazine. "It has this incredible lecture where Osho talks about his past life in Tibet. He says he went into this twenty-one day fast, preparing to die, and that three days before it was finished he had a disciple kill him. He says he promised his disciples he'd come back to help them, but if he'd let himself die he wouldn't have been able to. So he had this guy kill him." He looks up at me. "Wonder if he's back? The guy who killed him. He might be right here in Pune now!"

Conversationally speaking, a vow of silence is a greatly limiting factor. I smile and shrug my shoulders. Picking up the matches, I leave Prageet to his magazine. It sounds fascinating, but I can wait. The silence has only three more days to go.

At the next morning's discourse, sitting there with my eyes closed, I feel wonderfully at peace. The music of Osho's voice, the singing of the birds, the soft in-and-out of my breath, the cool morning air stroking my skin—everything is right and perfect.

Suddenly, inside, as if projected onto an inner screen, a face appears before me. At the same time, a tremor quivers through me, setting everything on edge. My body remembers first: it's the same sensation as happened in Lonavla that night before the mirror. Only then do I recall the face. It's the oval one, the one that seemed Tibetan. It's the one that looked back at me before the mirror went blank the second time. It's the last face before the wolf.

It hangs in front of me, suspended, bodiless. Then it is gone. Now Osho's face replaces it. Now Osho is gone and the Tibetan is back. And so it goes. First one and then the other, one and then the other, until I open my eyes and erase them with the light and the trees and the sannyasins around me. I have no idea what's going on.

After the lecture, Teertha approaches me. "I hear you have a typewriter you might be willing to sell?"

I nod yes.

"I also hear you're thinking about going back to the West?"

One night, Divy, Virag, Prageet, Rani and I had talked about going back and the idea of a meditation centre in Montreal had been mentioned. I presume it's this to which Teertha's referring. Rather than try to explain with hand signals, I simply nod.

"Why?" He's incredulous anyone would consider leaving.

I rub my thumb and forefinger together. Money.

He considers a moment. "Look," he says, "Virag tells me you used to write. We need some help. After this Hindi series Osho is going to give fifteen talks in English. They're to be published in a book especially to introduce him to the West. I'm supposed to edit it. I'm not a writer; I'm a therapist. We could use your help."

He reads my thoughts. "Money!" he laughs. "Look, Osho's vision is vast. He sees things we don't. If he says it's okay for you to stay, can you stop worrying about money and help us on the book?"

I nod again. Sure. Why not?

"I'll send him a note tonight and let you know what he says tomorrow."

As I turn to leave, Teertha touches my shoulder gently. He looks at me intently for a moment, his gaze direct. Then he starts to laugh. "Surrender," he says. "Just surrender."

When I arrive at the National Hotel for breakfast the dining room is crowded: a train must have just come in. I join Prageet and Virag at a table, but the second the bearer hands me the menu the idea of food makes me feel sick. I need to lie down. Outside, I try riding my bicycle, but my balance is off. I wheel it around the corner to the Green, collect my key and walk slowly upstairs to my room. I feel like I'm going to faint.

As soon as the door closes behind me I burst into tears. There is no reason to cry, but I am crying. And for the next six hours I lie on my bed and sob my guts out. When the flood finally abates, there is absolute stillness inside. But it is short-lived. All of a sudden I sense a presence, as if there is someone else in the room.

And then I'm looking at a scene, but it is so fleeting that I sense it more than actually see it. There is something about five days and disobedience, about three days and a metal weapon. And then my world fills with a voice that comes out of nowhere, loud and sharp and clear: "You killed Osho in his last life!"

When it fades, it leaves condemnation in its wake. And the tears start again until, at last, like sea spray on the wind, they are blown away and I am left in peace. I sleep, uncovered, uncaring, until the bearer knocks at my door with morning tea.

It's been almost five months since any of us have heard Osho speak in English and, after the morning's Dynamic before a curious crowd of Indians at Empress Gardens, we cycle hurriedly back into town, to the flat we moved into the night before—a fine, two-family, ground-floor affair off Boat Club Road, minutes from Koregaon Park. We've just under an hour before the discourse, time for a shower and a quick mug of Ness-coffee. We're all in high spirits this morning, and the flat is filled with song. From the shower come Prageet's bass rumblings; from the kitchen, with the kerosene stove roaring backup, Virag's high, sweet trill.

On the kitchen table lies Prageet's copy of *Sannyas* magazine. "Seven hundred years ago, in my previous life," I read, "there was a spiritual practice of twenty-one days, to be done before death."

Shit! This morning, of all mornings, I have to stumble onto this! I'd managed to shelve the voice from the Green. For the last day or so it had hardly crossed my mind at all.

"I was to give up my body after a total fast of twenty-one days," I read on. "There were reasons for this, but I could not complete those twenty-one days. Three days remained. Those three days I had to complete in this life. This life is a continuity from there; the intervening period does not have any meaning in this respect. When only three days remained in that life, I was killed. Twenty-one days could not be completed because I was killed just three days before, and those three days were omitted."

Prageet's sudden hand on my shoulder is like the grisly grip of death itself.

My stomach knots. "Ready?" he asks. Then, seeing what I'm reading, he adds, "Far out, huh? Wonder what'll happen when the guy who killed him shows up?"

I say nothing. My eyes are riveted on a paragraph further down the page: "Therefore, I have told many times in various discussions that just as Judas tried for a long time to kill Jesus, though Judas had no enmity with Jesus, the person who killed me had no enmity with me, though he was taken to be and was treated as an enemy."

"Krishna Prem!" Virag calls from outside. "Are you coming?"

"Two minutes!"

"That killing became valuable," I continue to read. "At the time of death those three days were left. After all my strenuous effort for enlightenment during that life, I was able to achieve in this life, after a period of twenty-one years, that which had not been possible to achieve during those three days. For each of those three days in that life, I had to spend seven years in this life."

"We're going now!" Prageet shouts. "Lock up after yourself!"

Cycling out to 33, my brain's going a mile a minute. "For each of those three days in that life, I had to spend seven years in this life," he said. And for the first time, the sensation of five days that accompanied the voice made sense. Seven times five is thirty-five. I arrived at Woodlands a couple of weeks after my thirty-fifth birthday. But nothing's any clearer. If anything, I'm more confused than ever.

Heading into Koregaon Park, I feel awful. Rattling in the pocket of my robe are a few fluted ten-paise coins. The sound of them is as unbearable to me as the chink of silver must have been to Judas. Rounding the last corner, I tear them from my pocket and hurl them into the gutter, as if the act might purge the confusion in my heart.

Ever since that afternoon at the Green I've been living a Scarlet O'Hara kind of existence, with "I'll think about that tomorrow" as the motto keeping me on even keel. By the time we're all seated in a semi-circle in front of Osho's chair I've calmed down somewhat. I soak in the peace around me, making it mine. That the balm is temporary, I choose to ignore.

I don't feel bad about shoving this whole thing aside. Not at all. In a way I feel obliged to—I have to work on the production of the book these talks will become. I have to be attentive, alert.

The team has already been established—all Kailash veterans. In overall charge is Teertha. His girlfriend Jagruti is to transcribe and I'm to edit. Virag's in charge of proofreading. There's no working space at 33, so Ma Shradha Bharti, an Indian disciple and Teertha's landlady, has donated the living room of her rambling, Raj-style bungalow a few compounds away from our flat.

The book is intended for the West, and Osho has asked that we prepare a series of questions, mirroring our own concerns, and that they be put to him. He is to respond spontaneously. The only thing we have been given is the title, *My Way: The Way of the White Clouds.*

For the past few days we've all been scratching our heads and scribbling down our queries. We've handed in questions on happiness and misery, sex and love, aloneness and relationship; on awareness and energy, meditation and enlightenment; on how a Master works on his disciples. Originally, Teertha suggested we each ask our own questions, but, deciding the passing back and forth of the microphone would be awkward, we agreed he should ask all the questions on our general behalf.

Suddenly the door to the house swings open and there is Mukta, her salt-and-pepper mane lifting from her shoulders as she sails to her seat. For a few breathless seconds the archway is empty and then Osho fills it, white and light and smiling, his hands folded in namaste. Vivek follows him, cool and mysterious, sitting to his left, facing inwards towards him.

Palms still meeting in greeting, Osho arcs a slow half-circle, his gaze caressing us, taking us all in. When he sits, crossing one leg and leaving the usual single sandal behind, Laxmi moves from the doorway, eyes downcast, and sits to his right. He looks at Teertha and nods. Laxmi's recorder clicks on.

"Osho," we hear Teertha's voice over the speaker, "why is your way called *The Way of the White Clouds?"*

His eyes drop from Teertha's face and there is a delicate, almost imperceptible turning inwards, as if he is moving towards some source that is hidden from the rest of us, available only to him. The air is charged, expectant, like the gap between lightning and thunder. And then, in a single motion of fluidity and grace, he opens upwards and outwards towards us, his hands lifting, index fingers touching, poised, ready for the coming illustration. He breathes in, and the sound is as soft and as faint as the murmur of a butterfly's undulating wings.

"Just before Buddha died," he begins, "somebody asked him: When a buddha dies where does he go? Does he survive or simply disappear into nothingness? And this is not a new question—one of the oldest, many times repeated and asked.

"Buddha is reported to have said: Just like a white cloud disappearing.

"Just this very morning there were white clouds in the sky. Now they are no more there. Where have they gone? From where do they come? How do they evolve, and how do they dissolve again?

"A white cloud is a mystery—the coming, the going, the very being of it.

"That's the first reason why I call my way The Way of the White Clouds. But there are many reasons, and it is good to ponder, to meditate upon them.

"A white cloud exists without any roots—it is an unrooted phenomenon, grounded nowhere, or, grounded in the nowhere. But still it exists.

"The whole of existence is like a white cloud—without any roots, without any causality. Without any ultimate cause, it exists. It exists as a mystery..."[2]

For the next ninety minutes he pours on us, this rare and beautiful man, showering his love and understanding, sharing his experience.

"Find out the way how your cloud moves, where it drifts," he is saying, "and allow it full freedom to move and drift. Wherever it goes, it will reach to the divine. Just don't fight—flow. Don't push the river—flow with it.

"A dance is beautiful. But you must be totally in it. That's the point.

"Don't reject anything—rejection is irreligious. Accept totally. Acceptance is prayer.

"Enough for today?"

And then there is silence. I fold my hands in front of me and watch his feet move past. Only then do I raise my head. My eyes are filled with tears, and my heart with gratitude. Whatever has happened between us in another time, he has accepted me again. Everything's suddenly okay.

The mornings become miraculous for me. I awaken with a sense of joy, as if the very day itself has been designed for me. The meditations at Empress Gardens are delicious. Daily, out of the silent stage, a new bliss bubbles and I carry it with me through the discourse into the day's editing at Ma Shradha's house.

The book is coming along beautifully. We are presenting Osho's words in a poetic format, and I feel part of a great and glorious work as each stanza rolls out of my typewriter.

And here, through the discourses and the day-to-day involvement in his words, I begin to see Osho from a new perspective. I am beginning to observe the Master at work, to watch him, slowly but surely, with infinite patience and compassion, setting in motion the transformation

---

2 *My Way: The Way of The White Clouds*

of his disciples. Up to now, it appears to me, he has provided the tools, the situations, but has left us pretty much to our own devices, left us to grind away our own roughest edges, be it through Dynamic, silence in Lonavla, the farm at Kailash, or a fruitless attempt at escape in Goa.

Looking at myself and at those around me, at people I've known for several months, it seems to me that heads are not so full, hearts are not so frozen, and that, for the first time, there's a real receptivity to Osho.

I feel as if my eyes have been blinded and my ears blocked up to now, as if everything that has ever been fed into them has been filtered, turned and twisted to suit me. For example, when I first came across the Hindi word maya and the concept that the world is illusion, I expected, when clarity began to come, for the outer to change, for the trees and the grass and the mountains to undergo some magic transformation. But now, sitting here with Osho, listening to his words, I see that it is *me* who is going to change, that it is my vision, my eyes, that will, with his help, become clear and unclouded.

But where am I right now? Who am I? The answer is obvious—mind. The mind is really all I know of me. I've had glimpses, yes, but my reality is the mind. And I am sitting in front of a man who's telling me that I am not my mind, not my body, that I am beyond both, that I am consciousness. But right now, I am my mind.

"Watch," he says in one morning's talk, "and when you watch you have to remember that while watching, don't judge. If you judge, watching is lost. While watching, don't evaluate. If you evaluate, watching is lost. While watching, don't comment. If you comment, you have missed the point."

At Empress Gardens, in the fourth stage of Dynamic, there's been a new presence arising, growing bit-by-bit, day-by-day. When the "stop!" comes and I freeze in place, it's there, intense and unwavering. The sensation is odd: it feels like an all-seeing eye somewhere back inside my head, staring, unfocused, into my inner space. Only now, listening to Osho, do I realize what's been happening. Watching, witnessing has been happening. My mind has been emptied of thoughts, and what

I've done is refill it immediately, trying to figure out what's going on, trying to grasp something infinite with something finite, something unknown with something known. I've been achieving what I've been striving for and destroying it at one and the same time.

And with this realization comes a new determination to be as alert as possible. I also see it is all up to me. He can indicate and inspire, but my transformation is up to me.

"And this possibility of your being near me can be used, can be misused," he is saying, "can be missed altogether. If you miss, then too it will not be for the first time. Many times you have been with me. It may not have been exactly with me—many times you were with a Buddha and that was to be with me. Many times you were with a Jaina, with a Mahavir, and that was to be with me. Many times you were around Jesus, or Moses, or Lao Tzu—that was being with me. Because a Lao Tzu or a Buddha cannot be defined in any way: they are two emptinesses, and two emptinesses have no qualities to differ.

"You may have been with a Lao Tzu and I say you were with me, because there is nothing to make any distinction. A Lao Tzu is an emptiness. Two emptinesses are just the same; you cannot make any distinction.

"But you missed. You have been missing many times. You can miss again."

That afternoon, at Ma Shradha's, I am distracted, disturbed. The talk about missing, about having been with him before and missed, has brought the voice from the Green roaring back, filling my ears to the exclusion of all else. Gone is the non-judgmental witnessing I vowed this morning to adopt. I am in turmoil.

Teertha suddenly crosses over to me, holding a sheet of paper in his outstretched hand—the next passage for editing.

"You are here with me," I read. "That is not so significant. You were with me in the past. That seems to be more significant. And you are missing this moment when you can be really with me, because to be with me is not a physical phenomenon. You can sit by my side and you may not be with me. You can cling to me for years and you may not be with me for a single moment. Because to be with me only means that you are not.

"I am not, and if even for a single moment you are also not there, there will be a meeting. Then two emptinesses meet. Remember, only two emptinesses can meet. There is no other meeting possible. Whenever you have a meeting, it means two emptinesses merging."

"I'll be back in a moment," I say to nobody in particular and, wandering out onto the terrace, drop into a corner chair in the sun, wishing the heat searing my eyelids would consume me totally. I feel threatened and, at the same time, completely impotent. Others have also read that same issue of the magazine and I've overheard all sorts of conversations about what will happen when the one who killed Osho in Tibet shows up in Pune. I've always been a loner; even with my family there was never any real sense of belonging, but for the first time I feel part of a family and I'd rather suffer in silence than risk what I've found. But the price is becoming more and more difficult to pay. It's becoming a festering wound, and it's eating at me.

"Tea, swamiji?" a voice behind me invites, and I turn to see Ma Shradha beckoning me into the shade of the covered veranda. She guides me to a sofa and sits me down beside her, putting a cup of tea into my hand. For a few moments she fidgets nervously with the border of her sari, rearranging it, refolding it. It is obvious she has something on her mind. It is equally apparent she is wary of broaching whatever it is she wants to say to me.

"What is it, Ma?" I ask.

"Forgive me, Krishna Premji," she begins tentatively, "I am not one to interfere in matters that do not concern me, but there is something I should like to say to you." She pauses, her eyes meeting mine briefly, as if to verify the ground upon which she's preparing to tread.

"Go on, Ma."

"You have been working here for well over a week now," she continues, "and I have not been able to help noticing that something is disturbing you. And I feel it has to do with Osho." Giving my knee a gingerly pat, she laughs. "You hide it well, but these old eyes are sharp. All I want to say is that I am willing to listen if you want to unburden yourself."

She settles back into the cushions and raises her cup to her lips. Her keen brown eyes, squinting slightly in the rising steam, are fixed on me.

I look into that soft, liquid gaze that reminds me of Laxmi, and I see compassion and understanding. And like a dam released the story gushes forth, seconds in the telling. Her eyes are as round as the saucer in her hand. "And you have not told him!" she exclaims, incredulous.

"I couldn't, Ma! I couldn't. I still can't!"

"But why?" she asks. "But why?" She moves closer to me, placing a hand on my arm. "You must tell him! You have no choice but to tell him. You don't know how he will use what has happened to help your spiritual growth. This is far too important for you to keep mum."

"I can't tell him," I repeat, explaining the fears that have haunted me, the fears of rejection, of retribution and as I speak it all just sounds ridiculous. "Of course I'll tell him, Ma. Of course I must," I say. And I head back inside to my typewriter, to write Osho a letter. Behind me on the sofa I leave Ma Shradha, blushing and giggling from the grateful kiss I have just planted on her matronly Brahmin cheek.

"Prem?" he invites, as I sit before him on the lawn the next morning.

"Did you read my note, Osho?" I ask nervously.

"Yes," he replies. "But don't think about things like this."

Shit! I shout silently. *Don't do this to me. After all I've been through, don't just slough me off like this!* On the surface, I am silent, watching him, looking for some sign, some indication.

He chuckles. I find myself reddening in embarrassment, wondering if he reads minds. For a moment, nothing is said. "You didn't do it," he says at last. "You were there; that's why you remember it, but you didn't do it. You were there, but you didn't do it. So don't worry about it." He turns to the sannyasin next to me.

I slink back to my seat on his right. My mind simply cannot grasp what he has just said. The rest of the darshan is a haze. Words pass back and forth between Osho and the other sannyasins, but nothing registers.

Suddenly he turns to me again, leaning sideways in his chair, his face inches from mine. "You didn't do it," he repeats. "You were there; that's why you remember it, but you didn't do it." Then he says it again: "You were there, but you didn't do it.

"And," he adds, preparing to rise from his chair, "many more things you will remember!"

And then our eyes meet. At first it's only the irises I notice, but then my focus shifts to the pupils, and the world as I know it crumbles around me. Osho's pupils are suddenly windows, and I look into his interiority and there is nothingness, only a vast expanse of space, as clear and as blue and as unending as the sky above.

And then he is gone and I am back outside the gate, my head buried in the nearest shoulder. And I hear the sound of my own voice coming from some place far, far away: "I was with him before, and he said I didn't do it. But there's nobody home. There's nobody in there at all."

Pune—Setting up a home

I've never known a grubby Libra, nor one who didn't like his creature comforts, and in getting the flat together while Virag and I have been busy with the book at Ma Shradha's bungalow and Divy has been off in Lonavla, Prageet's done his horoscope proud. He's had our new abode freshly painted, off-white throughout, and furnished the place. For the kitchen he's found six chairs, a generous table, an assortment of pots and pans, dishes and cutlery, and a brace of kerosene stoves. For our rooms, he's picked up chests of drawers, overstuffed cotton mattresses, mosquito nets and mounds of throw pillows. He's alerted the neighbourhood vendors, the vegetable wallah, the fruit lady, the milkman and found a Christian Madrasi maid, Rita, to come mornings and evenings when the Pune city fathers open the taps to flood the tin tubs and plastic buckets that line our bathroom walls.

It's an odd little flat. A central wall divides it in half, mirror-like, each side an exact reflection of the other, with a foyer and two rooms leading, New York City railroad style, into a common kitchen. Part of the kitchen floor is raised and tiled; the rest is brick. The tiled section is ceilinged; the bricked, open to the elements but for a wire mesh. On each side is a compact cooking cupboard—"room" is too kind a word—and a bathroom with a foot-washing tap, a shower and a toilet: Indian-style to the left, Western to the right. "Take your choice," Prageet says, "sit or squat."

Soon the flat is a home. Divy returns from Lonavla and after a few trips to Empress Gardens and the second-hand sari market, the kitchen is alive with ferns, the windows are flowing with silks, and there are gaily-patterned cushions and brightly-coloured bolsters for the morning transformation of sleeping spaces into snug and sunny sitting-rooms, ready for the day.

The kitchen is Virag's. Straw baskets are hung, rat-safe, for fruits and vegetables, and jars are filled with dried beans and chickpeas and lentils, honey and sugar, rice and spices, teas from Ootie and Darjeeling and Assam.

And one afternoon I come home to find her standing in the kitchen doorway, as pleased as can be, a still-warm chocolate cake in her hand. Behind her, all new and fresh and gleaming, perched atop a kerosene stove like a square-eyed gargoyle on a pillar of flame, is a minuscule oven with a little glass door.

The laughter is instant—at the tiny toy oven, at her child-like pride. But the cake is undeniably delicious. Giggling and guffawing, we stuff it into our cheeks, every last crumb, planning, as we chomp, to make another for dinner. This time with icing.

The cake that night, ambitiously marbled and iced high in peaking swirls, is not only a success but also a celebration. That very afternoon we'd put the finishing touches to *My Way: The Way of the White Clouds* and, somewhat dubiously, I had agreed to try my hand at writing the introduction for the book that is to introduce Osho to the West. Nervously, I share the news. Divy, Prageet and Virag are all thrilled. I am still not sure.

Over our final pot of tea at Ma Shradha's that afternoon, Teertha broached the subject. "You know," he began, "Osho asked me some time ago to write the introduction for this book. I'm not a writer. I've tried two different versions and it's just no good. I've suggested you. Will you give it a try?"

"Jesus, Teertha, I haven't written anything in years. Editing is one thing; writing is something else altogether. And when I did write it was basically press releases, that sort of thing. I'm not so sure I can do it either."

He's not buying my doubts; that I can see. He just smiles, appraising me with that piercing, knowing look. "Did Osho give you any guidelines?" I ask, capitulating.

"A few," he replies, relieved the task is out of his hands. "He wants himself introduced to the West, and he wanted me to tell what's going on here through what's happened to me. Now it's your story you have to tell."

A Libra as well, my surroundings are as important to me as Prageet's are to him, and so, to put my writer's sanctum together, I drag him downtown to the furniture wallah early the next morning. By afternoon, the creative setting perfect, I find myself sitting in a straight-backed chair at a desk-high mahogany table, looking blankly at the naked white sheet of paper staring back at me from my typewriter. All that's changed when Virag calls me to dinner is that the word "Introduction" has been neatly centred at the top of the page.

As teatime draws nigh the following afternoon I've had it with the blank piece of paper and that bloody single word, so I cycle out to 33 to see if Laxmi's free for tea. Mukta's standing in the garden, pondering placement of a pack of potted begonias. "Laxmi?" she says. "I think she's in her room." Around the house I go, across the patio where Osho gives his morning lectures, and knock at Laxmi's window.

"Laxmi?" I call.

We're good buddies, Laxmi and me. The window flies open. "Tea?" she asks the moment she sees me. "Sit. Laxmi's coming." And as the window shuts behind her I hear her shrieking into the depths of the house, "Gaghan Singh! Chai! Patio lao!

"So, swamiji," she says, pulling a chair close, her feet firmly planted, hands resting squarely on her knees in her typical tomboy stance, "what are the news? Introduction has happened?"

"Not yet," I confess. "I really don't know what to write."

"That I!" she pshaws, expelling the word like a spit. "That 'I' can do nothing. Become vehicle, swamiji. Let him write through you. Just become instrument to his work—like Laxmi." And for her the problem is solved. The introduction is as good as done.

"Now, swamiji," she says, leaning towards me confidentially, her deep brown eyes sparkling, "Laxmi has news. Last night number 17 happened!" She sits back, as pleased as punch with her pronouncement, surveying me, awaiting my reaction. All I can do is look back at her. I have no idea what she's talking about.

"Number 17 Koregaon Park!" she shouts, tapping her temple at my stupidity and indicating the adjoining property with a grand wave. "From today number 17 is with us. Now commune is going to happen. Gate at 33 will be walled up, and in-coming will happen through number 17.

"And in back of bungalow, space is also there for meditation camp," she adds. "No more Empress Gardens. Now camp, just like Mount Abu, can happen here. So, on tenth June night, he will introduce camp, and from eleventh morning, discourse, Dynamic Meditation, kirtan, whirling, everything!

"He is speaking on Zen and title for book he has already given Laxmi: *A Bird on the Wing*. He says Krishna Prem should be editor. So, swamiji," she laughs, slapping her knees in delight, "those are Laxmi's news!"

Back at the flat, back at the desk, back at the typewriter, riveted by "Introduction" like a cobra holds its prey, I feel inadequate, pressured by the rushing tide of events, and as blank as the empty page. And I can sense them coming, those roots and wings, ominous and foreboding, dive-bombing towards me, straight for my throat.

"June ten!" I croak at the typewriter. "June ten! You'd better get your act together. That's only four days away!"

Over the next couple of days the scope of my activity ranges from filling the wastebasket with crumpled bits of paper to hanging out at 17, watching the preparations for the meditation camp. The Foundation's new acquisition is a rambling, low-slung, four-bedroom bungalow, built in the fifties, a covered, marble veranda meandering across the front. It sits in the middle of a one and a half acre compound. There's a large, untended garden in front, a long paved drive down the left, and in the back, a spacious patch of bare earth, flanked, where it borders on 33, by servants' quarters, a squat, six-hovel construction in rain-stained cement, a cross between slum-row housing and a kennel for a pack of overgrown pets.

Tall pine poles, freshly planted in the soil, dot the back yard. And with twists of twine held in their teeth, a group of chattering Indian coolies clamber upwards, hand over hand, sure feet gripping the timbers, shooting themselves upwards with simian ease and agility. A lattice roof of lashed bamboo is fast taking shape, and just beneath the swarm of knot-tying labourers scampering over the framework, a plodding train of bullock carts pulls up, unloading sheet upon sheet of corrugated tin panels to be passed on high and secured in place—roofing for the monsoon, for the end-of-June rains. And off in one corner, treading, treading, a pair of intent Pune tailors bends over time-blackened Singers, stitching miles of white cotton panels into a billowing, cloud-like ceiling for the meditation camp marquee.

A makeshift stage for the musicians nestles against the house, and Ma Taru, Osho's gargantuan Bombay thrush, is already there, testing, belting Hindi bhajans into the mêlée, calling for more and more volume until, wobbling her head in satisfaction, the pitch is as great as her girth.

"So, swamiji," I hear a familiar voice behind me saying, "introduction is ready? Only this morning he was asking..."

I don't even let her finish. I am instantly on my bicycle and, fuelled by Laxmi's laughter, pedalling furiously down the drive.

Hours later, endless, empty, frustrating hours later, I push my chair back from the desk in despair, ready to drop the whole thing. My gaze falls on a picture of Osho hanging on the wall. There's a smile on his face. But the way I feel right now, it seems as if he's laughing at me. "You think it's funny, huh? Well, if you want this bloody introduction done you're going to have to do it yourself!"

I feel suddenly ashamed, as if I've been rude to him directly. "Osho," I say to the picture, "I need help with this."

I turn back to the typewriter and simply sit there for a moment, eyes closed, not trying, just remembering the discourses, just remembering him. And then, slowly, my fingers poise above the keys and the words begin to come:

"On fifteen May mornings in Pune, a large Indian city one hundred and eighty kilometres from Bombay, a group of Western followers gathered at his ashram to ask Osho a series of questions about himself and his path to enlightenment...."[3]

Over the next couple of days, my effort is not so much to write, but to allow. And out it flows—the coming to Osho, the taking sannyas, the discovery of meditation, the magic of the Dynamic, Kailash, Goa. And then I sense the introduction nearing its end.

"When I left Goa and came back to Pune," I watch the words materializing on the page, "I was taken to see Osho in the garden. As I walked across the lawn he said, 'I was with you in Goa.'

"For the first time I began, just began, to understand what working with a Master means. He once said, 'A Master follows you like a shadow.' I don't understand how, but he is always there, with me, guiding me. I am beginning to hear him more and more clearly.

"He tells a story about school children who were asked what they did to help at home. One washed the dishes, one made his own bed, and so on. But one little boy replied, 'Mostly I just keep out of the way.'

"It's difficult to do. The ego fights all the way. But I'm learning to keep out of the way."

3. For interested readers, a full introduction can be requested at info.allanach@retreatspace.com. It is not included in the current published version, but comes from the author's personal records.

I sit back. Finished. The ninth of June. And it is finished.

"Beautiful," Laxmi says to me the next afternoon, smiling at the sight of my noticeable relief. "He says it's beautiful.

"And tonight meditation camp begins," she exclaims, rubbing her hands together in unbridled glee. "Laxmi loves camps! 'Hoo! Hoo! Hoo!'" she shouts, jumping up and down, arms pumping like the wings of a crazed chicken. And, hopping and hooing, she bounds out of the room, leaving me standing there, this little orange loony whose life is his work.

"Laxmi," I say, savouring the taste on my tongue. "Laxmi." And, arms extended, head thrown back, I turn slowly, speaking to the air, professing to the empty room, "I love you, Laxmi."

"Laxmi loves you too, swamiji," I hear from the direction of the doorway. But when I swing round it is empty. All there is, is the sound of girlish laughter, echoing and disappearing down the hall.

There was a sense of adventure about the Mount Abu camp that isn't here tonight. There in the hills, a gutsy, pioneering spirit filled us all. There was a kind of raw excitement that charged the mountain air, as crisp and invigorating as a frosty Montreal wind on a mid-winter's morning. It energized us, that feeling. It triggered an explosion of revelry, into dancing and singing late into the night.

Where has it gone, that vigour, that vitality? Earlier, at the flat, we'd simply sat around—no visitors, no party planned, a night like any other night. And I look about me, at the sannyasins surrounding me, wondering. Where is the energy? Where is the enthusiasm? Where is that incredible intoxication at the prospect of embarking on a ten-day cosmic cruise with Osho? Where is it? Waiting for Osho to arrive, I wonder. Around me is stillness, silence. Around me, faces are closed, expressionless.

"But," I ask myself, "where is my own exuberance?" And I begin to perceive, first in me, that what I thought was missing is still very much there, very much indeed. It has simply turned in; it's all happening on the inside. And on the faces of my friends I see a subtle glow, an inner radiance shining through, fine and luminescent. I drop Mount Abu. I drop comparing. I let it all evaporate, dissolve, fade away.

My eyes close. And a settling comes. And I find the dancing and the singing and the revels in my own silence, in my own inner light.

"Osho," Teertha's voice sounds softly over the speakers as he begins the reading of the sutra for the first discourse of the camp, "the Japanese Master Nan-in gave audience to a professor of philosophy.

"Serving tea, Nan-in filled his visitor's cup, and kept pouring.

"The professor watched the overflow until he could restrain himself no longer: Stop! The cup is overfull; no more will go in.

"Nan-in said: Like this cup, you are full of your own opinions and speculations. How can I show you Zen unless you first empty your cup?"

During Teertha's reading Osho's eyes had been closed, his folded hands resting gently in his lap. Slowly his eyes open, the lids lifting languidly, taking Teertha in first and then, like a camera pulling back, his gaze widens, encompassing us all. "You have come," he says, "to an even more dangerous person than Nan-in, because an empty cup won't do. The cup has to be broken completely." His words startle me. It is not so much what he is saying, there is a quality to his voice I have never heard before. The tone is soft and loving, as seductive as always, but there is an undercurrent of something else—a new edge, sharp, almost severe.

"This camp is going to be a destruction, a death," he says. "If you are ready to be destroyed, something new will come out of it. Every destruction can become a creative birth. If you are ready to die, you can have a new life, you can be reborn.

"I am here just to be a midwife. That's what Socrates used to say—a Master is just a midwife. I can help, I can protect, I can guide, that's all. The actual phenomenon, the transformation, is going to happen to you...

"Empty the cup. That's what Nan-in said. That means empty the mind. Ego is there, overflowing. And when ego is overflowing, nothing can be done... From nowhere can the divine penetrate you; you have created such a citadel...

"The mind is unnecessary luggage. It makes no difference to this existence that is carrying you. You are unnecessarily burdened. I say drop it...

"Once you can put it down, even for a single minute, your whole existence will be transformed. You will enter into a new dimension, the dimension of weightlessness. And that's what I am going to give you: wings into the sky, into the heaven—weightlessness gives you these wings—and roots into the earth, a groundedness, a centring...

"This camp is going to be in many ways different. This night I start a completely new phase of my work. You are fortunate to be here, because you will be witnesses of a new type of inner work. I must explain it to you, because tomorrow morning the journey starts."

Then, slowly and carefully, he guides us through the meditation techniques to be used in this camp: Dynamic in the morning, kirtan in the afternoon, Sufi whirling for two hours in the evening.

"Another new thing," he is saying. "I will not be there... Only my empty chair will be there. But don't miss me, because in a sense I will be there. And in a sense there has always been an empty chair before you..." I nod, understanding, remembering when I looked into his pupils that day on the lawn.

"I will be there, and if you meditate rightly, whenever your meditation is exactly tuned, you will see me. So that will be the criterion of whether you are really meditating or not. Many of you will be able to see me, more intensely than you can see me right now, and whenever you see me, you can be certain that things are happening in a right direction. So this will be the criterion.

"By the end of this camp I hope ninety per cent of you will have seen me. Ten per cent may miss because of their minds. So if you see me, don't start thinking about what is happening. Don't start thinking whether it is imagination or a projection or am I really there. Don't think, because if you think, immediately I will disappear. Thinking will become a barrier... To be aware of the physical body is not much awareness; to be aware of the non-physical being is real awareness...

"This is my promise—I will be there in the empty chair. The empty chair will not really be empty. So behave, the chair will not be empty. But it is better that you learn to be in contact with my non-physical being. That's a deeper, more intimate touch and contact. That's why I say a new phase of my work starts with this camp..."[4]

The next few days are intense, rich and rewarding. I throw myself totally into the camp, keeping silent and to myself as much as possible. The Dynamic is amazing, better than ever—deep, gut-wrenching catharsis followed by high, soaring flights into the inner. And the afternoon kirtan is a delight: singing along with Taru—"Govinda Bolo Hari; Gopala Bolo. Govinda Bolo Hari; Gopala Bolo"—and clapping and dancing to a crescendo of exhaustion. And then, after forty-five sweat-drenched minutes, falling into the deliciousness of complete relaxation, of profound rest.

But the Sufi whirling! Agony. Sheer agony! Osho had said the Sufi whirling was to last two hours—one hour of whirling, building slowly to a peak, and a second hour of lying face down on the ground, one's bare navel in contact with the earth. But no matter how hard I try, the nausea and the dizziness and the armies of stinging red ants defeat me utterly. After the second night I simply sit on the sidelines with the others who have succumbed and watch, in open-mouthed admiration, the stalwart—spinning and spinning, swirls of orange and red and ochre, turning, turning, turning in the light of the rising moon.

Between meditations, nothing much exists for me but the book and the steady flow of Ness-coffees tiptoed in by Divy or Prageet or Virag with loving regularity. I've elected to do the whole thing by myself, the transcribing as well as the editing, and after discourse I collect the morning's cassette from Laxmi and hurry home, anxious

4. *A Bird on the Wing*

to get to work. The space it puts me in is exquisite. I feel immersed in him, absorbed by him. And tremendously grateful. The insights into my makeup, into the complexities of my emotions and the intricacies of my mind, are coming fast and furious, and I feel new—in strength, in commitment, in understanding. It is as if my life has taken a new turning. It is as if, at long last, I have finally begun to walk the road that leads to God.

And more and more, much to my surprise, it is "God" that draws me.

When I came to Osho I had believed my search was for wisdom, for wisdom with an esoteric capital W, but somehow, somewhere along the line it has all changed—God has become the goal, and nothing else will do. And I am amazed. Hedonistic, irreligious me, searching for God!

But my concept has changed. I find myself sticking with the word—somehow "Existence" or "The Whole" or "The Ultimate" just doesn't do it for me—but my vision has radically changed. Gone is the Christian idea of God. Gone is the great white-haired spy in the sky, the omnipotent peeker into bathrooms and bedrooms and little boys' secrets. But even more important, that whole idea of separation is gone—there is no more Creator and creation, no more God and the world. When the word "God" whispers in my heart now, it encompasses and includes all—me and the trees and the typewriter and the steaming mugs of Nesscoffee. Being with Osho, being with his words, sharing his experience, something hidden in me has surfaced. Some sleeping memory has been stirred and I know, unequivocally, that all is God or that God is all, that I am a wave and God is the ocean, that we are one, that me and the trees and the typewriter are just manifestations of him.

But I also see that knowing from the mind and knowing from the heart are vastly different from the experience itself, from the experience Osho has had and is telling us about. For Osho it is a reality, but for me it is simply an intellectual understanding. I find it hard not to give in to impatience.

"Don't feel bad," Prageet says to me over a philosophical glass of beer. "At least you know that now you can go to the toilet in peace!"

The next morning the sky is thick with clouds, huge, rolling white-capped structures, underbellies heavy with the darkness of imminent rain. By afternoon the air is hot and steamy, oppressive in its humidity. The crowns of white have gone, and any hope of relief is squelched by an upward glance—the cloudbank stretches from horizon to horizon, a ceiling of dingy grey. Here and there great black patches sag, aching for release. The flat is as dark and as dank as the sky.

I pack the typewriter away.

At 17, against the impending monsoon, roll-up bamboo blinds are being strung all along the front of the veranda by a crew of Indian workmen, straining in the heat with hammers and hooks and pulleys and lengths of deep-green twine. At the effort their bodies glisten, beaded with perspiration, rivulets of sweat coursing down their backs, staining their once-white pyjama pants an even darker grey. Around their heads are strips of coloured cloth, red and blue and yellow, tightly wrapped in a vain attempt to keep the salty sting from already smarting eyes. Oblivious of the heat, from the sheltered depths of the porch, I hear the voice of Laxmi bellowing a barrage of instructions in Marathi. Wisely, the workmen ignore her.

"Laxmi?" I call.

"Swamiji!" she shouts in reply. "Come, sit! Tea can happen!"

She pats the chair beside her. "So, swamiji, how goes the book?"

"Really well, Laxmi," I answer. "It's going really well. He's saying such important things, and it feels so good to be doing some really serious work for him."

"Serious?" she explodes, on her feet almost faster than my eyes can follow. "Serious? Serious?" she shrieks again and again, as if she cannot trust her ears. "Serious?"

And, spouting a stream of Hindi I am grateful I don't understand, she whisks into the house, virtually toppling a stunned Gaghan Singh who has appeared in the doorway with a tray of tea. He stands there, undecided how to proceed, whether to follow Laxmi or lay the tea for me. "Gaghan Singh!" a voice bellows from indoors, settling his indecision.

For a while I just sit where I am, glued to the chair. I doubt if my legs will support me if I try to leave. I close my eyes for a moment, to pull myself together. Suddenly there is a tap on my shoulder and I look up into the grinning face of Gaghan Singh. In his hand is a little scrap of paper. I take it. There are three words on it, each with a line to itself, scrawled in pencil in a little schoolgirl hand: "sincere never serious."

Leaving the flat for discourse the following morning I shove the scrap of paper into my pocket. I hadn't slept well—seriousness had even plagued my dreams.

I was back in Montreal, playing an after-dinner game of bridge with three friends. My partner had made a silly mistake, costing us the rubber, and I'd flown into a rage, berating him, going on and on and on. "For Christ's sake, Jack," he'd finally yelled, "it's only a game!" I awoke, covered in sweat, "It's only a game," ringing in my ears.

Suddenly, through my thoughts, Osho's voice penetrates. "You play a game. You play cards," he is saying. "Can you play cards without rules? There can be no possibility. If you say: I will follow my rules and you follow your rules and we play the game, there will be no game. We have to follow the rules. And we both know that rules are just rules, nothing real in them. We have agreed on the rules. That's why they exist.

"A game cannot continue if rules are not followed, but life will continue without rules. What rules are these trees following? What rules does the sun follow? What rules does the sky follow? The human mind is such that the human mind thinks they are also following rules, moving according to rules. The sun moves, it follows a rule, so there is a ruler, the God who controls everything. He is like a great super-manager. He goes on spying on everybody—who is following, who is not following. This is a mind creation.

"Life exists without rules; games cannot exist without rules. So real religion is always without rules. Only false religion has rules, because false religion is a game...

"Your ochre robes, your mala—these are rules. This is a game. This is not what I mean by real sannyas. But you are so accustomed to games, that before I lead you to a ruleless life, in the transitory period, you will need rules. Moving from this world of rules, of games, to that world without rules and games, a bridge has to be passed. Your orange clothes, your mala, are just for that transitory period. You cannot drop rules immediately, so I give you new rules.

"But be fully alert that your robes are not your sannyas, your mala is not your sannyas, your new name is not your sannyas. Sannyas will be there when there is no name, when you become nameless. Then there will be no rules. Then you will be so ordinary, you will not be recognized. Only then...

"But don't think that now it is okay, so no need to take sannyas and no need to take an orange robe. This is again a trick. You have to pass through this; you have to go through this. You cannot by-pass it. And if you try to by-pass, you will never reach to the other shore.

"Rules of the world, then rules of sannyas, and then comes a no-rule state."

A game? Sannyas, a game? I'd heard him correctly; there's no doubt. "This is a game," he'd said. But if it is a game, then my whole approach is wrong. A game is a game, to be played totally, to be played to the end, but not to be taken seriously. "Sincere never serious," the little slip of paper in my pocket says. I look over at Laxmi. Her eyes are closed but I am certain I detect the hint of a smile playing on her lips. This is what she was trying to show me, not to take Osho's work seriously, not to take the work on myself seriously. In my heart, as I watch her sitting there beside him, silent and glowing, a rush of gratitude wells up in me.

That afternoon, after a meditation, I open my eyes; there, in the empty chair on the platform before me is a shape, outlined in gold. The form is there, yet it is not there. There is nothing there, yet there is a presence. And all around it, where the head and shoulder would be, a shimmering aura of gold light dances, splendid and sparkling, like a fountain of water spiralling on high. And then, like a dark rain cloud obliterating the light, my mind moves in, questioning, doubting, destroying what my eyes have just seen. But it doesn't matter. Today, nothing matters at all.

July enters, bringing the real monsoon rains—heavy, battering outbursts from the darkness above, turning the open half of our kitchen into a jungle of lush, dripping ferns. But the rains don't last. They seem to have a pattern to them: they wash the morning clean and then return, just before evening, to freshen the world again before the coming night. And in between are long, welcome stretches of hot, delicious sun.

Rani has moved in, occupying the room next to Divy's and mine, and there's a new feeling in the flat. She's brought another kind of femininity with her, a female caring that's reflected in how our dinner table is set, in the presentation of our food, in the bouquets of fresh cut-flowers around the place, and in countless other little touches. After living with three men, all chauvinistically attuned to service, Virag is thrilled with Rani's presence. And they are a delight together—one plain, one fancy, one earthy and rooted, one right out there among the stars.

It's surprisingly easy with the three of us, with Rani and Divy and me. I've never really understood what made me ask her to come and live with us. Taking our history into consideration, it was the last thing I should have done. But, standing in front of her door at the Green Hotel one afternoon, it was as if I had no choice, as if I were only acting out something already ordained.

"It's worked out beautifully with Rani here, hasn't it, Divy?" I ask one evening after a particularly splendid repast the girls have put together.

"So far, it's fine."

"What do you mean?" I want to know. "So far?"

"Just that. So far, it's fine."

Typhoid

"Please, Osho, stop," I plead silently. "Please, please, just stop talking!"

I am sitting against the wall, my teeth chattering like loose dice rattling in a cup. He's speaking Hindi and there's no way I can tell how close he is to wrapping it up, how much longer I have to hang on. In English I know the cues; in Hindi I'm at a loss. I wonder if I can make it, if I can see the discourse through. To get up and walk out is unthinkable. Besides, I'm not so sure my legs will support me, they're aching so badly. I close my eyes, determined to wait him out, bringing all my attention to stilling the noise of my clacking teeth. To my ears the racket is so great I'm certain everyone around me can hear it too.

When he finally finishes and I somehow make it back to the flat, I am sweat-soaked and as sopping wet as if I'd just been caught in a sudden shower. Virag takes one look at me and trundles me into bed, covering me with blanket after blanket to ward off the cold. But the covers make no difference. They might as well be sheets of ice.

"I'm going to call Dr Tavildar," she says, leaving me curled up in a freezing, foetus-like ball, and dropping gratefully into blackness.

The next thing I am aware of is the doctor's voice. "Temperature is one hundred five," I hear in lilting Indian-English, as if from the other end of a long tunnel. "I say: typhoid." Then there's another sensation, the sharp prick of a needle in my arm. And then, again, there's the mercy of disappearance, of nothingness.

For the next week there's no real comprehension of anything much at all, just a vague awareness of things being done to me from time to time: an injection being given, a pill being administered, my brow being mopped, my body being shifted for sweat-soaked linen to be replaced with dry. At one point I surface sharply from the blackness, carried upwards to consciousness on waves of nausea. I hear myself crying, "Get it out of here! Get it out of here!"

Virag is suddenly there in the doorway, puzzlement on her face. "What is it? Get what out of here?"

A hand extends from under the blanket, the index finger pointing, rigid and quivering in accusation, towards a clay pot standing, covered, in the corner. "That! Get that out of here. I can't stand the smell!"

"But it's only water," Virag says.

"Water made me sick," I whisper. "Please, Virag, please take it away!" And the last thing I notice before the darkness envelops me again is the strange, unfamiliar scrawniness of the hand that has fallen, wasted and exhausted, onto the dampened pillow beside my aching head.

My first steps, a week later, are pretty tentative, and limited to teetering into the kitchen where I plop into a chair, drained and breathless. On the way I passed a mirror, and the reflection of my body gave me quite a turn. In the past two weeks I've become absolutely skeletal; there's hardly any flesh left on my bones at all.

"My guess is you've lost a good thirty pounds," Divy says.

Virag stands before me with a tray. "Let's see if we can start putting a bit of weight on with this toast and this nice clover honey from Canada that Mukta sent over. Rani's due back tonight on the Deccan Queen. Let's try to put a few ounces on you before she gets home."

The morning before the typhoid hit Rani had left for the mountains with her Danish friend Pathika, the wife of Land-Rover-Anup from Kailash. Someone had sung her the praises of Dalhousie, a hill-station in Himachal Pradesh, an Indian state to the northwest of Nepal and just over the Himalayas from China, and she and Pathika, adventurous memsahibs both, had trucked off by themselves.

And that night, cooing over my wasted frame, she paints a picture of snow-capped peaks and boulder-strewn valleys, of misty mornings and strolling Tibetan monks, of good food and fireplaces and crisp, clean air. "And it hardly rained at all."

That does it for me. I want a vacation from water for a while. "Shall we?" I ask Divy.

"Why not?" he agrees. "As soon as you're better, why not?"

"Us too," Prageet says.

Virag smiles in blissful accord.

Out of politeness we check with Osho. He tells us to have a good time and to be sure to be home in time for the next English series and meditation camp. Divy gets down to the booking of rail tickets while I, grateful it's him queuing and not me, move into the final stretch of editing *A Bird on the Wing*. I'll have no problem finishing it before we leave. At the Pune station, Divy's told we should be able to travel in eight days. Prageet and Virag can't get reservations on the same train and are to follow several days later. And, remembering the third class train trips to Kailash and to Delhi to collect Rani, we decide this trip is going to be first class. "We'll be broke soon anyway," Divy says philosophically. "So what the hell!"

In terms of earning money and coming back for a longer period, Canada seems the best bet for us all. Prageet and I both have Canadian passports, Divy has landed immigrant status, and Virag is fine: she's a New Zealander, but she's Prageet's wife. Rani wants to come too. "We can always get married," I offer jokingly.

We also talk about working for Osho while we're there, perhaps opening a meditation centre. I write to Osho, explaining that we're going to have to go back for a while, that we've been considering opening a meditation centre, and asking, because most of the people in Canada are either Christians or Jews, if he would perhaps speak about Jesus before we go. Rani is lunching with Mukta the next day, so I give the note to her, telling her to ask Mukta to pass it along to him.

And then, somehow, the whole discussion drops; we simply don't talk about it any more. We know we're going to have to leave at some point, that the infant commune can't support us yet, and that's that. I turn my focus back to *A Bird on the Wing*.

The train tickets arrive the day I finish the book. We leave in four days. There's an afternoon train to Bombay, connecting with a sleeper to New Delhi where we change for the twelve-hour run to Pathankot, the end of the northern line. From Pathankot, Rani tells us, we take a bus. It sounds like the ride to Mount Abu. "Four hours straight up," she says, "and you're in Dalhousie."

"And what about introduction?" Laxmi inquires when I hand her the completed manuscript. "Laxmi doesn't find introduction here," she says, fiddling with the pages. "Books need introductions! And what about weight?" she asks, prodding my still-protruding ribs with a sharp, emphatic finger. "Eat, swamiji. Eat. Eat and write beautiful introduction. For him!"

So, albeit reluctantly, it's back to the typewriter.

But this time nothing comes. I start and re-start again and again, but everything I write is dull and trite and stupid, doing no justice whatsoever to Osho or his words. "It's not working, Laxmi. I'm just writing crap," I tell her the eve of our departure. "I'll take my typewriter with me and write the introduction in Dalhousie."

It's evening by the time we check into the Rock View Hotel. Dalhousie is shrouded in a thick, opaque fog, hazy little halos of shimmering light dotting the darkness here and there, illuminating tiny circles of mist-wet greenery, leaving all else to the night. Dinner is long over, the hotel bearer tells us, so we settle for toast and tea. While he paddles off to fetch it, Divy totally rearranges the room, moving the beds to the wall and grouping a table and a pair of chintz-upholstered armchairs in front of the coke-filled fireplace. When the bearer returns, we are snugly ensconced in front of a warming fire, swathed in dressing gowns, freshly bathed and finally free of mud, a photo of Osho smiling down on us from the mantelpiece.

From Pathankot, which Divy swears is the sleaziest Indian city he's ever passed through, the ride up the mountain was reminiscent of the climb to Mount Abu. It was all steep inclines, impossible curves, and sheer drops that always seemed inches away from the balding tires of the exhausted, overcrowded bus. In the monsoon season the roads can be treacherous, and three hours up into the hills we come upon an enormous landslide, an impassable wall of rock and mud erasing the narrow road as if it had never been there at all.

"Getting down!" the Sikh driver calls to us. "Everyone getting down, please. But not to be worrying! Dalhousie is knowing. Other bus coming," he promises, waving in the direction of the mountain of slime blocking our way. And no sooner are all the passengers disembarked and clustered in a confused huddle beside the bus than the clouds burst. Within seconds we are ankle-deep in mud.

Typewriter in one hand, umbrella in the other, wrapped in a sodden shawl and wearing a robe that's soaking up water like a thirst-crazed sponge, I pick my way along the edge of the cliff, paying precise attention to my footing. I've never liked heights—the Eiffel Tower freaked me out—and traversing those twenty death-defying yards takes an eternity.

Locating the driest spot possible, we squat under a tree to await the arrival of the second bus. Through the pelting rain we watch the snaking string of passengers, followed by coolies with valises balanced on their heads, slip and slide towards us across the mound of mud and debris.

"Listen, Divy, I hear an engine. It must be the bus." But it turns out to be a lorry with a group of Indians in the back—a crew to begin unblocking the road. When they start to work I cannot believe my eyes. The scene doubles me over with laughter. "Look, Divy. Three on a shovel!"

Incredulous, we watch. Two lengths of rope have been fixed to the shaft of the shovel just above the blade, each length held tightly in the grip of an Indian workman. A third man, stationed at the handle, makes the actual shovelling motion. He scoops up a load of dirt, but doesn't follow through. He stops halfway, leaving the blade embedded in the soil. And then, in an awkward, uncoordinated attempt at unison, his two colleagues jerk smartly on their ropes, propelling the spade-load of earth less than a foot away. For a good half hour we watch this strange and painful process, amazed at the mindset that has, somehow, somewhere, figured out how to turn a perfectly efficient tool into such a joke.

One of the Indian passengers, drawn by our attentiveness to the workmen, asks what we find so interesting.

"Three on a shovel," I explain.

"Three on a shovel?" he repeats, not getting my point.

I elaborate.

He nods thoughtfully and then turns a sombre gaze on me. "We are seven hundred million," he says quietly. "One shovel means three jobs."

Suddenly, it's not funny any more. Rather sheepishly I offer him a bidi, which he accepts, and we smoke in silence, squatting on our haunches, watching the labourers making little insignificant dents in the mountain of mud until the second bus arrives to take us on up to Dalhousie.

"Krishna! Krishna, come outside! Hurry, come outside! I'm standing in a cloud!"

The shout is Divy's, but it takes me a moment to recall where I am and to locate the voice. I stumble out of bed and onto the terrace. There, spread-eagled, arms raised to the heavens, is Divy, standing, as he'd said, in a cloud. "My God," is all I can say. "My God!"

What lies before me is enough to bring a man to his knees. There is so much, so incredibly much, my eyes have no idea where to begin. They sweep back and forth, alighting first on this, then on that, powerless to pause anywhere, drawn onward again and again by something even more remarkable.

I am like a child faced with a box of assorted chocolates, wanting them all at once but forced by his very single-mouthed nature to select his candies one at a time.

The Himalayas win. I drop to my haunches, cloud-floss floating about my head and feet, and simply look, marvelling. Capped and crowned in the whitest of snows, they stretch out before me, peak upon peak, falling into each other, rising out of each other—crags and crevasses, pillars and pyramids, spires and steeples of raw, brute rock tumbled together in jagged symmetry, extending onwards towards the mounting gold of the morning sun.

Below me a yawning canyon extends, deep and long and funnel-shaped, its floor strewn with colossal rocks and boulders, a few here and there at first, but growing in size and number as the valley narrows, until they mass together at its apex, piled one atop the other like gigantic stepping-stones, like some ancient god's staircase leading upwards towards the peaks themselves. And cascading down the two walls of the valley is a profusion of greens, a manifold display of nature's hues. At the top of the sloping hills, forests of self-sown trees cluster, deciduous and coniferous, weaving a living carpet that travels, thick and unbroken, nodding in the mountain breeze, down the rolling ridges to where the greenery of man begins. And here my eye feasts on a new abundance, on fields of rice and wheat, of hops and barley, of cane and corn, an occasional orchard or thin, high stand of bamboo springing up between. There must be hundreds, literally hundreds of tiny plots of cultivated land strung out all along the two faces of the canyon, falling in orderly tiers from the trees above to the valley below. And each little field is neat and tended. I see generations before me, grandfathers and fathers and sons, placing stone upon stone in endless layers and rows to create flat, walled terraces to catch the rich, fertile topsoil carried down the mountain by the rains.

"Bed tea, sahib?" I hear behind me. And Divy and I, speechless in wonder and breathless in the thin Himalayan air, follow the white-coated, bare-footed waiter back into our room.

From our first day's exploration, we both agree the British had a knack for locating spectacular views and, with an unlimited source of subservient labour at their disposal, an equally impressive talent for setting themselves up, no matter how remote or seemingly inaccessible the locale, in truly grand comfort and style. Granted, like Lonavla, it has all faded, but the memory of the Raj lingers on.

All over Dalhousie we find the traces of the lifestyle of India's former rulers. Rambling colonial-style bungalows dot the hills, and, further down, smaller cottages, obviously for the lower ranks, bear names like Rose Cottage and Arbour Dell, like Bide-A-Wee and Dew-Drop-Inn.

Dalhousie is one of the north's best-known hill-stations, second perhaps only to Simla, where the British shifted the government in summer to escape the oven New Delhi became. Essentially Dalhousie is just that: a hill. A series of footpaths and laneways spiral upwards from the main square towards the summit, circling the hill itself, converging and connecting here and there in chowks, in little paved plazas where miniature arcades of restaurants and shops, reminiscent of Brighton, meet the needs of the Indian tourists who now frequent the place.

To anyone craving excitement or uninterested in nature, Dalhousie offers little-bordering-on-nothing. We discover that the Dalhousie Talkies, with an understandable eye to the rupees, is playing a Punjabi romance, all turbans and scimitars and buxom, veiled maidens, and that the much-touted Dalhousie Roller Skating Arena is a narrow, uneven hotel-ballroom floor with a pack of novices-on-wheels hurtling themselves unsteadily from one end to the other, smashing first into one wall and then, carefully turning themselves about on all fours, reeling to their feet again to launch an assault on the other.

And one afternoon, at the Rock View, we stumble onto a sweet-sixteen party, onto a group of doe-eyed, black-braided Indian lasses in floor-length skirts, dancing cheek-to-cheek to the scratchy sounds of Frankie Avalon. There isn't a boy in sight except for the herd of waiters huddled in one corner, watching and wanting but kept at bay by the no-nonsense stares of two monolithic matrons in starched nylon saris of disagreeable pink. Divy gives the birthday-girl a Rosemary Clooney cut-out book he found in a shop, more, I think, to pique the chaperones than anything else. The youngster is delighted. She flees in a paroxysm of giggles, her dancing partners in excited pursuit. The keepers scowl into their tea.

But over and above the phenomenal vistas that thrill us again and again with their grandeur, there is little to tempt us from the hotel. We spend more and more time in front of the fireplace, toasting our toes, browsing through moth-eaten rainy-day novels—with me, from time to time, making unfruitful attempts at the introduction to *A Bird on the Wing*. When Prageet and Virag arrive, the routine alters little. Instead of two people doing practically nothing, now there are four.

En route to joining us in Dalhousie, Prageet and Virag had taken a detour in Pathankot for a four-hour bus ride up to McLeod Ganj, to where the Dalai Lama and his court set up residence when the Chinese invaded Tibet in 1953.

"Wouldn't have minded seeing him," Prageet admits. "But he wasn't around. All there was in McLeod Ganj was a bunch of freaks with a lot of fleas."

The Tibetans are a presence in Dalhousie, as they are in many of the hill-stations that lie across the north of India in the shadow of the Himalayan range. Crossing the impossible peaks before the advancing Peking armies, with their women and children and laden yaks, they settled as close as possible to their high and windblown land, waiting in refugee camps provided by a hospitable India for the day predicated by their astrologers, for the day they will once more traverse the snows and glaciers to return home.

At first they're only noticeable in the bazaars, squatting by the roadside, with neat displays of stones and amulets, temple bells and painted tankas and prayer wheels spread out for sale. They seem aloof and enigmatic. Their round Mongol faces with wide, flat noses and cool, narrow eyes are appraising, dispassionate. Their mouths, broad and thin-lipped, are in a kind of perpetual motion, continuously mumbling their scriptures, their bodhi-seed malas twirling between thumb and forefinger, abacus-like, counting off the prayers like Catholic school children condemned to repeating the rosary for life.

And then we spy them on the hills above the chowks, sometimes perched in pensive solitude on a jutting knoll, gazes fixed on the distant peaks. Sometimes we see them manoeuvring private pathways, going about their business, a pack over a shoulder or a child slung low on one hip. And sometimes they simply hover, motionless and remote, like a rare species of bird reluctant to approach the strange and alien world that churns beneath it.

But they are not as inaccessible as we first believe. Walking among them, we find them warm and friendly, laughing easily, ever anxious to share from their always-steaming samovars of greyish, salted tea. Laced with a dollop of yak butter, one cup of the brackish brew is all I can stomach. From then on, whenever it's offered, I rub my belly and smile, indicating beyond language that I am too full to accept anything more.

They say the Tibetan plateau is so high and that the climate is so cold that bacteria cannot live, and so there's never any need to bathe. If it's true, they've carried the custom with them: there's a great deal of scratching and lice-gleaning going on. The men, in particular, seem a little the worse for wear. But the women are spectacular. They are tall and stately, immaculately groomed, and regal without exception.

I love to watch the women together, chatting, gossiping, a long-haired lhassa apso panting languidly on one arm. They wear the national costume, the long-sleeved, ankle-length Tibetan tuba with the wide side panels that tie, like an apron, in the back. They prefer dark tones—deep purples, midnight blues, rainforest greens. And peeking out from under each cuff and rolling down each tuba cleavage like the crest of a starched wave is silk, fine, delicate, hand-woven silk, repeating, in the softest pastel whisper, the colour of the ensemble of the day.

It's not so much their appearance that intrigues me, but more the way they are with each other. Being used to Indian women, to the bird-like cackle of the workers and the syrupy Englishness of the upper classes, the Tibetan women are as refreshing as the first monsoon shower. There is a quality about them I have rarely seen in women anywhere, let alone in India, and it takes a few days before it registers. They are real. It's that simple: they are real. I watch them closely, and I see no games, no masks. It is as if each of them is so at ease with herself, so at home in herself, that it has imparted to her very mien a naturalness, a fluid grace and beauty that, thirsting for it, we tend to turn from humanity to seek it in the mystery of a flower or the splendour of a tree.

And when they turn their gazes to me, to the odd, orange-robed foreigner with long brown curls and eyes the colour of the sea, nothing changes. There are no ripples of uneasiness in them. The contact is direct and open. There is no suspicion, no hint of closing; there is simply meeting.

For the first time, except for Osho, I feel that I have seen the reflection of nature in ordinary people. I have seen a kind of wholeness and it has touched me deeply. And somehow, that I have observed it in women is even more significant, although I cannot explain why.

Gradually, over the past several days, the Rock View has been filling up with Westerners, and we're informed we'll have to vacate our rooms by the end of the week. It's obviously time to start thinking about going back to Pune, about going home. Back down the mountain we go, fingers crossed, feet pressed against the bus floorboards, hoping, at each blind curve and precipitous descent that the brakes will hold. "This is still the sleaziest city I've ever seen," is Divy's only comment when we arrive in Pathankot.

Prageet and Virag manage to get themselves on a train to Bombay, but our reservations are still a few days hence, so, rather than stay in Pathankot, which Divy refuses even to consider, we mount another bus and ricochet upwards once again, straight up another set of hills.

Whether the Dalai Lama is at home or not is totally immaterial to me after ten horrendous minutes in filthy, flea-ridden McLeod Ganj. And I don't find our twenty-four soggy hours in Dharamsala much better. Apparently, after Darjeeling, it has the second highest rainfall in India, and this monsoon the water-god has obviously decided to give it all to Dharamsala in one dank and drenching day.

Three long and sleepless nights later back in Pune, gratefully drifting off in my very own bed instead of in a rock-hard berth on a rolling train, Rani suddenly pokes her head under the mosquito net. "I completely forgot to tell you," she says. "There's a message from Mukta. You know how I am; it slipped my mind. Anyway, she told me I should write to you, but I wasn't absolutely sure where you were staying. If I'd known you were at the Rock View, I would have written. But I thought maybe..."

"Rani," I plead, "please get to the point. I'm exhausted. I need to sleep."

"Sorry, sweetie," she coos. "About five days ago Mukta came to me. 'Write to Krishna Prem,' she said. 'Tell him after the next camp Osho's going to talk on Jesus, just like he asked.'"

Of all the techniques devised by Osho to wake us up, to shake us out of what he calls the somnambulistic state we think of as living, the Mandala meditation has to be the worst. Even the Mount Abu nightmare, the jumping up and down with our arms in the air for forty minutes while shouting Hoo! and looking at him without blinking—even this pales by comparison.

"This ain't a meditation," Prageet says cryptically, summing up the general attitude after the first morning of the August camp, "it's pure torture!" Rubbing our calves and holding our heads, trying in vain to massage the knotted charley-horses away and relax the tightness around our paining eyes, we agree to a man.

The new camp had begun as usual. Rested from the Dalhousie holiday, we cycled out to 17 just before six, the whole household, a slight drizzle misting our faces deliciously, and dived into the Dynamic with gusto. The discourse following had been a sheer delight, an exquisite ninety-minute voyage into the enlightenment of a Zen nun. It was so good to be back, to be sitting before him once again. When the discourse was over, we filed silently to the space behind 17, shedding superfluous clothing in little orange heaps, ready for introduction to the new technique, to the Mandala.

"The first stage," Teertha announces into the microphone with an underlying chuckle, "is fifteen minutes' jogging in place, as fast as you can, bringing your knees up in front as high as you're able. In the second stage, just sit and sway gently from side to side for fifteen minutes. In the third stage, also fifteen minutes, lie on your backs and rotate your eyes in a clockwise direction. For the last stage, stay as you are and relax.

"Ready?" he shouts with a wave of his hand to the musicians behind him, and like a pack of greyhounds after a stuffed rabbit, knees pumping up and down to the beat of the tablas, we're off to the races.

I've never been much for athletics—a leisurely skate or an ambling stroll could be considered a lot of exercise for me—and after the first few minutes I'm sure my legs are going to drop off. But I somehow manage to get through the whole fifteen minutes, the result of nothing less than teeth-gritting stubbornness on my part. In the second stage my swaying can hardly be called meditative; it's more like a Jewish widow's wailing at a funeral, except I'm mourning the death of my thighs. The third stage is equally hopeless. By the time I figure out which way is clockwise and discover that my eyes won't rotate, that all they're trained to do is flick furtively back and forth, the fifteen minutes are over. I spend the last stage, where I'm supposed to relax into the bliss of meditation, sinking into a black and bottomless pit of total frustration.

But we're a game and hardy lot, we sannyasins, and the next morning we're at it again, running on the spot, legs pumping up and down. "Osho says on the fourth day your legs won't hurt any more," Teertha calls encouragingly over the loudspeaker.

"Terrific!" I hear from a breathless Virag beside me. "But what about my tits?"

That afternoon, lying around the flat, kneading our aching muscles, we find we're all quite well disposed to the new techniques after all. There always seems to be something to dislike about every camp and in this one, it just happens to be the Mandala. "At least it isn't whirling," Prageet says, "and it doesn't make me puke."

The Shivanetra though, we all agree, is a winner.

We'd done the Shivanetra for the first time the evening before. And I'd loved it. A big circular light, some two feet across, was placed on the ground in front of the platform holding Osho's empty chair. We were instructed to look at it softly, not focusing, for ten minutes. The next ten minutes we were to close our eyes and sway gently from side to side, not more than a foot in either direction. Then there was to be ten more minutes of light, followed by ten minutes' swaying, and so on, for an hour.

The light was an incredible piece of machinery, and that it had been unearthed in India absolutely amazed me. At first, in the centre, a pale blue glow appeared and then, slowly, began radiating outwards in ever increasing circles, pulsating all the while, growing gradually in brightness and intensity until, at the end of the ten-minute sequence, the entire orb was filled with a vivid blue light.

What the Mandala was meant to trigger in me, what clarity or emotion or experience it was designed to invoke, escaped me completely and no matter how totally I did it during the next several days, its secrets continued to elude me. Only once did I get any sort of glimpse. One morning, attempting to rotate my eyes clockwise, I actually did it! I finally got it right and I found myself sinking, in and in and in, towards emptiness. It lasted a few seconds, and then I lost it. And it never happened again. But the Shivanetra! The very first time I tried it, something in me responded.

In Bombay and in Mount Abu I'd heard Osho talk about the third eye. I didn't quite understand it, but knew it had something to do with inner vision and that, for a seeker, its opening was quite an event. The third eye, he said, was not physical; it belonged to a subtle body, but it could be felt. He said something about closing one's eyes and focusing one's gaze inwards and upwards towards a single point in the centre of the forehead. He said this diverting of the eyes' energy acted as a kind of massage on the third eye and would help it open. He said that when it began to be activated one would feel a soft, pulsating movement. This began to happen after the first Shivanetra and, as the days went on, the vibration in my forehead grew stronger and stronger, more and more intense. And it made me greedy. So, one night, I decide to have a little chat with Mukta the very next day.

I find Mukta sitting on her own on the dais behind 17, straw hat, gardening gloves and pruning shears beside her, contemplating the area where we do the meditations. "Planning a garden?" I ask, indicating the tarpaulin-covered ground.

"One day," she smiles. "One day."

"Mukta," I begin gingerly, sitting alongside her. "There's something I'd like to ask you.

"Divy told me a story you told him, about how you once came back to Bombay from New York, feeling great, feeling really together, and you went to Osho and said, 'Enough of this piddling around. Let me have it all at once.'"

She grimaces at the memory and then asks, "And did he also tell you that after three days, almost on my hands and knees, I went back and said, 'Stop! I can't take any more?'"

"Yes," I admit. "But I don't care. Whatever it is, whatever I have to go through, I'm ready. Will you do this for me? Will you tell Osho that I'm bored, that nothing's really happening? There's a little something every once in a while, but nothing really important is happening. Will you tell him? Will you ask him just to give it to me?"

She looks at me intensely for a moment, her eyes questioning. Then she nods.

"Sure. Why not? But are you sure you can take it? That whatever he sends your way, you can take it?"

"I'm sure, Mukta. And I'm ready."

She starts to laugh, pulling at my beard. "For your sake, I hope so. But remember, you can always cry 'Enough!'"

Jesus

"Get ready to die, because that is the only way to be reborn."

So ends the first of twenty-one discourses on Jesus, on the recently discovered Gospel According to Thomas and when Osho is gone, no one moves. There is pin-drop silence. Even this morning's rain rolls off the roof soundlessly, as if the heavens themselves are loath to disturb the profound hush that lingers in his wake.

Jesus lives again. For this gathering of sannyasins, primarily products of Christian and Jewish traditions, Jesus lives again. But it is not as the "Son of God", not the offspring of some virgin conception; Jesus lives again as a flesh-and-blood Master working with his disciples, sharing his own experience with them, striving to lead them towards their own divinity.

I loved Jesus as a little child, but as I grew I turned away, fed up with his church, tired of his ministers with their moralistic tirades and endless appeals for money. Now, this morning, I've fallen in love with him again—but with a real Jesus, with a man flowing with life's juices, with a man who has transcended life's seeming limitations and helps others see how to do the same. He is demystified yet still mysterious, desanctified yet still sacred—and I love this new Jesus even more.

Jesus once said, "Give no thought for the morrow," but I am so excited, so totally blown away with Osho's Jesus that I honestly wonder if I can wait for tomorrow morning to come!

But when tomorrow morning arrives and I sit before Osho once again, I am in utter turmoil and confusion, exhausted from a sleepless night, trying to hold my act together, trying not to let what happened yesterday unhinge me, trying not to let it freak me out.

"When you come to a Master like Jesus you come for peace," Osho is saying. "You are blissfully unaware that you have come to the wrong person. As you are you cannot get peace. And if somebody gives you peace, that will be death to you. As you are, if you become peaceful, what will that mean? That will mean the struggle has ceased before you have attained anything. As you are, if somebody makes you silent, what will that mean? You won't have achieved any self, and you will be consoled by your situation.

"This is the way you can know a false master from a true Master: a false master is a consolation. He gives you peace as you are; he never bothers to change you. He is a tranquillizer. He is just like sleeping pills; you come to him and he consoles. But if you come to a true Master this is the criterion: whatsoever peace you have, that too will be destroyed; whatsoever at-easeness you have is going to the dogs.

"A true Master will create more turmoil, more conflict. He is not going to console you because he is not your enemy. All consolations are poisons. He will help you to grow. Growth is difficult; you will have to pass through many difficulties. Many times you will want to escape from this man, but you cannot because he will haunt you."[5]

"Well, Krishna Prem," I tell myself, gulping in trepidation, "you asked for it!"

---

5. *The Mustard Seed*

High from the discourse, exhilarated by Osho, overwhelmed at the rediscovery of Jesus, reveling in the sunlight peeking through the clearing clouds, I had whizzed through the Mandala, jogging away like a four-minute miler, rolling my eyes like a trouper from an old-time minstrel show. I felt fantastic, enraptured with everything, head-over-heels in love with life.

Lunch was spent alone at Empress Gardens, munching dry sponge cake, gazing moon-eyed at the flowers. And back at 17, when Taru and her girls struck up the band for the afternoon kirtan, I danced and clapped and sang like never before, becoming more and more ecstatic as the tempo mounted towards its final crescendo. But when the music stopped abruptly, the signal to fall to the ground and relax, I suddenly felt two slashes of light. One encircled the bicep of my left arm; the other tore down my left cheek, halving my eye. And lying there on the tarpaulin, drenched in perspiration, I knew beyond the shadow of a doubt that somehow, somewhere, in some other life, my arm had been severed and a sword had split my face.

My mind instantly jumped in, trying to negate the experience. But no matter: I knew it was not to be denied. It carried a familiarity: it recalled a particular afternoon in the Green Hotel. This time there was no voice, no sound, but, as before, there was a vision, a flash, so quick, so instantly come-and-gone as to be seen and yet unseen. But nonetheless it registered, imprinted on my consciousness as searing as a scar.

There was a night-time technique, the "O-meditation" we called it, that Osho gave us at Mount Abu. We'd all taken to doing it of late, each of us propped up in his own bed, the entire flat resonating with the sound of collective humming. The technique was simple: fill the lungs with air and then empty them slowly to the sound of "O" from deep in the throat. Eyes, of course, were to be closed. He told us to pay close attention to the gaps between inhalation and exhalation. "Watch these gaps attentively," Osho said.

"They come between each breath. Be alert to them: in-breath, gap; out-breath, gap. And stay with the gap as long as possible, as long as is comfortable for you. In these gaps the mind dissolves. So be alert. In these gaps you can encounter your inner emptiness directly."

A few minutes after we began, I found myself witness to a curious scene, to a brightly-lit tableau projected onto an inner screen, as if some hidden camera whirred inside my head. More surprised than shaken, I held myself in check, eyes tightly closed, simply looking. Masses of sun-yellow curls tumbled down a back. But the back! The despair in the back struck me like a blow. It was hunched forward, not from any deformity, but more in a posture of protection, as if to shield the heart housed within the chest. I watched, transfixed but uncomprehending. And then the inner camera made a slow pan to the left, and there, between the shoulder and where the elbow should have been, I saw the stump, a clean, neat, axeman's slice. And then I understood. It was me!

At first I thought my heart would burst, it began to pound so uncontrollably. And it ached with a wild and helpless hurt, like a forest animal's, frantic in a cage. But the scene held, unmoving, until the turmoil ebbed away.

Somehow I knew I could control the inner camera. "Man or woman?" I asked.

Immediately everything went black. But only for a second. Then a tiny light appeared in the centre, like an actor's follow-spot, revealing male genitals. And then, spreading outwards, the light filled the screen. A young man lay on a stone slab, chained, writhing in fear, straining to escape. He could not have been more than sixteen or so, and the terror on his face was agonizing. The arms! Suddenly I had to know about the arms! But they were both there. It had not happened yet.

And then in the foreground a face materialized. The persecutor. Tibetan!

Yet on his face I saw no anger, no vengefulness. There was no coldness or indifference, but a kind of sad compassion. And I understood. What was to be done had to be done. Something greater than both of them was at play. And as suddenly as the scene had come, it disappeared, dissolving into blackness.

Shaken, I slid beneath the covers and tried to sleep. But it was no good. All night long the faces came, one after another in an unending queue. They were of all ages, from infancy to dotage, and of all expressions, from rage to rapture, from misery to bliss.

Into the centre of my vision they would float, bodiless, appearing first in this corner and then in that, or, most terrible, shooting straight at me like a comet, zooming at me from the centre of the void. Some lurked in dark shadow, taunting; others were fully lit. Some were just eyes, a strip of white light beamed across staring orbs; still others were up-lit from below, as children do on Halloween, making themselves ghoulish with flashlights under their chins.

I knew nothing—not who they were, not what they wanted. I tried to stop them, to shut them out—but to no avail. They came and they came and they came. And when the first rays of morning finally banished them, I was depleted. As if the vampires had been, I was icy and trembling and incredibly, chillingly cold.

I splashed water on my face, downed half a cup of coffee, and raced to 17, just to be near him, just to wait for the discourse, just to hear that everything was okay.

Past into Present

That afternoon I come home to the flat to find a lean, fair-haired young man sitting at the kitchen table pulling away on a thin-stemmed clay pipe, puffs of foul-smelling smoke chugging upwards above his head. His long, equine nose is buried in a book. It takes a while before he even notices me.

"Hi!" he says, finally acknowledging me, but with the most cursory of glances. His eyes, set wide in an oval face, are deep and clear and emerald green. He looks at me for a second and then returns to his book, a collection of Sufi stories by Idries Shah.

"Who are you?"

"Shantidas," he mumbles. "It means servant of peace." He doesn't bother to look up again.

I'm really not in a mood to press anything—my fourth attempt at an introduction to *A Bird on the Wing* has been pooh-poohed by Laxmi—so I leave him to his reading and join Rani in her room. Surrounded by jars of fabric paint, she's lying on the floor, a brush in her teeth, contemplating a pastoral scene she's doing on a pillowcase. "Who's he?" I ask, indicating the interloper in the kitchen.

"No idea," she laughs. "He just sort of wandered in and sat down in there with his book. He's been reading for hours. But I don't mind. I think he's rather sweet. Does he bother you?"

"Not really," I shrug. I'm getting used to heavy traffic. Most of our friends live in rooms and the homey atmosphere of our flat seems to be a major Pune attraction. I head back to the typewriter for a fifth try.

When dinnertime rolls around Shantidas is still firmly planted in his chair and only puts the volume aside when Virag sets a plate in front of him. He eats with gusto but, conversationally, all there is from him is an occasional request to pass the salt or to hand him another slice of bread. But there's something very likeable about him and, as if an unspoken vote has been taken, we all accept his presence without question, as if he belongs.

Over the next few days, it appears he does belong. Except to sleep, he's at the flat constantly. Even Divy, territorial about his space, doesn't mind. Suddenly, our little family is six.

Soon we discover Shantidas can talk. How he can talk! But I love his tales: his childhood in Wales, above-ground and below; his contact with Idries Shah, who sent him to Turkey; his time with the Sufis there, until they shunted him East; his ride through Afghanistan, a rifle on his shoulder; his coming to Osho and his heartfelt knowing that at last he had come home. And I find I love the storyteller too. He is a beauty, a young man of a depth and a richness remarkable at twenty-two. And of all the people in the flat, he's closest to Rani and to me. When he's not talking to her, he's bound to be yakking at me.

With a surprise break in the weather the temperature soars and, shelving the introduction for the time being, I join the others poolside at Pune's only five-star hostelry, the Blue Diamond Hotel. There, lolling in deck chairs, swilling lime sodas to beat the heat and kill the pool taste of chlorine, we while away the hours, welcoming the sun. Rani and I, this particular afternoon, are reclining in towel-draped deck chairs at one end of the pool when Shantidas gambols into view, tripping a kind of light-fantastic across the lawn towards the water. I watch, enjoying his silliness. Then, with a sudden jolt, something inside me flips, like an old 45 in a jukebox, and I am looking at my son. My heart is filled with a pride and tenderness I have never felt before. But I recognize the feeling. Paternal. It's the relish of a father in his son.

I turn to Rani to tell her, but no words come. She is watching Shantidas too. And on her face, as clear as the sky, I see a mother's love. I look at him again and then back at her. And I know she was my wife. For me there's no need, but Rani simply has to tell Osho, and so she goes to darshan that very night. "What did he say?" I ask when she comes home.

Her eyes are shining. "He said it was true, that you and I had been married in a past life and that Shantidas had been our son!"

I know Rani. I know that romantic, abstracted look. "What else?" I insist.

"Well, he did tell me to be careful," she admits, somewhat reluctantly. "He said to be aware that what happened then was over and gone, and that only now is real. He said that connections continue from life to life and that recognitions from past lives were beautiful, but not to get hung up on them. He said just to see them for what they were and to let them go."

"And can you?" I inquire, not overly convinced at her capacity to drop the whole thing.

"Of course, darling," she says sweetly, patting my hand in reassuring dismissal. "Of course I can. By the way," she adds, that daydreamy look back again, "where's Shantidas? Has our son been by this evening?"

At this point money's becoming a problem. There just isn't much of it left. And for a while the entire household's been existing on what remains of Rani's nest egg from Sweden. Out of necessity, the conversation turns, with increasing regularity, to plans for Canada. A letter from Gustavo and Miguel, old friends from Madrid, seems to be the clincher. They're coming to India to visit us in October and want Divy and me to take a holiday with them in Goa, as their guests. We decide to go to Anjuna, come back to Pune for a while, and then head west. For me the decision is arbitrary, more a way of closing the discussion than anything else. In my heart I don't want to leave at all. But what to do about money is a quandary. With pure surface-enthusiasm I agree to Canada, but inside I keep hoping some miracle will happen so I won't have to leave Osho at all.

The idea of not being able to see him, to be with him, is painful and I find myself remembering how beautiful he's been with me during this year in India, just how much he's given to me. Something in me must know I really have to leave, because the memories of each and every darshan with him fill my thoughts these days, making writing an impossibility. And it's odd, but one particular meeting, perhaps the most insignificant of them all, is the one that somehow makes the prospect of leaving the most difficult.

Wandering through the Mapuca market on a steamy Goa afternoon, I spied a bolt of fabric in a shop, an amazing sun-gold cotton. I bought a few meters and had a robe made. One morning in Pune, before monsoon, when darshan still happened on the lawn of 33, when we could just drop by and sit with him whether there was anything to say or not, I wore it. That morning a lanky Englishman took sannyas. After naming him—Veetmoha I think it was—Osho had said to him, "And wear a robe. You will look beautiful in robes. Wear a robe. Just like Krishna Prem," he added, turning towards me.

He looked at me intensely for a moment. "Don't wear yellow, Krishna Prem," he said at last. "Yellow is the colour of death."

"But this is orange, Osho," I replied.

"No," he insisted, "it's yellow."

I couldn't argue with him. "I really thought it was orange," I replied. "I'm a little colour blind."

"Really?" he'd said, his eyebrows arching into an intrigued V. "What colours?"

"Greys and greens. And now," I added, "I guess yellows and oranges too."

"Hmmm," he murmured, closing his eyes and tilting his head back, pensively steepling his fingers. After the longest while he turned back to me. I was expecting something of import. "The next time you go shopping," he said, "take someone with you."

At the sheer unexpectedness of his reply, after those pregnant moments, everyone had fallen about, laughing. Including me. And I thought I'd even heard a chuckle from him as he rose and walked, Vivek alongside him, back towards the house. I don't want to go.

The memory of having been Rani's husband has also been nagging at me, and my suggestion we get married again, made in jest several weeks ago, keeps surfacing in my mind. I find myself wondering whether it was more of a premonition than a joke.

The recollection of being married to her is one thing—it can easily be digested and dismissed; I've done it before with other memories, but what I cannot shake is the underlying feeling that what happened between us was left unfinished, that there is still some drama to be played out. And a part of me wants to go ahead, to close the circle, to polish off the karma. But on the other hand, she frightens me a bit—primarily, it's her capacity for dreams, the fact that she seems more at home in the world of fantasy than in the clear light of day. Whether she can see things as I do, with an overview, and not get caught up in them is my dilemma. She's had a keen eye on me these days, and my suspicion is that the same thing is on her mind. One evening, she finally broaches the subject.

"I've been thinking about it," I admit. "But all this mother-and-son jazz between you and Shantidas makes me a bit nervous. Yet, still, there's something to be worked out; that I can't deny."

"Well?" she asks quietly, tossing the ball back to me.

Suddenly I have to go through with it. Apprehensive or not, my curiosity eclipses all else. We sit down and talk the whole thing over, me doing my level best to put everything into perspective, to make sure she understands exactly how things are.

When I finish, some twenty minutes later, it's difficult to know whether I've penetrated or not. She assures me I have, that she's got the picture clearly, and insists there's nothing to worry about. She's aware too, she tells me, that a relationship left incomplete has to be completed. "After all," she asserts, "I did talk to Osho and he was very clear with me. Everything's fine. Really it is."

"And no guarantees? Remember, I'm going through with this for something else."

"I understand," she insists. "Everything's fine."

A few days later, with Divy, Prageet, Virag and Rani's friend Pathika in boisterous tow, after an hour of faded carbons and triplicate forms in a squalid Pune municipal office, Rani and I are legally man and wife.

"Remember what this is all about," I remind her in the rickshaw on the way back to the flat. She smiles at me, all dewy, her bridal bouquet resting on her heart, but says nothing at all.

That night, the flat a chaos from the wedding-reception revels of some fifty or so friends, with scraped-clean plates and half-full glasses dotting every available surface, I go to bed in my own room as usual. But I cannot sleep. I feel as if I am caught in the crossfire of two energies—Divy's from across the room; Rani's from the other side of the wall. I don't know what to do. But my own energy? Looking inside, I see clearly it wants to be with Rani.

"Divy?" I whisper, checking to see if he's awake.

"I know, Krishna. I know," he says quietly. "You're going to move in with Rani."

"Is it okay with you?" I ask. "I don't want to hurt you, but I have to see this thing through."

He props himself up on one elbow and looks at me. I can see his face in the half-light and I am reassured—he is calm and undisturbed. "I love you, you know," he says, "and no matter what, I want you to be happy. Don't worry about me. You go to her."

And so I do.

Since the night of the wedding, since our first unexpected but inevitable night together as husband and wife, things have been very beautiful with Rani. Although I sense she'd like to hear it, I cannot say I'm in love with her. There is, though, a deep affection, a tenderness, a caring, and I'm not at all closed to the possibility that, one day, there may be love between us. There's a new air of tranquillity about her, an aura of wellbeing, a soft, round feeling of completion that wasn't there before. She looks fulfilled, like a woman whose juices are flowing. Sexually, we're still getting to know each other. We're at the stage of exploration, of getting to know each other's bodies and rhythms, but, basically, the love-making is good. And frequent.

Considering the fact we've been hanging out together for three years, Divy's attitude has astonished me and given me, as well as Rani, a whole new respect and admiration for him. If someone had left me for someone else, particularly someone in the next room and of a sex that precluded competition, I'd have been really pissed. But Divy has been incredible. Not only has he been totally accepting of the situation, he seems genuinely happy at what's going on between me and Rani, between two people he loves. I would have followed my energy anyway, I had no choice, but that Divy is understanding and supportive is a great relief to me. Something else is going on, and it is to this something else my attention has to go.

Where it came from I do not know—there was no recollection of ever having heard Osho talk about it—but the first time I went to Rani I was very aware that it was tremendously important not to lose myself during sex, but to remain detached, witnessing, particularly during orgasm. I knew it was not a question of holding back, that I could let the body do what it wanted to, but that, on the inside, I had to watch. Somehow I also knew the trick was to keep my awareness focused in the centre of my forehead, in the third eye. I was a bit surprised at all of this, wondering, as I opened the door to her room, where it could have come from. But the sense of rightness was undeniable. And, as

I went to her that night, I felt very much a seeker, more like a man approaching a temple than a husband going to his bride.

It was on our second day together that I began to notice something new going on in my body. At first it was almost imperceptible, but when I closed my eyes and watched, it became clearer, more distinct. Some kind of circuit was in motion in me. Beginning in my genitals, it curved inward and upward, turning, when it reached my heart, downwards again, completing the circle. As I watched, it kept turning over and over again like a Ferris wheel, tracing circles inside me. And even when my eyes were open and I was engaged in things, in reading or talking or eating, I could feel it still turning.

At eight the next morning, the sun skimming the treetops out of a cloudless sky, sitting in front of Osho, I hear Teertha read this morning's sutra. It captures my attention immediately—it is one of the strangest of Jesus' sayings yet.

"Jesus saw children who were being suckled," Teertha reads softly. "He said to his disciples: 'These children who are being suckled are like those who enter the Kingdom.'

"They said to him: 'Shall we then, being children, enter the Kingdom?'

"Jesus said to them: 'When you make the two one, and when you make the inner as the outer and the outer as the inner, and the above as the below, and when you make the male and the female into a single one, so that the male will not be male and the female not be female, then shall you enter the Kingdom.'"

When he finished, I glance around me and on every single face I scan there is the same puzzled look I can feel on my own.

"This is one of the deepest sayings of Jesus," Osho begins slowly, "and one of the most basic to be understood by a seeker. It is also one of the most difficult to achieve, because if this is achieved nothing more is left to achieve...

"A saint, a sage, becomes like a child in a totally different sense. He has transcended; he has gone beyond mind, because he has understood the futility of it. He has understood the whole nonsense of being a successful man in this world. He has renounced that desire to succeed, the desire to impress others, the desire to be the greatest, the most important, the desire to fulfill the ego. He has come to understand the absolute futility of it. The very understanding transcends. The very understanding—and immediately you are transformed into a different dimension.

"Then there is again a childhood. That is called the second childhood. Hindus have called that stage the twice-born, dwij. Again you are born, but this is a different birth, not out of a father and a mother. This is out of your own self, not out of two bodies meeting, not out of duality. It is through your self that you are born.

"This is the meaning of Jesus' birth; that he was born out of a virgin. But people take everything literally and then they miss. Out of the virgin means: out of the one. The other is not there, so who can corrupt it? Who can enter into it? The virginity remains absolutely pure because there is no other.

"Jesus is born out of sex like anybody else, and it is right that it should be so. Jesus is just like you in the seed, but in the flowering he is absolutely different because a second birth has happened: a new man is born. Jesus who was born out of Mary is no more there—he has given birth to himself. In the old Essene sect it is said that when a man is transformed he becomes his own father...

"A man is not only a man, he is woman also; a woman is not only woman, she is man also—because both are born out of two. Your father goes on existing in you, your mother goes on existing in you, because they both participated, they both met in your body and their streams go on flowing—you are two. And if you are two, how can you be at ease? If you are two, there is going to be a constant conflict. If you are two opposite polarities together, a tension is always going to remain. This tension cannot be lost, yet you go on trying to find out how to be silent, how to be peaceful, how to attain bliss. It is impossible! Because you are two!

"To be silent, oneness is needed...

"Right now, as you are, nothing can be done. Unless you are reborn, unless you become your own father, unless your duality disappears and you become one, nothing can be done.

"When the woman within you and the man within you meet, they become a circle. They are not fighting, they disappear; they negate each other, and then oneness is left. This oneness is virginity."

"So what is to be done?" I hear him ask, millions of thoughts later. "Inside," he says, "a circle has to be made." I snap to attention. This is not to be missed!

"Jesus," he continues, "has not said exactly what is to be done because those secrets cannot be given openly, those secrets can be given only to disciples. Jesus must have given them to his disciples, because just by saying 'Become one!' no one is going to become one. Just by saying that the male should be female and the female should be male, no one is going to become one—because this is the goal. What is the method?

"Jesus must have kept that method secret... I will give you a few hints, though, how it can be done...

"These methods are to be done only under a Master, so that the Master goes on continuously watching what is happening with you. I am giving you a few things because I am here, and if you want to work you can work.

"The first thing: Whenever you make love to a woman or a man, that is the right moment to look for the inner woman or the inner man. Whenever you make love to a woman, do it with closed eyes—make it a meditation. The woman outside always helps the inner woman to become awake. And when you make love, your inner energies, both male and female, come to a peak. When the orgasm happens, it is not between you and the outer woman, it always happens between you and the inner woman...

"At that crescendo, don't go on looking outside, otherwise you will miss something beautiful that is happening, something very mysterious that is happening inside: you are becoming a circle. Your male and female are meeting...

"If you do it a few times, you will immediately become aware that the outer woman or man is not needed. This can be done without the other because this is happening without the outer. The outer is just a trigger-point. That trigger-point can be created inside. And once you know how, you can do it inside. But this has to be experienced; only then do you know—I cannot say how. You have to observe, watch, and then you will know how the energies come, how orgasm happens; how they separate again, and again the two arise...

"So close your eyes and watch what is happening inside. Don't try to make anything happen, just watch whatsoever is happening... and a moment comes when this inner circle remains forever. With the help of the other it cannot remain forever because the outer has to separate; the separation is a must. But with the inner there is no need to separate. If the inner marriage happens there is no divorce...

"And this is what Jesus means: 'And when you make the male and the female into a single one, so that the male will not be male and the female will not be female, then shall you enter the Kingdom.' Then you have entered. You have become perfect. You are not divided. You have become indivisible. Now you have a self. Now you have freedom and independence. Now you lack nothing, you are complete in yourself. Unless this circle happens you will lack something and you will depend on others to fulfill it...

"Meditate on these words of Jesus, and what I have said, try. But if you want to try, let me know. If you start working for the inner circle, then let me know continuously what is happening...

"So remember that a very balanced effort is needed. And many other things. If you want to work on it I will tell you, but that can only be done personally. That is why Jesus talks about the goal, but never talks about the method. The method is to be given personally. It is an initiation."

That evening a group of us congregate at the gate to 33, waiting for Mukta to take us to Osho. As she leads us down the tree-lined, graveled drive towards him, she moves close to me and whispers in my ear, "He says to sit on his right."

I am taken aback, but there is no time to question her: we have rounded the corner of the house and he is sitting there under the carport,

Vivek beside him, his hands resting in his lap. We place ourselves in a semi-circle in front of him, me on his right as Mukta instructed. "Krishna Prem?" he invites softly, still looking towards the garden.

"Osho," I begin, "that circle of energy you spoke about this morning? Well, it's been happening to me for the past few days."

His head spins round, snapping towards me with the speed of a bullet. "You're on *absolutely* the right track!" he almost shouts, leaving me reeling from the sudden impact of all that energy. And then, more gently: "Tell me about it."

And so I do: about going to Rani the first night and about knowing I should watch and not lose myself but not knowing how I knew—at which he chuckles—and about realizing the circle of energy was somehow connected with making love. "And then you talked about it this morning," I conclude.

"You are on absolutely the right track," he says once more. "Just keep watching, nothing more is to be done, and slowly, slowly, the circle of energy will go deeper and deeper inside you. And one day your inner man and your inner woman will meet and there will be an explosion. That is virgin birth. But keep me informed what is happening.

"And one more thing. Create a beautiful atmosphere for making love—candles, music, incense. It will be a help.

"Good, Krishna Prem," he adds, patting the air above my head. "It is beautiful what is happening."

Rani is waiting for me at the gate, but before she can speak, I've crushed her to my chest, one arm encircling her waist, the other nestling her head into my shoulder. "It was so beautiful, Rani," I tell her softly in her ear. "It was so, so beautiful. He said we're on absolutely the right track. Those were his very words: on absolutely the right track!

"Come on!" I shout, taking off down the drive in a half-trot, half-jig, pulling her along behind me. "Come on! Let's go home!"

Suddenly I remember something. "Do you have any money on you?" I call over my shoulder.

"Some," she answers breathlessly.

"Good! I want to stop and pick up some candles and incense on the way!"

Gustavo's arrival, preceding Miguel's by a week, is as much of a shock for us as finding Rani and me together is for him. It's been almost a year since we've seen him, since Divy and I spent a month with him and Miguel in Tripoli, en route to India, when Miguel was posted in his embassy there. He's like a creature from another planet with his tight grey pants and patent leather shoes, his tapered blue shirt and short, styled hair. He's the same age as Divy but looks ten years older. His face is lined with tension and puffy from booze. He's the first sounding-board from the outside world we've had since coming to Osho, and the contrast is so staggering I'm convinced I'd rather starve here in India than go and live in the West.

"I don't know what to say to him," Divy confides. "When I saw him step off the plane in Bombay I thought, 'Who the fuck is that?' And we were such good friends in London, him and me. But I just don't know what to say to him any more!"

I'm equally at a loss. But Rani, bless her woman's heart, comes to the rescue. She throws out his razor—"All the men here have the most beautiful beards!"—and drags him shopping down MG Road. Soon, a few days' stubble sprouting on his chin, clad in pyjama pants and a T-shirt, flip-flop sandals on his feet, the speed of civilization disappearing from his face, his cocktail intake down to two at sundown instead of ten, and some dynamite discourses on Jesus spinning his head, things are much better, for him as well as for us.

But it's short-lived. After the next twenty-four hours, Gustavo is so freaked out that, on his own, he's back to a quart of vodka a day.

I was sitting at the kitchen table when it first began, me at one end, Shantidas and Gustavo at the other. Shantidas was reading, Gustavo was writing a letter, and I was still fiddling with that accursed introduction. Everyone else was out.

All of a sudden, there was a strange, pulling sensation in the top of my head. My eyes became unbearably heavy and began to close, rolling backwards in my head. And I could sense the energy of each eye probing, like antennae, until they met and settled together, converging in the centre of my brow. The moment this happened the upward pull increased. But now it was outside me, above the crown of my head, drawing me upwards like some giant vacuum cleaner trying to inhale me from on high. I could feel my body sitting in the chair, but on the inside, it was as if some kind of inner levitation was happening. And then I heard the voice. "This is the ocean of consciousness," it said clearly. "Jump!"

I hesitated for a moment. I recognized the voice. It was Osho! He can't pronounce "sh"; he always says "ss". And that's exactly how "consciousness" was pronounced. It was Osho!

I tried to jump and couldn't. I tried again and couldn't. But on the third try I jumped. And then I was no more. Then my whole body, every single cell, went into orgasm.

When the waves of ecstasy subsided, and I was back in my body, back in the chair, I simply sat for a while, too stunned to move. I knew Shantidas and Gustavo had been watching me, but there was no way I could talk about what had just happened. But, with Shantidas at least, there was no need. He came and stood behind me and, ever so lovingly, bent over and kissed the top of my head. Then, without a word, he left. I vaguely noticed Gustavo scurrying off behind him. He looked terrified.

Everyone is at the table the next evening, including a vodka-soaked Gustavo, and Shantidas, our very own man-who-came-to-dinner. On the way home, Virag and Prageet stopped by our favourite Chinese restaurant and loaded a trio of tiffins with steamed rice and sweet-and-sour veggies, and Rani tossed together a big salad, drenching it with the olive oil Gustavo had brought from Madrid. There's virtually no conversation; everyone's attention is on his food, but suddenly, I am aware of a distinct change in the energy around the table. It's Divy. Something is happening to him.

He is sitting bolt upright in his chair, his cutlery fallen in front of him. His arms are rigid at his sides and his head is bobbing back and forth, as if in a continuous yes. His lids have dropped, heavy and weighted, covering half his eyes and they catch mine for the briefest moment before they roll backwards, leaving only the whites staring at me. A strange smile plays across his lips, and from deep in his throat comes a tiny mewing sound, but whether it is from pleasure or from pain I cannot tell.

Suddenly he shouts "No! No!" and his arms lift. At the same time, his body jerks erect, leaving him half-suspended in the air, his heels digging into the floor, his neck crushing against the back of his chair. Prageet moves to help him, but I motion him back. Everyone else is stock still, mesmerized. Except for Gustavo. His mouth is wide in amazement; his eyes wild with fear. In panic, he reaches for the vodka.

It is Divy's hands that tell me what is going on. Slowly they begin to contract, to close inwards upon themselves, the fingers taut and trembling, but the palms are unmoving, as if they cannot move, as if they have been fixed, nailed in place. And I remember Dalhousie and Jesus and the discourses all in a jumble. And somehow I see and yet I don't see. Somehow I understand and yet I understand nothing. All I can do is watch.

The torment on Divy's face is awful to behold. His features twist almost beyond recognition, but then, in a single sigh that reverberates around the table, everything in him relaxes and his face is swept clean by a rush of joy. And his lips, dry and parched, form a muted "Yes" as soft as the whisper of an evening breeze.

No one says anything for the longest while. Divy just sits there, glued to his chair, his eyes tightly shut. Finally, Gustavo, unable to contain himself any more, breaks the silence. "Krishna," he says, turning to me in confusion, "what's going on with Divyananda? Please, I don't understand."

I reach across the table for his hand. "Shsh, Gustavo," is all I can say. "Shsh."

That night I doubt if anyone sleeps. Rani and I try to talk about the past couple of days, but it is pointless, and we simply end up lying together, lost in our own thoughts. From Prageet and Virag's room the sound of their voices carry: his, animated and questioning; hers, quiet and reassuring. From the other side of the wall, we can hear Gustavo crying until just before dawn.

When the time to leave the flat for the discourse arrives at last, we cycle out to 17 convinced that Osho will say something about what has happened, that he will give us some kind of clue. But there is nothing. It is a beautiful lecture, but there is nothing.

Divy is unperturbed. "Will you all stop worrying?" he says with exasperation. "What happened was far out! I feel fine."

Back at the flat, a cup of coffee beside my typewriter, I find myself drifting away from the work in front of me, my brain trying to figure out what's going on. But it's impossible. There's no foundation, no previous experience upon which my mind can construct any kind of hypothesis. I asked for it, that I have to admit. And whatever it is, it's happening. All I seem able to do is try to hold myself on even keel and ride it out. Thinking about it is exhausting, so I drop it, grateful I'm facing yet another attempt at the *A Bird on the Wing* introduction, thankful there's something to occupy my mind. Laxmi's been bugging me for the introduction of late, cornering me at every chance, but so far whatever I've written is garbage.

No sooner are my fingers poised above the keys than the upward pull starts again. Closing my eyes, I go with it. Once more there is the feeling of inner levitation, the sensation of boundless space. And then comes the voice: "This is the edge of the ocean of bliss. Jump!" As before, I try and can't, try and can't, and then, on the third attempt, I jump. Like a diver soaring off a board I plunge into myself, falling deeper and deeper, until there is simply silence.

Into the silence everything has been absorbed: my mind, body, everything, and only two things remain: witnessing and breathing. And with nothing else within or without, with all else gone, I watch my breath—in and out, in and out, in and out. The more my attention focuses on my breath, the higher my awareness rises until, suddenly, I observe something new, staggering in its immensity—*I* am not breathing! Not that my breathing has stopped; it is still very much there, but the breathing comes from somewhere outside me. It comes from somewhere distant, penetrating me, entering the mechanism of my lungs, feeding me, nourishing me. But *I* don't breathe! I am *being* breathed. Existence is breathing *me!*

And I see that we are not separate, we are one! Joined together by a common breath, we are one!

That night I'm back at the gate to 33. "Mukta," I ask, when she comes to take the darshan-goers to Osho, "may I come too? I'd really like to talk to him about something."

Sitting in front of him, I spill it all out—about the orgasms, about seeing that I don't breathe, but for some reason the voice goes unmentioned, as if it is too intimate to be spoken of before others.

He simply watches me, smiling occasionally, saying nothing.

"But now," I say, "I just can't write. I've tried the introduction to *A Bird on the Wing* at least a dozen times, and it just isn't working. Whatever I write is stupid and meaningless. I don't even breathe! How can I write? You keep saying the truth cannot be spoken. Osho, it can't be written either!"

"Then," he says with a matter-of-fact wave of his hand, "you just write beautiful lies."

Turning towards the next sannyasin he asks what's going on, but before he has a chance to speak, Osho turns back to me. "And edit *The Mustard Seed* too," he says. "You edit these talks on Jesus. It will be good, hmmm?

"Now..." he invites, his total attention on the man at my side.

The next morning it happens again. The only difference this time is that we seem to have left the oceans of consciousness and bliss behind for something new. "This is the edge of the abyss," the voice declares today. "Jump!" Again, a couple of faltering attempts; again, it happens on the third try. And I'm off again, spiralled away.

By this time nothing surprises me and I find I'm getting a bit blasé about the whole thing—it could stop tomorrow or go on forever and, one way or another, life has to go on. I spend part of the afternoon staring at a blank piece of paper, cursing the book I'm supposed to introduce and calculating how long it will take me to edit *The Mustard Seed.* I come up, ironically, with forty days.

"But what about Miguel?" Divy asks when I tell him. So, that night, it's back to darshan again. "Osho," I say, "I worked it out this afternoon: it will take me forty days to edit *The Mustard Seed*"—at which everyone laughs, including him—"but a good friend is here from Madrid and another is coming to Bombay shortly. They want us to go to Goa for a holiday with them. Couldn't I just drop this book? Couldn't someone else do it?"

"You really don't want to do it?" he asks.

"Not really," I confess. "I've done two books already, one after another, and I seem to have lost the knack. Like this introduction. I just can't get it. I've tried and tried, but I just can't get it. I feel I need a change."

"Okay," he replies. "You go to Goa."

"Thank you. With everything that's been going on, my mind is going nuts. It can't understand anything, but it keeps on trying. My mind needs a change."

"Then forget about Goa and do *The Mustard Seed.* It will keep your mind occupied. It will be better.

"And how about you?" he asks, turning to someone else.

Shit! He got me! He really got me! Why hadn't I kept my big mouth shut? I'd gotten out of the book, but somehow I'm right back in it again, with forty days of editing stretching out before me. I try to catch his eye, searching for an opening, but he's having none of it. Shit! Hooked again!

Before I open my eyes the next morning I know I'm pissed off. I hate the lecture, I hate the meditations, I hate lunch. Everyone avoids me, including Rani. She does what every wife does when her husband's in a grump—goes shopping.

After a nap the gloom has given way to resignation, and by the time Divy comes home I'm more or less back to normal. He makes a pot of tea and we stretch out in his room to drink it. It's been a while since we've had any kind of intimacy and I lock the door not to be disturbed. We talk; he tells me how he misses me and I see just how important he is to me as well.

At some point, someone had tried the door and, finding it locked, had gone round, through Prageet and Virag's room, into the kitchen. I knew it must be Rani.

When I walk into the kitchen later, I am greeted with a look of such venom that it brings me, in mid-stride, to a complete standstill. "Don't think I don't know what's been going on!" she spits. "Don't think I don't know what you've been up to in there! I won't stand for it, do you hear?" she screams, quivering with rage. "I won't stand for it! You're *my* husband and you belong to me and I won't stand for it!"

When the fuming finally abates, I say, "Rani, be aware of one thing: you don't own me. I'm not yours. I'm free. I'm free to do whatsoever I want—free to be with you; free not to be with you. It's up to me. But remember one thing and never forget it: I am not yours!"

I walk out of the kitchen, closing the door behind me. As I leave the flat, I hear the sound of dishes smashing against the wall. For the rest of the afternoon I don't go home. I shower at a friend's flat and borrow a clean robe. I must see Osho again!

Divy's at the gate when I arrive. We don't speak; there's nothing to be said. But Mukta can't resist. She spies me as she comes up the drive to collect us.

"Lots going on, Prem?" she laughs.

"To say the least, Mukta," I reply with an attempt at a grin. "To say the very least."

Osho looks up as we round the corner of the house. Seeing me, he suddenly raises his hand, pointing his index finger directly at me. "Ah,

Krishna Prem," he says loudly, and like an angler playing a fish, guides me to the spot on his right. "Hmmm?" he asks, leaning in my direction as soon as we're all seated.

Somewhat embarrassed, especially in front of others, I blurt out the tale of the day's events. I explain that things have been very good with Rani but, as the afternoon showed me, something with Divy is obviously still there.

"Don't make it a problem," he says when I finish. "Make it a three-way marriage."

A trill of nervous laughter ripples around the semi-circle. Osho's father, visiting from Madhya Pradesh and attending his first darshan in Pune, leans forward to peer at me, as if I were a carnival attraction on display.

"Make it a three-way marriage," he repeats. "Rani will understand. Tell her this is my suggestion and she will be fine—she'll understand. But, Krishna Prem, don't create any difficulties between Rani and Divyananda. Just follow your energies, moment to moment, and move wherever your energy takes you.

"And Divyananda," he adds, turning to Divy next to me. "You don't create any problems between Rani and Krishna Prem, hmmm?"

Divy nods. He's willing to cooperate. "Make it a three-way marriage," he says again. "Rani will understand. And Krishna Prem," he adds, looking directly at me once more, "if your mind interferes, if it starts asking questions and creating troubles, just sit under a cold shower!" To a background of laughter, he repeats, "And Rani will understand."

But she doesn't. On the contrary, she goes berserk.

"I don't care what he says," she screams, hammering her fist on the table. "I don't give a shit what he says! You're my husband and you belong to me and that's that. And if he thinks I'm going to share you with *this*," she snarls, curling her lip in Divy's direction, "then he's crazy. Just forget this three-way crap. You're mine!"

"Rani..."

"Shut up!" she shrieks. "Shut up! I don't want to hear any more. Don't think I worked to get you for this long to lose you now. When you two left me in London I made up my mind I'd get you one day, that I'd take you away from him, that I'd get even. And I did!" Her face is a mask of sneering pride. "I did! I waited and I planned and I did it! I am not, do you hear, not going to give you up—not in any way!"

For a few moments there is absolute silence in the kitchen. I cannot believe what I have just heard. I cannot believe that she has been scheming and conniving for over three years to get even, to have revenge. I feel like a fool, like a stupid fool. I feel like I've been manipulated, as if I'm not a man, but a wind-up toy. And suddenly I know it's over. In a flash it's apparent that whatever Rani and I had to complete has been completed. I don't want anything to do with her any more.

She must read me, because all at once she softens, her anger giving way to fear. "Krishna," she says, her tone telling me she knows she's gone too far, "I didn't mean what I said. I was angry and it was all such a shock at first. Let me go see Osho too. Let me talk to him first, and then I'm sure everything will be okay."

I can say nothing. I look into her face and I hate what I see. She reaches for my hand, but I pull it away. I don't even want her to touch me. Without a word I leave the flat. I need to be alone.

I don't go home to sleep. Land-Rover-Anup puts me up in his room at Ma Shradha's. And I don't go home the next day either. I drink gallons of tea and think and think until my head aches. Everything is unclear, except for one thing—between Rani and me it's over.

When I'm certain she's gone to darshan I come home. When she returns I'm at the kitchen table, staring vacantly at the wall. "Krishna," she says tentatively, dropping to her knees beside me, her hand on my arm, "everything's fine. I spoke to Osho tonight and I understand. Believe me, everything's fine."

"Rani," I beg, "not tonight. I'm so tired and so confused I can't listen any more, I can't talk any more. Please, just let me be."

"Okay, okay," she says, the words choking in her throat. "Let's see what tomorrow brings. But I'm sorry. I want you to know that. And I want you to know that I understand now and that everything's fine."

Late into the night I sit at the table, my head in my hands. Where do I go from here? He warned us in the discourses. "My whole effort is to kill you," he said. I asked for it and it has been given to me. And now look—my world shattered, my mind a chaos. I sit here and I can't even think. I try to put two thoughts together into something cohesive, into something substantial, and I can't even do that. They slip by each other, missing, like ships that pass in the black of night.

"I'm dying, Osho!" I tell him the next evening, hoping he'll fix it, hoping he'll make it all right. "I'm dying. I'm dissolving. I can't even think any more. I'm dying!"

"Good!" he says. And that's all. Not a single word more.

"I'm not coming to discourse this morning," I tell Virag after the longest night of my life. "But here's a letter for Osho. Would you give it to Mukta to give to him? It's about editing and introductions. I don't want to do it any more."

And the longest night of my life is followed by the longest day. Restless, I pace the flat like a caged tiger, filling one room with my discord and then another. Everyone but Gustavo is out. He hunches over the table, following me with frightened eyes and it drives me mad. I pick up a mirror and drive it at the wall, covering everything with tiny silver crystals, like frozen morning dew. Gustavo flees, leaving me alone.

And then, suddenly, enough is enough. Enough hurt, enough suffering, enough indulgence. And a feeling of coolness overtakes me. What's done is done and cannot be reversed. My life has to go on. But not with Rani. I've seen cunningness, possessiveness. I've seen their ugliness. And in a funny way I'm grateful. I've seen them so strongly that I swear to myself the next time I become involved with someone I'll be alert to them in the other person and I'll be alert to them in me. But right now I need space from all of this. I feel like I have to protect myself, give myself time to heal. And, sweeping the floor, I feel an armour forming over my heart. But I don't care. Really, I've had enough.

Divy's the first home. "So what are you going to do?" he asks. "Are you coming to Goa? Miguel arrives in Bombay tomorrow night, so if you're coming let me know. Gustavo and I have to go to the station to get tickets for the Deccan Queen in the morning. Are you coming or not?"

"Yes, Divy," I reply. "I'm coming."

"Where are you going?" Rani's voice asks from behind me. She has walked in, unnoticed.

"Goa. I'm going to Goa with Divy and Gustavo and Miguel."

For a moment she says nothing. She simply stands there, quite still. Finally she sighs, a long, deep, despondent sigh. "And what about me?"

"What about you?"

"What about us?"

"There is no *us*. There is no us any more, Rani. It's finished."

She begins to cry, pulling at me, telling me she's changed, begging for another chance.

"Understand one very simple thing: it's over," I say. "I'm sorry too. It was beautiful for a while. But it's over."

An hour or so later I am still at the kitchen table, pen in hand, trying to write a letter, trying to occupy my mind with anything but thought. I hear Rani come into the room, but I don't look up. She crosses behind me towards the bathroom. Somehow I know she has a razor in her hand. I don't look up, yet I know. She wants me to think she's going to slash her wrists, of that I am aware, yet I don't move. There's a gap between the bathroom door and the floor, and I keep my gaze glued there. I know she's not going to hurt herself, but still, I'm not taking any chances. Fifteen minutes go by before the door opens again. She stands there, framed in the doorway, eyes red and puffy and swollen—and totally bald. Except for a few tufts at the back she couldn't reach, there's not a hair on her head. For a while we just look at each other. "Why did you shave your head?" I ask at last.

"To show you I've changed."

For a moment I don't speak. A sudden conflict surges up in me and I don't know what to say. Part of me wants to reach out, to enfold her in my arms, to kiss her hairless head and make everything okay. But another part of me remembers the manipulation, the possessiveness, and this is the part that wins. "I'm sorry, Rani," I say as gently as I can, not wanting to hurt her but having to be true to myself, "the only change I see is that now you're bald."

Into the silence that follows, into the pained silence that fills the room, Virag comes, a piece of paper in her hand. "Here," she says, passing it to me, "Laxmi gave it to me. It's from Osho." Then, instantly sussing the situation, she rushes to Rani and takes her to her bosom, rocking her to and fro, like a mother comforting a stricken child.

I open the folded paper. The message is in Laxmi's hand. "No need to edit," I read. "He says fine to drop books for now." It is signed by her.

And then I see the postscript. It rips into me like an arrow shot from afar. Across the bottom is written: "Enough for today?"

Escape to Paris

Goa is hideous. The monsoon is still in full swing and we spend most of each day huddled in the only room we could find, four of us crammed in together, entering and exiting through a window because the landlord's ancient granny is living in the room on the other side of the only door. Even the Brie and the Camembert, the Pommard and the Beaujolais Miguel has brought from Paris do nothing to brighten the days.

But worst of all is the spectre of Rani. It's not enough that I have to deal with her in my head, but I also have to cope with her physical presence, with her solitary, stubble-headed figure perched on the hill whenever the clouds break for a moment and we rush to the beach.

She has followed us to Goa and is staying, we find out, on Baga, the beach next to Anjuna. She doesn't come near us, but looms, day after day, high on the cliffs above the sand, like an eternally-patient vulture. No matter how hard I try to ignore her, it's impossible. I feel like a bird in a cage.

One afternoon I've suffered this horrendous holiday long enough. I announce I've had more than I can take of Anjuna and the rain and that I want to leave.

My proposal is carried unanimously, and we catch the next day's flight from Panjim to Bombay.

"Well, Krishna," Divy asks, "what do you think? What would you like to do?"

We're sitting on a balcony at Shelley's Hotel, an old Bombay favourite of ours, overlooking strolling Indian families meandering down the seafront, along the Apollo Bunder esplanade to where the reclaimed Colaba Causeway juts out into the grey-green water, and then turning, to retrace their steps, towards the Gateway to India and the Taj Mahal Hotel.

I'm not so much concerned with the spectacle of the twilight promenade as I am in thinking over the proposal Miguel has made to us. As Divy has just done with me, he'd asked what we intended to do. He knew we'd run out of money and were planning to go back to Canada to earn enough to spend another year or so in Pune. He hadn't said anything in Goa but had obviously been thinking about our situation, because a few moments ago he'd asked us to come and live with him in Paris. He had a huge flat in the sixteenth arrondissement, he'd said, right across from the Bois de Boulogne. There was plenty of space, including a big guest room we could have.

"And don't worry about money," he added. "I earn enough to take care of your needs. I'll handle things like rent and food, and whatever you earn you can set aside for India. I know all sorts of people in Paris; I'm sure you won't have any trouble making money."

"So," Divy asks again, "what would you like to do?"

On the way to India over a year ago, after a stopover with Divy's parents in Stockholm, we'd gone to visit Miguel in Libya, where he was consular officer in the Spanish Embassy. He lived in a rambling Italian-style villa some thirteen kilometres outside Tripoli, on a large date and olive estate, with a Spanish cook and the occasional long visit from Gustavo, his closest friend for many years. We spent a very nice month with him, mostly lazing about the house.

Tripoli, under the Gaddaffi regime, had nothing to offer but overpriced goods in the shops, Pepsi Cola in the bars, boarded-up casinos, pictures of the revolution in the churches and a nervous, suspicious citizenry that scattered in all directions at our approach. I'd grown extremely fond of Miguel in Tripoli, and choosing between his warmth and hospitality in Paris and the freezing blasts of a Montreal winter is not, when I come right down to it, that difficult. "Let's go to Paris, Divy," I reply. "Let's go and live with Miguel and Gustavo in Paris."

And so, with a parting thousand rupees shoved into Divy's hands before they board the Paris-bound Air France jet at Santa Cruz Airport, and a pair of eighteen-month-old tickets from Bombay to Sydney—where I cannot remember really ever wanting to go—we begin the process of extricating ourselves from this country.

For the next few days I see nothing but backstreet bazaars and airline offices. At Gustavo's suggestion, for shops he knows in Paris, Divy gleans the market stalls for silk saris, second-hand but in mint condition. He also hounds the Rajasthani gypsies, bargaining over their panels and hangings, arguing and haggling with them until they succumb. In Paris, according to Miguel, Indian folk art is all the rage.

The excursions into the bazaars are fine—I've always enjoyed this aspect of India—but I'm sure the airline people are going to drive me round the bend.

It all begins at the TWA office in the Taj Mahal Hotel. We must sit for a good forty-five minutes before the painted, powdered Indian agent behind the counter even deigns to acknowledge our existence. "Yes?" she inquires, as if an offensive smell has just wafted under her ski-jump nose. "Is there something you want?"

"No, you stupid bitch," I mutter under my breath, "we're sitting here waiting for a bus."

"I beg your pardon," she says, examining a chip in the varnish of a long, scarlet nail. "I didn't get that."

"It wasn't important," I reply, laying the tickets on the counter. "Here. We flew from Athens to Bombay on TWA and these are endorsed to your airline. We want to go to Paris, but if they won't take us that far, then we want to get as close as we can."

Using two talons from each hand, as if contact with the tickets might soil her flesh, she raises them to eye level, holding them there for the briefest moment before she relaxes her claws and lets them flutter downward, back onto the counter. "These tickets have expired," she snorts, looking happy for the first time since our exchange began. And without another word she vacates her chair, leaving us staring in utter disbelief at each other and at the tickets lying on the counter where they've fallen.

"Fuck her!" Divy says finally. "Let's try somewhere else."

Air France, Air India, Lufthansa, SAS, Sabena; the Russians, the Poles, the Pakistanis, the Bangladeshis, the Iranians—we try them all. We even spend a whole afternoon encountering Islam—Kuwait, Egypt, Saudi Arabia and a host of sheikdoms and emirates I've never heard of before. To a white-robed, wimpled Arab, they turn us down.

Finally, standing in the midst of the milling Churchgate throng, hot and tired and frustrated, clutching the bloody tickets in my hand, I've had enough.

"Divy, it's pointless," I argue. "We may as well throw these away. They're expired, useless. Haven't you accepted that yet?"

Divy turns to me, the fire of determination still burning brightly in his eyes. "Look," he says, pointing over my shoulder. "There's one we haven't tried. Let's give the Brits a go!"

I could have kissed the man at British Airways. He was the first human I'd met in days of trucking through Bombay airline ticket offices. He sits us down, sends for tea, examines the tickets and says, "I think I can take care of this for you."

After a few rough calculations on his pad—in which hope is the only emotion I'm aware of—he looks up. "These tickets will get you to London," he explains, smiling at the waves of relief that sweep across our faces, "and you have a credit left over that should be enough to get you over the Channel to Paris. You can probably take the boat-train from Dover to Calais. Or the Hovercraft. Have you ever ridden a Hovercraft?" he asks, excitedly. "It's jolly good fun!"

Clearing his throat, as if taken aback by his own familiarity, he returns quickly to the affair at hand. "First of all, I shall have to telex the travel agent in Montreal where you purchased these tickets to make sure you bought and paid for them. It's just a formality, but one must stick to the rules, musn't one? We should have their reply by tomorrow and if everything's cricket I can issue your tickets."

Stunned, all we can do is nod.

"I've based these calculations on a special fare we have for Britons returning to England," he adds. "By the way, what passports do you carry?"

"British," Divy replies.

"Canadian," I answer, a lump forming in my throat and a knot starting in my stomach.

"Oh dear," he tuts. He ponders a moment. "Well, these rates also apply to foreign residents in the United Kingdom or to foreign students studying there." He looks me in the eye. "I don't suppose you fall into either of these categories now, do you?"

I have to admit I don't. I also admit I wish I did.

"Well then," he shrugs, flashing us a big twinkling smile, "let's just say you do, old chap. Let's just say you do."

To leave the country we need tax clearance, an odd affidavit affirming that one has not been employed in India—as if that were remotely possible. It's issued on the presentation of foreign exchange receipts, which Divy tore up months ago, or, failing that, one's sworn statement. Swearing is all we have to offer, but the clerk's a nice man and, after hearing our oath on the *Bhagavad Gita* he stamps the papers dutifully and wishes us bon voyage. That takes the morning.

The afternoon is devoted to some last-minute shopping for Paris and, a bit nervous at the prospect, to checking with our friend at British Airways.

"Everything is fine," he calls to us as we walk through the glass doors. "There's a flight to London in seven days. Will that be all right?"

And so, a few minutes past five, tickets and treasures stored safely in our luggage, we pull out of Victoria Terminus on the Deccan Express. Apart from one stop in Lonavla, it's a straight run to Pune.

During my last days in Pune I want to do anything but think. Some undercurrent of doubt nags at me, trying to force its way into my consciousness, but I don't want to allow it—so, occupying myself wherever and however I can, I manage to keep it submerged. Osho is speaking Hindi, which gives my mind nothing much to focus on, but at least there's a meditation camp in progress, and I throw myself into the techniques with a totality that borders on frenzy. Evenings, sometimes with Divy, sometimes alone, I visit this friend or that, avoiding, at all costs, the flat off Boat Club Road.

We've been staying at the Green Hotel since the night we arrived from Bombay. Running into Virag at 17 one morning, I ask her and Prageet to drop by. At first it's a bit strained with them, but they soon mellow, especially Virag. Prageet, I sense, is disappointed in me because of what happened with Rani. I don't have the energy to get into it with him, so I don't even try.

They're leaving India too, they tell us. They fly out of Bombay the day before we do, for Singapore, where they'll catch a ship to Australia. Rani, Virag tells me when I ask, is fine. "It was rough at first," she says, "with that insane trip to Goa and everything. But she seems fine now. Don't feel bad," she reassures me. "No one's blaming anyone for anything any more." I feel better, knowing Rani's okay. I don't want to be with her, but I don't want her to hurt either.

"We'll all look back on this one day and have a good laugh," Virag adds, hugging me tightly. "Take care of yourselves. I'll miss you both. And I'll write."

"See you, guys," Prageet mutters from the doorway. But when our eyes meet, it's just not enough. He crosses the room in one long stride and engulfs us both in a massive, heartfelt hug.

When Mukta hears we're going in a couple of days, she proposes a farewell dinner the night before we leave. "You'll be back in January," she predicts. "I don't know how I know, but I know. You won't be in Paris more than three months. You'll be back in January."

On the list of farewells that leaves the two most difficult: Osho and Laxmi.

"Osho," I say, sitting before him for the last time for a while, "we've run out of money and we're going back to the West, to Paris. I want to be able to come back with enough money to stay here with you for at least another year."

"And how long will that take?" he asks.

"I don't know," I answer.

"How long?" he asks again, leaning forward, as if he hasn't heard.

"I don't know," I answer once again.

He cocks an ear towards me, as if he still hasn't caught what I've been saying. "When will you be back?" he repeats.

All at once I remember standing with him in his room at Woodlands, the day I told him I was going to Goa when what I really wanted was to be brave and trusting and willing to return to Kailash. But I didn't let it out then, and whatever's going on inside me, I don't let it out now. My head goes into a jumble, mostly about money. How can I stay? Where will I live? What will I eat? I see no solution, no alternative. I see no other choice but to go. "I don't know, Osho," I say. "I really don't know." More to change the subject than anything, I add, "Mukta says January."

"Hmmm," he murmurs. "January." He looks upwards for a moment and then back at me. "It shouldn't take that long."

My heart sings. Deep down I really don't want to go at all and now he's telling me I'll be back in less than three months! Suddenly, I feel light and happy again.

Turning to Vivek, he asks her to go into the house and bring him two shirts, the knee-length affairs he wears over his lunghi. While Vivek is about her errand, he turns back to me. "Remember one thing, Krishna Prem, while you are in the West," he says. "If you let it, existence will take care of you, the same way it takes care of the birds and the trees and the flowers."

And something in me knows he is giving me a key, a way to keep growing while I am away from him. And I also know the key is to be found in the first part of the sentence, in "If you let it..." And I'm so freaked out by what's been happening that I don't even understand I'm missing again. All I have to do is to surrender and stay, to let existence care for me here, where I really want to be, and not go to the West at all. But I'm so caught up in my own drama that I miss completely.

"Here," he says, taking the white robes from Vivek and leaning forward to place one in Divy's hands. "Dye this orange," he instructs. "And if you need me, put it on."

And then there is a robe in my outstretched hands as well. "If you need me, Krishna Prem, put this on."

She is sitting on the ledge of her window when I find her the following afternoon. Her head is resting against the frame, her eyes distant, long, delicate fingers entwined around her knees. The headscarf has fallen to her shoulders, and her hair, without a trace of grey, shines black and sleek in the dappled sunlight filtering through the trees.

"Laxmi?"

"Ah, swamiji," she says softly, gesturing beyond the tiny mosaic terrace to the bare plot stretching out behind the house, "the brain was pondering. Much work has to happen...

"But you," she shouts, springing to her feet and clapping her hands together as if to break her reverie. "You are going, it seems?"

"Yes, Laxmi. To Paris. To earn some money. I just came to say goodbye to you."

"No need for goodbyes, Krishna Prem," she says. "Only bodies are separating for little time. Laxmi is in this heart," she adds, first jabbing my chest with her finger and then laying her hand on her own, "and Krishna Prem is in this one."

Bidding farewell to Laxmi is, in many ways, even more difficult than it was with Osho. She's always been a kind of embodiment of Osho for me, a living, tangible proof of what can happen by being with him. He's always been available, but somehow, he remains remote and distant. Laxmi, on the other hand, has always been close, real, more like a friend. There's a depth of love and height of awareness that emanate from her that are quite remarkable, as if she resides in some inner halfway house, at some mid-point between him and us. My love and respect for her are overwhelming—and I don't think I can take this much longer. I have to get this over with and get the hell out of here, fast. And she knows. "Laxmi, goodbye," I say, leaning over and kissing her cheek, holding my welling tears in check.

"Goodbye, swamiji. Remember, this is home. Come back soon." And she returns my kiss, planting an awkward little peck on the side of my head.

"Laxmi!" a woman's voice shrieks from inside her room. "Laxmi! You've never kissed a man before!"

She laughs. "It's not the Indian way," she confesses, a hint of red shading her brown cheeks, "but Laxmi is becoming international! Besides," she adds, shouting back, "this is Laxmi's boyfriend. And that's who kisses are for!"

I simply don't trust my emotions any more and turn to go. "Krishna Prem," she calls softly. I turn to face her again. She places a square, flat box lovingly in my hands. I open it to find a large, reel-to-reel tape inside. "Take," she says. "Gift. Twenty-one discourses. *The Mustard Seed.*"

At dinner that evening with Mukta and a few friends I feel more comatose than festive. The meal is a pleasant one—good food, witty conversation, silly repartee and lots of beer—but I'm rather relieved when it's all over, the bill is paid and we're out on the street, piling into rickshaws and saying goodbye. As Mukta prepares to leave she hugs us both, thrusting a slip of paper in Divy's hand. "Bring me some goodies from Paris," she calls as the rickshaw pulls away from the curb.

"Look, Krishna," Divy says in surprise, holding the piece of paper up for me to see. "It's a cheque for five hundred dollars!"

Our first meal in Bombay had been at Gourdon's, in Churchgate, a nice restaurant with good food and a bumbling pretension at French-style, spoon-and-fork service that always tickled my fancy. And so, before it's time to leave for the airport, we decide it's only fitting to close the circle properly, to have our last Bombay lunch at Gourdon's. As I dip into my vegetable rissole with one of the half-dozen unmatching forks flanking the left of my plate, something suddenly churns in my gut. I look up. There, standing in the doorway, is Rani.

At first she doesn't notice us. The head waiter leads her to a table on the other side of the dining room and hands her a menu. She peruses it for a moment and then, as if trying to decide what to order, glances around the restaurant. She sees us. Our eyes meet for a moment, but no one moves. After a bit, I return to my food.

But it's no good. I can't eat. The events of the past weeks rush over me, choking me, filling my throat with bitterness. Things I thought had settled, things I believed I'd come to grips with, they're all there again. I push my plate away. "Divy, I want to leave," I announce, signalling for the bill.

Rani gets up and crosses over to us. She stands beside our table, an odd, faraway look in her eyes, a strained, forced smile on her lips. She seems wan and gaunt and alien, her head coated in a fine bristle of inch-long hairs. I stare at her and I don't know who this is. It's as if a total stranger has approached me. I wait, as if I'm going to be asked for a match or a cigarette.

"Krishna," she says finally, in a cracked and unfamiliar voice, ignoring Divy, "I wanted to see you to say goodbye. I knew you were leaving today and I also knew I'd find you here. You see, I know these sorts of things now. I even know what Osho is going to say before he says them..." She drifts off, abstracted. With a visible effort she pulls herself back. "I hope you have a good time in Paris. And I want you to know that I'm different, that I've changed. I've really really changed, you know."

And she has. But what freaks me out, what shocks me to the core, sharply, like a slap, is that Rani is gone and Ulla is back. I scrutinize her face and all I can see is that woman in London. All I can see, bubbling under the surface, is the same madness I saw in the flat on Beaufort Street.

All at once a sense of urgency arises in me—a need to protect myself, to escape from this woman, to put my own survival first, to get as far away from her as I can. And I hate her hold on me. She still affects me, disturbs me, and I hate her for it.

"Can't you say anything?" she asks. "Can't you see I've changed?"

"Ulla," I say, tossing a handful of rupee notes on the table and standing to leave. "I'm sorry. All I see is Ulla."

She reels backwards, as if I have struck her. Her mouth opens, but whether it is to cry or to beg or to curse me, I never know. Before any sound can come from her I have turned on my heel and am gone.

"Tea or coffee?" the middle-aged stewardess with the Knightsbridge accent inquires sweetly as we level off, the smog and the slums of Bombay falling away beneath us.

"Neither, honey," I reply. "Just bring us a couple of bottles of wine and keep 'em coming until you roll us off at Heathrow!"

Chapter Three: 1975

PARIS

By the end of the second month in Paris I think I may go mad. I am sick of grey skies and grey people and grey underground trains, of stone-lined streets streaming with sombre faces and stagnant eyes, of shops and restaurants and cinemas filled with corpses bedecked and painted to pretend they are alive. I am sick of larger-than-life monuments, of triumph and glory, of deco railings and ormolu furniture and opulent facades. I am sick of syrupy shopkeepers and chic colognes and little bronze plaques that tell me who died here and when. I am sick of avenues and bridges and quays, of faubourg-saint-this and boulevard-général-that, of the Opéra and the Lido, of Nôtre-Dame and La Madeleine, of Place Pigalle and St-Germain-des-Prés. I am sick and tired of the whole morbid, miserable, death-obsessed place, from the first arrondissement to the sixteenth and way, way beyond.

"Divy," I tell him, meaning every word, "if I don't get out of this fucking graveyard soon I'll be as dead as they are!"

The first month had been more or less fine, as soon as I'd come to grips with the irrevocable fact that I had actually left Osho and India behind me, and that, no matter how much I might want to, the wherewithal was missing for me to be able to turn around and go right back.

It hit me the moment my feet touched British soil and I looked up into that dingy, cloud-filled morass the English call the sky. I knew, beyond the shadow of a doubt, I didn't want to be here at all, that I had never really wanted to leave India, that I had made a terrible mistake and, worst of all, I'd missed another opportunity to surrender.

And, standing in the Customs shed, watching a pair of HM's uniforms ever so politely tearing our luggage to shreds—"I suppose you realize we may ask to search your person, old chap. Looking for drugs, you know"—I see I have a choice here in the West: to use what Osho has shown me to rise above all this or, slowly but surely, to allow myself to sink back into the mire of unconsciousness I see churning around me.

It's not that I'm condemning what I see, it's more that I once belonged to this myself, to this sheep-like civilization, to this robot-like existence, to this world where one thinks and acts as one has been taught to think and act—and I just don't want to be a part of it any more.

Osho has given me a glimpse of my possibility, of every man's potential, of an inner world beyond the mind—but it's a realm as alien as Mars to these people I see milling about me. In Pune we had been sheltered, protected, encircled by light and love and laughter—but I see here that we are alone, Divy and me, and that what we have is delicate and fragile and, like a rose by a rock, easily crushed. But I will not allow it to be killed! I make that commitment to myself. One day life will take me back to Osho, but while I am here, I vow to do whatsoever I can to nourish what he has given me, to do my utmost not to let it shrink and wither, but to help it grow. "Divy," I promise, my voice firm with determination, "as long as we're here, as long as we're stuck in the West, I swear one thing: I'm going to do the Dynamic every single bloody day!"

Miguel and Gustavo are thrilled by our arrival. No sooner have we stepped through the door of the fourth-floor flat, overlooking, as Miguel had promised, the Bois de Boulogne, than a pair of Gustavo's famous frozen daiquiris are shoved, in welcome, into our hands.

Miguel, of course, hadn't met the train. "He's done it again," Divy remarks. "Let's find a telephone."

The last time Miguel had "done it" had been in Tripoli. A strike had held us up overnight in Zurich and Swissair had promised to notify Miguel, but arriving in the Libyan capital we found no Miguel anywhere. All there was, camping on the cement floor of the tin-roofed hangar the Libyans proudly referred to as an airport, was a mind-boggling collection of ferocious looking Bedouins, straight out of the desert, each patriarch surrounded by a mound of filthy bundles, a transistor radio, a donkey or two, an occasional camel, a gaggle of half-naked, runny-nosed children and a cluster of wives, all purdahed to the hilt except for one peering eye that coolly surveyed the reigning pandemonium like a periscope wrapped in a dusty sari.

"Let's find a telephone," Divy had suggested on that occasion as well. But when a quick scrutiny of the signs encircling the terminus revealed not one single letter in the Roman script, all I could venture was a nervous "How?" Finally, poking here and there under the suspicious stares of the Bedouins and their Cyclops-like spouses, we'd found a phone and, joy of joys, a directory. But, to my immediate dismay, I found it filled, as well, with the picturesque but totally unintelligible squiggles of the Arabic alphabet. But God—or in this neck of the palm groves, Allah—was with us. A sympathetic lady from the French Embassy rescued us and we soon found ourselves, as today, sipping Gustavo's favourite form of welcome, an ice-cold drink.

The flat opposite the Bois de Boulogne is ample for the four of us, as our first perfunctory tour indicates. There's a kitchen, two bedrooms, two bathrooms and an enormous living room. It is even more cluttered than the villa in Tripoli, if that's possible, and Miguel confesses he had difficulty fitting everything in.

"I see you managed, though," Divy comments, his sense of décor wincing at what Miguel has done, or rather not done, to the place. Sitting on a sofa dropped where the movers left it, with his drink resting on a cardboard carton bursting with files, is not Divy's idea of gracious living.

Miguel's father had also been a diplomat and carried with him, from one Latin American posting to another, a houseful of the ugliest Spanish furniture I have ever seen. Everything is of the heaviest oak possible, upholstered in leftover hides from some ancient corrida, and wherever the cracked and aging wood shows, carved to death.

On his demise—an event I would have wished more on the furniture than its owner—Miguel's papa had bequeathed the whole worm-eaten collection to his son, including a ton of silver that covered every possibility of elegant diplomatic dining from serving a fifty-pound salmon to peeling a grape.

Awakening to my first morning in Paris, I feel surprisingly good. Part of me would prefer to throw open the curtains onto a sky of clear Indian blue instead of dull French grey and be greeted by a sunbird's cheerful cheep rather than a taxi's brassy beep, but my faith in January as the home-to-Pune date buoys my spirits considerably. Since touching down at Heathrow, they had been on a steady downhill spiral. But last night, over a superlative meal in a tiny bistro in Les Halles, I'd purged that awful English weekend from my soul, pouring it into Gustavo and Miguel's understanding ears. "No missionary work in Paris," I resolved into my third snifter of cognac. "Just make some money and run!"

And now, padding sleepily down the hallway towards the kitchen, stark naked—my favourite form of attire since Goa—I wonder whether my memories of Ibiza summers include the mechanics of making a good cup of café con leche. After three or four coffees and as many Gauloises as it takes to get my lungs pumping, I figure I'll be ready to dive into the Dynamic and get the three months in Paris off on the right foot.

After a year of floor-level cuisine, of squatting on one's haunches over a kerosene stove, Miguel's modern range is as alien to me as the controls of an Air France jet. But finally, after ten head-scratching minutes and the better part of a box of matches, the stove explodes into action, a blinding column of blazing gas shooting on high, melting half the handle of the coffeemaker, singeing the tip of my moustache and blistering a hefty section of the ceiling.

But I've made coffee. And, like nectar on the tongue, I savour it. Alone, silent, smoking a Gauloise, I sit at the living room window, watching two early-morning riders galloping through the November-brown Bois on a matching pair of high-stepping roans.

When everyone else gets up, more coffee's ready and the kitchen's more or less still intact.

Miguel's as resistant to meditation here in Paris as he was to seeing Osho in India. There, he'd managed to convince himself that a Goan holiday was more important to his wellbeing than an encounter with a living Buddha. "If I see him," he'd confessed with a foresight that had surprised me, "I'll never be able to leave"—and he makes it clear our morning sessions of Dynamic are not to be graced with his presence. So, as soon as he leaves for the Embassy, Divy, Gustavo and I convene in our bedroom and, bare-assed and blindfolded, huff and puff as if to blow the walls down. Then, leaving Divy to fluff the flat, Gustavo and I set out for the market to shop for lunch.

Behind the apartment block, on a side-street leading off the main boulevard, a potpourri of shops pander to the neighbourhood's needs, the majority of which, in typical French fashion, have to do with ingestion of one sort or another. From sugared bonbons glistening in the windows to dripping sides of bleeding beef suspended above the sidewalk, from racks of wines to rows of peaches, from pyramids of tomatoes to towers of green-ripe avocados, the street is a gourmet parade that, after India, is almost too much to take. We'd decided on wine, cheese, bread and a salad for lunch, and I virtually whip Gustavo in and out of the shops, a bit sickened by the surfeit.

By the time we're back at the flat Divy has the table laid—crisp white linen, polished crystal, cutlery that actually matches and china that doesn't have a chip. But the food! Fresh, healthy food! A forgotten treat on the palate. After a year of curries and wizened, nutrient-starved vegetables, to raise a glass of wine and inhale the bouquet of the countryside, to smear a dollop of Brie on a cloud of bread, to actually taste the sweetness of a leaf of lettuce, a thick river of olive oil rolling down its crinkly valleys! The sensations rush to my head, delicious and intoxicating.

Being a Spanish household, luncheon over, it's time for a siesta. And it's no nap, the Spanish siesta. It's curtains drawn and beds turned down. It's a short night's sleep in the middle of the day.

Several hours later everyone's up again—Miguel, back to the office to wrap up the day; the rest of us, to peruse the city's cinema guide for an evening film. Andy Warhol's new *Frankenstein* is playing, supposedly a spectacular horror extravaganza in 3D, so we settle on that. And as soon as Miguel's home we pile into his Alfa and, skirting the Arc de Triomphe and scooting under the Tour Eiffel, cruise down the broad and glittering Champs Elysées towards the cinema.

The picture's a bore. Between struggling to hold the cardboard 3D glasses on top of my own spectacles and dealing with all the blood and guts and hacked-off limbs spewing into the auditorium, I'm relieved when it's over.

Back in the car again, Miguel announces we're off to a restaurant near the Tuilleries. The food's over-sauced and over-priced, the waiters over-effusive and over-cologned, the customers over-effete, overdressed and, for the most part, over the hill.

But actually, lying in bed later, I have to admit my first day in Paris hasn't been that bad. But what I don't know is that the next sixty days are to be exact replicas of the first: coffee, Dynamic, shopping, lunch, siesta, a movie and a restaurant.

After sixty films, sixty different restaurants and gallons of aperitifs in scores of different bars, I've had enough. Here, in the so-called capital of the civilized world, I've *had* the chic and sophisticated pursuits of the West. I don't want any more, not one tiny mouthful more.

I've also come to grips with another fact, as hard as it's been to accept, and that is that the money to return to Pune is simply not going to materialize in Paris, no matter what Mukta or Osho said. The silks and things we'd brought from India are gone, sold, the francs spent in dribs and drabs, and the idea of finding gainful employment is a ridiculous, unfunny joke.

"Montreal?" I suggest to Divy one blustery December evening.

"Montreal," he agrees without a second's hesitation. "On Mukta's cheque."

Miguel is upset by our decision to leave and, knowing the impetus has come from me, wants to know why.

"A few things," I begin. "First of all, I want to get back to Pune, back to Osho. We'll never find work here. And secondly, I just can't live off you any more. I feel like a parasite."

He tuts at me, his head shaking in an attempt to dismiss my argument. "Look," he says. "For me, money is paper with numbers on it. They give me a lot and I spend it. It's that simple. I don't feel bad about what you call living off me. Why should you?"

"It's not that easy for me to receive, Miguel," I admit. "I've seen that about myself here. Giving isn't a problem for me—in the old days I was always the one in your shoes, inviting people out, picking up the tab. But accepting... I never realized how difficult that is.

"But, most important of all, I'm putting nothing into life here. I'm contributing nothing—no work, no energy. And it doesn't feel good. I need to work, to do something. I'm stuck here. I feel static, stagnant. And so I have to go. To do exactly what, I don't know. But I have to go."

"Okay," he smiles. "I understand. And I won't pressure you. I'll miss you and Divy, though. When are you planning to go?"

"It'll take another three weeks or so. We have to wait for Mukta's cheque to clear." His eyes light with a twinkle. "Would you accept one more thing before you go?" he asks. I smile back at him, loving his generosity. "What's that?" I ask. "A New Year's holiday in Madrid?"

"You're on!"

The next morning Divy's father calls from Stockholm, offering to send us rail tickets to spend Christmas with the family in Sweden. It feels good. A final fling in Europe—and then North America and work. Already Osho and Pune feel closer.

Montreal

Jemima's gone respectable. I see it the moment we step onto the Montreal airport's snow covered tarmac and catch her welcoming wave. Instead of the wild African princess I'd expected, there's a tall, black matron, all solid and sensible in matching blue overcoat and tweeds. And driving into the city in her station wagon there's no mention of the plan to join us in Pune, of the sannyas taken by post. There's just the same old song she's been singing to Divy for years: "Let's open a shop together."

For the next couple of days that refrain is pretty much all I hear. Divy's all for it. I'm wary. All we have in the world is a one hundred dollar bill Divy's dad gave us in Stockholm, and I'm loath to blow it on a tune I know only too well, on a chorus that never progresses beyond the first few bars.

Jemima and Divy have always had a thing about working together, about coupling her spectacular sense of fabric design with his innovative and eclectic ideas for clothing, accessories and household furnishings. During the time we lived in Montreal before going to India there was lots of talk, but no action whatsoever. This time, the shop concept they're tossing back and forth is a definite winner and, watching the creative current buzzing between them, I begin to wonder if I haven't been misjudging her, if, now, something might actually transpire. We even get as far as looking for locations, finally finding the perfect spot on downtown Bishop Street. The rent is two hundred a month. We're ready to lay half down immediately, but Jemima hems and haws, as skittish as an untried filly at the gate.

But when the three of us do the Dynamic together one morning, I know it's time to call her number. Part way through the breathing I realize only two people are doing it. Peeking out from under my blindfold I see Jemima, just standing there, frozen, immobile—raw, stark terror on her face. "Jemima," I say afterwards, "it's time to piss or get off the pot."

She says nothing. The only sign she's heard me is the slight tremble in the hand stirring her coffee.

"Look," I continue, "once in Pune Osho spoke about science and its law of cause and effect. 'In religion,' he said, 'there's a deeper law: Create the effect and the cause will follow.' Do you get my point? First the location. Then the shop. Well?" I insist, wanting an answer. "Willing to take the gamble?"

After a moment she nods. Her face is composed, but her eyes are afraid.

That very afternoon we pay the rent. But it's the last step the three of us take together. Three days later, Divy and I move into Bishop Street, ready to open a vegetarian restaurant with Swami Shyam Chaitanya, my old friend Alex, the guy who first turned me on to Osho.

"I've no courage," was all Jemima had been able to say as we'd packed. And as we left, it had been impossible to tell whether she still felt threatened or was greatly relieved. She couldn't look at us. We'd walked away, leaving her framed in the doorway, her gaze fixed on a spot on the floor between her feet.

Alex and I had known each other for at least ten years when I'd moved to Montreal to open my company in the early seventies. We'd taken a little Westmount townhouse together—him, upstairs; me, down. The day I'd given my firm away to my partner it was to this house I'd returned, thrown a few things into a valise and headed for the airport. It hadn't been until I'd come back to Montreal almost a year later that we'd seen each other. He no longer called himself Alex, but Shyam. He wore the most awful day-glo orange robe all the time. And beads—with, as described to me by a mutual acquaintance, "an 8x10 glossy of his guru around his neck". The whole thing had turned me right off.

He dropped by my flat one afternoon and, for the first time, we talked. Sitting there at the kitchen table, listening to him, looking for the first time beyond the orange frock and the necklace, I was stunned by the change in him. There had always been two Alexes, and whether it was because he was a Gemini or a complete schizophrenic, I had never been certain. From my side ours had always been a love-hate relationship. I adored the mad, carefree, bubbling Alex, and, with an equal passion, abhorred the panicky, money-grubbing Jewish jewellery salesman who couldn't quite make it, who kept flagellating himself for his constant failures, whose childhood years in Treblinka had long since ceased being a valid crutch. But that afternoon, I really saw him, really heard him. And the negative part was gone, purged at last. I saw a man cleansed of his past, stripped of his ghosts. "How did this happen?" I'd asked.

He'd laughed, understanding my question immediately. "Actually," he'd replied, "through you."

"Me?"

"When you left, leaving your company like you did, it really shook me up," he began thoughtfully. "You see, you had everything I was working for. And you gave it away. Just like that," he said, snapping his fingers. "It really made me take a good look at my life. And I didn't like what I saw. I knew I had to do something, and fast.

"I tried a little hatha yoga, a few sessions with a shrink, stuff like that—but nothing changed. Then, one night, I was listening to FM radio, and they played a tape of an interview with Baba Ram Das—you know, the guy who wrote that *Be Here Now* book? Well, I figured if he had to go to India to find what he was looking for, I was ready to do it too. So I got on a plane and took off for Bombay. I was there for weeks and nothing happened. But about four days before I was going to leave to come back, this guy in an orange robe walked up to me on the street. 'You're looking for something, I can tell,' he said. 'Come with me.' It was that simple. I followed him to Woodlands and I met Osho. And that was that."

All of a sudden I remembered my car accident and knew that here, in front of me, for the first time since it had happened, someone was holding out to me the possibility of recapturing that space again. "Shyam," I said eagerly, using his new name, "tell me about this man in India."

He laughed. "I know your mind, Jack. I really don't know what to say to you." He dug into his shoulder bag, extracting a book. "Here. Take a look at this," he said, shoving it across the table towards me. "He puts it better than I ever could."

After he'd gone I'd reached for the slim, Indian volume. *I Am the Gate*.

I finished half a page when it abruptly felt as if something had kicked me in the stomach. "This man is telling the truth," I announced to the empty room. And I knew, there and then, that I had to see this man, face to face.

And now, two years later, Shyam waltzes into our lives once again. Divy and I, fed up with Jemima's vacillation, were wandering Ste. Catherine Street, money spent on the Bishop Street flat, wondering what to do next.

"Where are you off to, Shyam?" I ask, glad for a friendly face on this gloomy winter's day.

"I'm looking for a place to open a restaurant."

Within fifteen minutes we were back at Jemima's, beginning to pack.

"You're hungry?" Shyam asks with ironic Jewish rhetoric. "You just had lunch!"

"I know," I admit sheepishly. "But there's no money to buy food for tonight."

"Don't worry," he grins, patting my hand like a wise old grandfather soothing a fretting child. "You're not going to starve. When it's time for dinner there'll be something to eat."

"If you let it, Krishna Prem," Osho had said to me before I'd left Pune, "existence will take care of you, the same way it takes care of the birds and the trees and the flowers." And existence is doing it. Day after day it's doing it. Still my doubts persist.

Existence began to shower on us the very first morning on Bishop Street when it led Prasad to our door. We'd met in Pune, this young French-Canadian graphic designer and I, and had liked each other. "Heard you were back," he'd said. "What are your plans?"

I explained.

"You know," he said after a bit, "I have this government design contract I'm working on. There are three months left. But then I want out. I want to do something else. I'd really like to get involved in this restaurant so there'll be something to come to afterwards. But I guess it's not quite fair to ask. I don't have any time to help you guys get it together."

"Time?" I laughed. "Time we have. It's money we need."

"Money? I have money. Not much, but at least enough for

materials. How about it then? I'll put up the cash and you guys do the work?"

So it began. And it's as if Prasad's opening offer has set some other kind of flood in motion. In amazement, from our pre-sannyas friends, I watch the gifts pouring through the door—power tools, gallons of paint, boxes of nails and screws, table bases, pots and pans, all sorts of equipment for the restaurant. And for us, for Divy, Shyam and me, carried on the same tide, come packs of cigarettes, bags of groceries, take-out pizzas and cartons of Chinese food.

"Why do you keep on worrying?" Divy asks me in exasperation one night. "The moment Prasad walked in the door I knew everything was fine. Remember those little biscuits Vivek handed out at the Guru Poornima celebrations in Pune? Those were called prasad, 'gift of the divine'. And we have our very own Prasad right here, passing out the cash. Will you stop worrying?"

I have no answer to give him. For weeks there's been daily proof that existence is taking care of us, yet I still can't shake the doubt that one of these days it's going to let us down, that this can't go on forever, that it can't really be possible to live the rest of my life like this.

His question makes me take a good look at myself. And what I see is embarrassing—misgivings instead of gratitude, anxiety instead of trust. Lying in bed I try to recall the farewell in Pune. "If you let it," Osho had said, "existence will take care of you." Existence is living up to its part of the bargain, that I cannot deny. But me? I'm just in the way all the time, worrying, doubting.

And what's driving me loony of late is existence's maddening habit of meeting our needs only as they arise—and not one second before. It's driving my future-oriented mind to distraction.

The larder is primarily full these days and, although my stomach is always full, my mind is obsessed with food, with the next meal. And with a certainty that borders on the impossible, my first pang of hunger *always* coincides with the arrival of a feast or an invitation to put the hammer or paintbrush down and come out to dinner. It never, ever fails!

"This has got to stop," I groan into my pillow. "I can't live with this ridiculous, unnecessary anxiety one more day!"

The next morning, in the half-world between sleep and waking, there's a strong sense of Osho. I remember him speaking about physical work, about throwing oneself into it totally and about how, in the totality, the doer disappears. "That's it!" I suddenly realize. "The doer! Existence is doing everything, but I keep getting in the way. I'm so used to *doing* I just can't step aside and let life take care!" And Osho's "If you let it..." makes new sense. I feel I've finally got the point.

Bounding out of bed, I look for the first bit of physical work available. In the dining room, I find a can of paint and a brush. Dropping to my knees on the floor, I begin working on the baseboards, inching the day's first cup of coffee along beside me as I progress along the wall. And the trick I've remembered stays with me. As each thought presents itself, as each worry surfaces in my mind, I force my attention back to the painting, refocusing again and again, as totally as I can, on the strokes of burgundy enamel flowing from the brush onto the stained and aged wood. When Shyam calls me for lunch I am unable to grasp, for a moment, that hours have passed, that the morning has been and gone.

But it's worked! The technique I've recalled has worked! There's been no sense of *me* all morning, no feeling of any doer at all. And I flash on Laxmi, suddenly understanding her strange terminology, her odd questions like "Has introduction happened?" At the time I'd simply thought she'd been translating from Hindi, but now, cleaning the paint from my hands for lunch, I see something quite different. She'd been referring to the space where I've spent the morning, to a way of living where the mind as manipulator has been set aside and where things happen, where baseboards get painted and introductions get done. I had tasted it with the introduction to *My Way: The Way of the White Clouds*, but had forgotten. I am silent over lunch.

"Not anxious about dinner yet?" Shyam asks teasingly.

"Don't worry about it," I reply, poker faced. "When your body's hungry, food will happen."

"Well, swamiji!" Divy laughs, wobbling his head from side to side, Indian-style. "Well, well, well!"

For the next two months the effort is pretty much continuous. With each new task, be it hammering or sawing or sanding, I bring myself back over and over again to the job at hand, withdrawing my attention from my inventive and pig-headed mind. But as the restaurant nears completion, my tenacity begins to bear fruit—whole days float by in peaceful, worry-free activity, with more being accomplished, with more work *happening,* than ever before.

And much to our surprise, one blustery March morning, the restaurant is finished; there just isn't anything more to be done. We set the evening of the twenty-first, the anniversary of Osho's Enlightenment Day, as opening night.

The rest of that day it's as if I'm seeing what we've accomplished for the first time. For months I've been involved in details, in the minutiae of construction and decoration, and I've never seen, with any perspective, what the place looks like. Bundling up, I decide on an hour's walk, on a tromp through the snow-caked streets. I want to walk through the door and see the restaurant as a new customer, like someone who's never been here before.

And I am impressed. From the smiling life-size blow-up of Osho above *The Orange People* sign at the front door, down the narrow hallway that leads past the gleaming, compact kitchen towards the dining room, the place is spectacular—simple and elegant, warm and inviting.

But the dining room! Here, Divy the decorator has outdone himself. Looking at it anew, taking it in now in its entirety, I marvel at what we have put together from scratch.

A hand-painted Japanese cherry tree blossoms across one rich burgundy wall, facing the L-shaped banquette we fashioned from sheets of plywood, padded with foam and then upholstered in a deep rust brocade. The tables, some round, some rectangular, carry pink damask cloths with pale green overthrows and napkins, basketweave bentwood chairs in natural wood nestling under them. And the cabbages! Everywhere, the cabbages! The memory makes me laugh.

We had thirty Prasad dollars in the kitty the day Divy decided the floor had to be done, that he had to do something to mask the hideous grey-and-white linoleum tiles. Despite our insistence nothing suitable could ever be found for that amount, Divy had hit the streets. "I'll find something," he'd said, exiting with a conviction I knew well. A few hours later he'd come back, eight rolls of cabbage-rose wallpaper tucked under his arm.

"Jesus!" I'd exclaimed when I saw the huge pink roses, their nasty great tendrils clutching a lattice in matching hospital-green. "It's so awful! It's pure Earls Court, pure English bed-sit! What in hell are we supposed to do with this?"

"It's for the floor," Divy announced, his tone precluding argument.

From Shyam, Prasad and me had come, in one unified voice of amazement: "For the *floor*!"

But down it had gone. We not only covered the floor, but moulded it as well onto the woodwork and even into the interior of the now doorless closet where we housed the sweets-fridge and coffee-station. It looked interesting, we had to admit. But nine coats of clear plastic varnish later, it graduated from interesting to incredible. Even now, poised at the entrance, I hesitate to step on it, on the shining indoor rink where cabbage roses grin up at me, embedded it seems, under inches of transparent, glistening glass.

Once the construction was complete, Divy and I suddenly lost interest. We moved to a tiny flat down the block and he started to work on ideas for transforming the remaining empty room at the restaurant into some sort of boutique. My long-standing waiter-fantasy, grown out of years of patronizing trendy eateries, had evaporated with the first table I waited on—and, armed with *The Tassajara Bread Book* and a copy of the *Fanny Farmer Cook Book*, I jump into baking, into preparing breads and pies and cakes and delivering them, mornings and afternoons, to the dining room up the street. My neighbour from upstairs, Jane, spends a good part of the day hanging out with me, talking and laughing, and shoving me aside to dive into the mixing bowl herself whenever anything hands-on with chocolate is involved.

Shyam and Prasad are fine with the new arrangement. The day I quit as waiter, Bessie Lou is suddenly standing in the door in a Carmen Miranda costume, balancing a bowl of bananas on her head. "Need a waitress, honey?" she asks Shyam, barrelling down the hall towards him on a pair of roller skates.

Being alone most of the time with my doughs and pastries, the longing for Pune returns. Building the restaurant, it had faded from my mind. But now, baking by myself in this quiet little kitchen, the ache I felt in Paris is there again. I want to go back. I want to be with Osho again. I want to see Laxmi and Mukta and old friends again. Yet, looking realistically at our situation, I can see no way this tiny restaurant is ever going to generate enough cash even to buy tickets to India, let alone provide money to live there for a while.

In the weeks that follow, despite the fact I'm still doing the Dynamic every day, a kind of resignation sets in. I'm fed and I'm housed...and Pune might as well be on Mars. Once again the memory recedes and leaves me comfortable, but dull and lifeless and asleep.

And everything pretty much coasts as it does until the weekend Bessie Lou and I decide to close and clean the restaurant, top to bottom. Then, without a doubt, I know something else is at play. When Osho told me existence would take care of me, I thought he was speaking of physical needs alone. But lying in bed with twelve stitches in a thumb slashed straight down to the bone, the result of an unaware encounter with a glass jar, I see that existence has my welfare in hand on a much larger scale. Whatever it was that brought me to Osho in the first place, whatever it is that's been taking care of me has no intentions of letting me get comfortable, of letting me off the hook. When I stood in front of the sink, drenched in cold sweat with waves of nausea buckling my knees and the suds-and-blood-filled jar as shattered as my thumb, I knew.

That night I also realized there was no money for food the next day. "See," I said to Divy. "Somewhere I knew that existence wouldn't take care of me, that surrendering doesn't help at all."

"Trust, swamiji," he said. "Today's not over yet."

About a half an hour to midnight there was a knock on the door. It was Natalie, the cousin of Clyde who lived across the hall and owned a second-hand clothing store in the same building as the restaurant. "Do you know where Clyde is?" she asked. We replied we didn't and asked why she was looking for him so late.

"I've suddenly got to go to this party tonight and need a pair of black satin pyjama pants to wear. I know he has some in the shop."

"I've got a couple of pair here that I sewed last week," Divy said, heading for the closet.

A few moments later he closed the door behind Natalie and turned to me, waving a fifty-dollar note. "We eat tomorrow," he said.

In that moment, in a wave of emotion and embarrassment, I felt all fight and doubt fall away from me. "I surrender," I said. "I surrender." And it was total, complete.

The very next morning I turn over my share in the restaurant to Shyam. "It's enough for me too," Divy says when I tell him what I've done. "I can't be bothered either. I want to go back to Osho too. And this has been fun, but it's leading nowhere."

"Wonder what we'll do next?" I can't help asking.

"Something will turn up," Divy replies. "You know how Osho says you always have to let the old go to make room for the new."

An old friend of mine who'd fast become a regular at the restaurant was an importer of art supplies from his native Holland with a taste for the finer things and such an admirable capacity for living beyond his means that he had just moved into an art deco palazzo built by the celebrated French-Canadian architect Ernest Cormier on the side of Mount Royal in 1931 and eventually bought by one of Canada's most loved prime ministers, Pierre Trudeau. The house was so impressive and unique it had been declared a National Monument by the Quebec government, and apart from vague references to "restoration", how Jack managed to manoeuvre himself into living in it, I could never bring myself to ask.

His latest project was a play about Sarah Bernhardt. He had arranged to produce *The Divine Sarah* at Ottawa's new National Arts Center and, struck by Divy's décor for *The Orange People,* he asks him, the very day after we end our careers as restaurateurs, to work with him on the design for the set.

"And I can't live in that huge house by myself," he added. "Apart from needing company, I travel a lot and someone has to be there. The furnace is old and needs watching. Besides, you're going back to India anyway, so why not move in with me and save the money you'd spend on rent?"

It isn't until an Aussie sannyasin, fresh from Pune, passes through town that the longing really begins again. Sitting with her, hearing news of the commune, of old friends—including a report that Rani's in tip-top shape and has a new man—that it suddenly becomes important, once again, just to get it together to get back home, back to Osho.

By the time the Australian lady has arrived we've been living with Jack for almost three months. I've enjoyed the luxury of the house, the cooking and the baking, the people I've met, but am feeling stale and stagnant again. I want to do more with my life than make sure an archaic furnace doesn't overheat and blow us all to smithereens. And it just isn't happening for us in this city. We've worked on Jack's play, redecorated a nostalgia shop and I've done freelancing for a television station where I worked years before—but there still isn't enough money even to begin thinking about India.

Of late, Jack and Divy have been in Toronto, putting together a new art supply store. And when Divy returns one weekend, full of enthusiasm for Toronto's dollar-earning potential, my bags are half packed before he finishes asking me if I'm ready to move.

Toronto

For Divy, Toronto fell into place with relative ease. He decided he wanted to make clothes and, borrowing a sewing machine, had whipped a few muslins together one evening. The next day he trucked his samples to a Yorkville shop, hoping to sell the designs, but instead, found himself with an order for several dozen of each item. Within a few days he located a virtuoso seamstress from Argentina, and he and Beatrice, communicating in broken English and fractured Spanish, were stitching up a storm.

What I encountered in my search for gainful employment was a blend of fear and negativity. With the reception I received from former colleagues, one would have thought I'd returned from India with leprosy. I'd been warned about the orange and the mala, and had written to Laxmi, receiving word that Osho had okayed mufti for work but to continue wearing orange at home—so what I'd been encountering had nothing to do with Osho, it had solely to do with me.

For weeks I did the rounds, covering everyone I'd ever known in every advertising and public relations firm in the city. When I exhausted them, I hit the personnel agencies. Everywhere I drew the same blank.

One afternoon, after a particularly depressing but at least truthful interview, I had to admit I was wasting my time. "Look," this agency guy said to me, "I'm going to level with you. The word is out that you're back and that you're looking for work. But no one's going to touch you with a ten-foot pole. Your work is good; no one can fault you on that—but everyone knows you'll never stay around, that you'll hang in for a bit and then you'll be gone.

"But the *real* reason," he added after a moment's consideration, "is what you did in Montreal. Everything we're all striving for, you had—money, success, a good reputation, your own firm. You were the Canadian PR whiz kid. And you threw it all away. It's like you spat in our collective faces. So forget it. No one's going to hire you. No one wants you around. We used to be friends, but I have to be honest—that even includes me!"

But out of all this rejection I saw something new about myself, something that gladdened my sannyasin heart. I observed that whosoever I was with, I'd remained the same. Before Osho, before sannyas, especially in the PR game, I behaved with people as I thought they expected me to. To my surprise, I saw that had gone.

Remembering that Osho had spoken on this very thing, I searched it out that evening, finding it in *The Book of the Secrets,* a present from Shyam. "George Gurdjieff used to say that man is a crowd," I read. "Personality is just a deception because you are not a person: you are many persons. So when one person speaks in you, that is a momentary centre. The next moment there is another. With every moment, with every atomic situation, you feel certain, and you never become aware that you are just a flux—many waves without any centre...

"Tantra, yoga, religion—their basic concern is how first to discover the centre, how first to be an individual. They are concerned how to find the centre which persists in every situation. Then, as life goes on moving without, as the flux of life goes on and on, as waves come and go, the centre persists inside. Then you remain one—rooted, centred."

Be it self-congratulatory or not, I'm pleased at what I've seen, at what this situation in Toronto has shown me about myself. And now, with an assignment of the temporary office help agency in my hand, there's something else to look at—the ego of this newfound individual. There's a little fear and a lot of curiosity at how this one-time executive is going to feel as a lowly, bearded, middle-aged male typist in the giant steel tower that houses the city's largest stockbroker.

But it's fine. Actually, I find I rather enjoy it—the anonymity, the non-involvement of the work. I throw myself into it, as I did building the restaurant, and the result is the same. Alert to the typing, focused on accuracy, there's that feeling of emptiness and timelessness again—and riding the subway home at night I am quiet, contented, and quite, quite serene.

And coming home to the flat we've found in a reconverted brownstone in a downtown residential area is a joy. Our trio of rooms in the back half of the ground floor are bright and sunny, but it's the private, high-fenced back yard that really thrills me. The moment the snow melts, Divy and I are out there, spades in hand, digging flowerbeds and a vegetable patch, bringing home new seed packets from the supermarket almost every day.

It is here one evening, just before sunset, that I look up from the tomatoes into a pair of deep blue eyes and find, suddenly and unexpectedly, that I am falling in love.

Planning a selling trip to Montreal, Divy had been searching for a designer to make buttons and belts and buckles for his clothes. He'd been introduced to Maggie and had brought her to the flat to look at her work and talk things over. He brought her over a couple of times and, although nothing was said, it was obvious that what happened to me had happened to her as well. The morning he leaves for Montreal I call and ask her if she'd like to come for dinner. She'd love to, she says. After hanging up I feel a sudden urge to meditate, just to sit quietly by myself, and then something happens that tells me another hand is at play.

When I was a child my body would dissolve at night. And it terrified me. I used to pinch and bite myself; I used to smash my head against the wall—anything to stop it, anything to be normal again. And now, sitting cross-legged on my bed, the same warning signals, sensations I haven't felt in thirty years, are suddenly there again—the same feeling of painful denseness and euphoric lightness, the same sense of boundaries disappearing. And along with them, turning my heart to jelly, comes the childhood panic. But I feel Osho so strongly that I don't fight, I just allow. And then my body dissolves completely; it simply *isn't* any more. All that remains is bliss and space and a point of light. And that point of light is me.

That night he comes again. We'd eaten dinner, Maggie and I, talking and talking as new lovers do, trying to grasp each other in a moment. And then, suddenly, she said quietly: "There's a presence in the room." There's no fear in her whisper, only a kind of awe. "Is it your Osho?"

I hold her to me to keep from exploding. "Yes, Maggie. Yes, it's him."

When Divy returns we decide to spend a week in Montreal. We need time just to be alone.

But in Montreal it all begins to go sour. She wants some kind of commitment I cannot give. And strangely, especially after what's gone on, the big hassle is Osho. She cannot accept "this obsession with a guru". She wants marriage, children, an ordinary life. "I'm a seeker, Maggie," I tell her. "My first covenant is with sannyas, with the search for my own reality." Anything else, including the woman I love, comes after, follows suit. I see no contradiction, but for her it's one thing or the other; she cannot see how the two can walk hand in hand. I ask her to come with me to India and see. But every time I mention India a sudden panic grips her, and refusal comes with a vehemence that surprises me by its intensity. About Osho and India, she simply doesn't want to know.

Back in Toronto the situation comes to a head and it becomes clear that neither of us can accommodate the other's wishes. I reach out and take her in my arms, just holding her for a while. "Maggie," I say at last, "please come and be with me in India—with me and with Osho."

"I can't!" she cries, pushing me away sharply. "I don't want to! It's not for me! This insane idea about killing your ego, this obsession with dissolving your personality...I don't understand any of it. I hate it! It terrifies me!"

I reach out for her again, but she steps back, away from me. She just stands there, looking at me. For a split second there is a softening in her eyes. Then they go hard again. And then she is gone.

There's barely a chance to mourn. A sudden series of events, as unexpected as the August hailstorm that crushes our garden, shows me, without a doubt, that existence is setting new wheels in motion for both Divy and me once again. The first thing is a letter from Mukta. Amidst her news of Pune is the sentence, "Don't stay away too long. Just make a little money and come." And the second arrives the very next day. From Laxmi. "Now you are needed here," she'd written, "so come and share in the joy."

Laxmi's words trigger a delight so intense I think I'll burst. Behind her words I recognize Osho's hand. I know the source of the invitation is him. I know he's telling me it's time to come home. "But how?" I ask myself that night. "How?"

Later that evening the answer comes. The telephone rings and on the line is François. When he'd managed one of Canada's major symphony orchestras, Divy and I had both worked for him. Through him we'd made the money for the first trip to India.

"I've just moved to Toronto," he announces. "I'm opening an agency to manage classical artists. Would you be into doing some work for me? I need lots of stuff written—biographies, flyers, brochures, that sort of thing. Interested?"

"Sure, François," I manage to squeeze out. My throat is so dry I can hardly breathe.

"And there's all kinds of design work too. Do you think Michael—or whatever he calls himself now—would like to get involved?"

Assuring him he would, I hang up, promising to call him tomorrow. I can only stand there, immobile, frozen in time and space, staring in disbelief at the phone. I've been waiting so long for this, so very, very long. And it has come. I have no idea how long this process will take, but it really doesn't matter. At last I know the exile's over. At last I know I'm going home.

Once he absorbs my news, Divy gives me his own. "You'll never guess who I ran into on the street?" he says. "Ramesh!"

"Ramesh? Ramesh from Goa?"

"None other," Divy replies. "He says he wants to see you, so he's coming over tomorrow afternoon."

Ramesh has come a long way from Anjuna Beach. He's graduated from trinkets to treasures, from baubles to bijoux, and he's here in Toronto on a three-month selling trip before returning to Pune. With the cash he raises, he'll buy office gadgets for Laxmi, the calculators, electric typewriters and the Western machines she loves so well. Like Columbus carrying plunder to Queen Isabella, Ramesh's greatest expression of his love for Laxmi is to lay his gifts at her tiny feet.

He and his girlfriend Nirupa have taken over her aunt's empty flat for their stay in Toronto and, to cut down on our collective expenses, he asks us to move in with them. I love our flat and everything in me revolts at the idea, but not to insult him, I agree to think it over and give him an answer in a day or so.

"You know," he says, turning back at the doorway, "I don't know where this is coming from, but I have the feeling one of the things I have to do while I'm here is make sure you two get back to Pune. And I have the strange sensation that if you don't come and live with me and Nirupa that you won't get back to Osho for a very long time. Laxmi told me to be sure to see you. Well, I've done that. Now it's up to you."

And I can tell, in a lightning flash of knowing, that Ramesh is absolutely right.

When the work for François is nearing completion and nothing new is showing up to augment it, I begin to wonder about Ramesh and his intuition. I take to perusing the want ads, hoping against hope there might be something I can do. One morning there's a call for writers, but they want samples and I have nothing at all. I sit down anyway and compose a cute reply, saying I don't believe in saving what I write, but that if they're willing to give me a chance, I'm willing to try something on speculation. Posting the letter, I forget about it. For the price of a stamp I've had a good time.

A few days later the telephone rings. "Your letter intrigued me," a husky female voice informs me. "Would you care to drop by?"

The company Husky Voice works for manufactures educational packages for children, and her current project is a series of game cards housed in a little red cardboard schoolhouse and designed to teach children grammar and punctuation. She gives me the comma and the exclamation point to play with over the weekend.

"I've had literally hundreds of applications," she tells me Monday afternoon when I hand in my assignment. "But if I do hire you I'll pay you for what you've already done. I pay ten bucks an hour, and I'm a trusting soul. You can bill me for twenty hours a day if you want. If your work is good I'll pay for it." She turns back to her desk in dismissal. "I'll let you know in a few days."

By the third day I'm on pins and needles, driving everyone to distraction. Days are unbearable; nights, sleepless. Every time the telephone jangles I almost leave my skin. Finally, late that afternoon, it rings again. It's Husky Voice. Asking for me. "Speaking," I reply.

"I suppose you've been waiting to hear from me?"

"Yes, I have," I confess, feeling the suspense is going to kill me, as if everything that matters in my life rests on this woman's next few words.

"Well," she says, "I won't keep you waiting any longer. I've hired twelve writers and you're one of them. And whether it matters or not I'm going to tell you anyway—I think you're one of the best. We're meeting at eight tonight."

It isn't until the phone is back in its cradle that my heart starts to beat normally again. And with it, loud and clear, come Osho's words: "Create the effect and the cause will follow."

Within ten minutes I'm on the subway, heading for the British Airways office. Without a penny to my name, I book two one-way tickets to Bombay for December 29.

That night I tell Divy when we're leaving.

"How do you know that?" he asks, puzzled.

"I've created the effect."

And I obviously have. Because we do.

Chapter Four: 1977

PUNE

In the mind's eye things remembered never seem to change, but remain suspended in the static sea of memory, until revisited once again.

Darshan had always been like this for me while we'd been away. Imprinted on my mind was the vision of Osho under the carport, a half dozen or so of us gathered at his feet. And despite news of thousands of sannyasins coming and going the scene had persisted. Now, sitting some twenty tightly packed orange rows away from his empty chair, I am stunned at the size of this darshan, at how everything around me has changed and grown.

Arriving in Bombay on New Year's Eve, we slept, as of old, at the sleazy, steamy Rex Hotel, and took the afternoon Deccan Express to Pune, a little unbelieving all the way. It hadn't been until we settled into the Green Hotel once again that my mind really began to absorb the fact that I was finally home.

Showering as quickly as possible, we scurry into the street, hailing the first rickshaw we spy. When I first came to Pune, most of the drivers had no idea where Koregaon Park was. Things have changed. "Ashram?" the rickshaw-wallah confirms, more a foregone conclusion than a question. And on the sidewalks, where the women's saris once provided the only colour, the orange and red of sannyas are everywhere. Gone is the Anglo-Saxon majority. Obviously, while we've been away, Osho's message has spread like wildfire. Whizzing through the streets, I catch glimpses of Latins, Mediterraneans, Nordics, lots of unidentifiable nationalities and, to my surprise, an incredible number of Japanese.

Number 17 Koregaon Park has also changed. Beyond recognition, in fact. Where once a scraggly hedge of crimson lantana sprawled, a massive teak gate stands, brass-studded, a white marble kiosk flanking either side. And looming majestically above it arches a great white portico, crowned with a Kremlin-style cupola and Osho's name emblazoned in chiselled black lettering. And smack in the centre I detect Laxmi's hand. Hanging there, pure glitz and glitter, is a tear-drop crystal chandelier, looking for all the world like she's purloined it from the lobby of some Beverly Hills hotel. "I don't believe it!" Divy chokes, caught between dumbfounded laughter and homecoming tears. "It's pure Hindi-Hollywood!"

The transformation inside the front gate is as unbargained for. The original four-bedroom bungalow that was 17 has mushroomed into an edifice the size of a residential hotel and the newly acquired next-door property now boasts a gigantic oval lecture hall, roofed in a tarpaulin befitting a massive circus tent. And then Divy and I are swamped by old friends, hugging and kissing us in welcome. The love is almost too much to take. I've been away from sannyasins for so long I'd forgotten the openness—the genuine, unabashed, easily-expressed gestures of love. Through the forest of someone's hair nestling into my shoulder I catch a glimpse of Veda and Pyari. In a single glance, the hard times of Kailash slip away and nothing remains but affection and love. Teertha, Jagruti, Kaveeta, my Australian friend Pratima, and dozens of others enfold us. It's a family, a beautiful, loving, far out family saying it's happy we're home.

But the commune itself! When we left there had been numbers 17 and 33 and a bare patch of earth between. Now there are four compounds on six acres and a thriving community bubbling with activity, bursting at its seams. The bookstall, the boutique, the cafeteria, the residences, the darkroom, the design studio, the warehouse, the group rooms and therapy chambers—it's all too much to absorb! And Osho's named everything. Number 17 is Krishna House, 33 is Lao Tzu House, and the patch in between has been roofed, floored, and renamed Radha Hall. And all the new names! Jesus House, Francis House, Eckhart Village,

Buddha Hall, Chuang Tzu Auditorium, Vrindavan—I've no sooner heard them but forgotten not only which is which but also which is where. It's a bewildered, bedazzled Krishna Prem they lead to Laxmi.

I stand for a moment in the doorway of the new administration office, watching this woman I love, just savouring the sight of her. She sits in a high backed chair at the centre of a cyclone of activity, dealing, as she's always done, with everything at once. She's tinier than before, even more frail and bird-like, but still, an energy of dynamic proportions emanates from her—mercurial and volcanic, but at the same time, centred and alert.

She does not look at me right away—she's involved in something—yet I am aware she knows I'm here. And when our eyes do meet, seconds pass before anything transpires. Like old lovers reunited, we simply look, saying nothing, as if the wordless gaze erases the time spent apart. Finally, with a sweep of one little arm, she indicates the stool beside her, patting it, inviting me to sit.

"So, swamiji," she says, "at last homecoming has happened!"

I can only nod.

"Have you visited commune?" she asks. "Much growth has happened, hmm?" She spreads her hands to include the women seated on either side of her, one Indian, one European, each dealing with someone. "And now, you see, secretary has secretaries!" She introduces me. "This is Ma Arup," she says, turning to the statuesque European. "Dutch lady." Arup flashes me a toothy smile. "And this is Ma Sheela," she adds, her voice all at once motherly. Sheela returns my gaze directly, with a straightforwardness rare in an Indian woman. "Gujarati," Laxmi whispers. "From Baroda." I'm not quite sure what Sheela's native state and city have to do with anything, but to Laxmi they seem as significant as university degrees. I just smile, too blown away to do much else. "Cat has tongue?" she asks, prodding me in the ribs.

"When can I see Osho, Laxmi?" I manage at last.

"Speak to Ma Arup," she says, suddenly business-like. "Now appointment is necessary. Many more friends are there, as you have seen."

"If you want to *talk* to Osho," Arup says, pulling a diary out of a drawer, "you'll have to wait a few days. But if a silent darshan is okay, you can go tomorrow night."

Uncertain what a "silent darshan" is, I agree to one anyway for Divy and me, for tomorrow night.

I find Divy sitting in the garden opposite Laxmi's office, looking as stunned as I feel. After I tell him we're seeing Osho tomorrow night, he tells me he's seen Mukta and she's invited us to dinner this evening at the Blue Diamond. Suddenly I'm wiped out. "The Green?" I suggest.

"The Green."

On the way to the row of rickshaws standing outside the front gate, I ask nervously, "Any news of Rani?"

"Nothing really. She is in Pune, though. I gather she's still with the guy we heard about." He chuckles softly. "But don't worry. I know Rani. She'll find us."

Rani's Saga

He's right. Before the bearer arrives with the pot of tea I ordered as we collected our key at the desk, Rani is framed in the doorway. She looks great. In all the years I've known her, I've never seen her so vital, so alive. "Well," she says, perching casually on one of the beds, "you're back!" Lighting a cigarette, she takes a long, deep haul, eyeing us for a moment. "Let's clear the air right off. I don't know what you've heard, but let me tell you what happened after you left."

"Before you do," I interrupt, "am I correct in assuming everything's okay now?"

"With me, you mean? Between us?"

I nod.

"Of course it is, darling. You know mama never holds a grudge."

She pulls on her cigarette and leans against the pillows, her eyes on the ceiling, moving back in memory. "Gourdon's," she says, her voice distant. "It was at Gourdon's in Churchgate where I last saw you. Where you called me Ulla, Krishna," she continues, shifting her gaze to me. Then she turns her gaze to the ceiling again. "I took the train back to Pune in a kind of haze. Everything was shaky, unreal. I couldn't stand the flat. I couldn't stand the commune. I couldn't stand being in my own body. I thought I was going crazy."

"Did you see Osho?" I ask.

"Yeah, I did," she admits, accepting tea from the bearer. When he's closed the door behind him, she resumes. "He said I wasn't crazy but was just playing a game with myself because I didn't want to face things as they were. And he warned me about madness. I remember he said that when you play at being mad a point comes when you can't stop playing any more and the madness takes over."

"Then what happened?" Divy asks, but softly, gently.

"I went mad," she says simply, shrugging her shoulders. She looks at me intently, as if she knows what's going on in my mind. "I know what you're thinking," she says, slightly accusing. "You think I never did listen to him, right?"

"That's all over, Rani," I reassure her. But she'd been right. As she'd been talking about Osho I recalled the time she'd gone to him about Shantidas being our son, about our having been married before—and how he warned her not to get caught up in it. She hadn't been able to. But it's all water under an ancient bridge. "Forget all that, Rani," I tell her. "That's all over. Tell us what happened next."

"Well," she goes on, "I just couldn't handle Pune. I was just so paranoid all the time. I thought everyone was after me, that everyone was out to get me, so I ran away to Bombay. I checked into Shelley's Hotel. Remember? Just down the road from the Taj? I hid under the bed for two days."

"What!"

She laughs, shaking her head in disbelief, as if the story she's relating is someone else's. "Remember that opera singer fantasy I always had? Remember how I always sang arias in the second stage of Dynamic when everyone else was screaming and crying and freaking out?"

Divy and I both laugh, recalling Rani's assaults on Puccini and Verdi while the rest of us were catharting all over the grass.

"At Shelley's," she continues, "I had this thing about being a famous opera singer and about being a prisoner of the Mafia, so I hid under the bed. Finally, on the third day, I couldn't take it any more. I wanted to be rescued, so I threw the telephone out the window and started screaming into the street. They called the police."

"The police!"

She shudders. "Yeah, the police. I spent two days in a cell—no food, no water. I was so scared. They promised to let me out if I gave them something, so I handed over everything I had—my rings, necklaces, even my crystal mala. But they just left me there. I remember writing 'Help!' on the wall with my own shit at the end of the second day."

"Jesus, Rani!" I blurt, filled with compassion for her and shame at my role in the ordeal. "I had no idea..."

"Let me finish," she interrupts. "Let me tell it all." She lights another cigarette. "The commune tried to do what it could," she says, "but the police just wouldn't cooperate. Finally, Laxmi arranged for a lady from the Swedish consulate to come and see me. She must have pulled some strings or something, because they let me out of jail. But the Indians just wouldn't forget it; they shoved me into this mental hospital in Bombay." Her face screws in disgust. "It was awful—filthy, all kinds of rats, real maniacs and food so disgusting I couldn't even bring myself to touch it. They kept me pretty well drugged and I think they gave me shock treatments, but I can't be sure.

"But the thing that frightened me most of all was that I knew this was the hospital where they just locked the crazies away and forgot all about them. I really didn't know much else. I even thought the lady from the Swedish consulate was the soprano Beverley Sills. Apparently I kept trying to talk her into coming to Pune to sing for Osho!

"At last, one morning, they came and gave me an injection. I remember I didn't want it, and kept fighting them. But they held me down and gave it to me anyway. If I'd known what was going on I wouldn't have fought at all."

"What do you mean?"

"It's so bizarre," she answers, laughing again. "You wouldn't even believe it if you saw it in the movies. When I regained consciousness I was sitting in an airplane on a flight to Stockholm, with this very dishy Italian at my side!"

My brain can barely absorb what she's telling me. "My God!" I say after a moment, "that's enough to snap anyone's mind!"

"That's exactly what it did," she says. "It snapped me right back. All of a sudden I was me again. All of sudden I was fine.

"Imagine," she adds, turning to Divy, "arriving at Bromma Airport in the middle of winter, barefoot, in a torn orange robe, with hair three inches long!"

"Were your parents waiting for you?"

"They sure were!" she chuckles. "You should have seen their faces! Freaked right out!"

"How were they with you?"

"Awful. They shoved me into a mental hospital outside Stockholm. But I wasn't there long. They pumped me full of insulin for a bit and I got very fat, but the psychiatrist finally admitted I'd been fine all along and they released me."

"Then what did you do?"

"Went back to my old job, made some money and came back to Pune. I met Ajit, we fell in love and here we all are."

There's nothing I can say for the next few moments. I feel guilty, responsible for everything she's been through. "Rani," I venture at last, "I'm really sorry. Really, really sorry. I feel like everything you've been through is my fault."

She looks me straight in the eye. "There's no need, Krishna," she says matter-of-factly. "I blamed you too for a long time. I really hated your guts. But Mukta flipped things for me. We were talking one day and she set things straight. She told me that all the madness was in there anyway, that it was all old, all mine, and that it really had nothing to do with you. You were just the trigger that released it." She smiles. "Actually, if you want to know the truth, now that it's over I'm quite grateful to you."

"Really?" I can hardly believe such absolute exoneration from her.

"Really," she answers sincerely, crossing the room to enfold me in a hug. And in the embrace I feel no resentment, no holding back. There is only warmth and affection and love. "Have you seen her yet? Mukta?" she asks, leaning back into the pillows again.

"This afternoon," Divy replies. "We're having dinner with her tonight at the Blue Diamond."

"We live in a flat in the building right next door. Drop by and have a drink first. You can meet Ajit. I think you'll like him. Actually, Krishna," she adds with a giggle, "he looks a bit like you. But darker. He was born in England but one of his parents came from India. He's quite beautiful. And he's *very* curious to meet the pair of you."

"Your two ex-husbands," Divy laughs. "I'm sure he is."

The dinner with Mukta is just like old times. We spend a couple of hours nattering, gossiping, exchanging stories, and in many ways it's as if we've never been apart. Within the first five minutes she'd asked if we'd seen Rani. She loves us all, Mukta the Greek, and what I told her pleased her. "I'm glad," she'd said. "There's no room for grudges with Osho."

For a while I'd made my contribution to the chit-chat, but had soon run down, leaving her and Divy to go it alone. I found I was just happy to sit back and listen, basking in Mukta's after-darshan glow.

She looks incredible, more radiant and shining than ever. And she's still close to Osho, although, she tells us, no one sees him privately these days except for Vivek and Laxmi. As she'd done when we left, she still lives in the large upstairs room in 33, now Lao Tzu House, still does her discourse doorman bit every morning, and still goes to darshan each night. "And," she adds, "I'm still in the garden. But it's not just Lao Tzu garden any more. Now I've got five gardeners and six acres. Walk around and have a look. It's all getting quite lush and beautiful. And one of these afternoons I'll take you through his private garden, through Lao Tzu. Remember how it was all sand and rock. Well, you should see it now! He likes the jungle look!"

She stifles a sudden yawn and, checking her watch, announces it's time for bed. As she summons the waiter for the bill, Divy places a bag on the table. "Goodies from the West," he says. "Sorry it isn't five hundred dollars' worth," he apologizes, "but it's the best I could do and still get back here." She brushes him aside with a laugh. "Don't worry, Divyananda," she says, pulling the bag towards her. "I love presents, no matter who paid for them. I'll open this at home by myself. Want to walk me back to the front gate?

"By the way," she asks as the waiter deposits her change on the table, "when did you arrive in Pune exactly? What was the date?"

"January first," I reply, knowing what she's getting at. "Your month was right, Mukta, but you were a couple of years off."

"Come on, Prem," she laughs. "If I remember correctly, I never did mention a year, did I?"

Wrapped in shawls, huddled against the chilly January night, we stroll slowly towards the commune, saying little. I'd forgotten the tranquillity of India at night—the gentleness, the silence that follows the harshness and the cacophony of the glaring, crowded, sun-scorched days. And, tonight, Koregaon Park is hushed and at peace. The soft winter moonlight, filtered through the ancient arching banyans, dapples the road before us in faint, flickering pools. Shadow-gardens line our way, silhouetted boughs and branches, serene and sleeping, bend over darkened walls. Through high iron gates, down long winding drives overcast in night-shrouded greenery, the hazy lights of huge rambling bungalows shimmer. Some are inhabited, but most are empty—great colonial mansions, abandoned, their heydays over and gone.

"We were going to buy these two," Mukta suddenly says, breaking the silence. She points to a pair of big houses at the end of the street. "But then we realized we're growing so fast that two more properties just wouldn't make any difference at all."

"And now?" I ask.

"The country," she replies. "Laxmi's looking for land in the country for a big rural commune. In Gujarat, I think."

"Has she found anything yet?" Divy wants to know.

"I don't think so, but she and Sheela are on the road a lot these days, looking at palaces and big estates. Okay, boys. Time for bed." To my surprise, I find we've arrived at the great teak gate.

Reconnecting with Osho

In Canada I'd heard tales of the groups in the commune, awful stories of angry encounters, and the possibility Osho would ask me to participate in them had plagued me from the first moment I knew we were returning. Primarily a private person, the idea of dumping my problems in the middle of a room filled with strangers, all of whom I was convinced would be hostile, didn't appeal to me at all. Actually, whenever I thought about it, it struck terror in my heart. But, I decided, if Osho wanted me to do groups, I was ready.

Returning to the Green after a morning's shopping I find a note to see Arup at the commune before darshan tonight. Groups! I am immediately convinced she's going to tell me Osho wants me to do a whole series of horrific groups! But I give myself as little time as possible to freak. I grab the first rickshaw I can find and hightail it out to Koregaon Park.

"Here," she says when I'm ushered in, holding a little volume in her hand, "Osho wants you to rewrite *From Sex to Superconsciousness*."

I open my mouth to speak, but words won't come. I'm relieved, I'm flattered, I'm surprised—I'm a dozen mixed emotions. I'm also speechless. Arup watches me, grinning. Then, with a laugh, she waves me out of the office with a sweep of her hand. "Thanks," I manage at the door. She nods, still grinning. She understands.

On the way back to the Green, the compliment my Master is paying me begins to register. After being away for so long, without even seeing me yet, he's trusting me with *From Sex to Superconsciousness,* with the one book of his that virtually every educated Indian has read! I don't know what to say—not even to myself!

Laxmi had told me about *From Sex to Superconsciousness*. It contained a series of talks Osho had given in Hindi in Bombay in 1968. And they'd been real blockbusters.

Osho had been living in Jabalpur at the time, Laxmi said, and a group of Bombay admirers, mostly Jains, had invited him to come and give a series of talks on a specific topic: Love.

According to Laxmi, Osho literally blew them away. By the time he finished his first talk, not one of the organizers was to be found in the auditorium. Shocked and scared, they'd all split. What Osho had said that evening was that love was one rung on a ladder that began with sex and ended in samadhi, in superconsciousness. And in no uncertain terms he told them that before they could hope to know anything about love they first had to come to grips with its lowest form, with sex itself.

Laxmi laughed at the memory, of the scandal of Osho's having mentioned sex in public. The talks had been cancelled and he'd gone back up north, to Jabalpur. But some people had wanted to hear more and a month later he'd returned to finish the series.

"It was before fifteen thousand people at Gowalia Tank Maidan in Bombay," Laxmi told me, her eyes shining. "One night, the rain started pouring like anything. People began getting up and moving about. Then came Osho's thrilling voice, booming over the microphone, commanding like the thunder. 'Don't move!' he said. 'Just remain where you are and listen to what I am saying. What difference does it make if you become a little wet or not? I am ready to be wet! Just go inside yourselves and listen!'

"There was a pin-drop silence," she said. "And people just stayed where they were. And his voice! Beautiful, musical, pouring, just like the birds singing!" Then she reached out and took my hand. "Ah, Krishna Prem," she said, "those talks in Hindi were so, so beautiful."

Nearing the Green, thumbing through the pages of the volume Arup has given me, I am amazed at the mess the Indian translator has made, at the terrible, stilted English he has produced. "Those talks in Hindi were so, so beautiful," she said. And I vow, for Osho and for his little secretary Laxmi, to do my utmost to make them beautiful in English as well.

"What kind of darshan do you have?" the young lady with the clipboard inquires at Lao Tzu gate, checking her list for my name.

"Silent," I reply.

Locating my name and checking it off, she motions me onward to where two other women stand, nostrils flared, ready to check whether or not I smell of any scent. It appears, while we've been away, Osho's body has developed allergies. But I don't smell, it seems, and I am passed on to yet another young woman who seats me on a bench to await the signal that darshan is about to begin.

A half hour later, seated cross-legged on the sleek mosaic floor of the new Chuang Tzu Auditorium, at the back of a crowd of at least two hundred sannyasins, I look around at what has happened during my absence to the tiny patio and barren yard I remember. An enormous, semi-circular lecture hall has been built, huge marble columns supporting a curving roof, in the centre of which, I observe with amusement, Laxmi has plonked another of her ghastly chandeliers.

Mukta's touch is also apparent. Ringing the auditorium are tall, stately ashokas, Osho's favourite tree, and spreading casuarina pines lean inwards, in the evening breeze, as if they too are expecting him at any moment.

As it has always been, he is suddenly just there, moving through the doorway, as white and shining as ever, gliding towards his chair. Seated, he turns to Mukta, nodding. She calls a name, the first person taking sannyas tonight. My old friend Vishnu, now the bodyguard, indicates where the young man should sit. Osho tells him to close his eyes. For a moment he looks at him intently and then, accepting a clipboard and a pen from Vivek, begins to rename him, as he'd done in Woodlands when I first came to him. He calls the young man close, telling him to look into his eyes. The mala is placed about his neck, his third eye is touched and then, directed gently by Vishnu, the young man moves back slightly. Osho begins to speak, explaining the meaning and potential of the young man's new name.

With the next several people the format is the same. And what strikes me is the formality of the affair. After the casual intimacy of earlier days, it all seems so structured. Yet, with so many people coming now, I can understand the need.

Next, Mukta calls people who are leaving and those who have just come back. And for a moment I'm sad. This is where Mukta would have called for Divy, where she would have called for me. But it's fine. I'm not sorry I didn't wait a few more days. Just being here, just seeing him, even with twenty rows of sannyasins between us, is fine.

A few commune residents are called up to talk to him and then, suddenly it seems, darshan is over. Even before he turns to Mukta to see if there are any others for tonight and she shakes her head, I can tell it's over. And then I think my heart is going to burst. I hear him say to Mukta, "Call Krishna Prem and Divyananda."

Within seconds, even before Mukta finishes calling my name it seems, I am at his feet. But when I raise my eyes to him I am shocked. It's as if he is hardly there at all. When I left Pune I had said goodbye to a man—to my Master, yes, but to a man. But now, looking at him, I can barely find a man at all. There is an overwhelming sense of transparency, of insubstantiality, as if he's on the verge of dissolving. And in this moment I somehow understand. Concepts like flesh and spirit, form and formlessness fill my head, but something way down inside me really understands—I am standing at a gate, I am standing at a doorway, I am gazing on a window that leads to the divine.

He simply looks at me for the longest while, saying nothing, just smiling at me, just loving me. And at last he speaks. "Do you have anything to say to me?" he asks softly.

I can only shake my head. There are no words.

And for Divy, who follows me, what transpires is the same.

Apart from the afternoon shower of soot that floats down from the boiler exhaust on the hotel roof, smudging my typewriter, my manuscript and me with huge black flakes, the balcony of our second floor room at the back of the Green is the perfect place to work on the book.

Spoken, Indian-English is difficult enough to follow at the best of times; written, it is virtually impossible. The translation is atrocious. It is stilted, a strain to read. Subjects don't match verbs, prepositions don't relate, sentences are incomplete, ideas belonging to one paragraph spill over into the next. At times the text borders on gibberish.

Yet, underlying the translator's abortive but, I'm certain, well-intentioned attempt, I can still find Osho—and it's obvious to me I'll have to wade through this book, phrase by phrase, sentence by sentence, digging into myself to render as faithful and accurate a rewrite as I possibly can.

It's slow going at first. Coupled with the garbled, convoluted and almost infantile English is my own nervousness at the responsibility of bringing real sense and meaning to Osho's words. But he obviously trusts my abilities, or I wouldn't be doing this at all. And soon I begin to relax, the work falling into an easy rhythm, into a daily flow I enjoy more and more as each one dawns.

And a kind of pattern to the work unfolds. Each sentence is considered, restructured and then set down, part of a continuous, uninterrupted stream. Finally, when a chapter is complete, I go back over it, querying, refining, polishing, breaking it down into paragraphs, making sure it's clear and concise and easy to read.But the more deeply I move into the book, the more disturbed I become.

And I begin to understand, or at least I think I do, why he's given me this particular volume to edit. What's happening to me is dissatisfaction with myself, a tremendous frustration with my own sexuality. I've never yet had a really fulfilling relationship with a woman. Osho is talking about climbing a ladder, about moving from sex to superconsciousness. And me? I haven't even planted one foot firmly on the first rung!

That old fear of missing plagues me constantly. I remember what happened with Rani; I remember the glimpse; I remember him saying "You're on absolutely the right track!"—and I know something has to happen. And soon.

That evening, I walk by Radha Hall when the evening dancing meditation, the Nataraj, is in full swing. I pause to watch for a while.

What strikes me is the variety of movements, the tremendous diversity of expressions to a single piece of music. It's as if no two dancers are hearing the same tune.

And what comes home to me in a sudden flash, carrying with it a significance that surprises me, is the uniqueness of each of us, the complete and utter individuality of each and every human being. I see how I've been comparing, sitting in judgment on myself for being different—how I've never been able to accept my own sexuality just for what it is.

The next day an Indian friend, Kavya, drops by the Green. We've known each other since the Bombay days and I always enjoy her company. She's built like one of those roly-poly Japanese statues of Buddha, with a belly to match—and whenever I hear Osho mention laughter, it's invariably Kavya's chubby, bubbly image that springs to mind.

We talk for a while about this and that, and I guess I've been a bit complaining, because in the midst of a sudden fit of giggles, obviously aimed in my direction, I can discern, between the gasps and the gurgles, the word *problems* again and again.

"You Westerners and your problems," she finally sputters, a resounding slap on one rotund thigh. "It's so funny! Everything for you people is a praw-blem," she laughs, dragging the word out in long, embarrassing syllables. "So many praw-blems!"

"What do you mean?" I ask, a little disconcerted. "I'm not sure I understand."

"Indians don't have praw-blems," she says. "Not like you people do. If we're hungry, we're hungry; if we're unhappy, we're unhappy, but it's not a problem. That's just the way it is. You people spend so much time thinking and worrying, chewing things over in your heads. You make problems out of *everything*."

The fallout from the Green's rooftop boiler had been pretty heavy earlier, and just before Kavya's arrival I'd moved my work inside, installing the typewriter on the mirrored dresser, the only desk-high surface in the room. When she's gone I return to the manuscript. But

I feel a bit strange inside. Kavya's touched something. Some kind of chord has been struck.

I look up from my work and meet my own face in the mirror. And the bottom drops out of everything! It's as if the carpet under my feet has been sharply and abruptly pulled, and I am poised, teetering, on the brink of an abyss. But the clarity, the perception!

And suddenly I see, with a lucidity that astounds me, that I invented my homosexuality, that it had started as a convenient avoidance, an easy escape; that it had nothing to do with my fundamental energy. And looking back, I see the exact moment in my life I decided that that was what I was, that I applied the label to myself, saying, "This is me." And with the acceptance of that word had come all the guilt and social condemnation the word implied.

"But this word has nothing to do with me!" I say aloud, remembering Kavya, remembering Nataraj. "I'm not this word. I'm not this label. I'm just me!"

Then comes another realization, carrying another great chunk of me away. I see that if I invented this idea of homosexuality, then the same is true for all my other so-called "praw-blems". And in this seeing, in this direct confrontation with myself, they have all been washed away.

Sitting there, watching my face in the mirror, I vow I will never invent another problem again. And all at once there is a new energy in my body. I want to make love to a woman again. But the idea of the game is still unappetizing. And I figure I'll just wait. After all, life brought me Maggie. If I'm ready, there's no reason it won't bring me someone once again.

So, for the next several days, from dawn to dusk, *From Sex to Superconsciousness* is pretty much all that exists. And the moment it's finished I deliver it to Laxmi, introduction and all. "What's next?" I ask.

"Come tomorrow," she instructs. "Tonight, asking will happen."

The following afternoon she passes me another Indian-English gem, *The Path to Self Realization.* "His first camp," is all she says. "1964. In the hills of Rajasthan."

Turning to Arup, I ask when I can come to darshan. "There's something I have to tell him."

"Tonight," she answers. "There's been a cancellation."

"Osho," I begin when I'm seated in front of him that evening, "I don't know whether you remember or not, but a couple of years ago during *The Mustard Seed* you spoke of a wheel of energy and said if it was happening to anyone he should come and tell you right away."

He nods, watching me intently. I cannot tell whether his nod is one of recall or encouragement, but I keep going. "Well, when I came to you, you said to me, 'You're on absolutely the right track.' And then I ran away. At the time I thought I was leaving because of money, but I've just now seen why I left. I was scared. It's taken me two years to see it, but I ran away because I was frightened to surrender, because I was getting close to something that terrified me." I sit back on my heels, relaxing now. "And I had to come and see you tonight to tell you this—and to tell you that, no matter what happens, I'm not afraid any more."

He chuckles, a low, pleased rumble. Then he leans forward in his chair. "Have they told you what book I want you to do next?" he asks.

"Yes," I reply after the split second it takes me to recover from the fact that my great insight has earned no more than a brief chortle.

"It was my first camp," he continues, settling back in his chair, re-crossing his legs. "It was held in Rajasthan in 1964. And they hired a professional translator to do the book in English. But he was a South Indian and he didn't speak Hindi very well. Besides, he never met me. He didn't know me."

He suddenly leans forward again and fixes me with a look of an intensity that takes me aback after the casual way in which he's been speaking. "You do what you want with it, Krishna Prem," he says. "*You* know me." And then, with the customary "Good," he turns to Mukta, indicating his readiness for the next sannyasin.

I walk back to the Green after darshan. Alone in Pune's crowded streets, "You know me" reverberates in my ears. Something significant has been given to me tonight, of that I am aware, but I'm incapable of computing it. All that's really real is the feeling inside. There's a familiarity to the feeling, a quality I've felt before when certain doors have opened, when memories have flooded me, when something of the beyond has penetrated my world.

The first thing next morning I dive into the book. It's an even worse mess than the other. But I don't mind. I welcome the challenge. I know him, he said. And I know the words will flow like a river in the spring.

Devika

Divy has a new playmate these days, a slim and lovely Dutch sannyasin with dark, enigmatic eyes. Her name is Devika. The two of them are in and out of the Green several times a day, occasionally convincing me to set the book aside for a while and join them for a swim at the Blue Diamond. One evening they tell me Devika's babysitting a flat in Koregaon Park, a few streets behind the commune, taking care of it for an American couple returning to the States for six months. "You must see it, Krishna," Divy says. "It's far out."

"Let's cook breakfast there tomorrow," Devika suggests. "Meet us there about ten."

The next morning when the rickshaw drops me in front of number 84 I am quite unprepared for what faces me. Devika has done herself proud—the flat is part of a genuine maharajah's summer palace, hardly faded at all. The house is white, low-slung, two wide wings spreading out on either side of a colossal, vine-covered porte-cochère. In front lies an Indian rarity, a real green lawn. A half-tended garden of overgrown shrubs and flowerbeds encircles it, and in the centre, topping a dry, weed-filled fountain, a little chipped cupid surveys it all.

The flat itself is wonderful. After the Green I feel I'm in acres and acres of space. Apart from the compact but fully-equipped kitchen and bath, it's one vast room, marbled, columned, high-ceilinged, casement windows flooding it with light. Covered mattresses and cushions are the only furnishings, except for a bookcase, a wardrobe and a hand-woven Kashmiri carpet lying luxuriously in the middle of the floor. "It was the maharajah's bedroom," Devika explains.

After a delicious home-cooked breakfast of eggs and toast and filtered Western coffee, Devika suddenly suggests Divy and I let the room at the Green go and move in with her. "There's plenty of space," she says. And, pointing to an alcove in one corner, adds, "And it's a much nicer place to work on your book."

I don't go back to the Green at all. Divy and Devika, on their way from the market that afternoon, simply pack our things and check us out of the hotel.

That night Devika and I become lovers. "I heard you say one day you were ready for a woman again," she murmurs into my shoulder. "I decided it was going to be me."

The next morning there's a powerful urge to see Osho, so right after discourse I book an appointment with Arup. But by the time I'm actually there I cannot remember, for the life of me, what it was that had been so imperative, what it was I'd wanted to say. I sit, waiting like a first-nighter with the stage-fright jitters, my lines forgotten, listening to Mukta call name after name, dreading the moment I'll hear my cue.

"Krishna Prem!"

Up on my feet, moving towards him through the rows of sannyasins, I feel more and more ridiculous, my mind a total blank. "Hmmm?" he inquires as I settle on the floor in front of his chair.

"Osho," I begin, honesty the only avenue open to me, "when I made the appointment to come here tonight I thought I knew why I had to come. But now that I'm here, I don't know why I've come at all."

Silence. Nothing. Not a word. He just looks at me.

"Do you?" I suddenly blurt, my voice sounding sheepish. I figure he's the Master and if I don't know why I'm here then he certainly must.

"No," he replies to an immediate and general explosion of laughter that I cannot help but join, despite the fact I feel like an ass. "But it doesn't matter," he adds mercifully. "You come to me whenever you want to. Now tell me, has anything been happening?"

I shake my head. Somehow I know he's not asking about Devika, but still I have nothing to tell him.

"Surely something has been happening?" he insists.

"Taps in my head," I say, remembering all at once an odd occurrence at the Green several nights before, grateful I've been able to come up with *something*, no matter how insignificant or stupid. His eyebrows arch in interest. He leans towards me. "Tell me about them. How many? Which side of the head? What did they feel like?"

"The left side," I reply, quite unprepared for the extent of his interest in an incident I'd practically forgotten. "Quick and sharp, like the tap of a ruler. And they happened over three nights—one the first, two the second, three the third."

"Hmmm," he murmurs again, as if considering. Then he motions to the spot directly in front of his knees: "Come close to me."

He places my head in his lap, positioning it slightly forward. My chin juts out and up towards him. "Look up," he instructs. "At the ceiling."

From the corner of one upturned eye I can see him make a fist, pyramiding his second finger. Drawing back, he swings downward sharply, hitting me on the left temple, a short smart blow. Then he does it again. After a brief pause, down comes the knuckle a third time, much harder than before.

"Good, Krishna Prem," he says, releasing my head and moving it gently off his lap.

I return to my seat in a daze, surprised stares following me. Except for the occasional pat on the head, Osho rarely touches us. I've never known him to do anything like this before. I don't know what to make of it. Throughout the rest of the darshan and walking home later, there's a strange burning sensation in my temple, at the point of contact, as if a dot of light were quivering there. There's also an odd sense of harmony, a new kind of balance, but it's something I can't quite get in touch with, can't quite explain.

The next afternoon, standing in the bathroom, dripping wet from the shower, the bottom drops out from under me once again, exactly as it had done a week or so earlier at the Green. This time there's neither insight nor realization, but a tidal rush of energy that nearly knocks me off my feet. It courses upwards from somewhere deep inside, like a sudden gust of wind blowing wide a door. And it's exactly that—a door.

It's a door that I closed on women when my mother died some thirty-eight years before.

The need to lie down is acute—my whole body is shaking uncontrollably. I get as far as the Kashmiri rug and collapse, icy with sweat, unable to make it any further. My chest is in upheaval. I feel constricted, suffocating, desperate for air. And space. I need space! Finally I spreadeagle, my limbs stretching outwards—and touching nothing, finding no confinement, the panic subsides. And I just allow. I allow the energy to tear through me, spasm after spasm convulsing through my body, pouring upwards, being thrown from me in painful, wrenching gasps.

During Dynamic I'd experienced energies unblocking but never anything like this! Long after the tremors cease I simply lay there on the carpet, depleted, unable to move.

When, at long last, I stand and take my first tentative steps, it's almost as if I'm in another body. There is a new quality of maleness in the way I walk, in the way I move, in the very way my body feels. And I find myself wishing Devika would come home.

That night, making love, we seem to be moving more deeply into each other than ever before. There is a singleness to everything, to our rhythms, to our breathing, as if our bodies are melting, being joined, becoming one. We seem to be dropping through layer after layer, distinctions disappearing, boundaries, like vapour and mist, being spirited away.

We had slipped beneath the net as Krishna Prem and Devika, but then, moving into the dance, the tempo heightening, a sudden sense of namelessness surrounded us—and there was only man and woman, raw and primal, elemental natures coupling in a bed. And then this too changed. Watching, witnessing the play, I feel yet another dimension open, welcoming us—and then there are simply energies, currents intertwining, male and female fusing, unifying, becoming one.

And then Devika is no more. There is only light and openness, a formless receptivity, womb-like, inviting me, accepting me, absorbing me, bringing me home. Devika, the archetypal woman, the female—all is gone. I am making love to existence, to the universe itself!

Now, for the first time, I understand words of Osho from *My Way: The Way of the White Clouds*, spoken years before. "Then the lover becomes the door," he'd said. "The beloved becomes the door, and they both reach to the one."

And in the midst of this miracle, this discovery of the divinity of sex, I hear a voice, soft and tender, as if coming from a great distance, whispering in my ear. "I love you," Devika is saying, calling me back to the woman in my arms. There is a quality to her voice that is new to me, a different depth and timbre that tells me something significant has happened to her as well.

I say nothing. There is no need. Still inside her, still joined together, I hold her to me and we drift, united, into sleep.

I awaken before her in the morning and lie there for a while, watching her sleep, amazed and touched by the beauty of the face on the pillow next to mine. It is not the same face I took to bed. Not at all. It is as if what has transpired between us during the night has transformed her, imparting to her a new grace, a new radiance. I feel I am seeing Devika's real being, gazing upon her original face.

Throughout the day she is exquisite, glowing, overflowing with love. And I am happier than I have been in ages. This is something I have wanted for a long time, this communion with a woman. And I feel complete, fulfilled. We spend the evening outside, watching the stars, listening to the wind in the trees, not speaking, sufficient to each other, her on the step beneath me, cupped and sheltered in my arms.

Devika's history with men is not unknown to me. She's been a bit of a ball cruncher, as if she's been out for revenge. Daddy had a streak of the bastard about him, I gather, but what she's been getting even for, specifically, I've never asked. Her past holds no interest for me.

But over the next several days I can see she's in turmoil. I watch her struggling, fighting to stay open, to remain vulnerable, not to fall back into old patterns, into old ways. And it saddens me to see her losing the battle, to see the games slowly starting once again. But there's nothing I can do. She's closing faster every day. And whenever I try to say something about it, she says it's my imagination and simply doesn't want to hear.

Then she begins to turn on me.

She starts to flirt outrageously whenever I'm around, one eye on me, watching my reaction, checking to see if she's getting through to me. Day after day it becomes more blatant, more provoking, as if she's trying to push me to explosion, trying to force me over the edge.

I get jealous and I get hurt, but I've been with Osho long enough to know that she is just the catalyst, that the jealousy and pain are mine. Remembering Rani, I can't point the finger at Devika; I have to deal with this myself. Each time she triggers these emotions in me I head off by myself and sit, my eyes closed, letting the energy rise, be reabsorbed, turned in.

But I'm only human. And one night I crack.

We'd gone for a drink to friends on the other side of the compound. And with a burly Scotsman who'd dropped by, Devika had begun her eye-contact game. It was one of her favourites. And she was good at it—she could easily have outstared Peeping Tom. Finally, fed up with the whole thing, I just came home, leaving her there.

And then I get angry. Red-hot, showdown angry. Like a blast of thunder I roar across the compound, pick Devika up and carry her home, screaming and kicking all the way. She won't stop cursing me; she goes on and on, shouting abuse. Beside the chair I shove her into is a bouquet of roses I'd brought her in the morning. Ripping the roses from the vase, I drive them against the wall and splash the water in her face. "Shut up!" I yell. "Just shut up and listen to me!" Stunned, she is suddenly silent.

I tear across the room to the table where I've been trying to work for the past few days. "Listen to this!" I shout, crossing towards her. She says nothing. She simply watches me, frozen, her eyes like ice. "Listen to what Osho has to say!"

"Do you *really* want to see the truth about yourself?" I read from the manuscript. "Do you want to meet the person that is really you?"

I look up. She hasn't budged. Her eyes are still cold, steely.

"I ask you to uncover what is hidden in yourself," I go on. "Uncover yourself and know your self. Do not run away from yourself. And escaping from yourself is not possible. Where will you go? What will you achieve by running away? No matter where you go, you will be with you. You can transform yourself but you cannot run away from yourself." What needed saying said, I slam the sheet of paper onto the table, hard, insisting. "How much longer are you going to keep playing these stupid games with yourself? How much longer? Tell me, Devika," I push, "how much longer?"

The air between us is electric, the silence crackling in the aftermath of the storm. My eyes are fixed on her face, watching, waiting. For a moment it seems as if she's rallying, preparing for battle again, but all at once the fight simply drains away, visibly, like sand from an hourglass. She lifts herself slowly from the chair and walks softly and unspeaking past me, bent, spent, moving towards our bed. She lies there on her side, curled into herself.

Going to her, kneeling beside her, my anger gone, I stroke her forehead, her still damp hair. "Devika, let's try again," I croon. "You can be so beautiful, so exquisite. I've seen the beauty and the love in you. Can't you just stay like that? Why do you have to put on these masks? Why do you keep on playing these ugly games? Can't you just stay open? I'll help you. I promise I'll help you."

"Fuck off!" she spits, pushing me away. "I hate myself. And I hate you! I'll never forgive you for showing me what I can really be. I despise you for that. And I don't *want* to change! I'm scared. Can't you understand that? I'm scared. Just leave me be. Just leave me as I am. And get the fuck out of my life!"

Out of the sense of finality and hopelessness her words trigger in me a new rage arises, a rage at existence itself. It keeps taking my women away—two mothers, my lovers—and now Devika too! Fury and bitterness fill me, demanding direction, a target. Osho!

I rip the armoire open and on the bottom shelf find the robe he gave when I left Pune before. "If you need me, Krishna Prem," he'd said, "put it on." Pulling it over me, wearing it for the first time, unable to bear being inside, I head for the open sky, "You want me too, Osho?" I shout into the stars. "You've taken everything else away, why not me? Take me too! I'm ready. Come and get me!"

In silence I wait, uncertain for what—for my breath to cease, for my heart to stop, for an all-consuming flash of fire to carry me away. But nothing happens. The night is still and windless. Nothing stirs. I stand there in the moonlight, impotent and ignored.

"It's all a fraud," I say quietly, turning back towards the house. "The first time I really need him, he's not there. It's all bullshit. It's all a fraud." I take the mala from around my neck and lay it sadly on the table. Across the room Devika sleeps. Or pretends to.

The sense of desolation, the feeling of abandonment, is utter, absolute. But slowly, as the night passes, a new understanding begins to surface. And with it comes a new appreciation of what I've just been through.

I've been asking the impossible. I've been asking Osho to make it all better, to make it like it was. Fundamentally, underlying my histrionics in the yard, that's what I've been doing. And like a silly, pouting child trying to punish an unyielding parent, I removed my mala. Weary with myself, embarrassed at the faithlessness, I retrieve it from the table, putting it back around my neck where it belongs.

I've been asking the impossible. My Master's a mystic, not a magician. I've been unfair, unjust—testing him out of my frustration, trying him out of my rage. Unless Devika really wants to change; unless she opens, cooperates, even Osho is helpless. And she's made it abundantly plain. She's stuck where she is—at least for now. "Am I willing to wait?" I ask myself. "Am I willing to hang in—patient, hoping?"

I look across the room to where she lies, and in the curve of her sleeping back there's a tightness, a stubbornness, a rigid obstinacy that answers me, more eloquently, more directly than weeks of confrontation, more than weeks of words.

And I just accept. This is how it is.

Yet I am grateful. I'd felt I'd lost everything, but see that's not true. Through Devika I've had a glimpse. I've tasted the possibility, the potential between a man and a woman. I've drunk of that divine meeting. And nothing and no one can take that away.

The next morning I bring Devika her coffee in bed and say goodbye—no malice, no regrets, just goodbye. An hour later I'm back with Divy at the Green Hotel. Fed up with the drama, he'd split days before.

And sun-scorched and soot-stained, it's back to the balcony. Back to the typewriter. Back to the book for Osho. Back to aloneness. Back to me.

Staveley Road

For a pair of paupers, Divy and I have done surprisingly well. For a month we've been the proud tenants of a fully-furnished three-room flat that runs the entire top floor of an old Parsi mansion a few streets up from the Pune cantonment's main thoroughfare, Mahatma Gandhi Road.

An Australian couple we met at the Green had found it and invited us to live with them despite our confession that we were flat broke, couldn't pay our hotel bill and had nothing coming for a couple of months. No matter, they said. The Green's manager was equally generous. "When money comes," he told us, "then you give." We all moved in and, unexpectedly, three weeks later, the Aussies had left for Greece, leaving us with next month's rent stashed securely downstairs in the landlady's safe. And when Virag had written—another of her backwards epistles that always sent me scurrying to a mirror—to say they were coming back to India, I cabled immediately about the flat. Back had come the prompt reply: "Save the space for us."

For India, the flat is the height of luxury. Not only is it furnished with an eclectic collection of tables and chairs and sofas and armoires, it has a refrigerator. And if the fridge isn't miracle enough, there is also a gas stove. To live without the smell of kerosene! Just to be able to turn on the gas! Ten years on a waiting list, or a bequest from one generation to another—that's about the only way. In this country, to have a gas bottle is, for the householder, the greatest prestige of all. The right to ours and the right to have it refilled, the landlady Mrs Barucha had confidentially confessed, had begun with her grandmother. "They still don't know she's passed away," she told me furtively. Divy and I both swore not to tell.

Compared to our old home on Boat Club Road, this flat is a dream. The rooms are large and airy, high-ceilinged, stone-floored, with French-style connecting doors. Others, paned with frosted glass, give onto the covered walkway that skirts the flat, meeting in the centre in a walled, mosaic terrace, the roof of the main house's porte-cochère. A bright green Rangoon Creeper, bursting with pink and white floral stars, spills over onto the floor.

And all around, on all sides, as far as the eye can see, are the incredible flowering trees of Pune. Raised in a land of green, where the forest's only splash of colour comes in autumn, when the maples turn to rust and orange before the snows, the spectacle that spreads before us, canopying Staveley Road, is awesome in its majesty.

Apart from the myriad greens of the banyan and ashoka, fig and mango, eucalyptus and palms, the sea of swaying giants is a blaze of reds and yellows. Only the lavender pyramids of the jacaranda's flowers temper the sensation the treetops are on fire. "The Gulmohar," Mrs Barucha said, indicating gigantic gnarled trees heavy with orange and crimson bouquets carried on branches like great feathered fans. "And its cousins, the Tamarind and Colville's Glory," she'd added, pointing to similar trees with delicate nosegays of creamy yellow and grape-like clusters in startling orange and red.

And from the Flame Tree and Indian Coral—also introduced by her—their flowering past, long black seedpods dangle, pointing like so many twisted satyrs' fingers towards the reddish brown earth below.

Down in her own garden, in front of the house, rows of potted begonias and oak-leaf geraniums line the drive, ringing a gambolling bed of variegated foliage with streaks of white and yellow, pink and purple, silver and bronze veining the green of their leaves.

The rest of the yard is haphazard, a mélange. Growing as if at random through a dense carpet of Wandering Jew, are hibiscus and ixora, oleander and honeysuckle, clumps of ratty elephant ears and a thicket of Love-Lies-Bleeding on its very last legs. There's scraggly bougainvillaea everywhere, plus those awful, showy Canna lilies, but around the porte-cochère are the signs of Mrs Barucha's private passion. Between the columns, flanked by a pair of enormous papyrus umbrellas, is a collection of ferns, dozens of varieties so fresh and feathery and healthy they could put the finest Western nursery to shame.

"Just look at all that," Divy mutters to no one in particular, thoughtfully curling a tendril of the Rangoon Creeper around one finger. Since he's started to work for Mukta in Lao Tzu garden, he has plants on the brain. "And there's this great big empty terrace right here," he adds, turning towards Prageet and Virag and me. "Just think of the incredible pot garden we could have!" And so, once again, the four of us embark on the creation of a home.

Prageet and Virag have some money and I have a tax rebate on the way, and we're soon best friends with the Pune plant-wallahs. But the day we count two hundred and seventy-six pots ranging over three rooms and one terrace, it's obviously time to be getting into something else. "I saw the most incredible bamboo begonia this morning when Mukta and I went to the nursery," Divy begins the evening Virag announces the tally. "Shut up," we say. "You can hardly move around here the way it already is."

And so we shift inside the flat, painting, reupholstering, making things cosy for the coming monsoon. Madhura, an eccentric Englishwoman we met while at the Green, takes to dropping by, pitching in, helping get the place together. Stage-managed by a speedy Divy, it's a decorating blitzkrieg. When it's finished, we get into cooking—I'm resident baker once again—and we seem to have guests almost every night. Mukta's number one. Sometimes she comes with Arup; sometimes, with one of her crew of gardeners. Other nights are Kailash reunions, a mix of old friends. And Madhura. Always Madhura. Like Shantidas of yore, she's pretty much a permanent fixture, sitting in the corner, casting caustic English comments about, knitting needles clacking like Madame Lefarge. She only lays them down for food or for the silly after-dinner games we get into playing. It's usually Mukta who starts things rolling. No sooner has she spooned the last cream-soaked stewed fig into her mouth than she wants action. We shoot dice, play cards, squabble over Scrabble or turn out the lights and play hide-and-seek, hooting and shrieking like a houseful of children at a birthday fête.

Path to Self-Realization has been finished, retitled *Pointing the Way*, and now I'm wading through one hundred and eighty letters and anecdotes and excerpts from talks, trying to turn two old collections, *Earthen Lamps* and *Seeds of Revolutionary Thought*, into one cohesive volume. And the book is progressing beautifully. After the morning discourse I cycle home and, naked and alone in the flat, the maid gone, I boil the day's milk, set out bread to rise and, Ness-coffee in hand, get down to it. There are some exquisite pieces in the volume I'm editing, real little gems, and my days are inspired, filled with the vastness of his vision and the wonder of his words.

I've been alone since Devika, and whenever the loins stir with the sweet ache of wanting I take meditation over mating every time. In the last book I'd done at the Green, Osho had spoken of two avenues for sex energy: "Downwards into sex; upwards into meditation." And when the energy begins to assert itself I sit, cross-legged, eyes closed, inner gaze focused on the third eye, and let the energy rise. Within seconds I can feel it start to move. Groin, navel, heart, throat—following the chakra map it climbs, pulsating and delicious, until it settles in my forehead, making me stoned. When it settles, subsiding again, it's back to the book. Right now I'm not interested in women. Right now I'm interested in me. Life, it seems, is as well. One morning, during discourse, it hands me a gift—more with an iron fist than a velvet glove.

Over the past few weeks Osho has been giving a series of discourses called "The Tantra Vision", based on the sutras of a buddha called Saraha—described by Osho as the father of Tibetan Tantra. "My old love affair," he'd said in the first lecture of the series. And for me these talks carry a particular significance, a strange evocative quality that both pursues and eludes me, at once tremendously real and frustratingly vague. Two things keep surfacing for me during the discourses—having been with Osho before in Tibet and that wheel of energy that had happened with Rani—but there's nothing specific I can put my finger on.

Ever since that darshan where he'd whipped that penetrating look at me, and his "You're on *absolutely* the right track!" sent me scurrying back to Canada, there had been this distant feeling, lurking somewhere in my inner shadows, that Tantra and I were old acquaintances, old friends, and that one day we'd get together again. But I'd seen I'm still not ready. It's as if something in me knows my potential, my destination, my door—but how to get there? Rani, Maggie, Devika—glimpses. But, really, I don't even know how to take the first concrete step.

Lying in the dappled sunlight on the path to an overflowing Chuang Tzu Auditorium, listening to him share the immensity of *the* Tantra vision, I slowly begin to see the stupidity of my impatience. He's speaking of a search that can consume decades, even lives, and I'm feeling despondent after just a few years. Looking inside, I see I've already rid myself of much, that three years of Dynamic have not been in vain. And now these books. In a way that's still unclear, I feel the work on the books is erasing me for him, replacing my tiny understanding with his greater view. I suddenly feel better, less impatient. All at once I feel ready for something new.

And it comes—blasting, like dynamite.

Near the end of the discourse come four words that trigger an inner explosion so shattering I am lifted off the ground, literally. Some interior depth-charge has been detonated, fathoms beneath my surface, and the shock waves jolt through me, sending tremors through my body into my fingers, into my toes.

And my eyelids! I simply cannot hold them still. They begin to flap, madly and uncontrollably, like the desperate wings of a struggling butterfly. No matter what I do I cannot halt them. Everything around is fluttering, strobe-like, and my seeing is as if from a great distance, as if from some inner place far away. Stuck on automatic they keep flapping, on and on and on.

"Intelligence becomes your meditation," he'd said. And my body had gone berserk.

The rest of the lecture I hear nothing. I'm just trying to hold myself together. I'm scared to death I'm falling apart.

After a couple of cups of strong coffee in Vrindavan, the commune canteen, I'm sufficiently recovered to try to absorb what's happened. Why I reacted so strongly to those few words evades me, yet I can't shake the sense that they have struck some very old, once-familiar chord. And I recall something else he'd once said. He is speaking for millions of people, he'd told us in one discourse. "But one day," he said, "you will hear something that is exactly right for you." Today, I know, that's happened.

I want to hear more. Before cycling back to the flat, I write a question for discourse: "Beloved Osho, yesterday when you spoke of intelligence becoming meditation, there was such a rush inside, it felt as if my heart would explode. It was as if you had said something I'd been waiting to hear. Can you elaborate?"

"The first question," I hear him say as he begins the following morning's discourse. And I know the question is mine.

Holding a slip of paper in his hand he begins to read: "Yesterday when you spoke..." and my body goes mad again, the same convulsing spasms, the same wildly beating eyelids. "The question is from Krishna Prem," he adds. And then there's a pause, almost as if he's waiting for my chaos to subside.

"Intelligence is intrinsic to life," he says. "Intelligence is a natural quality of life. Just as fire is hot, and air is invisible, and water flows downward, so is life intelligent.

"Intelligence is not an achievement—you are born intelligent. Trees are intelligent in their own way; they have enough intelligence for their own life. Birds are intelligent, so are animals. In fact, what religions mean by God is only this: that the universe is intelligent, that intelligence is hidden everywhere. And if you have eyes to see, you can see it everywhere.

"Life *is* intelligence. Only man has become unintelligent. Man has damaged the natural flow of life. Except in man, there is no unintelligence. Have you ever seen a bird you can call stupid? Have you ever seen an animal you can call idiotic? No, such things happen only to man. Man's intelligence has been damaged, corrupted, has been crippled.

"And meditation is nothing but the undoing of that damage. Meditation will not be needed at all if man is left alone. If the priest and the politician do not interfere with man's intelligence, there will be no need for any meditation. Meditation is medicinal. First you have to create the disease, then meditation is needed. If the disease is not there, meditation is not needed. And it is not accidental that the words 'medicine' and 'meditation' come from the same root. It is medicinal."

For the next quarter hour he elaborates on how this innate intelligence is destroyed by the status quo. "The society," he tells us, "has done something wrong with man—for certain reasons. It wants you to be slaves, it wants you to be always afraid, it wants you to be always greedy, it wants you to be always ambitious, it wants you to be always competitive. It wants you to be unloving, it wants you to be full of anger and hatred; it wants you to remain weak, imitative—carbon copies. It does not want you to become original Buddhas, original Krishnas or Christs, no. That's why your intelligence has been destroyed.

"Meditation is needed only to undo what the society has done. Meditation is negative: it simply negates the damage, it destroys the illness—and once the illness has gone, your wellbeing asserts itself of its own accord...

"The intelligent way is to bring intelligence into everything that you do. Walking, walk intelligently with awareness; eating, eat intelligently with awareness...

"Whatsoever you are doing, bring the quality of intelligence into it. Do it intelligently. That's what meditation is...

"An intelligent person will make his life in such a way that it will have a poetry of spontaneity, of love, of you. It is your life, and if you are not kind enough to yourself, who is going to be kind enough to you? If you are wasting it, it is nobody else's responsibility. I teach you to be responsible towards yourself—that is your first responsibility. Everything else comes next. Everything else! Even God comes next! Because godliness can arise only when *you* are. You are the very centre of your world, of your existence.

"So, be intelligent. Bring in the quality of intelligence... Then there is no need for any religion, no need to meditate, no need to go to the church, no need to go to any temple, no need for anything extra. Life in its intrinsicness is intelligent. Just live totally, harmoniously, in awareness, and everything follows beautifully. A life of celebration follows the luminousness of intelligence."[6]

His answer hadn't been the blockbuster I'd expected, considering the intensity of my reaction to his words yesterday. It was more subtle, this gift of his to me. But I get it. Sitting there, in Chuang Tzu, after he's moved on to the next question, I understand why his statement of yesterday had felt so familiar. The car accident. Saying "Okay" in that spinning, smashing car, surrendering to death because there was nothing else to be done, had been an act of intelligence. I hadn't seen it at the time but that's exactly what it had been—an act of intelligence. That act of intelligence had brought me the greatest experience of meditation in my life to date. And it had set me on the search that led to Osho.

I feel he's set me back on course, back on the "right track" once again.

I hadn't known how to move. Now it's clear. One step at a time. And the first step: "Bring in the quality of intelligence..."

The issue of money has raised its head again. The same old boring trip. It's been proven to me time and time again that there's no need to worry, that existence really does take care, but I can't stop my mind from fretting. Despite what I've been through in Montreal, in Toronto and here in Pune, my mind keeps on and on, nagging at me, trying to convince me

6. *Intelligence: The Creative Response to Now*

starvation is just around the corner. I know it's ridiculous, but these days I'm stuck with a one-track-mind with a paranoia all of its own.

"Bring in the quality of intelligence...," Osho said.

In Montreal, at Jack's house, I'd read a book, *Secret of the Atom* by Vera Stanley Alder, an English portraitist who set out for the East, in the 1920s or thereabouts, in search of what she termed the Ancient Wisdom—capital A, capital W. One passage in particular had stuck with me. She wrote of thoughts as subtle forms of matter. Being matter, she explained, they required food. And their food, she said, was our attention. Withdraw the attention and they starve. And, although he had expressed it differently, I'd heard Osho say exactly the same.

If the withdrawal of my attention is what I have to do to stop this constant preoccupation with money, I reason, I obviously need to give my attention somewhere else to go. I don't have to look far. The destination is sitting there, waiting for me, on the table in my room. The book.

For the next week I work anywhere from ten to fifteen hours a day, depending on how tenacious my mind is on any particular day, on how stubbornly it clings to this anxiety about money. And one morning I find the technique has suddenly worked. I'm thinking about the trees and the plants and the first monsoon rains—and there's not a single rupee note fluttering in my head.

Moving to Gujarat?

"Train to Gujarat—December 4," announces the small, hand-lettered sign at the entrance to Krishna House garden, a bright red arrow pointing towards the table where tickets are up for a hundred rupees a throw.

"Castle is ours!" Laxmi had shouted triumphantly, bursting into Mukta's kitchen in Lao Tzu where we had just polished off plates of spaghetti topped with one of the Greek's tastier culinary atrocities—ketchup-and-water sauce with a token tomato tossed in for body.

"Let's see the key," Mukta asked immediately, all Greek practicality, knowing well Laxmi's inveterate bent for ballyhooing beforehand.

"Key?" Laxmi cried in wide-eyed innocence. "Key?" And, grabbing the locket of her mala in one tiny fist she waved it on high. "Key? Here is key! Where is trust, Ma Mukta? Here!" She held the locket out. "Here! *He* is key!"

"Laxmi," Mukta laughed. "You're an incurable optimist. But I know you! I'll believe we're moving to Gujarat the day I see the key."

The castle in question, a rather rococo Moghul affair, lay a little inland from the Arabian Sea on a two-mile stretch of sea near the Pakistani border, in the quasi-peninsula of Kutch. It was the result of a long and arduous search by Laxmi and Sheela. Both Gujaratis, they were thrilled with the find. The rest of us weren't quite so sure. According to Veetmoha, Laxmi's driver, it was barren, treeless, waterless and resplendent with flies. But it was isolated. And it would be private. The two Ranns of Kutch, the Great and the Little, would see to that. Except for a single road through the walled city of Bhuj to the main part of Gujarat, it seems we would be pretty well separated from the rest of the world—in summer by a desert of parched earth, during the monsoon an ocean of waist-high mud.

But one way or another, a move is definitely in the wind. And so is talk of contributions. Money is needed to build the new commune. I have none. Nor does Divy. It's panic-time all over again.

"I can't stand this suspense any longer," Divy announces in exasperation one evening. "I'm going to talk to Laxmi. I want to know one way or another—whether we're going to be taken along when the commune moves or whether we'll have to go back to the West to make money again. I'm going to make an appointment to see her tomorrow morning. Will you come and talk to her with me?"

"Okay," I agree, relieved he's taking the initiative. "You know how easily I freak out over money. This whole thing is driving me nuts as well."

The day we see her, the commune grounds are as wet and as messy as both of the Ranns are purported to be. The mid-August rain is virtually one solid stream, and by the time we kick off our sandals at the entrance to Laxmi's office we feel and look, despite our orange plastic ponchos, as if we've just braved the deluge of Niagara's Horseshoe Falls. Every chair in her office is full, each vinyl armchair cupping a sannyasin in lotus posture. But no one's in any great state of meditativeness. It's a case of pure self protection. Soaked bare feet are tucked under damp, mud-splattered robes to escape the blast of air-conditioning and the aching iciness of Laxmi's marble floor.

Sitting there, chilled to the bone, waiting for her attention to fall on either of us, I keep feeling more and more insecure. Smatterings of conversation reach me—talk of donations, of ready cash and heavy equipment, of selling houses and liquidating businesses—but worst of all, and total torture to my ears, is the terrible sentence: "Laxmi's suggestion is to go back to the West and earn." Next to me, I can sense Divy's growing uneasiness and impatience. "Laxmi!" he finally blurts.

She turns to him with a coolness of gaze that throws me for a moment. "Yes, swamiji?" she inquires politely, with an aloofness as chilling as the floor. And I realize that here, in the office, I'm not facing my old friend Laxmi. Here, in the office, I'm about to encounter Ma Yoga Laxmi, the Foundation's Managing Trustee. But it turns out there's no need for me to say anything at all.

"Laxmi," Divy says simply and straightforwardly, "we want to know about Gujarat, about moving to the new commune."

"Money is there for contribution?"

"No. We have about three thousand rupees between us—enough to live on until December. And that's it."

"And in West? Anything is there?"

"No."

"And Krishna Prem?" she asks, turning towards me.

"Nothing, Laxmi. I burned all my money-earning bridges behind me before I first came to Bombay."

She leans back in her chair, her eyes half-closing. And I swear she's checking with Osho. I've never seen this happen before, but I get the distinct impression she's waiting for him to tell her what to say. It's as if there's some kind of telepathic hook-up between them, some sort of psychic radio connecting her and him, linking her office in Krishna

House with his room in Lao Tzu. And she hasn't done this with anyone else! While we've been sitting here, she's dealt with everyone quickly, easily, on her own. It's as if she wants to tune in to him first before replying to us.

There's a pause, extremely pregnant with our anticipation. I watch, fascinated and anxious at one and the same time. Finally, her eyes re-open, normal again. "Come back tomorrow," she says. I figure he must be having a nap or a bath or something, but whatever he's doing, he's obviously unavailable. Leaving her office, I know she's going to talk to him about us tonight.

The following afternoon, more apprehensive than ever, Divy and I are back, face to face with the Managing Trustee. "Well?" Divy asks, taking the initiative once again.

"Oh!" she laughs, slapping her forehead with the heel of her hand, "Laxmi forgot. Come tomorrow."

"Laxmi!" Divy shouts, leaning across her desk. "Don't do this to me! I can't take another sleepless night!" There's a fraction of a second where she scans the pair of us with a look as penetrating as an X-ray. Then, as suddenly, her eyes become soft and liquid, gentle, like melting snow. "Not to worry," she says, her voice loving, reassuring. "When new commune happens, you bring what you have and come."

"Thank you, Laxmi," we reply together. But she waves our thanks away with a sidelong smile, her single-pointed attention already riveted on the sannyasin in the neighbouring chair.

The next day I'm still in the commune by lunchtime. After discourse I'd delivered the finished manuscript of the book to Pratima, head of publications, and as had become the pattern, taken the introduction straight to Vivek. It was as if the introductions had become my way of telling Osho what's been happening to me, of keeping him up to date on my growth. I find Vivek in the kitchen, putting together a tea tray to take to Osho. She takes the introduction straight in, telling me to wait. A few moments later she comes back down the hall, smiling, holding four little paperbacks in her hand. "I know," I say before she can speak, "he wants me to make these into one book too. Right?"

"Right," she laughs, turning into the kitchen again.

"And how goes the book?" Laxmi asks the next day as we have tea in her office, empty except for me and her for a change. I bring her up to date on what I've finished and show her the four books I'm now going to start editing. "But I'd like to be closer, Laxmi. Is there some place here in the commune where I could work?"

She reflects for a moment and decides it would be fine for me to use the lounge across from her office. "Sometimes it is needed for guests," she explains, "but Laxmi's feeling is it might be okay."

A week later my back is killing me. The lounge is just not the place to work on a book. Laxmi's away in Bombay for a bit, so I leave her a note, thanking her but no-thanking her, and trundle my typewriter back to the flat, to my comfortable chair and my nice little table, to the peace and solitude of Staveley Road.

But before there's a chance to start on my latest assignment, a very special treat comes along. Maneesha, Teertha's girlfriend and the editor of the new one-a-month darshan diaries, asks me to attend darshan one evening and write my impressions. I hardly bother to say yes—all I want to know is when!

And it's far out. I'm positioned right behind Vishnu and Mukta, not three feet away from him, and I find myself watching him with the greatest intensity I can muster as the parade of sannyasins passes before him. He is so incredibly, unbelievably beautiful, and I can literally feel his love showering, pouring down on each and every one in the same measure, indiscriminately, like the falling rain.

Real. Sitting here, I find that word about sums it up for me. It's the all embracing word that describes my search, my relationship to him. He is the only real man I've ever encountered. Real. Really real. Like a tree, like the ocean is real.

"I liked your commentary very much," Maneesha tells me a few days later. She holds out a bulging file to me. "Into writing an introduction for the book as well?"

I write it that very evening.

The next day Maneesha finds me once again. "I thought you'd like to know how much I enjoyed your introduction," she says. "And Osho liked it too. Vivek told me after he read it he said, 'He writes very well.' Just thought you'd like to know," she adds, turning into Lao Tzu driveway, leaving me standing there, grinning from ear to ear. Words like that from Osho are even better than the gold stars I used to get on my report card as a kid.

A few moments later, on my way to Vrindavan, I'm waved into Laxmi's office again. "Bombay-coming just happened. Lounge not okay?" She's still perusing my note under her owl-eyed magnifying glass.

Miming back pain, I groan in reply.

"Give Laxmi two, three days," she says. "Something else may happen."

It takes four. "Laxmi spoke to him last night," she tells me. "Just off library, balcony is there. There, your work can happen. On balcony. In Lao Tzu."

"Jesus," Prageet whistles when I run into him, hose in hand, watering the Krishna House garden, "you couldn't get much closer!"

Lao Tzu Balcony

The balcony, accessible only through the library, runs along the front of Lao Tzu House, overlooking the gravel drive we used to walk, years before, towards darshan—in the days when a half dozen or so would gather around him on the lawn or, during monsoon, under the covered car port leading to the main entrance of the house.

Osho, Laxmi told me, reads up to ten books a day. As food was for Ramakrishna, my feeling is that books are Osho's anchorage, his grounding, his way of staying in the body, something, he's told us from time to time, that becomes more and more difficult for him as time passes. I also recall him saying once that his reading, his books, had helped him prepare for the deluge of Westerners he always seemed to know would one day come. "Your authors," he'd said, "are the mirrors of your minds."

There'd been a lot of books in Woodlands, but compared to the Lao Tzu library the Bombay bookshelves had been bare. There must be thirty thousand books at least, from Freud to Raymond Chandler, Sri Aurobindo to Mark Twain. Long ago, the original library had spilled over into floor-to-ceiling cabinets that line the corridors of the house, inching, with each new shipment, down the hallway, closer and closer to the back door. The books are arranged helter-skelter by the colour of their bindings, and located through a complex card system—the Master's device, swears the Italian librarian Lalita, to short-circuit her once ordered, logical mind.

Half the balcony is used by her to air the books before Vivek takes them in to Osho. The allergies again. Explaining why we were all sniffed before seeing him, Laxmi had told me the doctors had warned her that the sannyasins either had to be spotlessly clean, wool- and dust- and perfume-free, or Osho would have to be enclosed in a glass bubble for discourses and darshan. In the daytime heat, even I find the pungent printers' ink a little nauseating.

I share the rest of the space with Veena, my old Kailash pal, my Dynamic Meditation mentor. She divides her day between editing discourses for Pratima and, under Vivek's supervision, sewing things for Osho or bits and pieces for his room.

The room, *his* room, is not fifteen yards away, just across the library and a little down the hall. And his presence permeates the house. It's as if, sitting at the typewriter working, he's standing beside me, cool and silent, all the time.

And here, working in the house where my Master lives, I begin to see something new about him, something I've never seen before. I see it through Vivek. Ordinariness.

On many occasions I'd heard Osho talk about enlightenment, saying that we are already enlightened, that buddhahood is our intrinsic nature, but that we'd simply forgotten, that remembering is all that's needed. Yet it never made sense to me. He always appeared so distant and different. And whenever I recalled that morning on the lawn when I looked into his eyes and encountered his emptiness, that vast expanse of his inner sky, any attempt to equate his state with mine flew straight out the window.

But sitting here at the typewriter, watching Vivek come and go from him to Lalita or to Veena, not eavesdropping but unable to help overhearing phrases like "fussy today" or "grumpy this morning", I begin to glimpse, albeit insubstantially, the paradox that is my Master.

One afternoon something starts to register. A gift arrives for him, a block of English cheddar and a big, glossy art book. I hear Vivek tell Veena we'll have the cheddar for tea. "If I give it to Osho and he likes it," she says with a laugh, "I'll have no peace. He'll want it all the time." And she tells Lalita to put the book away for the time being. "I'll save it until he's ill," she decides. "About the only way I can keep him in bed is with picture-books. When his body's sick it's like taking care of a little child. He can be so stubborn," she adds, her green eyes suddenly dewy and maternal.

"You locked him in once, I heard?" I venture, feeling it's okay to take a step forward now that she's opened a door.

She nods, giggling at the memory. "He was really sick. He'd been up coughing half the night. He told me in the morning he was fine, but I knew he wasn't—I'd heard him from my room. I said he shouldn't give a discourse, but he insisted. His body looked terrible, so I went out and locked the door behind me. I went to Laxmi and told her there'd be no discourse that morning." She shudders slightly. "I thought he'd be really angry with me, but he was far out. Since then he's much easier to take care of. When he's sick he lets me know."

At first, particularly over the cheddar and the art book, I'd been a bit taken aback. I don't know Vivek, but I do know her love for Osho and her total devotion to him. But thinking things over, I see she's recognized something in him that has eluded me and most other sannyasins—the ordinariness and the innocence of enlightenment. Being a Master is something else, but enlightenment, I am beginning to see, is ordinary, perhaps the only state of man that really is. As I'd put it to myself when I'd written that darshan commentary for Maneesha—like a tree, like the ocean is real.

Sitting here on the balcony, overlooking the garden, watching Mukta pottering among her plants, I am reminded of a saying of Jesus:

"Unless ye become like little children..." And a paragraph from *A Bird on the Wing* comes back to me as well: "I can make you most ordinary. I can make you simply human beings. I can make you like trees and birds. There is no magic around here, only religion. But if you can see, this is the greatest miracle."

"Veena," I ask, interrupting her sewing. "The book is finished and I've just done the introduction. It's quite brief. Would you read it to me and let me hear how it sounds?"

She reaches over for it, adjusts her glasses. "Some things in life are as ageless as the stars, as enduring as a smile," she reads. "Some things soar above impermanence and change and carry you to everlastingness. Truth is like this. And the words of Osho are like this.

"This volume is a mosaic, a mixed bag of tricks. There are one-liners to shock you, anecdotes to shake you and questions to stir your heart. There are tales to provoke you, talks to inspire you and treatises that will turn you into the very thirst for your own transformation.

"This book has everything. It's a tranquil lake; it's a roaring waterfall. It's the nightingale's song; it's the hornet's sting. It's a garden in the sunshine; it's the jungle on the darkest night.

"It's the long and the short and the all."

"What was that?" I hear behind me. I turn to see Vivek standing in the door.

"The introduction to the last book," I explain. "I've just finished it."

"I'm just on my way in," she says, whipping the sheet of paper from Veena's hand and turning on her heel. "I'll take it in and see what he has to say."

A few moments later she's back. "It's fine. He says you should title the book as well."

Masking my surprise, I look at the introduction she's returned to me, hoping for instant inspiration. "It's obvious," I say. "I'll just call it *The Long and the Short and the All.* Did he say what he wants me to do next?"

"Laxmi's coming back from Gujarat tonight and he wants to talk to her first. I don't know what he has in mind, but he said to tell you to take the rest of the day off. You know," she laughs, "in all these years this is the first time I've ever heard him tell *anyone* to take a day off!"

To say my curiosity has been piqued is an understatement. The next morning Laxmi tells me the deal for the palace in Kutch has, at least for the moment, fallen through. And so, it seems, has whatever new task it was Osho had in mind for me. I'm given a translation of a Hindi series on the fifteenth century weaver-mystic Kabir to edit.

After almost a year of Indian-English I face the twenty handwritten notebooks of Kabir without much enthusiasm. And I find myself wishing Laxmi's ardor were more infectious. Despite a disastrous press conference in Gujarat where she'd gone too far, offending the local Jains and delaying the move, she is undaunted, her optimism unscathed. "Let the dogs bark!" she poohs, dismissing the negative press reports. "Kutch will happen!"

Then, I resign myself, so will Kabir.

It's hard going at first, but I keep plugging away. Actually, when it comes right down to it, I'm finding a lot of things difficult these days. The flat's still a beautiful place to live, but we're all getting bored with planning menus, with shopping lists for the maid, with cooking, with making bread, with boiling milk every day. And now, working here in the commune, the distance is becoming a bit much, particularly during the lunch break. The library's closed from noon to two-thirty, and with it, access to the balcony. There's just nowhere to be, nowhere to go. For the first time, I'd really like to move into the commune now—and not have to wait for Gujarat.

Standing at the ironing board at home that evening, touching up a tablecloth and some napkins before Mukta, Arup and a few other friends arrive for dinner, I wonder just how much about us Osho really knows. Does he know, for example, I'd like to move into the commune now?

"Why are you bothering with that?" Virag asks, indicating the things I'm ironing.

"Why not?" I reply. "I like a nice looking table."

She laughs, heading towards the terrace with a handful of cutlery. "I'll bet you're the only sannyasin in Pune who sets the table every night with a tablecloth and napkins!"

The very next afternoon, Vivek appears on the balcony carrying a rust lacquered box. "House cleaning," she sighs, wiping a loose strand of hair out of her eyes. "Here, Veena," she says, setting the box in front of her and opening it to reveal an exquisite, hand-painted Japanese tea service, "Osho says this is for you."

She disappears, leaving Veena, Lalita and me lost in admiration and, on my side, a little envy.

"Here, Krishna Prem," I hear a moment later. "From Osho. For you." In my hand she lays, to my stunned amazement, an embroidered Kashmiri tablecloth and six matching napkins. He knows! He *does* know!

And, within a week, awaiting his arrival at discourse one morning, I suddenly feel a pair of hands on my shoulders and a mane of salt-and-pepper hair tumbling about my face. "Laxmi came to see me after darshan last night," the Greek's throaty voice whispers in my ear. "She'd just been to see Osho, and asked me to give a message to you."

"What is it?"

"Are you ready?" she teases.

"Mukta! Will you stop! Just tell me."

"She said to tell you that you and Divyananda can move into the commune today."

It's what I've been hoping for, what every sannyasin living outside hopes for—the call, the invitation to live in the commune. And yet I can hardly trust my ears. Even though I've been longing for this, the news is so unexpected and Mukta's laughing so hard, my immediate reaction is she's having me on. "You wouldn't joke about something like this, would you?" I ask, looking up at her anxiously. I can't get a word out of her—she just keeps on laughing. But the light shining in her eyes tells me it really is true—we are moving into the commune and, what's more, the invitation has come directly from him.

A sudden wave of relief washes over me. And it has nothing to do with economics, with being fed up trying to hold the whole rent and food trip together. It'll be beautiful to be cared for, not to have to think about money any more, but it's not that. It's something else. It's that I missed before. It's that I'm being given another chance.

In the early days of Pune, Osho had tried to bring me close. He'd paid me all kinds of attention, given me all sorts of juice—and I'd run away, terrified at the possibility of disappearing, of dissolving into his emptiness. Since I've been back I've worked for him and for the commune, but I've been peripheral, stuck in hotels and flats, skirting the edges of the community growing around him. Yet the moment I'd asked to be closer he'd put me on the balcony of Lao Tzu. And he must know what's been happening to me there—because now there's this.

When at last he arrives for the discourse, I wait until he mounts the podium and turns, in greeting, in my direction. Whether he sees me or hears me is irrelevant. "I'm ready now, Osho," my heart calls silently. "This time, whatsoever you ask of me, I'm ready and I surrender."

Divy is equally prepared when I tell him. "Just get out of the way," he shouts, tossing our suitcases into the centre of the room. "And go get a rickshaw. I'll be ready long before you get back!"

A new home, a new job

There's no need for an alarm clock in the commune—the music of Dynamic Meditation rocks me out of bed, dot on six. And by seven-thirty, lecture cushions tucked under our arms, Divy and I join the residents' queue as it inches its way under the noses of the sniffers into Buddha Hall.

Since the July Guru Poornima celebration, a whiz-bang wingding of Indian kirtan and Western rock, we've been using the new auditorium for English discourses. After the close confines of Chuang Tzu, where darshan and the smaller Hindi lectures are still held, the space in Buddha Hall is wonderful. It's just so nice to be able to sit with Osho, listening to him, without a pair of knees poking me in the back.

They're cold, these end-of-November mornings, and everyone's huddled under cotton shawls, edges carefully secured under cushion corners as extra protection against the cement chill of the floor.

What's happened during monsoon to the plants and trees that ring the oval hall is remarkable—things have doubled, tripled in height and lushness, filtering the early sunlight and sheltering us from the cool winter breezes blowing in across the high Deccan plateau.

The silence is the best. "Pin-drop," Laxmi always calls it. It is full, expectant; it is the love that beats in two thousand hearts. Utterly still we sit, in shades of orange and ochre, red and rust, arranged in arching rows before the white marble podium and the empty armchair that, like us, await Osho.

The crunch of approaching wheels on gravel is the sign. A shiver of anticipation runs through the hall. A few heads turn to watch the orange Impala pull up to the marble walkway that leads into the auditorium, to watch Vishnu open the car door, but most prefer the moment he is suddenly there, at the top of the stairs, beaming, glowing, gliding towards the platform.

I like to watch him greet us best of all. And every morning I make for a certain spot that affords me a particular angle. It's the favourite part of the day for me, those few seconds it takes him to turn a slow half-circle, palms meeting before him in greeting, in namaste.

In many ways, that tiny fragment of time says everything to me. In many ways, it's what being with him is all about. It's so faint as to be almost imperceptible, but he's reeling. Blissed right out. Stoned on God. Drunk with the divine. For me, it's a daily contact-high. Every morning, before he speaks, as attentively as I can, I watch his drunkenness. Then I close my eyes. And it carries me away.

Sitting there, his voice reaching me over the speakers, I am newly amazed, each day, at what flows out of the space of oceanic blissfulness. To speak, he'd said, is torture for him, but that, as we are, it's the only way he has to contact us. But he only speaks, he's said, to seduce us into silence.

And despite his staggering clarity, his faultless reason, his exquisite poetry, I find myself less and less able to focus on his words. What I'm beginning to hear, more and more, is the gap between them, the silence out of which they come.

He has a peculiar way of trailing his words, of leaving a wake behind each one, and this is where my attention is. It's as if I'm being carried along in his current, along some cosmic chute, dropping, as each word ends, over a waterfall, into the pool of his silence. I am lifted and dropped, lifted and dropped, over and over again, until I am immersed, floating in stillness, his words far away, like distant music. All that seems to reach me are the jokes. I rise on wings of laughter, bubbling upwards, and when the joke ends I fall inwards again, back into the silence.

And even when the discourse ends with his "Enough for today?" and he's gone, the silence remains. Each sannyasin carries it with them, softly and tenderly, out of Buddha Hall. It takes me a couple of cups of coffee in our room before I'm ready for people.

For most of the day, Buddha Hall is the focal point, its sophisticated PA system filling our six acres with the sound of its activities. As I sit down at the typewriter on the balcony in Lao Tzu, I can hear the morning's Sufi dancing, the slightly off-key voice of Aneeta, the blonde Californian "Sufi princess", mingling with the blare from a room, where a band of boutique seamstresses twang along with Dolly Parton on cassette. And from the roof of Krishna House, when Aneeta gives it a rest, there's the laughter from Prasad's Centring Group, or, from Radha Hall just below, the intermittent change-your-partner gong of Enlightenment Intensive and the leader's persuasive tones as she guides participants through the question, "Tell me who you are."

Afternoons are somehow quieter, more subdued. From the taped discourse in Buddha Hall, Osho whispers through the trees, followed by the gentle, soothing hum of the Nadhabrahma meditation. Even the groups seem more tranquil—the only sounds of growth, the muffled cries of catharsis filtering from the basement therapy chambers into the Vrindavan garden when we break for tea.

On the balcony the days course by. Lalita's inside for the most part, occupied with the library, and neither Veena nor I are much into conversation of late. As a break from proofreading, Virag's weeding Lao Tzu lawn for Mukta every once in a while. She's still living at the flat and we have the occasional little chat through the shrubbery. But, for the most part, it's just me and the book, just me and Kabir.

At five-thirty, when the cascading notes of the Kundalini meditation in Buddha Hall signal the approach of the end of the working day, I'm always surprised it's over, wondering where it's gone.

With his usual decorating aplomb and an early but well-timed hundred Christmas dollars from his dad, Divy's transformed our room, making it cosy and comfortable. When Mukta first showed it to us, we were a bit dismayed. It was one of the row off Radha Hall that had reminded me, when Laxmi had bought Krishna House, of a series of kennels for giant dogs. Dark and dismal and reeking of dhal, it had just been vacated by an Indian couple who'd gone back to Rajasthan to open a meditation centre.

We repainted it right away, a vague shade of mushroom, and Divy splashed another Japanese cherry tree across one wall. Mukta had given us some leftover white enamel for the single window and the door, and we'd used it in the shower stall as well, only to watch it peel off in great gobs from the humidity the very same day it finally dried.

We'd brought our mattresses and bolsters from the flat, and in the khadi shops down Laxmi Road, found nubbly hand-loomed cotton to cover them, a grainy neutral shade to match the new sisal matting on the floor. We'd rented a low cupboard, reminiscent of French-Canadian country pine, and between the beds, Divy placed a lamp he'd made, resting it on a sheet of glass floating on legs of lacquered bamboo. I love it. It's a beautiful room to come home to.

And after the hustle and bustle of the day, commune evenings are surprisingly quiet. Once the muffled melodies of the music group in Buddha Hall fade away, almost no sounds reach the room at all. Except for an occasional peal of laughter or the hushed tones of a strolling couple's conversation, there is total silence.

Apart from Mukta and sporadic visits from Virag, Prageet or Rani, guests are rare. It's as if those who live here in the commune are so satiated with people during the day, with people in groups, with people doing meditations, with people just milling about, that when night falls they seek the company of a few intimates or the solitude of their own rooms.

Mukta's a great walker and, knowing my love for wandering through the velvety Indian darkness, she's taken to dropping by most evenings to invite me for a stroll. One afternoon I send her a note asking if she'll be dropping by tonight. There's something I want to talk to her about.

"Want to tell me now?" she asks, after we've meandered up and down a few tree-canopied streets.

"A few days ago in discourse," I begin, "Osho looked at me as he left. At least I thought he did. But then I just told myself not to be silly, that everyone in this section was telling himself the same thing.

"But the next morning it happened again: he looked at me as he left. And a little voice in my head asked, 'Get it?' I spent the rest of the day wondering, 'Get what?'

"And then another strange thing happened. That very afternoon three separate people talked to me about the bad publicity the commune's getting in the Indian newspapers and magazines. But what struck me as odd was that not one of these three people had any idea I used to do public relations work in the West before I took sannyas.

"And I still can't shake the feeling that they're connected—his looking at me, the voice saying 'Get it?' and the people talking to me about publicity."

"Have you written Osho about it?" Mukta wants to know.

"No. Do you think I should?"

"I do," she answers. "I most definitely do."

Before getting into bed that night I write to him, outlining what's been happening, telling him what I did in Canada and asking if I'm right in feeling there's something in the area of public relations or publicity he wants me to do. Running into Vivek on my way to the balcony the following morning, I hand her the note. A bit later I look up from the typewriter to find her standing beside my desk, a big grin on her face. "He said to tell you, you got it. He said that's what he was trying to tell you. Journalists are starting to come and more are on the way. He wants you to set up a press office to handle them."

And I knew that if I hadn't understood his non-verbal message, I wouldn't have been ready to do what it is he now wants me to do.

Vivek and Veena's laughter following me, I'm off down the Lao Tzu corridor, skipping and jumping in glee, heading for the gardens to find Divy and Mukta. I locate them in the little vegetable garden near Buddha Hall. "Hey, you guys!" I shout the moment I catch sight of them. "Guess what? I've got a new job! I'm going to do PR for God!"

Chapter Five: 1977-1978

THE PRESS OFFICE

Before I know it, the fledgling press office has a staff of two—me and Mangala, a bosomy, English-born ex-journalist from New Zealand, an office-warming present from Pratima's publications department. Veena's been relocated, Elna sewing machine and all, and we have a whole half of Lao Tzu balcony to ourselves. In the beginning the library hours had driven me to distraction—we would want to work; they would want to close—but after a hassle with Vivek, intervention by Osho and a nod from Mukta, one of the gardeners had built us a series of stone steps, and we enter and exit our office with a swing of a leg over the balcony railing, as if we were boarding or jumping ship.

While I continue with the yet-unfinished book on Kabir, Mangala wades her way through a tall stack of English, American and Indian magazines, looking for possibilities for articles on the commune. A few bits and pieces, shallow and inaccurate, have appeared in small-circulation yoga and new-age periodicals in the UK and in the USA, but nothing of any import or value. We're pretty much an unknown quantity to everyone, it seems, but ourselves.

One chilly December morning, however, I see we're not as invisible to the outside world as I'd thought. "Krishna Prem," one of the Lao Tzu gate guards calls down the driveway, "can you go to the office right away? There's a journalist here from *TIME* magazine."

"*TIME*?" Mangala says, swivelling around in her chair. "Well, KP, nothing like starting at the top!"

Larry Malcolm is cynical, opinionated, a know-it-all. He's obviously very fond of himself, and I find I rather like him too. He informs me that, as *TIME's* New Delhi correspondent, he's more at home with Afghani wars, Bangladesh famines and Pakistani coups than "spiritual India". I sense the put-down immediately. Although he feigns openness, pretending there isn't a preconceived idea in his head, I see he's already decided we're a bunch of Western drop-outs on a dead-end street and that Osho is taking the lot of us for a very profitable ride. He's going to be a challenge, and I look forward to several days of mental jousting, of good old parry and thrust. After my in-depth editing of all those books, I doubt there's a topic in existence I couldn't grace with Osho's view.

His partner is Parsi, Jehangir Gazdar from Bombay. "Jungo," Malcolm tells me, encircling his colleague's shoulder affectionately, "is one of India's top international photographers. In my books, he's the best. I always use him for *TIME*."

The next couple of days are spent squiring them around the commune. We sit through Dynamic, Sufi dancing, Kundalini, music group, Malcolm and I quietly nattering while Jungo clicks away. And we go through each and every department in detail. We watch cutters snipping fabric, potters throwing clay, weavers threading looms, children learning numbers, jewellers grinding stones, instrument-makers stringing guitars, woodworkers fashioning boxes, bakers kneading bread, photographers developing film, artists sketching layouts, proofreaders checking galleys, silk-screeners printing stationery, books of Osho's discourses being crated and shipped from the warehouse. It's a hive of non-stop activity—creative, productive and filled with happy, loving people. And I can see that, in spite of himself, Malcolm is very impressed.

The reports he's heard of sexual perversities and permissiveness he deals with himself. "I'll bet there's less fucking going on here than in any other six acres in the world," he says one afternoon, puffing hungrily on a bidi. "You people work so hard, where would you find the time and energy?"

But about looking in on the therapy groups he's more insistent. So am I. I just say no. When Osho had been told *TIME* was here he'd sent me a message. "He says," Laxmi informed me, "tell Krishna Prem to be loving and friendly with them and to show them what they want to see, but he should also make them aware that it doesn't matter to us what they write, positive or negative. Whatsoever they write, the work will continue." And about visiting the cathartic groups, Laxmi herself draws the line.

Once, long before the press office began, she had allowed a *STERN* photographer to shoot in Teertha's Encounter group. The journalist with him, *STERN's* Andrees Elten, had done the group to write an article, and both he and the photographer, Jay Ullal, had taken sannyas. When this happened, she agreed to the photos. But after the article had been through the hands of *STERN* editors, the photos, inadequately explained, just looked bizarre, frightening to anyone who didn't understand what was going on. And a decision had been reached—no journalists or photographers in cathartic groups. Apart from the obvious risks of misrepresentation, this one experience showed Laxmi it wasn't fair to the participants either, being put on display like monkeys in a zoo. I explain all this to Malcolm and take him to a few non-cathartic groups—Centring, Zazen, Vipassana, Enlightenment Intensive. He's not satisfied. I shrug my shoulders: "This is how it is here." I tell him he'll have to make do with interviewing Teertha, leader of the Encounter group, and also suggest Geet Govind, the former Dick Price, a new sannyasin and founder of California's famous Esalen Institute.

The interview with Geet Govind is a bit dreary. He's still too new to have the unique sannyasin sparkle, but I can see talking to him is doing something for Malcolm. The fact that the respected founder of Esalen has come to Osho is giving us a new standing in his jaundiced journalistic eye.

Teertha, on the other hand, is bang on. He answers Malcolm's questions quietly, unhurriedly and with intelligence, explaining how the Encounter technique is different here with Osho, and putting the few breaks and sprains that have happened into their proper perspective. Malcolm, for once, is attentive. I can feel he trusts and respects

Teertha. Sensing it as well, Teertha suddenly begins talking to the man, forgetting the journalist. It's nothing terribly overt, as in a group situation; it's just that beneath the surface of his words are messages for Malcolm, mirrors in which, if he wishes, he can encounter himself. He allows Teertha in for a few moments—and the feeling in the room is beautiful—but I watch his fear beginning to arise, and then there's an abrupt cut-off, both to the interview and to his introspection.

He's silent for a long while after Teertha leaves, as if he's digesting. I wait, saying nothing. Finally he coughs, as if to break his reverie. "Impressive," he says. "Impressive."

He needs rescuing. "Tonight's your last night. You've already been to discourses and seen Osho there, so this evening I'll take you and Jungo to darshan," I say. "But first, let's go spend some time with Laxmi. You've been asking about money. She'll tell you what you want to know."

Malcolm will be Laxmi's first contact with the press since the Gujarat debacle where she berated rather than beguiled, and, escorting *TIME* into her office, I find myself hoping she'll behave. She has a naughty streak as wide as the ocean and as unpredictable as it is deep. But with Malcolm she's polite and friendly, playing the hostess to the hilt, pressing more tea and cakes on him with each bite he takes. Jungo photographs while they talk.

"This is a charitable trust, I gather," he opens.

"Yes," Laxmi replies. "Registered in Bombay."

"And you are the Managing Trustee?"

Indian-style, she wobbles her head from side to side in assent.

"And how long have you been with, uh," he hesitates, as if the strange name is sticking in his craw. "With, uh, Osho?" he manages at last.

"Lives."

He looks at her as if she's from another planet.

"He means *this* time around, Laxmi," I interject, throwing her a meaningful glance.

Her eyes twinkle. "One forgets what time means to you people," she says, her tone intended to be apologetic, at least to his ears. Me, she's not fooling for a second. "For us, you see, time does not exist," she says. "But one understands your questions. In your terms, twelve, fifteen years perhaps. Something like that. One isn't so concerned with these things."

"And you administer this whole show?" he asks, waving grandly, as if to encompass the entire commune in one sweeping gesture.

Like an arrow, a finger darts towards Osho's picture. "It's him! On the outside, Laxmi may be instrument—that one doesn't deny. But it's him. And Laxmi is *in* him!"

He doesn't have a clue what she's talking about. "You've only been here in Pune a few years," he tries again. "And all these books of his talks?" he asks, indicating the brimming bookshelves behind Laxmi. "And everything that is made in your workshops. How does all this happen?"

"Love."

He leans forward, one ear cocked, as if he's heard her incorrectly. "Love?"

"Love."

She offers nothing more. She just sits in her chair, at ease, totally relaxed, smiling at him. His discomfort is almost painful. I realize I'll have to try to explain what she means to him later. The funny thing is that she's right, that love is what makes all the work and creativity happen—but with a journalist, a little background's in order.

I'm enjoying the repartee, but it's not getting the work done. I shoot Laxmi the closest thing to a dirty look I can muster. And I dive in after Malcolm again. "He wants to know where the money comes from, Laxmi."

"Money?" Her arms lift towards the heavens as if to catch the rupee notes as they fall. "Money? Money happens."

This time my look *is* dirty. She gets it. "Look here," she begins, leaning towards him with an intensity that propels him backwards in his chair, "in this commune, psychological approach is used. A small charge is there for discourse. This keeps curious, uninterested away. At one time no charge was there. And what did we have? Rickshaw drivers coming to put hands up dresses of our women. This is not the way. So now, five rupees. Five rupees is nothing, but enough to make these people stay away.

"But one thing we tell you," she adds, warming to her subject, "if someone comes who is thirsty for Osho and no money is in the pocket, Laxmi is the last person to turn him away. Over fifty per cent of people in discourse and meditation camps are admitted free of charge.

"This gate is never closed. Many people are coming now from all over the world. We are practical people—we need money to live; we need money to grow. And no one who comes here for Osho can be turned away. Who are *we* to say this one can be allowed to search for God and this one cannot? It is up to us, his children, to make sure that thirsty people from all over the world can come and drink him. Thousands have come and thousands more are on the way.

"Commune *must* grow.

"And meditation camps," she continues. "Ten days' meditation; one hundred rupees. This is also nothing, but it is also psychological. If someone has paid for cinema, even if he does not like the film he will remain to the end. This is how human mind works. Same with meditation camp. Five meditations a day are there, his morning discourse, taped discourse in the afternoon. If someone has paid his hundred rupees, he wants money's worth—and he will put his total energy into the techniques. And Osho's techniques are *very* scientifical. Something *will* happen for him.

"But remember one thing." She wags her finger sternly at him. "We have never and will never go to public for money," she says proudly. "We never beg!"

"And the groups?" he asks. "You charge for them?"

"Of course charge is there!" She's getting impatient and I figure it's almost time to usher Malcolm and Jungo away. "But much less than in America or in Europe. Laxmi is told that for one weekend in Esalen, in America—for same cost, mind you!—one can fly to India, do groups and even pay hotel expenses! And, we tell you, cream of world's group leaders are here."

"One last question," he announces to my relief. "What is your major source of income?"

"Books."

"But how, in such a short time, have you managed to build this commune and print so many books? How have you done it?"

"You see," she replies sweetly, leaning back in her chair and retying her bandana, "it just happens. Nobody *does* anything. It just happens."

Malcolm's face is a study in consternation. "But how?" he insists. "How?"

"Laxmi already told you," she answers simply. "Love."

The boys from *TIME* have invited me out for a farewell dinner after darshan, an event photographer Jungo adored, and journalist Malcolm abhorred. Watching him squirm as sannyasins came and went before Osho, it was obvious he was getting nothing out of it and couldn't wait for it to end. After darshan I send him and Jungo on ahead, agreeing to meet them at the restaurant. I invited Mangala to join us and, frankly, am ready for a few moments on my own before another bout of questions.

But there aren't any. Only conclusions. Malcolm must cry "I've got it!" a dozen times throughout the meal, his fist raised in jubilant self-salute. And each and every time, from something that has happened to me, out of my own experience with Osho, I send his theory flying out the window.

A long time ago, in darshan, Osho had spoken to me about borrowed knowledge. "Unless knowledge comes from your experience, Krishna Prem, don't befool yourself by speaking as if you know," he said. "Nothing is wrong with not knowing. But this does not mean you can't speak either. Just be honest—give a credit, quote your source." As a result, back in the West, my conversations must have been excruciatingly boring, peppered as they were with "Osho says..." But as the years went by and more and more glimpses happened for me, I found I didn't need to quote Osho so often, that I began to speak out of my own experience. "When you speak out of your own direct experience," he told me that night, "there is an authority in your voice, an authority that comes from your very being. It is an authority no one can argue with, no one can shake, no one can dispute."

Tonight, with *TIME,* I see the proof.

"Let all workers hear Meeta's darshan in Buddha Hall at lunchtime," I hear Laxmi say to Arup one morning during their daily post-discourse get-together.

At noon, a curious and somewhat apprehensive commune work force, some five hundred strong, gathers to hear what Osho said to Meeta, one of the office typists, in darshan the night before. Arup, with her usual Dutch punctuality, briefly explains Osho wants us all to hear the tape.

Over the loudspeakers comes Meeta's thin, child-like voice: "I've been typing for a year and a half now and my heart isn't in it. And it never was. And I've been doing it because it needs to be done. I just feel I'd rather be doing some sort of work I'd enjoy more."

There's a pause. Then Osho's voice comes. It's stern. "If everybody is going to enjoy, then who is going to do the work?" he asks. "Only I? It is perfectly good—enjoy—but then you don't share any work with me. Everybody wants to just go into the garden; nobody wants to work anywhere. Then why should I? I can also go into the garden!

"This idea arises because the commitment, the involvement is not there. You are working just for your own sake, not for my sake; otherwise there would be no trouble and no problem. Once that starts happening to you, that you are working for me, then it is not work—this is your way to help my work; this is your love towards me. Then there is no problem. Otherwise, do you think Laxmi would like to be in the office? Everybody will be in the garden except me!" His deep, rumbling chuckle rolls over us, sparking a few nervous giggles here and there. "Then how am *I* going to do everything? I have been inviting thousands of people here and much work is going to happen and everybody wants to escape from the work.

"Just change your attitude and see. For two months, work for me—forget yourself. If that doesn't work then I will change you from there. Then you can do whatsoever you feel like doing, hmmm?"

Leaving Buddha Hall, everyone is silent, thoughtful. "We sleepy people," Laxmi often says of us—and I see today how easily we lose sight of what Osho is trying to do, how we forget, immersed in our own wee worlds, the role each of us has to play in our Master's game. And walking back to the balcony, to the press office, I'm reminded of a piece from one of my Indian-English re-edits. Speaking of Swami Vivekananda, Ramakrishna's apostle to America, Osho had said he'd died a disappointed man, unable to find a hundred men with the courage to step forth and be transformed. "I have no intention of dying like that," Osho had said. "And when I die," I also recall him saying, "I don't want there to be anyone in the world who can say, 'How come I missed him? How come I never heard of him?'"

And it's abundantly clear to me what I have to do. News of his availability is already spreading—through books and tapes, a monthly magazine and a fortnightly newsletter, and a growing network of centres around the world—and now he wants to use the media. And it's up to me. As Laxmi says: "Word must reach!"

One morning in discourse, just exactly what his work is, just exactly what we're involved in, is laid out for us with crystal clarity. I'd seen "the work" as telling the world about Osho, and taken it no further. But he has something else up his sleeve. And the magnitude of it boggles my tiny little mind.

In recent months he's been speaking a lot on Buddha. Now it's *The Diamond Sutra.*

"Twenty-five centuries before, just some day, early in the morning, just like this day, this sutra was born," he had told us in the opening discourse of the series. "Twelve hundred and fifty monks were present. It happened in the city of Sravasti.

"Buddha must have loved this city of Sravasti, because out of forty-five years of his ministry, he stayed in Sravasti twenty-five years. He must have loved the people. The people must have been of a very evolved consciousness. All the great sutras of Buddha, almost all, were born in Sravasti.

"This sutra, *The Diamond Sutra,* was also born in Sravasti. The Sanskrit name of this sutra is *Tajrachchedika Prajnaparamita Sutra.* It means, 'Perfection of wisdom which cuts like a thunderbolt'. If you allow, Buddha can cut you like a thunderbolt. He can behead you. He can kill you and help you to be reborn.

"A Buddha has to be both—a murderer and a mother. On the one hand he has to kill; on another hand he has to give a new being to you. The new being is possible only when the old has been destroyed. Only on the ashes of the old, the new is born. Man is a phoenix. The mythological bird, phoenix, is not just a mythology, it is a metaphor. It stands for man. That phoenix nowhere exists except in man. Man is the being who has to die to be reborn."

That had been his introduction. The thunderbolt came a few days later.

This particular morning's sutra reported a dialogue between Buddha and Subhuti, a disciple who'd become a bodhisattva, the last stage before buddhahood. Near the end of the discourse, Osho repeats the sutra, referring to it again: "Subhuti asked: 'Will there be any beings in the future period, in the last time, in the last epoch, in the last five hundred years, at the time of the collapse of the good doctrine, who, when these words of the sutra are being taught, will understand their truth?'

"Now you will be surprised," Osho says. "*This* is the time Subhuti is talking about, and you are the people. Twenty-five hundred years have passed. Subhuti has asked about you." It's as if an earthquake has hit Buddha Hall. My eyes fly open. All around me, everyone is rigid with attention, focused on Osho, on the unbelievable, wonderful thing he is saying.

"Buddha has said," he continues, "that whenever a religion is born, whenever a buddha turns the wheel of dhamma, naturally, slowly slowly the wheel starts stopping. It loses momentum, hmmm? You turn a wheel. It will start moving. Then by and by, by and by, a moment will come when it will stop.

"When a buddha moves the wheel of dhamma it takes two thousand five hundred years for it to stop completely. After each five hundred years it goes on losing momentum. So those are the five ages of the dhamma. After each five hundred years, the dhamma will be less and less, decreased and decreased and decreased, and after twenty-five centuries the wheel will stop again. It will need another buddha to turn it for the coming twenty-five centuries.

"Buddha is talking about *you.* The sutra is being read to you. Twenty-five centuries have passed. Subhuti has asked about *you.*"

My whole body is shivering and at the same time I'm on fire. But it's beautiful. There's nothing standing between him and me—I'm just open, attentive, expanded, letting him in.

"The other day," he goes on, "I had told you that many of you will become bodhisattvas. Many of you are on the way. It is strange that Subhuti should ask such a question. And more strange is that Buddha says, 'Those people after twenty-five centuries will not be less fortunate than you but will be more fortunate.'

"Why? I have been telling you many times that you are ancient ones, that you have walked on this earth many, many times, that you are not listening to dhamma for the first time, that you have come across many buddhas in your past lives—sometimes maybe a Krishna and sometimes maybe a Christ and sometimes maybe a Mahavir and sometimes maybe a Mohammed—but you have come across many, many buddhas, many enlightened people.

"And you are fortunate to know so many buddhas. And if you become a little alert, all the seeds that have been sown in you by the past buddhas will start blooming, will sprout. You will start flowering...

"The wheel that Buddha moved has stopped. The wheel has to be moved again. And that is going to be my and your life-work. That wheel has to be moved again. Once it starts revolving it will have again twenty-five-centuries' life. Once it starts moving it goes on moving for twenty-five centuries at least.

"And it has to be done again and again and again because everything loses momentum, everything functions under the laws of nature—entropy. You throw a stone, you throw with great energy, but it goes a few hundred feet and it falls down. Exactly like that, dhamma has to be made again and again alive. Then it breathes for twenty-five centuries and then dies. Everything that is born has to die.

"And you are the people Buddha is talking about. And you are the people I am depending on. The wheel of dhamma has stopped. It has to be turned again."[7]

Life-work. The word moves me strangely. Puffing on an after-discourse bidi in my room, I find myself, in the midst of pondering the scope and grandeur of my Master's vision and design, wondering why that particular word touches me so. And then, all at once, a memory from my childhood comes rushing over me. I'm surprised, in a way, that I'd forgotten it—it had been of such significance when I was young.

At what age it was most intense I can't recall, but I can see, in my mind's eye, the fat little kid I then was, in the privacy of his attic sanctuary, gleaning glossy magazines for pictures of Indian sadhus. And I remember the knowing, that almost mystical knowing many children have, that one day I too would be a holy man in India. And coupled with it was the knowledge that I would also, some day, meet a Jesus face to face. And they've happened. Both boyhood presentiments have come to pass.

"You are ancient ones," he'd also said this morning. "You have come across many buddhas in your past lives." I know I've been with Osho before, in Tibet, and it's suddenly apparent that this feeling about India and Jesus as a child was not really a precognition but, in actual fact, a vague remembering that Osho had promised to return in some future time and bring us together again. And what he's gathered us to do makes me marvel. He made it clear today: our task is to bring religion back to the world. But not religion as we know it. "Why be a Christian," he'd asked one day, "when you can become a Christ?" That religion. *Real* religion.

---

7. *The Diamond Sutra*

And my role in all of this? Exposure. As much exposure as possible. I've got to fill the press with him. "If you want to help somebody," I remember him saying when he spoke to me about starting a press office, "the first thing is they have to know you exist." Well, TIME isn't a bad start, I admit. But it's just the beginning. I want more for Osho. Much, much more.

The First Car

Almost overnight, it seems, the press office doubles. There'd been a spate of Indian journalists all at once, including a delightful Parsi lady, Bachi Karkaria, from the country's biggest English-language rotogravure, *The Illustrated Weekly of India*—all rushing to have a look at the Mercedes Laxmi had bought for ten-lakh rupees to ferry Osho the few hundred yards from Lao Tzu House to Buddha Hall and back once a day.

It had been his solution to a problem Laxmi couldn't resolve. Money was low—she confessed to me one evening there was just enough left in the kitty to feed him for a week—and she had been turned down by every bank she approached. Despite the obvious profit potential, no one was interested in financing the operation and its expansion.

When she explained the situation to Osho, she told me, he said to go to New Delhi and buy the most expensive car in India. As usual, she took his advice without question. She travelled to Delhi, toured the imported car dealers and, with the help of a wealthy local sannyasin, returned to Pune with a Mercedes the colour of Dijon mustard. The very next morning we were on the front page of *The Times of India* and every other major daily in the country. And three bankers dropped by with offers of assistance that very afternoon.

But whether it was the car or curiosity that was drawing the journalists here, I didn't miss a chance to give the grand tour, the grand rap. "Blabber!" is Laxmi's only guideline. Well, I figure, if hot air will help turn the wheel of dhamma, Osho's certainly picked the right guy.

Sparked by news about the luxury car, requests start pouring in from magazines, mostly Indian, for excerpts from discourses, for photos and articles on the commune and our activities. Mangala has just about all she can handle already, editing, coordinating—and we need a writer. Madhura packs in her knitting needles and says she'll give it a try, but her promise outweighs her performance and, with a graceful English upper lip, she abandons the Muse for typing and the files.

There is a journalist around, a thin, balding, former House of Commons reporter, but Laxmi's told me not to touch him with a barge pole. He'd apparently written a couple of pieces so negative and awful that Osho, after he'd read them, had sent him a message, saying he could drop sannyas if he wished. But Subhuti, distraught yet tenacious, had tried again—this time with an article for *The Guardian* on Pramod, a one-time British diplomat and EEC official. He'd sent it in to Osho. And it must have been his redemption. When I ask for him again, Osho agrees, making it clear that he still has reservations but that the decision is mine. Subhuti joins us on the balcony. And now we're four.

The BBC

"Krishna Prem!" the Lao Tzu gate guard shouts down the drive. "Now the BBC is here!"

"How do you do? I'm Tony Isaacs. From the BBC. Executive Producer of *The World About Us.*" My hand is engulfed in a massive fist and pumped heartily up and down. "I was just on my way back to London from China and I thought I'd drop by for a chat." I start to laugh, liking him right away. He makes it sound as if he's just come from MG Road. "We've heard rather a lot about you chaps at the Beeb, you know. Wouldn't mind coming and doing a film on you."

Laxmi also likes this big, burly Englishman with the short curly hair and the hefty Jewish nose. She spreads her hands in a gesture of welcome. "Our gates are open."

He invites me to join him that evening for a drink in the Blue Diamond bar. Mangala's out for a few days with a kidney infection, so

I take Madhura along. And she floors me. She is absolutely spectacular, right in her element. As the evening progresses, it's quite obvious that Madhura has a new role in the press office and that we'd better find another secretary.

The next morning, straight after discourse, still excited about last night, I rush into Laxmi's room. I tell her what happened with Madhura, how well we worked together, and how effective it had been, having a man and a woman dealing with journalists together. "We had a wonderful time, Laxmi," I say. "Whenever I shocked, she soothed. When I was hard, she was soft; when I appealed to his logic, she went straight for his heart. It was fantastic. We had such a good time. And so much happened—for the work."

"Fine about Madhura," she laughs. "So find another secretary. Now, swamiji, tell Laxmi about BBC man."

"His program is a big one, Laxmi, *The World About Us.* It's shown in England first, then syndicated worldwide—America, Australia, New Zealand, Canada, all over. It reaches millions and millions of people.

"What he wants to do is go back to London, put together a proposal and submit it to the Indian government. You know, ever since that 1969 Louis Malle documentary on Calcutta, permission to film in India is needed.

"He's also aware that another BBC program wants to come. You know, those letters we've had from Peter Armstrong of *Everyman,* the BBC's religious series? Well, Tony thinks they *both* might come—looking at us from two different angles.

"He wants to send a film crew here, about eight people, for at least three weeks. They'll stay at the Blue Diamond and we'll only have to handle them during the day. And I really like his idea—he wants to put someone through the process."

"Through the process?" Laxmi repeats, not getting the point.

"The process—meditation camp, groups, the whole thing. There's a reporter called Jack Pizzey Tony wants to send. He says he realizes the risk, that Pizzey might take sannyas, but that's the way he wants to do it. The whole thing sounds terrific to me."

"You said okay?"

"I said okay."

"Good," she says, standing to go see Osho. "Laxmi will let him know."

"One other thing," I add, stopping her at the door. "I asked him what made him want to film us. He said, 'You people are becoming a force the world can't ignore any longer. It's time to take a good look at you and assess what you mean to society as we know it.'"

"Hmmm," Laxmi murmurs. "Interesting."

"I asked him if people looked on us as some kind of a threat, because that was the implication."

"And what did he say?"

"He said, 'Not yet.'"

"Smart man," Laxmi calls over her shoulder as she heads down the hall towards Osho's room. "As world is, love *is* a threat. This Tony Isaacs is smart man."

I wish I could say the same for Larry Malcolm and his editors.

"Don't be too disappointed in it," Jungo warns me by telephone from Bombay. "Larry was very impressed and wrote quite a favourable article—I saw the draft. He just called from Delhi. He's seen an advance copy and is pretty unhappy with what they've done with it. You know how *TIME* works—reports come in from correspondents and then they're rewritten in New York to suit the magazine's style."

After the issue hits the stands, Jungo calls again. "What did Osho think of it?" he wants to know.

I pass along what Laxmi had told me: "He said, 'At least they didn't call me a charlatan.'"

Jungo laughs nervously. "And you? What did you think?"

"I thought it was a piece of shit."

But the article in *TIME* shows me one thing—in the game of religion, negative publicity attracts more than positive does. Within the next week I meet dozens of people who've come to Pune as a direct result of the snide, sneering, smart-ass *TIME* report. "When I read the article," one lady from Texas tells me, "I figured if *TIME* is putting it down, something really incredible must be happening there. So here I am."

Vasumati

"Krishna Prem," Madhura says, introducing me to a plump, curly-haired girl in her mid-twenties, "this is Vasumati."

Standing outside the front gate, we talk for a while. She's a trained librarian, had been a secretary at the Architects' Association in London, and is in Pune to stay. This is her second time here, she tells me, and she's done all the groups Osho's suggested. "Now I'm ready to dive in, to work," she says. I like her. She's cocky.

"Fine with me," I say. "When can you start?"

"This afternoon, if you want," she shrugs. She has strikingly beautiful eyes, green and clear and piercing. They've been on me since we've been talking. All of a sudden, fixing me with a gaze so penetrating it takes me aback, she says, "You look like the devil." And then she laughs.

I don't know what to say. I look at her for a moment. She returns it, unwavering. There's an undercurrent of something I can't quite put my finger on. All I know is that I feel uncomfortable. "Madhura," I say, turning away, "arrange for her to work with us on Lao Tzu balcony."

She lays a hand on my arm. "My name is Vasumati."

"Vasumati," I repeat as I stride back through the gate.

Apart from a whirlwind visit from the German film-maker Charles Wilp and a slow trickle of Indian journalists from small magazines, things in the press office are quiet. Mangala's kidney infection has laid her flat, Madhura's off with a crew to book fairs in Madras and Bangalore, and Subhuti's involved in an article for *East-West Journal* on Aneeta, the Sufi dancing lady. He's rarely on the balcony. I spy him around the commune from time to time, trailing Aneeta like a lovesick puppy. This leaves Vasumati and me. And Kabir. I'm down to the last couple of chapters and typing like a madman.

I like Vasumati. And I find myself really enjoying the time with her. She makes me laugh. She'd been born in London and raised in

Rhodesia (now Zimbabwe), a Jewish Princess with five servants, a big house, a swimming pool and acres of garden. Her dad's a doctor; her mother, a speech therapist. She has one sister, studying gourmet-cooking in Paris, and a brother, a novice journalist in England. She's the eldest.

She has a great love for Africa, and spends hours telling me of riding through its wide expanses, visiting the tribes, watching giraffes and gazelles galloping across the veldt, spying on a pride of lions from the cover of the bush, watching a herd of elephants rumbling down to the river for their nightly drink. Her eyes still intrigue me; they are so deep and clear—and when she speaks of Africa, I can almost see its vastness mirrored in them.

She'd gone to university in South Africa, in Cape Town, and studied anthropology. "Then I went to Israel, like every good Jew, and lived on a kibbutz." She grimaces at the memory. "I hated it. All I did was feel miserable and get fat.

"And then, London. In many ways I hated London too, especially the living conditions. The C and the D—you know, the cold and the damp. I lived in this squat in Hampstead and every night, wrapped in this ratty fur coat I owned, I'd scour the bins for fuel. I'd find all this furniture, sometimes quite good antiques, drag them home and chop them up for the fire." She shivers. "I was raised in Africa. My whole time in London was about keeping warm."

Finally she'd come across Somendra, one of the well-known European group leaders now practicing in the commune. She'd begun to do groups with him and had eventually taken sannyas. "And now, I'm here for good." I'm glad. She's brassy and ballsy and I enjoy her company.

But I suddenly begin to get the feeling she's beginning to see me in another way—not as a boss; not just as a friend—and I pull away, discouraging anything more than what's already happening. I've been on my own since Devika, and I'm certainly not going to get involved with this one, I tell myself. I like her, but, romantically, she's not my cup of tea. A friend, yes; a lover, no. She's a bit too much. And she's a bit too fat.

The Allan Whicker Show

It's like an oven on Jesus House lawn. By the time the television crew has checked the sound level and camera focus, dark red stains are creeping outwards from under each arm, spreading towards the pool of water forming in the centre of my chest. The Englishman in the blue seersucker safari suit is no better off.

He drops his sodden handkerchief onto the grass in disgust. "Rather pointless effort, what?"

"Let me know when you're ready," I call to the cameraman. "I want to put on a fresh T-shirt. At least I'd like to start the interview dry."

Waiting, we eye each other, the Englishman and me. We don't like each other very much.

"The Allan Whicker Show," a technician shouts. "Interview with Krishna Prem. Take one." The sign-board clacks. "Camera rolling."

So is the sweat. I needn't have bothered changing at all.

While the first question formulates in what I've come to view, over the past day or so, as a pea-brain, I wonder what it is about this man that's so terrific he's worth his own television series—and one that's so popular it's telecast all over the world. The man's conceit is stupendous. He's constantly primping and preening; he obviously thinks he's the cat's meow. He's been doing his best to put us down, in that polite and condescending manner the English seem to monopolize, and maybe, I figure, that's what his audience enjoys. He travels the globe, knocking everything, making them feel how lucky they are to be snug at home in the good old British Isles. I find I really don't give a shit, one way or another. I just wish something would surface in that mind—the heat's a killer today. His pinched nostrils and furrowed brow reassure me—I can tell he's trying.

All in all, the show's visit has been a smooth one. The interviews have gone well, the Mariam Canteen tea party with the Limeys was great fun, and even the darshan filming went without a hitch, except for Whicker's loudly-voiced resentment at being told he smelled of cologne and would have to wear a headscarf to see Osho. That had pissed him off no end.

I chuckle at the memory.

My giggle seems to remind him I'm here. "Krishna Prem," he says at last, checking his profile in relation to the camera, "what are all these young people seeking when they come here? Themselves?"

"Who they really *are*," I reply. "Does that make sense?"

"It makes about as much sense as most of the things I hear here."

"Well," I begin, taking a deep breath and feeling a sudden burst of energy inside, a rush that gets me going, "in the West people are multi-faced. You have one face that comes up in anger, one that comes up in greed, one that comes up in lust, one that comes up in jealousy—and so you're never really one whole person. And it's hard to live that way. It's not satisfying at all to live that way.

"Through association with Osho, through living with us here, through meditation techniques, group therapies, all those false personalities start to fall away, until you're left with one, until you're just the same all the time, wherever you are.

"And it really frees you. Your identity no longer depends on what's being fed into you by the outside world or by the person you're talking to.

"Osho once said that religion was the last luxury. And for us in the West, we've had the fridges, we've had the cars, we've had the television sets, and we've seen that they don't have anything to do with making you happy.

"But the Indians, at least the middle-class Indians in this country, still haven't come to that yet. They still want them and they don't know yet they don't make you happy."

His smile is pure plastic. "How does your hard-core permanent staff react to the suggestion that the commune is just a bunch of affluent Western kids looking for a packaged, Madison Avenue-style guru or Master?"

It sounds like he's memorized a script. "Obviously, that's an outside opinion," I reply. "When you come here it's hard to see what's going on. I suppose it can look like a holiday camp or something like that, or a summer resort. There's a lot of work going on inside.

"People think we've dropped out or something like that. And it's not that at all. It's just that, with most of the people here, it's a very aware, conscious decision that what they saw ahead of them in the West was leading nowhere."

"A lot of people I was speaking to yesterday were very spaced out," he says, his voice suddenly provocative. "I thought..."

I jump in right away. I know what he's implying and I'm going to say it before he does. "...were spaced out?" I repeat. "That's not drugs. The people who live and work in here?" I'm as condescending as he is for the moment. "It's meditation. I mean, you get very stoned when you meditate."

The director gives him the wrap-it-up signal. He tries a new line. "Your publications are excellent and beautifully done, but you package them rather like a beauty product."

"Well, it is for the West," I say matter-of-factly. "I mean, why not package religion attractively? Everything else is packaged that way."

There's a pause; his pinched nostrils flare for a moment, like a hound that's picking up a scent. I can tell he's revving up for his last question and that he's going to do his best to get me. He grins smugly, quite pleased with himself. "I do detect here," he announces loftily, "an air of suppressed hysteria."

"Of suppressed *hysteria*?" My tone is one of studied incredulity.

"Mm," he nods, relaxing, settling back against the bench, his eyes daring me to get out of this one.

"Oh, no!" I answer, laughing at the silliness of his suggestion. And as Laxmi did with Larry Malcolm of *TIME*, I just lay the truth on him, knowing that, even on television, it will shine through. "It's called *love*!"

"Cut!" the director calls. Whicker mutters an icy, "Thanks" and strides off. The moment he's out of range, the crew collapses in laughter, to a man. Madhura begins distributing bottles of cold soda and we lay on the grass, them and us and a few other sannyasins drinking and talking, just friends, sharing. "It's true," the cameraman says, "you really *do* have it here—that thing called love."

Chapter Six: 1978-1979

ENGAGING WITH THE GOVERNMENT

"Laxmi! Look what came in today's post!" I rush into her room, waving a letter, ignoring the fact she's in the middle of a conversation with Sheela. "The BBC's application has been turned down!"

"Show Laxmi," she commands, all attention. Magnifying glass poised, moving slowly from left to right, silently mouthing the words, she digests the news from Tony Isaacs. "Hmm," she says. "Difficulties with new government are going to be there." But she rallies fast. "But this cannot be allowed!" she shouts, the call to battle stirring the blood in her fighter's veins. "This is democracy! This is not Morarji Desai's country. If Indira were still in Prime Minister's chair this would not have happened. Government has no right to keep people from Osho. And visa problems too. Public must become aware!"

"We can send out a news release and get the story into the newspapers," I suggest.

"Will they print?" she wants to know. I assure her they will. "Okay, swamiji," she says, "let it happen."

Heading for the balcony, I call to Madhura and Mangala to drop everything and put together comprehensive lists of the entire Indian media, including the foreign correspondents in New Delhi. "Come on, Subhuti," I shout. "We've got work to do." The BBC's refusal isn't the first, but the others haven't had any news value. Now we've got a hook to hang our gripes on. In India, whether the Brits are gone or not, the BBC still carries a great deal of weight.

By mid-afternoon, Subhuti's draft is ready. We take it to Laxmi for approval. "Reading is slow," she says, indicating her magnifying glass. "You read to Laxmi, Subhuti."

In the modulated tones of an announcer, as if he's broadcasting the evening news to the nation, Subhuti begins: "Indian government Vetoes Foreign Filming at Osho Commune."

He clears his throat. "Osho and the international community that has grown around him in Pune have become the object of a determined censorship campaign by the Indian government."

Laxmi loves the opening. She bounces up and down in her chair, rubbing her hands together in glee, as if she's readying for a punch-up.

"So far," he continues, "two separate applications by the BBC to film Osho and commune activities have been turned down by the government. Similar requests from an Australian film team and the Spanish national television network have also been rejected.

"Visa difficulties have also been reported by Osho disciples and other visitors from Western countries, once they have stated their intention to visit the commune. In Holland, Switzerland, Germany and the United States, some have been refused visas, while others have been granted entry into India with the warning that if they go to the commune they will not be allowed into the country again.

"The two BBC film units involved are from the religious program *Everyman* and from *The World About Us.* Requests by the BBC for an explanation from the Indian Embassy in London have met with no response, and inquiries made by the Osho Foundation itself in New Delhi have also drawn a blank."

"Now we quote from Isaacs' letter," Subhuti says. "'It's incredible to me that after all the protestations we had about a free press and allowing journalists access to anything they wanted in India, that the first time we put in an application for something as unpolitical as the commune, we get held up,' a senior BBC spokesman said in a recent letter to the Foundation.

"About a dozen more film and television companies from England, Italy, Germany, Canada and the United States have written to the

Foundation in the last three months, expressing their intention to film at the commune later this year."

"Letters are in the files?" Laxmi wants to know.

"They are," I answer. "Some of the requests are vague, but what we're saying is true. At least a dozen TV crews have said they want to come."

She waves to Subhuti to continue. "This sudden flurry of interest by the media," he reads, "reflects the increasing influence in the West of Osho. His message is spreading fast. Four years ago he was virtually unheard of abroad; today he has an international following of fifty thousand disciples, with two hundred meditation centres worldwide. Books compiled from his discourses are available in many languages and in most countries.

"'If I were a Hindu they would have loved you all,' he told his disciples during a recent discourse at the commune. 'They would have bragged about it in their papers, magazines, books, radio stations, TV. But I am not a Hindu, I am not a Mohammedan, nor a Christian, nor a Jain, nor a Buddhist. So naturally all these people are against me. The more my work spreads, the more trouble will be coming, because the more they will be afraid.

"'Journalists are being prevented from coming here—the world should not know what is happening here; people should not come here. But the reason is clear, obvious. The reason is that whatsoever they have been thinking is religion, I say is not religion. In fact, what they say is religion is exactly anti-religion.

"'I am teaching you a new religion, a new dispensation. A new flower is opening up here, and the so-called religious people are against it. They will try to crush this opening bud. That's the risk you take by being with me.'"

Subhuti expels a long breath. "Finished," he says. "That's it."

"Beautiful," Laxmi compliments him. "Foundation's first press statement is beautiful, swamiji." She turns to me. "Now what?" she wants to know.

"Simple," I say. "We send it out all over India, foreign correspondents included. But to Bombay journalists, I want to go with Madhura and deliver it by hand."

"Why by hand?"

"I want them to get to know us, Laxmi. I want to meet them, talk to them, intrigue them. I want to pique their curiosity so that they come here and write about us."

"Laxmi knows Bombay journalists from old days," she sneers. "They're not worth much."

"They're strictly a stepping stone," I explain. "My aim is fixed on something else. What I'm really after is the foreign correspondents in New Delhi. It's through them we're going to reach the world. They read the Indian papers and magazines," I continue, "and if we begin getting a lot of coverage here, they'll become interested. Osho's taught me to start with what's available. Thanks to Morarji, we've now got the makings of a controversy. And Bombay's right next door. It's too good a chance to miss. I want to deliver this news release personally."

"Okay," she agrees. "Laxmi likes this thinking. When you want to go?"

"At six tomorrow morning. We can be at the newspapers when the offices open at ten."

Later that evening, Mangala comes to my room with the material for Bombay. "And you'd better take a look at this," she says, handing me a copy of *STERN*, opened at a double-page spread. "I ran into a German sannyasin with it, grabbed it and split."

It's one of the photos Laxmi allowed Jay Ullal to take ages ago. I know, the second I glance at it, that our troubles in India have just begun.

The photo was taken in Somendra's Leela group, and he's the only person wearing anything. And all he's got on is a tatty lunghi knotted around his waist. Everyone else is stark naked. Grey beard flying, Somendra stands in the middle of the room, his arms raised on high like a voodoo priest caught in the moment of incantation. Around him swirl a mass of writhing bodies, faces twisted in catharsis. One woman stands, spent, sweat-tangled hair covering her face, her body sagging in exhaustion against two nude, dishevelled men. And the photographer's been clever—the viewer's attention is drawn straight to her pubes!

"Someone read the article by Andrees Elten, by Satyananda," Mangala says, "and they say it's very beautiful and very moving. It's his account of doing Encounter and taking sannyas."

"Terrific," I mutter, a bit sarcastically. "Indians don't read German, but they're sure going to love these photos. Sex. That's all they're going to see. Sex. Now they'll be totally convinced we're all in the clutches of some mad sex-guru. I'll bet this is all over Bombay already."

"Well," she says, heading for the door. "It's bed for me. Good luck," she adds, pointing at the magazine. "You may need it."

"We'll survive," I promise, checking my watch. It's not too late. "Guess I'd better show this to Laxmi."

She's in her dressing gown, getting ready for bed. She studies the photographs for a while. "This is what happens in groups?" she asks, as if she's never really known.

"You had no idea?" I say.

She shrugs. "Laxmi knows Somendra's work is beautiful. Energy-magician, Laxmi calls him. But in photograph it looks so ugly. It surprises Laxmi, that's all, how beautiful work can look so ugly. Ah well," she sighs with resignation, setting the magazine aside, "this will set the dogs in Delhi to barking."

"I'll call from Bombay and let you know how things go with the press."

"You do that, swamiji," she says. She suddenly sounds tired.

The Bombay Press

"This is news!" The young Goan *Times of India* news editor comes to life. As Madhura and I had walked in, he looked as if he wanted to crawl under his desk, but the moment I handed him the release and he scanned it, things had changed. "Take this to the rewrite desk," he says, passing it to an assistant. "I want it in *Evening News* tonight, the *Times* tomorrow morning. And send it out on the wire service," he adds. "I want it all over the country."

We chat for a moment, but he's not interested in us or in Osho. We invite him to visit the commune anyway. "Too busy," he says, indicating the piles of paper before him.

For the rest of the day, we're in and out of one rickety, steaming taxi after another. Up and down filthy staircases stained betel-spit red and crammed into elevators reeking of hair oil and sweet talcum powder, we see *Indian Express, Free Press Journal, Bombay Samachar, Navbharat Times, Maharashtra Times, United News Of India*—all the Bombay biggies. We consume endless cups of spicy chai in grubby, overcrowded offices, the stale and musty air, as depleted as the decrepit buildings themselves, swirling ineffectually about our heads, set in token motion by ancient, creaking fans. Under the shower that night, at the sannyasin-couple's flat where Laxmi has billeted us, the water coursing through my hair runs black.

The next morning, bright and early, I buy the papers. "Commune persecuted," says *Evening News* and "Censorship of commune activities," is the headline in *Indian Express*. Absolutely everyone has picked it up. When I call, the papers haven't yet reached Pune. I give Laxmi the gist of the coverage over the phone. "Excellent, swamiji," she says, sounding pleased. "What's next?"

"Now we'll spend a couple of days visiting the magazines," I tell her. "We might as well strike while the iron is hot."

And, considering it's our Bombay debut, it goes surprisingly well.

We secure the publication of a couple of discourse excerpts in the two biggest weeklies, *Current* and *Blitz*—on sex, naturally—and orders for special material from *Youth Times*, the girlie-mag *Debonair*, and *Mirror*, a kind of sub-continental *Reader's Digest*. We arrange a visit to the commune workshops with *Eve's Weekly*, a national rag for the ladies, a let's-see-it-for-ourselves report in the newsmagazine *Onlooker*, and score amazingly well with the Hindi, Marathi and Gujarati press. The rest nibble—curious, interested, but wary and somewhat apprehensive.

Everyone gets a news release and a verbal blurb on the injustice of the government's stand. To an editor, the pervading view is that Prime Minister Morarji Desai is a loser and that his Janata Party is the worst thing that's happened to India since the British left. I begin to wonder how Morarji was elected. No one seems to have voted for him.

But, for the most part, it's sex. Sex, sex and more sex. By the end of the third day I'm so bored with talking about sex I begin to wonder if I ever want to get laid again. All this lofty palaver about moving into sex with awareness, meditatively, prayerfully; all this high-falutin' confabulation about sex being the lowest rung on the ladder to transcendence, is giving me a headache. They're obsessed with sex, the Indians. And beneath the intellectual veneer gilding the conversations, they're getting some sort of vicarious thrill, just talking about it. And whatever we say, they don't really hear us. I can see visions of wild orgies dancing in their eyes. "Jesus," Madhura mutters on the way home that evening, "doesn't anyone in this country ever get a good fuck?"

"You're up against five thousand years of culture and tradition," Bachi Karkaria says, toying thoughtfully with her vegetable cutlet. We're lunching at Gourdon's, my old Churchgate favourite, and she's explaining why, in some quarters, the reception we've received has been so strange.

"You've seen the sadhus by the side of the road, the Jain munis, the Buddhist monks, the Brahmin priests. These people are accepted as religious seekers. This country is ancient. We Parsis have been here almost a thousand years and we're still considered newcomers.

"People just don't know what to make of you lot. You don't fit with their ideas of religion. You dance, you sing, you laugh, you make love, you drink a beer, you smoke a bidi—you *enjoy* life. Your Osho is right when he says religions in India negate life. I'm not surprised some people are against you, like Morarji Desai and his government. You show them how dead and dull they are. I mean," she adds, shaking her head in disbelief, "CBS in America gave Morarji ten minutes of television and what does he do—talks about his favourite obsession, auto-urine therapy! What must the world think?"

"I understand all this, Bachi," I say, "but what exactly is going on in the *Times of India* building? Every time we've been in there, there's a very weird vibe."

She spoons more mango pickle onto her plate, considering. Madhura and I remain silent, waiting. "If this gets back, I'll be in trouble," she says at last. "But I like you people. And I liked your commune when I was there.

"First of all, the editors have been told not to do any features on you. News is okay, but features are a no-no. The *Illustrated Weekly* isn't going to publish my article; it's been cancelled. And that makes me angry, because it's good. And the same thing happened with the report by Minhaz Merchant. Do you remember him? The young man from the *Sunday Times* who came just after I did? His article's been cancelled too. And the reason is that Indu Jain, the wife of the *Times* owner, is a devotee of your Osho's. The editor felt she might be offended. He's afraid to make waves. They just fired Khushwant Singh, my editor on *The Illustrated Weekly* for years, and everyone's scared."

"Indu Jain?" I repeat, the name ringing a bell. "Does she live in Calcutta?"

"Yes," Bachi confirms.

"Then, don't worry. I've heard Laxmi speak of her. They're friends. Just leave this with me. Your article will be published, Bachi."

She smiles, pleased, and at the same time, impressed. "You know the right people."

"And what else is going on in relation to us?" I want to know. "I have the feeling there's more."

"Does the name Jay Ullal mean anything to you?"

The *STERN* photos! So far, no one had mentioned them, but I'd been wondering when they'd pop up. "Have you seen the latest issue of *STERN*?" I ask.

"No," she answers. "But I did hear, though, that there was a big article with some outrageous photographs. No, these are *other* photos Jay Ullal took when he was at the commune.

"What I've heard is that Khushwant Singh contacted Ullal in Germany and asked for photos for the *Weekly*. Ullal sent some, but they were just too shocking for us to use. Khushwant kept them locked in the safe in his office, but not before they'd been passed around the building from editor to editor. They wouldn't show them to any of the women, but I overheard them talking and snickering among themselves, like a bunch of schoolboys over dirty French postcards."

"No wonder they look at us strangely," Madhura says dryly.

"Finally *STERN* contacted Khushwant, saying Ullal had had no right to send them to India, that he'd just helped himself from the *STERN* files. They asked for them to be returned. By then Khushwant had been fired and the photos had disappeared.

"And where's Khushwant Singh now?" I ask, knowing full well the photos could surface one day and, when they do, we'll have quite a number on our hands.

"In New Delhi. He's editor of *The National Herald,* the newspaper Mrs Gandhi's father, Jawaharlal Nehru, started."

I file the tale away. Something else to tell Laxmi.

It's almost two o'clock and I ask the waiter for the check. Bachi's made us an appointment with Dr. Bharati, editor of the huge Hindi roto, *Dharmayug,* the largest and most influential publication in the country. It's time to get back to the *Times* building, to face the veiled sneers once again.

"All of this makes me ashamed to be Indian," Bachi says a little sadly in the taxi. "I saw such beautiful people at the commune. And there's all this." Her hands flutter helplessly in the air.

"Don't worry about any of this. And I'm grateful you've been so direct and honest with us. But don't worry. I remember one discourse on the Sufis. Osho said the Sufis say that when a man has had a glimpse of God, everything he does succeeds. People may not get it, but we're doing God's work. Everything will work out fine. It always does."

Riding the lift to the *Dharmayug* offices, I sense the other passengers pulling away from Madhura and me, as if even this slight proximity to us might somehow contaminate them. India, it appears, has a new caste of untouchables. It's unpleasant and vaguely threatening, this feeling of being disliked and unwelcome.

But how often have I just said "Enough" and moved on, walking out on jobs, apartments, on cities and love affairs? And here in this Bombay elevator, it hits me suddenly that there's no loophole, no exit any more.

For the first time in my life I'm into something where there's no way out. I'm totally hooked, irrevocably committed, utterly Osho's.

Okay, I say to myself. Okay. And a new sense of freedom bubbles up in me. Stepping from the lift I feel giddy, light-headed. The workers, the desks, seem miles away. I start to laugh. Heads turn, but it doesn't matter. I sail towards the *Dharmayug* offices, grinning all the way.

Dr. Bharati is cool and reserved. He reminds me of Somerset Maugham. He has that same look of disdain, as if there's an unpleasant smell under his nose.

"I don't like your Acharya," he says immediately. "Who does he think he is to call himself 'divine'?"

My hackles rise. "Because he is! So are you and so am I. We're all divine!"

He snorts scornfully. "I suppose you want me to publish his words in my magazine? Well," he continues before I can even admit I do, "there's no point in asking. None whatsoever. I think our Prime Minister has done a very good thing, keeping foreign film crews away from you people. This is not the kind of thing we want to show abroad. It would not be good for India's prestige."

"And what do you know about our commune?" I ask, rather enjoying this straightforward encounter after several days of the usual Indian wishy-washiness. "Have you ever visited it?"

"No. Nor will I ever," he states emphatically. "But I know people who have—people I trust—and I know what is really happening there, no matter what you people say. Who does he think he is?" he asks again. "Setting himself up like some god, living in luxury, being driven in an expensive foreign car! He should be out, consoling the poor."

"A Master is not a consolation," I quote, thankful, at last, those weeks of Kabir have finally come in handy.

"You know Kabir?" He seems surprised. And, bowing his head slightly, he admits defeat. "But your guru is no Master!" he suddenly sneers, rallying. "He is not of the calibre of Ramakrishna, Raman Maharshi, Nanak. Or Kabir. He is not to be compared with any of the illustrious ones of our great Hindu tradition." His lip curls. "He just gives you Westerners licence for sex."

"And pray tell," I ask, "who do *you* think you are? Who are you to sit in judgment when you have never been to the commune? I have been with Osho for years now and I tell you, he is authentic. Things have happened to me that have shown me, through my own experience, that I am the disciple of a true Master, of a twentieth-century buddha!"

And then Osho comes. From somewhere deep inside an energy begins to arise, filling me, shoving *me* aside, demanding expression. And as it happened that day at the typewriter, I find myself stepping aside. I open my mouth and out pours a river of words. For the next ten minutes, non-stop, the ring of authority resounding in my voice, I let Dr. Bharati have it—every experience, every glimpse I've had through Osho. But what is even more incredible to me is that the energy is tangible. Not only do I feel it, I can see it. It is invisible yet it is visible.

I watch it, as if it were a cloud, moving up and out of me, across the desk, enveloping the still, unmoving man facing me. Despite himself, as if powerless in the face of this energy, he is hearing me; he is letting me in.

When it is over, no one says anything. I just keep watching him and, slowly, ever so slowly, he begins to gather himself together again. The process is uncanny, bizarre; I've never seen anything like it before. Like a child building a house of blocks, I watch him reconstruct himself, piece by piece. Finally he speaks, his voice hoarse: "These experiences are subjective. To me, this is not proof."

"And what about truth?" I ask. "Osho once said, 'When you hear the truth, don't consider the source.' The truth has just been given to you, Dr. Bharati. Don't look at *me*—look at what's been given to you."

"It may be your truth, but it is not mine. I sit in this office and wait for truth to come."

"What ego!" I say, amazed at the man's conceit. "Who are you that truth should come to find you here, sitting in this grubby office? At least we are searching for truth, not just sitting around waiting!"

"You can call it ego if you wish, but it is my way," he replies. "Enough of this," he says, waving his hand as if to clear things away. "Let's get down to business. I've made it clear I don't like your guru, but I'll tell you one thing: I will never print anything by him in my magazine, but I will never print anything *against* him either."

His tone softens slightly. "I met him once, you know. Twelve years ago. I asked him a question. I asked him, 'Why do you bother with the rich? If you really are an Acharya, a teacher, why do you not go out and spread your message to the poor?' And do you know what he did?" he asks, his voice hard again. "He leaned back in his chair, your Acharya, closed his eyes and said, 'One day I will answer you.'"

"That day has come, Dr. Bharati," I say. Among the discourse excerpts we've brought to Bombay is Osho's answer to *exactly* that question. "You see, Dr. Bharati, truth *has* come to find you in your office after all. Here's the answer Osho promised you twelve years ago. Madhura and I are just the messengers."

Laying the transcript on his desk, we stand to leave. "I'll come back tomorrow," I promise, "to see if you have the courage to publish this or not."

The following afternoon, on the way to Victoria Terminus for the train to Pune, we stop by Dr. Bharati's office. I go in. He is hunched over his desk, bare except for the transcript. He doesn't look up; he doesn't acknowledge me in any way—he simply moves the sheaf of papers across towards me, to the edge of the desk. His voice is quiet, but unyielding. "I won't publish it," he says.

Outside his office, the door closed behind us, I look at Madhura. There are tears on her cheeks. "Poor man," she says. "Poor man."

Film Veto Official

When Parliament is in session in New Delhi, *The Times of India* devotes a daily column to happenings in both houses, the lower and the upper, the Lok Sabha and the Rajya Sabha. Checking the papers one morning, a few days after the Bombay expedition, I spy, in bold face, halfway down the parliamentary report: "No to film at Osho commune."

En route to Laxmi's office I read it. Finally, it seems, the government has said something official: "Foreign television and film units have been refused permission to document the activities of the Osho commune at Pune as 'It is felt that a film on activities there would not reflect favourably on India's image abroad,' the Lok Sabha was informed."

"We're news right now," I tell Laxmi. "I'm going to put a question in for discourse. And if Osho answers it, we can do another news release. We've got a little fire going right now—I want to fan it into an absolute conflagration!"

"Now this urine-drinking Prime Minister is helping the Indian image abroad?" Osho asks in discourse the next morning. The whole of Buddha Hall explodes with laughter. Mine's among the loudest. I can already see the headlines!

He also suggests a commission be appointed.

"So don't appoint a commission of some senile, retired judges," he says. "That won't help. Remember that what is happening here is something so scientific that only people who know something about modern developments in humanistic psychology, who know something about encounter therapy, gestalt, psychodrama, primal therapy, about est, Arica, who know something about Vipassana, Zazen, Sufi whirling—only they will be able to understand what is happening here. This place has great intelligence, great talent...

"So send some educated people—not your MPs! They won't understand a thing. And then you decide."

By six the next morning, Madhura and I are on the road again, another news release in hand, heading for a second round with the Bombay press. And I know, without a doubt, that Osho's challenge to the Janata Party will be in every single Indian newspaper tomorrow morning.

Not for a second do I think the Prime Minister will appoint a commission. And, although I'm second-guessing my Master, I suspect Osho doesn't either. I feel he's just using the situation, turning it to our advantage.

"Do you think you will be able to prevent me from reaching people?" he'd asked. I think of Morarji Desai in New Delhi and chuckle. The Prime Minister wants to hinder us, but what he's really doing is helping us more than anyone else in this country. It's Morarji's antagonism that's opening the doors of the media. It's his hatred of us that's going to make Osho a household word.

I'm looking forward to reading the papers over the next few days. I can't wait for the government's reaction. I want more fuel for discourse questions. I can't wait to give Osho another chance to strut his incredible stuff.

Germany's Yellow Press

Whips, chains, belts, forced sex. All that's missing are the jackboots and the burning cigarette ends. Day after day the clippings pour in from Germany, sensational, savage—the actress Pia Renti's*[8] nightmare in the love temple of the Indian sex-guru.

No one even knows who this woman is, this ageing German starlet upon whom we're supposed to have inflicted these unspeakable yet vividly documented abominations. A little detective work is obviously in order. On one of the cuttings I'd noticed three lead letters—DPA—indicating some wire service as the source of the story. They meant nothing to me, but Satyananda, the ex-*STERN* reporter knew the signature well. "It's the Deutsche Presse Agentur," he explained. "A big German news agency. Head office in Hamburg."

I find DPA listed in the New Delhi directory and phone. The bureau chief, Helmut Räther, is out of town, his wife informs me. When I push, she tells me what she knows. This Pia Renti had called her husband from Bombay one evening, telling him she'd been badly beaten in one of the commune groups, and that she wanted to warn people in Germany about the horrors of the place. She said she'd be in Delhi the following day to show Räther her bruises as evidence. She didn't show up but Räther sent the story out anyway. I must admit Mrs Räther takes my blast about irresponsible reporting quite well. She apologizes on her husband's behalf and tells me

8. All names marked with an asterisk (*) have been changed and are fictional

she'll have him ring me as soon as he returns. I don't plan to hold my breath.

The call to Delhi gives us an idea of when all of this was to have happened and, checking the group records, we find that a Pia Renti enrolled in Prasad's Centring group a week or so before. "Centring!" Laxmi is incredulous. "Centring is awareness games! Call Prasad."

Prasad, the group leader, remembers her—an aggressive, angry woman who wouldn't cooperate, who kept disturbing the other participants with her argumentativeness, with her unwillingness to follow the structure of the group. "At last I told her," he remembers, "that this wasn't the right group for her, that she had so much pent-up violence in her she needed something like Encounter. She walked out in a huff. I never saw her again."

"Get Teertha!" Laxmi shouts to the receptionist.

Teertha recalls her as well. He'd been on his way to his group in the therapy chambers when this woman had stopped him on the staircase and said she'd been told she should do Encounter. "She didn't mention who'd suggested it," he says, nodding in Prasad's direction. "I assumed it had come from the office, from Arup. Anyway, someone had just cancelled, there was a free space, the group was about to start, so I told her to come along. She stayed one full day and left the following morning."

"And this sex and violence she talks about?" Laxmi asks, checking the translations of the clippings under her magnifying glass. "She says she was forced to spend the night with some Dutchman, that she was beaten the next day and ran naked from the commune back to her hotel."

"All untrue, Laxmi," Teertha reassures her. "In the morning, the Dutchman spoke to the group about what had happened the night before. They'd gone back to the Blue Diamond and sat, talking, in her room. He wanted to spend the night with her, but she wasn't into it. He slept in his room and she slept in hers. He was upset, I remember, at the way she'd rejected him, but she was there in the group all the time he was telling us about it and didn't contradict anything he said.

"And the only violent thing that happened had to do with another woman in the group. Later in the morning session, Renti started berating the Germans, screaming at them, calling them Nazi pigs. One German woman got angry. She slapped her face—more to stop her hysteria than anything else. Then she left."

"And locked door? Newspaper says door was locked."

"The door to the group room is never locked, Laxmi. When this Renti woman said she wanted to leave, I told her she was free to go. She walked to the door, opened it, and left. Fully clothed.

"It's strange," Teertha adds with a wry smile, "but, usually, when someone wants to leave the group, I always ask them to sit in the centre and then we try to talk them out of it, try to convince them to stay and face whatever it is they want to run away from. I didn't do that with her. Something told me just to let her go."

"This Pia Renti is actress. Laxmi's feeling is this is publicity stunt." She turns to me. "Get statements from everyone in group, from Teertha and Prasad too. And from this Dutchman. Signed, witnessed, notarized. Laxmi is going to call our sannyasin lawyer in Munich and tell him to sue.

"And make extra copies," she adds, something else dawning on her. "This news will have reached to Delhi. Police are bound to come."

And they do. Within a few days the CID, India's version of the FBI, is at the gate. After calling Räther, Pia Renti had contacted the newsmagazine *India Today* and poured her tale into the ears of none other than the former *Times* reporter Minhaz Merchant. I'd spoken to him between interview and publication and he'd said nothing. I am really pissed. He'd *been* to the commune; he'd *seen* what happens here. In front of the CID man, I get Minhaz on the phone and let him have it, duplicating, word for word, the blast I'd levelled at Mrs Räther.

According to the CID, the *India Today* article has New Delhi's dhotis in a twist, particularly Morarji's. "The CID is all yours," I tell Mangala, dumping the statements and the parading of witnesses in her lap. Suddenly, Madhura and I are up to our ears in German journalists.

And in all my years of dealing with the press, it's my very first contact with real sleaze.

The worst is Joseph Kammer* of *Bild-Zeitung*, the yellow rag four million Germans devour daily. He's ensconced, two reporters from the sister publication *Bild-Am-Sonntag* tell us, in a room at the Blue Diamond. His commission is to write an exposé, *German Girls in Pune.*

"You're such nice people," they say, "we just had to tell you. It will all be pure fiction. That's Kammer's style. He won't find any facts for the scandal the editors want, so he'll make things up."

And most of the other German reporters can't find any facts either. One after another they show up at the commune, confessing to fruitless days spent nosing around Pune, posing as tourists or businessmen or newcomers here to see Osho. "I couldn't find anything," one of them said to me, "so I figured I might as well identify myself and find out what's really going on."

Kammer's subterfuge is a challenge, so one evening Madhura and I join the two *Bild-Am-Sonntag* boys at the Blue Diamond's outdoor coffee shop. I'm ready to confront Kammer and invite him to come to the commune to see what's happening instead of sitting in his room making it up. We check at the desk, but are told he's out. "There he is," one of the reporters says when we sit down in the coffee shop. "That's him. Sitting over there by the pool." I stroll over to the man they've indicated. "Mr Kammer?"

"No," he says in heavily-accented English, his eyes narrowing suspiciously behind thick glasses. "You have made a mistake. My name is not, uh," he pauses, as if having difficulty remembering the name I've used, "uh, Kammer, it was you said?"

I apologize for my error and return to the others. "Of course it's him!" the German reporter says. "I work in the same building with him in Hamburg. I see him at least twice a day!"

With renewed determination I head for the pool again. He sees me coming and stands, starting towards the lobby with a studied casualness. By the time I reach the foyer he's standing in front of the elevator, waiting for the door to open. I say nothing until he steps in. "Mr Kammer!" I call. "Yes?" he asks, turning. When he sees it's me his face hardens.

There are only a few seconds before the door slides closed, but it's enough for what I have to say. "There's no reason for this dishonesty, Mr Kammer, no reason for this ridiculous game of hide-and-seek. We've nothing to hide. Instead of writing lies, why not come to the commune and see for yourself. The truth is much more interesting..." The door slams on me, in mid-sentence.

And when at last his stories appear, eleven in all, a macabre new tale of sadomasochistic horrors every day, they reveal a very ill and perverted man. He has the kind of evil, fiendish mind that, had he been born earlier, Hitler's SS recruiters would have been delighted to find. But a few respectable German newspapers begin to take a more in-depth look at us, and some intelligent articles start to appear. Renti, on the other hand, begins to get slammed, her colourful past catching up with her. There are reports of nervous breakdowns, of treatments for schizophrenia, of outrageous tantrums on movie sets.

Osho is beautiful. In one discourse he speaks of his compassion for her and invites her to come back, telling her this is the only place in the world where she can be helped.

"And don't be worried by what is happening in Germany," he tells us in response to questions by anxious German sannyasins. "It is going to help my work tremendously. I know my business and how to do it. You don't be worried about it. Now it is all over Germany—everybody knows my name. This is something great!" I laugh, recalling something he'd once said: "If you want to help people, the first thing is they have to know you exist." Well, I think, Germany sure does now!

With Laxmi's go-ahead, Subhuti and I do a mass mailing to the German media, inviting them to come and look us over for themselves. The CID has also given us a clean slate, dismissing Renti as a publicity-seeker—a few semi-nude photos in German magazines convincing their puritanical minds her moral fibres are, to say the least, a little loose—and we decide, as long as the pendulum's swinging our way, to have another go at the powers-that-be.

Subhuti trucks out Delhi's refusal to let the BBC and others show the real picture as licence for journalistic lies in a bombshell entitled, *Osho Commune Lays Responsibility on Indian Government for Sensational Stories in German Press.* Everyone picks it up. There's a growing anti-Desai feeling in the country, and these days, we seem to be champions of a national cause. We're on the front pages almost every day.

Not only in India.

One morning, long before Renti, Laxmi, fresh from Osho's room, had brought me a message: "He says to get ready for waves of journalists from Germany, Holland and Italy."

Pia Renti had certainly triggered a tide from Germany—young and old, from factory-workers to university professors, they'd been pouring through the gate like breakers spilling on a beach. And then, tall and blond and solid, in stalk the Dutch.

Renti's Dutchman, the ogre who was supposed to have forced his unwanted attentions on her, had turned out to be one Swami Deva Amrito, greying, fiftyish, a former shrink. And that was that. But in the Netherlands, we soon discovered, he was the country's most celebrated psychiatrist, a well-known and popular personality and author of a bestseller on psychiatry that had been translated into eight languages. And when the news travelled from Germany to Holland, with a universal "What! Our Jan Foudraine? Impossible!" the Dutch press had rallied behind him. Overnight he'd become a maligned national hero.

"God," Madhura moans wearily one night after another evening of booze and blabber with a handful of Hollanders at the Blue Diamond bar, "I hope he gives us a little rest before he turns Italy on!"

Morarji Takes the Bait

I've been wondering for a while how long it would take to get a rise out of Morarji Desai. Since Osho's public invitation to set up a commission of inquiry, there hasn't been a peep from New Delhi. Finally, opening the paper one morning, I find, at last, Morarji's stuck his finger in the fire.

There's a report from Ahmedabad where a group of Gujarati sannyasins had invited Morarji to present him with a memorandum asking for his help in allowing us to establish our new commune in Kutch. "Why have you come to me?" the newspaper quotes him. "Your Acharya has been heaping abuse upon me and the Janata Party. Now he has even started talking of a comeback of Indira Gandhi. If you believe it all, why do you come to me?"

"You are the Prime Minister," one of our sannyasins said. "We have come to put our case before you. You should help us."

"How can I help in a cause in which I have no faith?" Morarji is reported to have replied. "Your Acharya styles himself as divine and you also call him one. Nobody should style himself as divine—this is my basic objection."

About Kutch he said, "I cannot help you. On the one hand you want help from me, and on the other hand your Acharya speaks about me as he likes. You call me a urine-drinking Prime Minister and in the same breath you want my help?"

He referred again to Osho's book *From Sex to Superconsciousness*, saying he'd found it repellent. He then dismissed the disciples, saying he had no more time for them in Ahmedabad and that if they wanted to discuss the matter further they would have to come to New Delhi.

The Missing *STERN* Photos

"So this is God's joke for today," Laxmi says wryly when I lay the latest issue of *New Delhi* magazine on her bed-side table. "Suddenly it seems the photos Jay Ullal sent to Khushwant Singh are no longer missing."

Missing they're not. In a full-colour spread, albeit off-register in typical Indian style, the *STERN* photos, plus a few others so horrific even the Germans rejected them, are laid out for all the country to see. And the editor's been clever. Under the simple title, *Total Love,* there are just a few words: "The Pune Acharya allows disciples in his community to practice what he preaches. The group therapy 'sessions' are a means to achieving the ultimate bliss and freedom." If he were here right now, I'd throttle the schmuck.

"So, swamiji," Laxmi asks, "what do you suggest? Something has to happen so the work doesn't suffer. And there is new commune to consider."

I don't hesitate for a second. "We take the bull by the horns. We call press conferences in Bombay and in New Delhi. We invite the press, telling them we'll be dealing with these photos. What else to do? You've taught me we have to use whatever challenges come our way—and this is one of the biggest yet."

By afternoon, reservations are made. The Bombay conference will be at the Taj Mahal Hotel; the Delhi one, at our Raj Yoga Meditation Centre. And Subhuti's at the typewriter, a press kit already taking shape.

It's decided that Madhura and I will handle the conferences, and that Satyananda and Somendra, stars of the *STERN* article and photos, will come along. Osho also suggests Divya accompany us. She's attractive, articulate and a long-time therapist. She's also used to dealing with Indians, having done Tata Management seminars in the past.

We give ourselves a week to get ready, but if I think for a moment we're going to get any rest before the upcoming trip, I'm kidding myself. Osho's on the government's case these days—and he's not letting up for anything.

"He's really after this government," Satyananda says to me after one particularly powerful discourse. "I've been to Delhi dozens of times for *STERN*, but I have the feeling this trip is going to be a whole new experience."

Anything more? I wonder. And yes, there is.

The next morning, in discourse, his first question comes from a journalist, Harivallabh Pandey of the New Delhi bureau of *United News of India*, the country's largest wire service. "I have always thought that you are against the politicians," Osho reads, "so I was very much surprised to know that you have blessed Indira Gandhi. Osho, would you like to say something about it?"

Madhura, sitting next to me in Buddha Hall, leans over. "Do you think anybody could stop him?" she whispers.

Bombay/New Delhi

"Madhura, are you asleep?"

"Hmm?" comes a groggy voice from the other bed.

"I'm going to start with the tape tomorrow."

"What?" She's sounding a little more awake. "What tape?"

"The one where Osho blesses Mrs Gandhi."

The light suddenly flashes on. Madhura's sitting bolt upright, the sheet clutched to her bosom, her face puffy with sleep. "You're not!"

"I am."

"Krishna Prem, you're mad. They'll go berserk. We're supposed to talk about groups. You know how they feel, especially here in Bombay. You know they keep saying Osho has no right to talk about politics, that he should stick to religion. They'll go mad!"

"I don't care. I've been lying here for hours telling myself the same thing. But it just keeps coming to me again and again—play them the tape. So I'm going to. First thing."

"Laxmi will freak right out."

"She's the one who gave it to me. Before we left Pune she passed me the cassette and said, 'Play this if chance is there.'"

"And you're going to *start* with it? Right off the top? It'll be like tossing a bomb into the middle of the room, especially that bit about the press! I doubt if that's what she meant."

"I don't care. Something keeps telling me to do it. Maybe it's Osho; I don't know. But I have to do it like this. The Bombay journalists are so fast asleep, maybe it'll wake them up."

"I can't speak for them, but you've certainly woken me up." She reaches for a bidi. "Let's listen to it and then decide. You set up the tape recorder and I'll make some coffee."

"I have blessed Indira Gandhi because to me she seems to be the least political amongst the Indian politicians," we hear Osho say. "It will look strange to you—because whatsoever has been said about her, spread about her, rumoured about her, is just the opposite. But my own observation is this: that she has the least political mind.

"And why do I say so? These are the reasons:

"First. Had she been really a politician and only a politician, she would not have tried to do anything that goes against the Indian tradition...

"Indira Gandhi tried to do something, sincerely tried to do something... She annoyed the rich people of this country because she was doing something for the poor. And she annoyed the poor because whatsoever she did went against their traditions. For example, imposed birth-control. The Indian masses cannot tolerate it. For thousands of years they have thought that it is God that gives children—and who are you to prevent it? It is a gift from God—that has been their idea. Now the gift is becoming very dangerous. The gift is becoming so dangerous that it is almost suicidal...

"Second. She started succeeding in her programs. That is dangerous. You should not succeed... She was succeeding in raising people's standards of living. She was succeeding in helping people to be more productive and less destructive. She was succeeding in many, many ways... Politicians only pretend—they never really do anything. But she was sincere; she really tried to do something for this country. That's why this country can never forgive her.

"Thirdly. Indian bureaucracy is the worst in the world. No work ever happens—files just go on moving from one table to another table, for years and years.

"If you want to *do* something in this country, with such a bureaucracy it is impossible. You have to force this bureaucracy to do things.

"The bureaucracy was angry. It was really the bureaucracy who deceived Indira Gandhi. She was given false reports that her position was perfectly okay—that she could allow an election, she was going to win. She depended on the reports of the bureaucracy. Those reports were false. The bureaucracy was absolutely against her. Nobody had ever forced them to do anything, and she was forcing them to do things...

"Fourth. She imposed an Emergency. She was straightforward. Had she been a politician she would have done everything that is done through an Emergency, without imposing an Emergency. That's what is being done now—everything is being done just as it was done in the Emergency, but without declaring it. The cunning politician always works indirectly, not directly. He is not straightforward...

"Indira was straightforward. She declared Emergency. She was honest. Emergency was needed. This country can only be changed if things are to be taken very seriously—as if the country is at war... She risked her power, her prime-ministership, to change the course of the history of this country. This Emergency angered the journalists and the other media people. And no politician ever likes to anger the journalists because much, too much, depends on them."

"They're going to love this part," I hear Madhura muttering under her breath.

"It can safely be said that fifty per cent of Indira's fall was made possible by the Indian journalists. They were getting angrier and angrier. They were not allowed to gossip; they were not allowed to make rumours; they were not allowed what they call 'freedom of the press', so when the Emergency was removed they took great revenge. It is how the human mind functions. A politician would have been alert about it.

"Fifth. Her son, Sanjay Gandhi, entered politics. A real politician, a cunning politician, would have allowed him to enter only from the back door; otherwise, others become jealous. She allowed him to enter from the front door, and the whole country became jealous... She functioned more as a mother and a human being than as a cunning politician.

"Sixth. She made the greatest error that a politician can commit, a very fundamental error and very obvious—Indira Gandhi forced all the political parties into jail together. That is so absurd! Even a man like me, who has nothing to do with politics, can see that it is absolutely absurd. If you put all your enemies into jail together, you are forcing them to be united against you.

"They became friendly. And they saw the point—that if they could become friendly and get together, then Indira would be gone... The Congress Party had ruled for thirty years because the enemies were divided...

"And seventh. After an Emergency, immediately after an Emergency and after a great effort to impose birth-control on the people—when rich people, poor people and the journalists and everybody were annoyed and angry—immediately after an Emergency, declaring a general election! That is again incomprehensible.

"If she had asked me I would have told her, 'Wait for at least one year. Remove the Emergency. Wait for one year.' That one year would have done. The steam of the journalists would have been released, the people would have forgotten the imposition—people's memories are very short—and the enemies, all the political enemies, after one year, would have again fallen into their old habits, would have started quarrelling with one another again.

"Immediately giving a general election to the country was utterly un-political. That's how she got defeated.

"Because of these errors, I say she is the least political of all the Indian politicians.

"Hence I have blessed her. I have blessed her, and I bless her again."[9]

Madhura proved to be right. The next afternoon, albeit edgy, the press is polite and attentive throughout the playing of the tape—but the moment Osho hits the journalists is the moment they explode. I like to stir things up—it's the naughty Krishna in me—but I'm not quite ready for this, for this barrage of anger. It's as if I've detonated a ton of emotional TNT.

Madhura leans over, whispering. Her voice is singed with sarcasm, but, mostly, she sounds afraid. "I hope you're enjoying yourself, Krishna Prem," she says. "I think, all by yourself, you may just have started a mob."

---

9. *Unio Mystico*

It had all begun smoothly. Veetmoha had arrived in Bombay early, with Divya, Somendra and Satyananda, and with all the efficiency of his African safari days, had taken charge. He'd sent the Taj Hotel bearers scurrying here and there, fetching easels and tables and linen, until he'd mounted, to his discerning satisfaction, an impressive display of Foundation books, tapes, newsletters and magazines. In one corner, he'd set up a screen for the slide show on commune crafts, finding a bearer who, for five extra rupees would keep an eye on him and pull the curtains on cue. Madhura, with equal ease, had slipped into her hostess role, arranging the seating informally, chairs grouped around low coffee tables, and instructing the waiters how and when she wanted refreshments served. At the front, under a huge colour photo of Osho in discourse, Divya, Somendra, Satyananda and I are positioned.

The press was prompt, most arriving well before four o'clock. "They've been looking forward to this one," Bachi Karkaria tells me. "They're usually a good half hour late—if they bother to come at all. I've never seen a turnout like this!"

As soon as they're seated, I call for their attention and introduce the four of us, mentioning the material in their press kits—an incredibly comprehensive opus by Subhuti, *The Role of Therapy Groups in the Great Experiment of Osho,* geared to an Indian audience. We all know why we're here, so I get right down to it.

"You've all undoubtedly seen the photographs published in *New Delhi* magazine," I say. At this, many of the men snicker and the women lower their eyes. "We've come to talk to you about these photographs. They were taken as part of an article Swami Satyananda was writing for *STERN* and have been used out of context, as well as illegally, by *New Delhi.* The photos were removed surreptitiously from the *STERN* files by Jay Ullal and sent to India. Now, we are told, *STERN* is suing *New Delhi.*

"In any case, some of the photos were taken in Swami Somendra's group and he will explain to you what is actually happening in these photos. We hope to help you understand, since group therapy is new to India, exactly what is going on in Pune.

"But before we begin..."—it keeps nagging at me; I just have to do it—"I'd like to play you a tape from yesterday morning's discourse at the commune. It's Osho's reply to a question from *UNI*—why he has blessed Indira Gandhi."

The first ten minutes or so are fine. Everyone's interested, attentive. Some nod their heads, clucking their tongues in agreement with Osho's words; others are stiff and disapproving, their mouths turned down in displeasure. But the second Osho swings his punch at the press, all hell breaks loose. The room is suddenly in pandemonium. Some journalists protest, shouting angrily; others shoosh them into silence, wanting to hear; several simply get up and leave. I begin to wonder if I've made a terrible mistake. Osho just seems to be going on and on. I keep wishing he'd talk faster; now all I want is for the tape to end.

When his voice finally stops, my relief is short-lived. If anything, things get worse. I sit there, one of a row of uncomfortable sannyasins, each trying to mask his nervousness behind betray-nothing poker-faces, and watch the Bombay press divide itself into two warring camps—one condemning Osho vehemently; the other defending him, saying he's right, saying it's time someone in this country spoke the truth.

Those on our side are primarily reporters, like Bachi, who've visited the commune, and those against us are rehashing the same old rumours—mostly to do with sex. When I hear the words "*New Delhi* magazine" a few times, I know it's time to jump in and do my best to bring this debacle to some semblance of order. It's hard, but at last I manage.

Satyananda takes the floor. And he is beautiful. He may be a sannyasin, but he's been one of their brotherhood for years, and they listen. Clearly and concisely, he explains how he came to India, to the commune, and what he found there. He speaks, openly and honestly, of his participation in the groups where the photos were taken. He tells of his decision to take sannyas.

Somendra is next. As he begins to talk, endeavouring to clarify the scenes portrayed in the photographs, trying to explain how he works with people's subtle energies, I can see we're losing them fast. His vocabulary is psycho-spiritual—a good ninety-nine per cent haven't a clue what he's on about. And when Somendra's wound up it isn't easy to pull the plug. Finally he senses my stare and glances in my direction. My face is relaxed and smiling, but my eyes are telling him to shut up. He does.

I turn to Divya. She's pale and obviously very distraught. I'd like to forget about her, but I can't. She's lined up with the rest of us, one of the conferenciers, and cannot be ignored. I mention briefly Osho's statement, included in the press kit, that the groups are primarily geared to Westerners and not intended for the Indian psyche and—crossing my fingers in my lap with a final reference to her Tata Management experience, I bow to Divya.

She is awful. She's on the verge of hysterics and it shows. Instead of explaining, she begins berating, telling them they're hypocritical in their condemnation of the commune's group program, that they're just jealous, that they're sexually repressed. She's scared and she's attacking. And I'd like to do the same to her. From the pitch of her voice I can sense she's on the brink of tears, seconds away from falling apart completely. "Enough, Divya!' I spit through clenched teeth, past caring whether anyone overhears me or not.

The room is in uproar again, they aren't taking this from her and I don't blame them. Another group stalks out.

Then, miraculously, it's quiet. It happens so fast it stuns me. The dozen or so who have remained all at once begin to ask questions, and we're suddenly having a dialogue with these people. Madhura stirs the waiters into action again, and we break up into little groups, talking, discussing, like buddies, like friends. Veetmoha even gets to show his slides.

"It was a flop!" Laxmi shouts at me over the telephone when she calls the Raj Yoga centre in New Delhi the following day. "Have you *seen* Bombay papers?"

"Not yet," I reply, the tone of my voice telling her how sheepish I feel. There's still an underlying feeling that playing the tape was somehow right, but I decide not to get into it with her, to let sleeping dogs lie.

"Have you learned anything?" she wants to know.

"Yes," I answer. "We discussed the format on the plane this morning."

I outline how we'll proceed here in the capital.

"Good," she says. "But Krishna Prem," she adds, softening, "don't feel bad when mistakes happen—if you learn. That's how God teaches us. And," she adds, "call Laxmi after the conference so we can tell him how it went."

I agree. Then, jokingly, I add, "And you might tell Osho the press conference is at four tomorrow. If he's not busy he might drop by. After Bombay we could use his help."

"Okay, swamiji," she laughs. "Laxmi will tell him."

Good old Madhura. In a day she transforms the bare, cement roof of the meditation centre into a setting worthy of the finest English garden party. After we'd calmed the local sannyasins down a bit she'd fanned them out into Delhi for palms and PA systems, for dishes and cutlery and tables and chairs, for all the paraphernalia we needed. She'd tackled the tent-wallah herself, coming back, hours later, with a crew of coolies, a great rust carpet and a gigantic cloth pavilion of Rajasthani panels, all bright and festive and geometric in blue and red and green and gold.

But cooling out the Delhi sannyasins had been the real task. For the most part they're simple, unsophisticated people, and the publication of the photos had been difficult for them; they simply hadn't known what to say to their friends and families, to their business associates and customers. We were like saviours to them, like archangels sent by God himself. They'd been at Palam Airport en masse, touching our feet, namaste-ing, weighing us down with garlands of marigolds, dancing and clapping and singing, with "Govinda Bolo Hari" reverberating through the terminal. It had been very loving and very touching. And terribly embarrassing. I thought the luggage would never arrive.

The morning of the press conference, leaving Madhura to her arrangements and the others to shopping, Satyananda and I taxi into the centre of the city, to the offices of *The National Herald*, to the den of the infamous Khushwant Singh. He's a rather pompous old fart, this grizzled Sikh who's been one of India's top journalists for decades, but I rather like him. As far as the photos are concerned, he doesn't tell us much we don't already know. Of course he has no idea how they disappeared from his safe. I don't push. What's the point? What's done is done.

Yet, in his own way, he obviously wants to help. *New Delhi,* he informs me, has just been acquired by one M.J. Akbar of the Calcutta English-Bengali chain, *Ananda Bazar Patrika*. I tell him Madhura and I are going to Calcutta after Delhi and we'll drop in on Mr. Akbar for a chat.

"Whether it's true or not, I can't say," he tells us, "but under Indian law, those photos are considered obscene. Now, the word is that Akbar showed them to Morarji first and Morarji promised him the government wouldn't prosecute. True or not, I can't say. But that's what I've heard."

He suggests we try to get the question of the film ban on the commune raised in Parliament by the Opposition, by members of Mrs Gandhi's Congress Party. He's convinced Morarji's on the way out. "It could help us both," he says. "I want Mrs G back in power. She's not against your commune at all, and if this issue comes up in Parliament it'll only help discredit Morarji even more. He's always saying how democratic he is. I'm interested in doing whatever I can to show the country he's full of shit. You are news. The timing couldn't be better."

I've never played this kind of game before. "How does one go about getting this issue raised in Parliament?" I ask.

"I'll arrange for you to meet Maneka Gandhi, Sanjay's wife, Mrs G's daughter-in-law," he says. "She'll see that it happens."

We've an hour to go. Madhura's clucking about like a mother hen; the rest of us are in our room, relaxing, awaiting the arrival of Swami

Vinod Bharti, better known to India's film-going millions as Vinod Khanna, the country's number one male box-office star. Laxmi had called to say Vinod was in Delhi and would join us. I'd been pleased. It had seemed odd in Bombay to have only Westerners representing an ashram in India.

The room is still; no one's saying a word. Divya's moisturizing her elbows, Somendra's writing a letter and Satyananda's buried in a book. I'm flat on my back, gazing at the ceiling. Suddenly, there's a presence in the room—and a silence, deep, profound and familiar. I sit up with a start. It's Osho! He's come!

The others sense it too. I watch as Divya drops her pot of cream, Somendra's pen trails off the paper and Satyananda looks up over the edge of his book, his nose twitching like a hare that's just picked up a scent. The book falls on his chest, as if he's read himself to sleep. My eyes close, almost on their own.

There's no sense of time, but we must sit like this for at least a half hour, enveloped in the silence. And then, as abruptly as he came, he's gone. As one, we open our eyes; as one, we begin to laugh. "I asked Laxmi on the phone last night to ask him to come," I say. "But it was just a joke. I never thought for a moment she'd really ask him."

"Well, she must have," Divya says, her eyes shining like she's just been to darshan. "Because he certainly did!"

Khushwant Singh was right. We are news. Stepping onto the roof, I am amazed at how many people there are. Every journalist in Delhi must be here. And there's also a good collection of foreign correspondents. The only face I recognize belongs to Larry Malcolm of *TIME*. "Hello, Rasputin," he murmurs as I pass him, "I see you're still selling snake oil." I'm still laughing as I make the introductions.

And I feel filled with Osho this afternoon. Really filled with him. As I talk about him I can feel him. It's as if he's standing next to me.

"Every Master, every buddha," I tell them, "has his own unique ways of working with his disciples—and this is where we are facing difficulties with society. Osho's methods, particularly his use of Western therapies, are unorthodox as far as this country is concerned. But," I want to know, "does this give the government the right to hassle us?"

I can sense the fire mounting inside. "India," I say, "has a long and time-honoured history of keeping her doors open to seekers after God." A few of the foreign correspondents wince at the word, but the Indians don't bat an eyelash. "India has something that is not available anywhere else in the world—the science of meditation—and she has *always* welcomed the world's seekers. But what is happening now under the Desai regime shows, without a doubt, that democracy is dead in this country. What is happening with us is nothing more than an attempt by the Prime Minister to impose his own personal morality on others. For the past two years our commune has been subjected to a continuing and escalating campaign of harassment by the Janata Government, and we are convinced it has only to do with the personal views of the Prime Minister. He's made it clear he doesn't like us and is doing what he can to keep people away."

Through the list of grievances I go: the film ban, visa refusals, mail censorship, the commission of inquiry saga. "And," I add, "Government officials are visiting our meditation centres around the country and asking for lists of sannyasins. What for? And personnel at the army base in Pune have been told they'll be discharged if they visit the commune. And you call this a democracy?

"This underhanded, undemocratic treatment of our commune has to be brought to the attention of the public. It's up to you. As a visitor to this country, you may feel I have no right to say it, but I do anyway: for the government you have elected, you should be ashamed!"

For a second, I wonder if I'm going to have another mob on my hands, but when I mention the *New Delhi* photographs, curiosity triumphs over national pride. Everyone's all ears.

Satyananda, Somendra and Divya are spectacular—brief, lucid and convincing. And it helps, having Western journalists in the audience. When the questions begin, their understanding of therapy gives us a credence that wasn't there in Bombay. For a good hour the dialogue goes on, back and forth, direct questions and honest answers. Everyone seems to be having a great time.

Larry Malcolm wants to know about Geet Govind, about what happened with him. He'd disappeared from Pune one morning after finishing the Encounter group with Teertha, and the next contact with him had been copies of negative letters about us to *TIME* on Esalen letterhead and signed with his old name, Richard Price. I'm straight with Malcolm: I tell him what I know.

"Osho had suggested he do the Encounter and the Tantra groups," I explain. "He did Encounter and told everyone how great it was, but the day before the Tantra group he left without a word to anyone. The next morning I heard he'd admitted to one of the commune group leaders that he was afraid to do the Tantra group. That's all I know." At this there's a general laugh, but Malcolm doesn't press it any further. I'm glad. It's the kind of thing I'd rather just let go. And from the look Malcolm gives me, I'm happy to see he feels the same.

For almost another hour the questions continue, and except for the staunch Hindi press everyone seems positive and sympathetic to us. When it becomes apparent the conference is drawing to a close, I tell them that Madhura and I will be in Delhi for the rest of the week and that, if any of them are interested, we'll be happy to drop by for further discussions. We're swamped with business cards and invitations.

When I call Laxmi that night, she's thrilled. I tell her about Khushwant Singh as well, saying he wants to set up an appointment with Maneka Gandhi with a view to our being discussed in Parliament.

"Go!" she says. "Opportunities are not to be missed. And you and Madhura go see Indira too."

"Go see Mrs Gandhi?" I am amazed. "How?"

"Laxmi is arranging it. She will tell you when appointment is fixed. Take her a nice book on Zen and diary. And invite her to visit commune. And then," she adds with a laugh, "you go see Morarji."

This is too much. After today's press conference! "Laxmi, have you lost your marbles?"

"You remember B.P. Mandal, the MP you met in Laxmi's office?"

"I remember."

"He telephoned Laxmi last night and wants to arrange meeting with Morarji to clear misunderstandings. He belongs to Janata, to Morarji's party, and since invitation is coming from their side, Laxmi said okay. Mandal will telephone and tell you when."

"But what are we supposed to say to him? After all those discourses, after everything Osho has said, what are we supposed to say?"

"You just be straight," she says. "Show him Osho's sannyasins are open, honest, loving people—not like politicians. Be polite but be straight. Tell him what we feel about his government. Tell him on the face. And be generous. Take few books. Take diary and take *Gita Darshan* in Hindi. He fancies himself expert on *Bhagavad Gita* but has only memorized, like stupid parrot..."

"Okay, okay," I interrupt, knowing, once she gets rolling, she can go on about Morarji for hours.

"And take copy of Patanjali's yoga sutras in English. He thinks he is yogi, with all his blabbering about celibacy. He has only suppressed his sex for thirty years and he calls himself..."

"Laxmi! Okay! I get the point!"

"And one more thing, Krishna Prem. If Morarji says he's too busy to read Osho's books, take books back. We are practical people and books are costly. No need to waste."

"Okay," I agree. Anything to get off the phone. I can't wait to tell Madhura the news.

"Who was that on the phone?" she wants to know, coming out of the bathroom, her hair wrapped in a towel. It takes me about ten seconds to fill her in. She flops on the bed, her face buried in a pillow. Her shoulders are shaking, but I can't tell whether she's laughing or crying. My suspicion is it's a mixture of both.

"Morarji Desai!" she shrieks, surfacing at last. "I don't believe that woman is really sending us to see Morarji Desai!"

"Well, Madhura, you might as well believe it. Because she is!"

"And Mrs Gandhi too?"

"And Mrs Gandhi too."

"My God," she shouts, her eyes wide with panic. "What am I going to wear?"

Indira Gandhi and Morarji Desai

Indira Gandhi looks exhausted. The strain of imprisonment, of endless court cases, of the current re-election campaign in Chikmaglur—all have taken their toll. It's apparent even now, in the dim evening light, as that distinctive shock of white hair moves towards us across the veranda of 12 Willingdon Crescent. Deep circles are etched under her eyes; her face is drawn, almost ashen. Her palms meet in namaste as she approaches, but she suddenly stumbles from fatigue and reaches for the wall to steady herself. My first impulse is to step forward to help her, but I check myself. This is India. The scores of supporters and supplicants on the lawn at my back would kill me if I touched her.

Watching her, seeing how haggard and depleted she appears, I am amazed at the price people pay for power. But yet, with this lady, I sense something else—the strength of an inbred conviction, of the no-matter-what determination of one who has been raised to rule. This is Indira, daughter of the House of Nehru, groomed from childhood to sit on this strange, unworkable democracy's non-existent throne. Her enemies haven't tagged her the Empress of India for nothing.

In the hour or so Madhura and I had been waiting, I'd been watching the people gathered around her—not the ones pow-wowing inside the house, mapping out campaign strategies; not the fat industrialists and financiers, rice-bellies bulging under white polyester shirts; not the stream of file-toting functionaries scurrying back and forth, stopping, ant-like, to consult, in hurried whispers, before rushing on.

I've been watching the common, ordinary Indians, lean and gaunt in sun-faded saris and threadbare dhotis who've come to pay respect to her, to touch her feet. Every once in a while she would leave the indoor meeting and come out to them. "Maji," they would call her. "Respected Mother." Or "Mataji," elevating their reverence even more. They would bow down, gingerly touching her feet with their bony, working fingers, or reach up tentatively, with awe, to place a ring of wilting marigolds about her neck.

And yet, observing this, not once did I have the sensation I was watching an Empress receiving the tributes of her subjects. Scrutinizing her face, almost as white with weariness as that famous band of hair, I saw love on it. And I remembered Osho's words: "She really tried to do something for this country." Jawaharlal Nehru raised his daughter well.

Now, as she stands before us, I'd like to say something to help her, to tell her I've seen their love for her and her love for them. But I can't. It's not the time and it's not the place. And it's not what I'm here for.

"Mrs Gandhi," I say, namaste-ing, feeling rather like an envoy from another state, "my name is Swami Krishna Prem and this is Ma Prem Madhura. We're from Osho commune in Pune. Ma Yoga Laxmi asked us to give you these." I hold out the diary and the book on Zen. She accepts them, holding them against her.

"Thank you," she says. And she falls silent. Her eyes betray a slight suspicion, as if she's waiting to see what we want, what we're going to ask for. I'm certain she knows of our meetings with her daughter-in-law, with Maneka, and that Maneka is arranging for the subject of our harassment to be brought up in the Rajya Sabha—but nothing is said. The gap needs filling. "Ma Laxmi asked us to invite you to visit the commune," I say.

"I will," she replies. "But later." She waves a hand towards the meeting in the house. "Now there's this campaign in Chikmaglur..." She is silent again.

I don't quite know what to say next. Madhura's equally at a loss. Suddenly I want to make a human overture. "Mrs Gandhi," I blurt, without thinking, "you look exhausted."

The eyes narrow again, in displeasure, as if I've breached protocol. But she seems to recognize I've only spoken as a friend, because the look softens. "I am," she says. Again, the silence.

It's obviously time to go. "We won't keep you from your people any longer."

"Thank you," she says, indicating the books. "Give my fond regards to Ma Yoga Laxmi and tell her that when I can, I will visit your commune." She turns away, towards the doorway, where a cluster of campaign workers has gathered, waiting to escort her back into the house.

After Khushwant Singh's tale of Morarji's guarantee that *New Delhi* wouldn't be prosecuted for obscenity, apart from days spent with Indian editors and foreign correspondents from a dozen countries, I've been nosing around a bit. Like Dr Watson and Sherlock Holmes, Madhura and I are looking for evidence of government interference with the press in relation to the commune. A visit to *New Delhi* proved to be a bust, except that I enjoyed how the staff freaked the second we walked in, as if they were afraid we'd come to wreck the place. Only at *UNI* do I find any hint of Morarji's finger poking in the pie. The first few times we call, we're told Harivallabh Pandey, the reporter who'd asked Osho the question about Mrs Gandhi, is "out of station". A couple of days later he's been "transferred". According to the grapevine, Pandey's been shunted to the provinces because of his question, something, we're told, had incurred great displeasure from on high.

After several pushy attempts, I manage to find myself with the *UNI* general manager. Mr. Pandey, he informs me, had asked the question personally and the news agency is under no obligation to use it. I say I have reliable information he's received orders from Morarji to suppress the story, and his dark rust blush tells me my intuition is right. Relieving him of the burdensome transcript, Madhura and I beeline for Khushwant Singh's office. The next morning, *Why I Bless Indira Gandhi* is on the front page of *The National Herald.* And a few hours after the paper hits the streets, B.P. Mandel telephones me to confirm our appointment with the Prime Minister. Morarji, he tells me, has agreed to the meeting on the condition whatever passes between us is not released to the press. I agree.

"Aha!" Laxmi shouts triumphantly down the phone when I call her. "He's beginning to fear Foundation! He's beginning to see Foundation is force to be reckoned with! He's beginning to learn that to play with Foundation is to play with fire! He's finally..."

I cover the mouthpiece with one hand. "Madhura, she's off again."

"Give me the phone."

"Laxmi!" Madhura yells, trying to get a word in. "Laxmi! It's Madhura. Yes, he's still here. Yes, he knows what to say. Yes, he knows to be straight and tell him on the face. Yes, he knows all that. Laxmi! Just *listen* to me for a moment! I need some advice. I haven't a thing to wear!"

Almost the next thing I know the two of us are sitting in the back of a car being chauffeured to the Prime Minister's office in Rastrapati Bhavan. Madhura's swathed in a sunset-orange sari of South Indian silk; I'm in a dark red robe of hand-loomed khadi. As the Bhavan comes into view we look at each other and explode. "Isn't this the most ridiculous thing you've ever done in your life?"

I sputter.

"It is!" she hoots. "It really is! I've been sitting here thinking the same thing. I've been asking myself what in the name of God I'm doing here—a part-time actress and part-time typist from a middle-class English family—about to see Morarji Desai, the Prime Minister of one of the biggest countries in the world!"

"Me too. It just blows me away! Here I am, fat little Jackie Allanach from Campbellton, New Brunswick, on my way to see the Prime Minister of India in a red dress! It's just too insane!"

At the checkpoint, showing our passes, we somehow manage to hold it together. But the laughter won't stop. It keeps bubbling up, spilling over, getting more and more raucous. We park in front of the entrance a good ten minutes before we're sufficiently in control of ourselves to get out of the car.

Morarji Desai looks like the taxidermist has just finished with him. He's left him propped up in an armchair, held in place by a starched kurtah and dhoti—with a sleeveless charcoal vest for added support. As a finishing touch, he's perched a jaunty Gandhi cap atop the ancient, hairless head.

It takes him a while to realize we're in the room. He doesn't move, doesn't avert his gaze from the blank wall he's focused on. It gives me time to look him over. The profile is classic Brahmin, lean and hawk-like, tight and pinched. Like Dr. Bharati of Bombay, it's Somerset Maugham in brown-face. When it finally registers that there's someone else in the room, he turns, looks at us, and stands. His eyes are small and mean, like those of a bird of prey. He's surprisingly tall.

He does namaste first and then shakes our hands, all terribly East-West. I can't take my eyes off his face. His complexion is incredible. He's eighty-three and has skin like a baby. It seems there's something to be said for not getting laid for thirty years and having a glass of pee for breakfast—if you're into good skin—but I decide, no matter how impressive the epidermis, to stick to coffee and a morning bidi.

Sitting, he eyeballs Madhura. "What about those pictures in *New Delhi*?" is his opening line.

"Deceit, Mr Desai," she says. That's all she's giving him and I love her for it.

I'm next. "And why does your guru say all those terrible things about me?" he asks.

Without thinking, I reply, "Prasad, Mr Desai." I am amazed at my cheek.

I don't know where that word came from but it hangs there between us like a challenge, like a slap in the face. I wonder if he'll take it from me. To have answered prasad, to have answered "gift from the divine"—and in Hindi no less!—is to have replied, in a single, smashing word, that Osho is only saying what he sees, only telling him what he really is, and that from a Master it is a gift, a gift to be used for growth. My audacity shakes me a little. But Morarji recovers quickly. "And what about sex in the commune?"

"Rumours, Mr Desai." And I say no more. But the interview cannot go on like this, in nothing more than monosyllabic answers. "That view is based on uncorroborated reports in the press," I add. "Many of the sannyasins are celibate; in my case, for example, there has been no sex in my life for almost a year."

I decide to let it go at that. There's no point in telling him it's not from choice, that it's just because no one turns me on—and what with all the work I've had because of him and his bloody government hassling us I wouldn't have time even if someone did.

He dismisses me with a wave. "I don't believe you."

"Then who do you believe?" I ask.

"I have sent people."

"Who?"

"People."

"And you believe what they have told you?"

"Yes, I do."

"They are deceiving you, Mr Desai, telling you what they think you want to hear."

"I don't believe you."

It gets boring after a while, this taciturn repartee. He asks a question and I answer. Then he says, "I don't believe you." It just gets boring. "Why have you banned the BBC?" I ask. Anything to change the pattern.

At the mention of those three letters he shorts out. It's as if someone has pulled his plug. For the next thirty seconds there's no one home. Madhura and I exchange sidelong glances. She shrugs, equally at a loss. But suddenly he's back again, as if he's just woken up. "About the BBC," he says dryly, "there is nothing more to be said."

"Then," I ask, "what about Indian embassies all over the world denying visas to people who want to come to Pune?"

"I have given no instructions," he replies. "No word of this has reached me. If this is happening—which I doubt—it is happening at other levels of government. I have given no instructions."

It's my turn. "I don't believe you."

He isn't pleased. He looks down at his desk, rubbing his hands together thoughtfully. He reminds me of Pontius Pilate. "Why are you against the commune?" I inquire, pressing him. "Why are you so against allowing us to set up this new rural commune? Why do you block us at every possible turn?"

"We have had a bad experience with this sort of thing before, at the Aurobindo ashram in Pondicherry," he replies, referring to recent reports of conflicts and violence between factions there.

"But this is not the same thing at all!" I retort. "Both Sri Aurobindo and The Mother are dead. There is no living guide at Pondicherry any more. Osho is very much alive!"

"Who does he think he is to call himself divine?" he spits at me across the desk. He's angry now.

"He is divine, Mr Desai. So are you and so am I. You call yourself a religious man, so you *know* that nothing exists but the divine. The only difference is that Osho has recognized it and declared it. The rest of us, you and me included, are still asleep."

There's nothing he can say, but he's not pleased. The look he gives me is hard, full of hatred. "Why are you against us?" I ask again.

"I have to protect Hinduism. I have to protect India."

"And do you see us as a threat?" I ask, my voice light, amused. I'm beginning to find the whole thing a bit funny. And I can't help wondering how the millions of Muslims, Parsis, Buddhists, Christians and Jains in India would appreciate his concern for Hinduism and for Hinduism alone. Osho is right: he is a Hindu chauvinist.

"No," he answers coldly. "I am making certain you do not become a threat. Not in any way whatsoever." He leans across the desk, bringing his face closer to mine. "I won't interfere with you as long as you remain where you are in Pune, as long as you are confined there. But this new commune I will not allow!" His tone is suddenly menacing. "Remember one thing. I could have banned you. But I didn't." He settles back in his chair, confident now, as if he's just won something.

Although I betray nothing, the realization that he could, with his parliamentary majority, ban us, make us an illegal sect, throw us into prison for wearing the mala, quite takes me aback. It's new for me, confronting this kind of power. All at once I've had enough of this horrid old man. And he's obviously had enough of Madhura and me as well. In the silence that follows his pronouncement he fixes his beady eye on the clock suspended on the opposite wall.

I take the hint. "Thank you for your time, Mr. Desai," I say politely. I place the books we've brought on the corner of his desk. "Here are some books of Osho's discourses for you. We felt they might interest you. The English book is on Patanjali; the Hindi, on *Bhagavad Gita*."

"I am a busy man," he says. "This is a large country to run. I have little time to read."

"Then I'll take them back."

A gnarled claw shoots across the desk, pinning them down. "Leave them!" the Prime Minister of India commands. "I will look through them." We make it through the anteroom, past the battery of secretaries and into the corridor before the laughter takes us over once again.

Laxmi enjoys the report. She wants it word-by-word, blow-by-blow, to pass on to Osho. When I tell her what Morarji had said about banning us, I can feel her bristling along the wire. "Stubborn old fool. India would never allow."

She chuckles. "Laxmi remembers meeting him in Delhi also. Laxmi showed plans for new commune, showing scientifically how much foreign currency it would mean for India. He just brushed plans aside with big 'No!' He didn't even read. Laxmi told him on the face he wasn't worthy to be Prime Minister of democracy. He didn't like Laxmi either.

"Anyway, swamiji," she adds, changing gear, "Calcutta keeps calling. Indu Jain wants to know when Madhura and Krishna Prem are arriving."

Calcutta

A young Indian in a white uniform reaches for our luggage. "Good morning," he says politely. "I am Mrs Jain's driver. You are Swami Krishna Prem?"

Whatever I knew of Calcutta was from books and movies, and driving towards the city, phrases like "teeming millions" and "Black Hole" run through my head. But no mental picture prepares me. It is the saddest, filthiest place I've ever seen. And there are people everywhere—a seething, milling mass of people. By contrast, Bombay and Delhi are ghost towns.

That Calcutta was once beautiful is apparent. The shadow of the Raj is still here in the huge Gothic structures that line the broken, pot-holed streets. But what is paramount is the sense of irreversible decay. A huge chunk of mortar, a section of brick, a broken gargoyle's head, a corner of a chimney, a window frame—all manner of things lay scattered on the sidewalks, fallen from buildings eroded by a century of driving east-coast monsoons and the burning Bengali sun.

I have the feeling it's all too much to cope with, that no one has the energy to bother any more, not even to care.

In the midst of this debris, tens of thousands seem to live—some under the sun and the stars; others under bits of burlap tied to spindly bamboo poles. It's the hour to collect the day's water, the only time to bathe—and the mains are open. Through gaping holes in the sidewalk, small fountains bubble, one or more per block. The water is grey and dirty, as if it's surfacing from some sour subterranean source. But it's all there is and they use it gratefully.

Driving in the air-conditioned car, we watch mothers wash their children, splashing cans of the brackish water over their cropped or shaven heads, letting it spill over their tiny limbs and round, protruding bellies. Then they wash themselves, bit by bit as Indian women do, washing one part first and then re-covering it with the sari before moving on to the next. Stripped to their shorts, the men—lean, muscular coolies and rickshaw-wallahs—cascade the water over their heads, rubbing vigorously, shoving their hands shyly into their underpants to wash their private parts. But, no matter how much the possession of genitalia embarrasses Indians, here, as in the rest of the country, the morning shit is open, exposed, unabashed, the spill over of the washing water carrying the faeces a few feet away, along the clogged and stinking drains.

The central part of the city is soon behind us and we skim along past gigantic tended parks dotted with beds of bright flowers and avenues of stately, silver-trunked Royal Palms. And suddenly, we're in a residential area, driving down a narrow street, lined, on both sides, with high cement walls and the occasional gate. In front of one of them we stop. When it swings open I can hardly believe my eyes. There, in the middle of an enormous park-like estate, sitting in the centre of an immaculate lawn and surrounded by an exquisite garden, is the most spectacular art deco mansion I have ever seen.

"Wow!" Madhura mutters softly under her breath. All I can think of is Jack's house in Montreal. If he could see this, he'd faint.

As we pull under the porte-cochère, a woman in a snow-white sari bordered in blue steps out of the house. She is strikingly beautiful, with the kind of easy, classic beauty that needs no adornment. And she wears none, except for the simple gold chain of marriage about her neck. She has the bearing of the born aristocrat. After Indira Gandhi, she's my first glimpse of India's ruling class.

"I am Indu Jain," she says in a firm, clear voice as we step from the car. "Welcome to Calcutta."

For the next week Indu Jain takes care of us. We are given a comfortable room in a guest cottage and a bearer to look after our needs. A driver is placed at our disposal for visits to the press; a telephone connects us to the central switchboard. It rings every once in a while to summon us to meals or to invite us to join Indu for tea.

She's a devotee of Osho's, an avid reader of his books, and she shows us the room where he used to stay whenever he visited Calcutta in earlier years. It's obvious she loves him. "But I cannot become a sannyasin," she says, explaining her duty as a wife and mother prevents it. She has been bred to a role and wed, in an arranged marriage, to one of India's wealthiest industrialists, to a vast empire of jute and cotton and paper and publications and God-knows-what-else.

Duty. It's a word I've heard often in this country, and it's usually accompanied by a martyred resignation mixed with an unshakable acceptance. Duty. Five thousand years of culture and tradition stand behind that word. Indu's eyes seem a little sad, yet she appears to be neither happy nor unhappy. "This is my duty," she says plainly, a gesture of a delicate hand encompassing everything around her. For her, everything is explained in the one word. For her, it says all.

Ashok Jain, the husband-industrialist, doesn't like us. He's recovering from an operation and in our single visit to his chambers he makes himself quite clear—he doesn't like Osho, he didn't like him blessing Mrs Gandhi, and he doesn't care too much for us either.

Nor does the rest of Calcutta. The Bengali and local English press are simply not interested in us or our commune. Pune is too remote, too far away to have any meaning or interest. And looking about their dying city, I somehow understand. Calcutta has other, more pressing concerns than us and our commune. About the only thing I enjoy is meeting M.J. Akbar from *Ananda Bazar Patrika*.

Within the first thirty seconds of our get-together, after I've given him time to recover from the shock of seeing us walk into his office, I thank him for having the courage to publish such photos in India and for the tremendous help he's been, helping us bring the work that happens in therapy groups to the attention of the Indian public. He doesn't know what to say. Maxdhura doesn't either. She keeps coughing so she doesn't laugh. But by the time we leave his office, he's agreed to send a reporter to Pune to do an in-depth story for *Sunday,* his widely circulated, national newsmagazine.

"It's high time," he says earnestly, as if he'd thought of the idea all by himself, "that someone told India what's *really* happening in your commune!"

During my nightly call to Laxmi I tell her that, except for Akbar, Calcutta's a bust. She tells us to meet her in New Delhi the following day. Madhura and I catch the morning flight and, for the next two days, sit huddled in Delhi, freezing, waiting for her to come. She doesn't show. Finally, she says to come back to Pune. "Something exciting is happening," is all I can get out of her on the phone.

Back in Pune

Walking into her office the next afternoon, grateful to be home after three weeks on the road, I find that "something exciting" is a German film crew composed of a sannyasin called Veet Artho and three of his friends.

"Project is wonderful," she explains, overflowing with enthusiasm. "Since Pia Renti, all of Germany is thirsty for Osho. Film will reach hundreds of thousands."

"What angle is he taking?" I want to know. "What's the film to be about?"

"Groups."

"Groups," Sheela says, echoing Laxmi. "Can you believe it?"

"Which? Zazen, Vipassana?"

"No. Encounter and Somendra's Leela."

"What?" I can't believe what I'm hearing. "After what happened with the *STERN* photos from the Encounter and Leela groups, you're going to let someone *film*?"

"Swamiji," she says, fixing me with a look that tells me plainly I should stop while I'm ahead, "Laxmi does not need you to tell her what to do or what not to do. Laxmi is Managing Trustee. And Laxmi likes this Veet Artho. And Laxmi likes this idea." She lowers her voice to a whisper. "Besides, Laxmi has arranged for mock groups to happen. Participants will all be hand-picked people who have done these groups before."

"And you think that's okay?" I insist. "You think that's going to make things look nicer? Laxmi, if you want my opinion, I think this is a terrible idea and we shouldn't get involved at all."

"Did Laxmi ask for your opinion, swamiji?"

I give up. "What's the film going to be called, Laxmi?"

"*Ashram in Pune,*" she announces. "Beautiful, huh?"

"Beautiful," I agree with as much sarcasm as I can muster.

The Kansas City Milkman

Jonestown. The name sends chills up and down my spine. The morning I open the papers to see those ghastly, grisly photos splashed across the front pages, I know a lot of flak is going to come our way. The office is besieged by overseas calls and telegrams from anxious parents. And I get the Kansas City milkman.

At the New Delhi press conference, cassette recorder whirring in the front row sat a young, clean-cut American collegiate-type. He asked good questions; he seemed sharp, bright, keen. He later introduced himself as Harry Schindler* of Associated Press. Now, here he is in Pune, prize-winning photographer Eddie Adams in tow.

Harry drives me crazy. He has a two-track mind and he's unbudgeable. Jonestown and the Kansas City milkman. Jonestown and the Kansas City milkman.

Jonestown I can understand. It's big news. But the Kansas City milkman! "That's AP's average reader," Harry tells me for the hundredth time. "That's who we have to write for. We have to give the Kansas City milkman what he wants to read at breakfast. And he wants sensation."

"You won't find it here."

"I have to. The Kansas City milkman wants it."

And then, as if the homogenized half-wit weren't enough, there's the list of AP subscribers. "We've got editors all over America to keep happy too," he tells me with wide-eyed Yankee sincerity. "They want local reference otherwise they might cancel the AP service and go with UPI or someone else. Now, you've got to find me people to talk to," he consults a sheet of paper, "from Minneapolis, Chicago, Des Moines, Houston..."

"And Kansas City."

"Yeah, from Kansas City too. And from Duluth and Portland and..." I feel like I'm listening to a Greyhound schedule.

"If Osho asked you to kill yourself, would you?" he asks everyone he meets.

"He never would," is the standard reply. But Harry isn't satisfied. "Look," I finally say to him in exasperation, "why don't you ask Osho if he would ever ask us to do it? That's the crux of your question. Write out a question and I'll send it in to him. I'm pretty sure he'll answer you."

The following morning, sitting in Buddha Hall with a fidgety Harry at my side, the moment I hear Osho say "The first question," I know what's coming.

"Some people," he reads, "have drawn parallels between your commune and Jonestown. Could what happened in that jungle clearing in Guyana happen here: a mass suicide? Would you ask your sannyasins to make symbolic or real sacrifices for you or your beliefs?"

A pause. Then: "Harry Schindler, I also teach death." I love Osho for this. He couldn't have picked a better opening line. And he's got Harry's attention totally. The Kansas City milkman's favourite writer's bolt upright, pencil at the ready. "But it is a different kind of death," Osho continues. "It is the death that Jesus taught. Jesus said, 'Those who want to enter the kingdom of God will have to be born again.' They have to die on one level and be awakened into another. They will have to be free from the body and will have to spread their wings in the sky of consciousness. This is what I call the *real* death.

"The body keeps on dying; it dies on its own. To kill the body is the same as killing something that is already dead. It is the mind that has to be killed—the mind which continues to live in spite of many deaths. After each death the process of rebirth starts again. I am for the death of the mind, not of the body. I want my sannyasins to die, but that death will be at the material level so that they can live on the spiritual level. They should die as mud so that they can bloom as the lotus. Throughout history this death has been taught by all the true Masters."

I glance at Harry out of the corner of my eye. I can almost hear the wheels of his mind churning. Osho's tossing things in there that Harry's head has never had to try to compute before.

"Harry Schindler, you have asked whether the mass suicide that has happened in Guyana is also possible here.

"Here, the one who becomes a sannyasin has already committed suicide. Sannyas means: I die to what I was so that I can live as I am. I drop my masks. I let my personality drop so that my soul can emerge. Sannyas is suicide, suicide in the true sense, because only then does true life begin. Here, there is no room for any other kind of suicide; here, there is no other way. Here, there is utter silence and peace. Here, out of this peace, the song of bliss arises. It is not that the sannyasin is singing, he is simply allowing existence to sing through him.

"And, Harry Schindler, you have also asked whether I will ask my sannyasins to make any symbolic or real sacrifices for me and my beliefs. I do not teach beliefs; on the contrary, I teach *freedom* from beliefs. I teach you how you can be free from the clutches of knowledge. I do not give you knowledge but take it away from you. I want to give you emptiness.

"Another name for this silence is meditation. As long as knowledge is there, meditation is not possible. Only when all knowledge is dropped does meditation come into being. Meditation is that state of innocence in which there is not a speck of dust on the mirror of your consciousness.

"I am not teaching you any beliefs. I do not even ask you to believe that God exists. I do not ask you to believe that there is rebirth. I do not stand for any sort of belief. I only ask you to know that which is right here and now. My emphasis is not on belief. Whatsoever makes you believe does so just to enslave you. To make you believe is to lead you towards lies.

"That which is not within your experience is a lie. My experience is truth, and your experience will be your truth. My experience can never be your truth. What I have tasted cannot be the same for you. If I have listened to music, you cannot have the joy of it. If I have eaten, how can your hunger be satisfied? Similarly, how can my sannyasin know godliness merely because I have experienced it? If the hunger of the body cannot be satisfied in such a way, how can the hunger of the soul be satisfied?

"So remember, whenever truth is passed from one who knows to those who do not, in the very process it becomes a lie. The truth of another is not your truth. That is why I am not giving you any beliefs. If I am imparting anything, it is awareness, wakefulness—so the question of making any sacrifices for me and my beliefs simply doesn't arise. Sacrifice and renunciation have no place in my lifestyle. I do not ask you to renounce anything for me; I cannot. Yes, that which you see as false will drop on its own, and that which is meaningful will stay with you. This will happen in your innermost core. You will be its observer and its owner. I am not your owner. At the most I am your friend...

"When your own lamp will be lit, all beliefs will disappear. You will not find me a guru and yourself a disciple. There will be no more I and thou. Then, only godliness remains—no Master, no disciple. When both disappear, the first encounter with truth happens."[10]

When Osho finishes I turn to Harry. And I see that this beautiful, moving, profound reply has been wasted on this man. He smiles at me, as if he is pleased with Osho's answer, but behind the look lurks the journalist, the reporter who, no matter what, is going to give the Des Moines editor and the Kansas City milkman exactly what they want to read. I know, without a doubt, that when Harry's article circles the world, tapping out on teleprinters in thousands of newspaper offices in hundreds of cities on several continents, millions of readers will be utterly convinced there's another potential Jonestown here in Pune. He won't say it directly, of that I'm also aware. It'll be implied through insinuation, through innuendo, but it'll be said. I can see it in his eyes.

Suddenly there's a bad taste in my mouth. Suddenly, this morning, I don't like my job all that much any more.

The Illustrated Weekly of India Article is Published

"God," Madhura says, handing me back the magazine, "what was all the fuss about? How could anyone be offended by this?"

Bachi Karkaria's suppressed article has finally surfaced in *The Illustrated Weekly of India*. And it's beautiful. It's intelligent, honest, impartial, light-hearted, and the first thing published in the country that comes close to portraying us as we are.

"You people still don't understand," Laxmi says, wagging her finger at the two of us. "For two thousand years Indians have been slaves, and this kind of thinking does not die easily. Indians are afraid to take risks, scared to offend whosoever sits on the chair above. *Illustrated Weekly* article is case in point. Editor knew Indu Jain loves Osho—and no ashram in India before ours ever welcomed publicity—so editor was afraid to publish in case owner got offended.

---

10. *Philosophia Perennis, Vol. 2*

This is how it is in India. And same is true everywhere. Look at problems with Morarji. All of Indian bureaucracy knows Morarji is against commune, so they are all against—and thousand-and-one delays and hindrances happen. So long as Morarji sits on the chair, commune will never have justice in India."

"Do you think he'll ever budge, Laxmi?" I ask, remembering the meeting with him in Delhi. "He's a stubborn old fart."

She makes a rude noise with her lips. "Old fart," she laughs. "Laxmi likes that. Fart. Laxmi likes new, modern words. But, swamiji, no, Laxmi thinks old fart will do nothing. Anyway, we tell you Morarji won't last. Soon he will be gone and Indira will be back on the chair. And then all this will stop; then new commune will happen. Just a few more months, Laxmi feels. So we keep on hammering. Laxmi told him on the face: to play with Foundation is to play with fire!"

Bernard Levin

Trim and neat in his beige cotton twills and plain white shirt, Bernard Levin, at forty-odd, still has the air of an English schoolboy. Walking him around the commune, the clear brown eyes behind the donnish horn-rims missing absolutely nothing, I feel like I'm escorting David Attenborough on one of his zoological expeditions, touring him through the hitherto-unexplored habitat of newly discovered species of yeti or yak.

He says little and asks less. The star writer of *The Times* hasn't come from London to ply us with questions. "I've read your press kit and some of Osho's books," he tells me. Bernard Levin is here to observe.

When Savita, one of Pratima's book editors, had excitedly brought me a Levin clipping a couple of months ago, she'd been aghast I had never heard of him. Vishnu, on the other hand, had been more surprised by Levin himself.

"The most acid pen in English journalism," Vishnu had said by way of introduction, and then proceeded, in capsule form, to describe the career of a writer and television personality who fought fearlessly for the underdog, went for the establishment's throat with bared fangs, called a spade a spade in no uncertain terms and who could, with a few choice phrases, prick the most pompous of British balloons. "I'm amazed, laddie," Vishnu burred thoughtfully, handing the clipping back. "Something's obviously happened to Bernard Levin. If I were you, I'd invite him here."

The article in question was a report of a visit Levin had made to the Festival of Mind and Body at the Olympia in London. In a nutshell, after years of battling the establishment, Levin had come to the conclusion that, essentially, nothing was going to change, that we were all headed down the drain, and that it was time for intelligent individuals to start looking about for personal alternatives. He'd gone to the Festival to check out what the spiritual supermarket had to offer. And he'd come away impressed, sharing his feelings in a sincere, sensitive and thought-provoking article written in some of the finest English prose I'd read in a very long time. He'd spent time at the Kalptaru booth, at the display mounted by London's major Osho meditation centre, and had liked what he'd seen. It was his description of Osho as "a truly remarkable Indian sage" that had prompted Savita's mum to despatch the cutting to Pune.

That very afternoon I took Vishnu's advice. I wrote to Levin, inviting him to visit us, and included a copy of our press kit. He replied promptly, saying that as chance would have it he would be in Pune in January, covering an Anglo-Indian conference, and that he'd stay on a few days after completing his assignment and visit us.

A few days ago, he had arrived. In mid-conference. "Much more interesting here," he said. And he had a journalistic bonus in tow—Peter Jenkins of *The Guardian*.

"Not bad," Subhuti commented, "getting London's two biggest papers at once." I handed Jenkins over to Subhuti. One of Subhuti's old House of Commons cronies was now news editor at *The Guardian* and had given Jenkins Subhuti's name. I like Levin at first glance. I don't mind having him to myself at all.

Osho never grants interviews, but so far he's been very cooperative with journalists, answering whatever questions they submit to discourse. I suggest Levin ask something, but there's nothing he wants to know. Subhuti has better luck. He shows me Jenkins' question before sending it in.

"What does your movement signify about the condition of society?" Jenkins wants to know. "Is it an escapist and self-regarding cult? Or do you propose through changing human nature to change society and the world?"

"Peter Jenkins," Osho begins the next morning, "what is happening here is not a movement, it is a mutation. It has no concern with the society; its whole concern is with the individual. It is a revolution in the true sense of the word. There is no idea of changing the society or the world, because there is no society at all. Only individuals exist. Society is an illusion. And because we believe in society, all the revolutions have failed. The belief that the society exists has sabotaged all efforts to change man, because the belief is rooted in illusion."

Beside me, Bernard Levin nods in agreement. His whole attention is focused on Osho, and there's a totality about him that is rare in people who are not sannyasins. I like him even more.

"The individual needs a mutation," Osho continues. "And what we are doing here is utterly individualistic—it is not socialistic at all. It may look as if it is an escape, but the word 'escape' in itself has nothing wrong with it. If the house is on fire and you escape from it, nobody calls you an escapist. You are simply intelligent, that's all.

"We are not escaping, we are simply trying to understand what is the case. We are not avoiding problems. In fact, just the contrary: we are facing all the problems that the society has avoided. We are trying to encounter all the problems that the so-called society has been teaching you to repress.

"They have told you not to accept yourself in your totality. They have told you that much is wrong in you—in fact, the major part of your being, of your wholeness, is wrong. That wrong part has to be denied expression; that wrong part has to be repressed. And once you start repressing anything in yourself, a rift is created. Then you go on repressing all your problems and you go on sitting on the volcano thinking everything is okay—and knowing all the time that nothing is okay. Deep down there is fire, and it is going to erupt any moment.

"Then people become neurotic and psychotic. Then people suffer millions of diseases unnecessarily. But it serves the vested interest... It serves all those who are in power.

"My effort here is not to change the society but to transform the individual—to help the individual to become whole, to help the individual to drop this rift between the conscious and the unconscious, to help the individual not to repress any more but to accept himself, not to condemn but to love himself.

"The person who really loves himself, who is in tremendous love with himself, cannot do any harm to anybody, because he cannot do any harm to himself.

"So in a way we are escapists—because whatsoever you call real life is not real. It is a distortion of life; it is something else in the name of life. And we are *certainly* self-regarding, because out of that regard, regard for the other is born.

"If the individual can be helped, if the individual can be enlightened, if the individual can be persuaded to celebrate life, to enjoy life, only then will we be able to change the climate around the earth. But that is not our purpose; that is not our goal: that is going to be just a consequence.

"Now the time has come that if buddhas are not tried, then there is no future—man is doomed. Because man has slowly, slowly invented so many violent forces, man has discovered such dangerous weapons, the next war will not be the third, it will be the last.

"The next war will be the total war. It will destroy all life—not only human life, but all life, life as such.

"Before it happens, please give one opportunity to those who have been saying again and again—Krishna, Christ, Buddha, Lao Tzu, Zarathustra—that the individual has to be transformed. And once the individual is transformed, society automatically changes. That is a consequence.

"So we are not proposing any social revolution here. I am not at all concerned with the society; my whole concern is the real individual...

"You ask me, 'Do you propose through changing human nature to change society and the world?'

"I don't propose it. That's how it can happen—the only way it can happen. But that is not our goal.

"When you kindle a light, darkness disappears of its own accord. You need not look for darkness with a light to find out where it is and force it to go out of the room. You need not do anything like that. If light is there, darkness is not there.

"If man is transformed he becomes a light—unto himself first, and then for others too. That's a natural consequence.

"We live in the present; we live in meditation. We allow ourselves to be full of love, so that it starts overflowing. But this whole thing is non-utopian. We are not searching for a utopia. We are not searching for a golden age to come into the world, although the golden age can only come this way. There is no other way. All other ways have failed."[11]

I don't know why, but throughout Osho's reply I've had the distinct feeling he's been speaking more to Bernard Levin than to Peter Jenkins. It's as if Osho's answered all the questions Levin himself posed in the article that first brought him to our attention. Throughout Osho's reply, Levin sat silently beside me, making the occasional note in the little spiral pad resting on his knee—and, unlike the other journalists I've squired to discourse, I feel he's missed nothing, that every single word has been allowed in. Of the two British reporters, Levin is by far the more influential, the more far reaching, but, as well, he's also the deeper, the more sensitive, the more intelligent man. Spending time with him, I've sensed his vision of life is simple, direct, uncomplicated. He seems basically at peace with himself and the world around him. Perhaps I'm right. Perhaps Osho has been speaking, through Jenkins, to him.

But whether I'm right or not, Levin is a gift for me. After the caustic, cynical collection of journalists that have paraded through the press office since it began, he's like a breath of fresh air. To talk to an intelligent man, to one who stretches me, is far out. To have to

11. *Philosophia Perennis, Vol. 2*

dig inside myself, into my own experience of Osho, and to translate it into worldly terms—and to see I can do it well with a man of Levin's calibre—thrills me, makes me fall in love, all over again, with Laxmi's abiding passion, The Work.

Jenkins is off to Bombay a couple of hours after the discourse. He's catching an evening flight to London. We promise to forward the transcript of Osho's answer to his question within a couple of days. Levin's going to stay on. "I quite like it here," he says. "Besides, there's no rush to get back. *The Times* is on strike and I have no idea when I'll be able to write about the commune anyway."

And he sees it in detail—each and every department. He chats with dozens of workers, sits in on the meditations and the evening music group, and even gets himself hauled into Sufi dancing for a little whirl. We spend hours gossiping with Laxmi and wander through most of the quiet groups, through Centring, Enlightenment Intensive, Vipassana and Zazen. After a couple of days he's pretty well seen it all. "There's not much left to show you, Bernard," I say. "I'll take you to darshan tomorrow night, before you leave. Is there anything you want to do, anyone you want to meet?" I ask.

"I wouldn't mind chatting with the two English group leaders involved in the *STERN* article," he replies.

Later that afternoon, Teertha and Somendra join us for tea. And they all get on immediately. They both like Bernard as much as I do.

For the most part I'm redundant. They're talking group processes, explaining how they work, what happens with people—Teertha, soft-spoken, gentle, a bit reserved; Somendra, excited, voluble, his hands waving all over the place. Actually, it's not that they're excluding me, it's that my attention is elsewhere. On our waitress. It's Vasumati. Between groups, she's working in Vrindavan.

Apart from one brief meeting the day she and her girlfriend Aneesha had moved into the commune, I haven't seen her since she left the press office. She looks good: working with people agrees with her. It turns out Bernard Levin's name is quite familiar to her—his best pal, Herbert Kretzmer, the English drama and television critic, is her father's cousin. She sets her tray aside and joins us. Watching her, listening to her, I have to admit to a certain pang, to a kind of aching nostalgia for something that might have been. I find myself wishing she'd put down that cake and lose a few pounds.

Throughout his visit, I sense, more from his demeanour than from his words, that Bernard Levin knows exactly what is happening here, that he is observing a twentieth-century buddha's mystery school at work. I feel he understands Osho—as much as anyone can understand a Christ or a Buddha or a Lao Tzu.

Sitting with him in darshan, glancing occasionally in his direction, I feel my intuition has been right. Bernard Levin *does* recognize Osho. The only thing that makes me a little sad for this man I like so much is that his recognition is an intellectual one, and not one that's coming from his heart. Bernard Levin is observing a phenomenon, not participating in it.

Later that evening, after darshan, in answer to my signal, a rickshaw sputters to a halt in front of the main gate. Bernard Levin reaches for my hand. "Thank you for everything," he says. "You've made me feel very welcome, very much at home. I'll write about the commune as soon as the strike is over. I'll let you know."

I tell him it's been beautiful having him here. "And I hope you'll come back one day," I add. I mean it. I'm quite sincere.

"I'm sure I shall."

The question sits on the tip of my tongue, burning. I can't resist asking. "Bernard, you really do understand what's happening here, don't you?"

Our eyes meet. For a moment, nothing passes between us but this look. "Yes, Krishna Prem," he says at last. "Yes, I do."

The rickshaw coughs into motion, heading down the street, ferrying Bernard Levin towards the Blue Diamond, towards Bombay, towards London. He leans out once, waving. I wave back, in farewell. But not so much to a journalist. More to a newfound friend.

Chapter Seven: 1980

WHAT ABOUT ME?

I'm suddenly lonely. Incredibly, achingly lonely. It's not friendship that's missing. There's Divy and Mukta and Laxmi; there's Madhura, Subhuti, Mangala, the whole press office gang. There are afternoon teas, evening beers at the Blue Diamond, parties in people's rooms, sorties into Pune for South Indian snacks or a Gujarati thali—always something going on. It's not companionship I'm lacking, it's intimacy. I'm craving that special something that only happens one-to-one. A lover is missing in my life.

And everywhere I look these days, lovers are all I see. Embracing after the discourse, kissing hello at morning tea, lying in each other's arms during lunch break, strolling around Buddha Hall in the evening, entwined under the stars on the bridge out back—it's all I see. And at night, lying alone in my bed, the sounds of love-making are the worst. From all over the commune they come, driving me, some nights, to distraction.

Yet I do nothing. A part of me says just to sit and wait, that someone will come. But another part of me, sometimes as strong, despairs. I begin to wonder, at times, if it's all over for me, if Rani, Maggie and Devika were it, if there isn't going to be anyone else. Sex is available, but I'm not interested. It's something else I want.

When I'm in this space of wanting, I find myself turning more and more to Laxmi. She intrigues me. Nothing, absolutely nothing seems to be missing for her. Osho is her lover. Not in any physical sense, but he is her lover—like Krishna was for Meera, like Jesus was for Theresa. And as mortal lovers express themselves in kisses and caresses, Laxmi's love manifests in her utter dedication to Osho's work. "The Work", she always calls it, somehow capitalizing the words by her very devotion.

The Work. Is this what it has to become for me? Everything? Do I have to let all ideas of a special woman go? Is she never going to come? Do I have to marry myself to the work and forget everything else? Is sex, I begin to wonder, finished for me? Osho often says things drop away and it takes the mind a while to catch up. Is it gone? There's no real driving urge in my body. Have I transcended sex and not realized it yet?

It seems I'm not the only person in the commune wondering if sex has dropped away. Sampati, a friend from Berlin, a cleaner, has been asking herself the same question. And she puts it to Osho one morning.

"Transcendence is possible only when you have known the whole secret of sex," he says.

Okay, there's the answer. I've transcended nothing. Whether this is a period of preparation or limbo or whatever, I don't know. But one thing's clear—I can drop this idea of transcendence. I've transcended nothing.

"The secret is," Osho continues, "it is a biological, natural device to make you aware of meditation. It is through sexual orgasm that meditation has been discovered. The first person who must have discovered meditation is bound to have discovered it through sex. There is no other way—because sex is a natural phenomenon. Meditation is a discovery; it is not a natural phenomenon. It is going beyond nature; it is transcendence...

"Repression cannot help you towards transcendence. Only expression can take you to transcendence...

"Going beyond sex, you go beyond the animals. Going beyond sex you shatter the biological prison cell around you. Going beyond sex you go beyond the earth. For the first time you start looking at the sky and the stars, and the faraway lights start showering on you. And faraway, distant music is heard, and you are moving towards your real destiny, towards your real fulfilment.

"Animal, human, divine: these are the three layers in you. The animal layer consists of sex, the human layer consists of love, the divine layer consists of prayer. It is the same energy expressing itself in higher and higher forms—the mud, the lotus, the fragrance...

"Sex has to be learned, and there is nobody to teach; no schools exist. No schools are allowed to exist. Everybody is allowed to poison you against sex; nobody is allowed to teach you the right way to sex. Nobody is allowed to make it an exquisite art. It is...

"Experiment freshly again. Go into it meditatively. It is prayer. It is one of the most sacred things, the holiest of the holy—because it is through sex that life arrives and it is through sex that you can penetrate to the very source of life.

"If you go deep into sex you will find God. You will find God's hand somewhere deep in the world of sexual experience.

"Sex has to be a meditation and you have to learn the art of it. Sing, dance, celebrate. Sex should not be a hasty affair. It should not be a hit-and-run affair—as it is.

"Savour of it. It should be a great ritual. That's how Tantra rituals arose... Don't enter with lust, enter with prayerfulness; then you will be able to know the secret of sex. Don't enter to exploit the other, enter to share with the other. Don't enter as if sex is just a kind of relief—that's the lowest form of sex. The highest form is not relief but ecstasy. Relief is negative.

"Yes, sex unburdens you of certain energy, but if it simply unburdens then you have missed the positive part. The positive part is when that energy nourishes you, creates something higher in you. When sex is just used as relief, like a sneeze, it is the lowest form of it. The highest form is tremendously creative—energy is not just thrown out of your being, energy is recirculated on higher planes. Energy takes a flight; it starts rising above gravitation. It starts penetrating your higher chakras. It is not only a release but a tremendous, ecstatic flight. And then only will you know that at the deepest moment of orgasm, ego and time disappear. Once you have known that, you will not need sex any more. Sex has revealed its secrets; it has given you the key, the golden key. Now you can use that golden key without going into any sexual activity. Now you can sit silently in Zazen, Vipassana.

Now you can sit silently, dropping your ego and forgetting time, and you will reach to the same heights and you will stay on those heights longer and longer.

"And a day arrives when you become a permanent resident on those peaks. That day is the day of great rejoicing: one becomes a buddha."[12]

Osho's words brought something back to me, something that had slipped into the recesses of my mind. For so long now I've been immersed in the world of journalists and politicians I'd forgotten. His words brought back the darshan when I'd told him what had been happening with Rani. "You're on absolutely the right track," he'd said.

"She *will* come," I tell myself, trusting again. "I just have to be patient. She *will* come."

The Desperation of Lovelessness

Across the room—I can't even make it across the room. The moment the door closes behind me the tears burst upon my cheeks in a flood. My knees buckle under me and I fall to the floor, sobbing. I can't even make it across the room to my bed.

I don't know what's going on. All I'm aware of is that a root's been cut. In this morning's discourse, he's severed something. And it hurts.

The question had come from Chandana, the head of the photography department. "Osho," she'd asked, "my mind has difficulty understanding the existence of beginninglessness. Would you please talk about it?"

"Don't try to do the impossible," he said. "Trying to understand reality through the mind is like pulling yourself up by your own shoestrings. Maybe you can hop a little bit, but that hopping is not going to help—you will be back on the ground again and again... That is not going to give you wings.

12. *Philosophia Perennis, Vol. 2*

"Slowly slowly, learn the art of contacting reality without the mind interfering. Sometimes when the sun is setting, just sit there looking at the sun, not thinking about it—watching, not evaluating, not even saying, 'How beautiful it is!' The moment you say something, the mind has come in...

"The mind has its limited uses. Use it. When you are working in your office, I am not telling you to be a no-mind...I am saying be *perfectly* a mind. Use the mind, but don't carry it continuously, twenty-four hours, day in and day out, with yourself. Don't go on dragging it. Use it as you use a chair. You don't go on carrying your chair everywhere, wherever you go, just because you may need it.

"The mind is a beautiful instrument—if you know how to be a no-mind too.

"The mind is impotent, incapable of knowing the beginningless and the endless. The mind exists between birth and death. It knows nothing beyond birth and death.

"You were here before you were born, and you will be here after you are dead. The mind has a very limited existence, very momentary—one day it comes; another day it is gone. You are forever. Have some experience of your foreverness.

"But that is possible only through no-mind. No-mind is another name for meditation.

"If you really want to understand, you will have to lose the mind."[13]

Alone in my room, lying on the floor, crying, I'm surprised at the intensity of my reaction to his words. In the discourse itself, I'd simply sat there listening, attentive but unmoved. But now, through the tears, I see how I've always relied on my mind, on its ability to grasp, to comprehend. And now he's telling me it's impotent, that if I really want to understand, I have to let it go.

I know what he's talking about. I've heard him say many times we have to start living from our hearts, from that deeper centre. But my

---

13. *The Book of Wisdom*

heart feels dry and barren. I beat the floor in frustration. "Where is she?" I want to know. "Where is she?"

And suddenly a great anger arises in me, a rage against Divy. All at once he's the barrier. All at once I just want to be free of this man. Unless this happens, something in me knows, I won't be ready when she comes.

Friendships come and go, of that I'm aware, but what makes accepting that this one has run its course difficult for me is the memory of my having been his mother before. Ever since that night in Lonavla when the memory had surfaced, when I recalled his being taken away from me, I'd known that, in this life, I had to make it up, that I had a debt to repay.

But one thing that's been nagging at me, making me uncertain, is the way it is between us. Divy's not my only experience of relationships that span lives. There's been Rani, Shantidas, Wakil. And with each, no matter what's been worked out, there's been an exchange of gifts and a parting in a space of gratitude and love.

But about Divy, I'm at a loss. I've given myself headaches trying to figure things out. And why it needs resolution so badly, I'm unable to say. I've been feeling I've got to understand what's happening so I can deal with it.

And now, this morning, Osho says it's impossible—the mind's impotent.

I don't know what else to do. I write Osho a note, telling him everything. "Is the relationship finished?" I ask. "Is the debt repaid?"

The next morning, sitting nervously in discourse, knowing my letter will go in with Laxmi when he's finished, I suddenly hear Osho say Vasumati's name. She's asked him something about relationship.

He talks to her about accepting happiness and unhappiness both, about accepting harmony and discord, agony and ecstasy, about saying yes to whatsoever life brings. He is tremendously gentle and tender with her. And what he says about love moves me deeply.

"Love can have three dimensions," he tells her. "One—that of dependence. That's what happens to the majority of people. The husband is dependent on the wife; the wife is dependent on the husband. They exploit each other; they dominate each other; they possess each other; they reduce each other into commodities. In ninety-nine per cent of cases, that's what's happening in the world.

"That's why love, which can open the gates of paradise, only opens the gates of hell.

"The second possibility is love between two independent persons. That too happens once in a while, but that too brings misery, because there is constant conflict. No adjustment is possible. Both are so independent and nobody is ready to compromise, adjust with the other...

"And the third possibility is of interdependence. That happens very rarely, but whenever it happens, a part of paradise falls on the earth. Two persons, neither independent nor dependent, but in a tremendous synchronicity, as if breathing for each other, one soul in two bodies. Whenever that happens, love has happened. Call only *it* love. The other two are not really love, just arrangements—social, psychological, biological—but arrangements. The third is something spiritual."[14]

I hope she finds it, I say to myself. I know that desire. It's what I want too.

Laxmi has just come from Osho, and in her hand is my note. She waves it at me as she heads for the bathroom. "He says: 'Talk to Teertha'," she announces as she closes the door.

By mid-afternoon I'm still fuming. I feel ignored, put off, hurt, insulted. How could he treat something so important so lightly? "So, swamiji," Laxmi asks, "how do you feel?"

"Hurt," I reply sullenly.

"Hurt!" she exclaims, looking at me like I were a child, and a

---

14. *The Book of Wisdom*

retarded one at that. "Hurt? By Osho!" She clicks her tongue at me, as if I've let her down.

The following morning I'm waiting in her room with some press office work when she comes from Osho. She tells me he'd asked how I reacted to his answer to my letter. She told him. "He laughed," she says. "He said to tell you there's no need to talk to Teertha if you don't want to."

"It doesn't matter," I shrug. "I've already made the appointment. It doesn't matter. I get the point. It's just Osho's way of giving me a slap in the ego. Anyway, I've never had a therapy session before. And I've already made the appointment. I'll talk to Teertha." I'm no further ahead in relation to Divy, but, for me, the affair is finished. Osho, though, I discover the next morning, has a bit more to say.

Savita's mum, the lady who'd sent the Levin clipping, is visiting her daughter, and she's submitted a question about the orange and the mala.

"This is a device, dear lady, to keep unwanted people out...," Osho tells her. "Orange is as good as any other color, or no color. It has nothing special about it. I could have chosen any—green, black; that would have done. But its purpose is that it is a device. It is for people who are ready to do a few mad things—because, later on, bigger and bigger mad things are waiting. If you cannot do such a simple, silly thing as wearing orange, a locket and a mala; if you can't gather enough courage to look foolish, a laughingstock, and feel absurd and ridiculous wherever you go—if you cannot do this much then this place is not for you, because bigger and bigger things will have to be done.

"As you move deeper into intimacy with me I will demand more and more illogical things, because only through those demands can the mind disappear; there is no other way. Those demands are like electric shocks. Only then can your cultivated mind, cultivated for centuries, be shaken to the foundations.

"This is just a simple device to help freak out people who are not meant to be here. They simply escape. Seeing such a mad crowd, seeing people in orange, they become afraid and they escape...

"These are small devices. And sometimes small devices work very deeply, because you cannot detect them. Big devices you can detect. They are so big, any stupid person can see them.

"Just the other day..."

Jesus Christ! I know what's coming! I know what he's going to talk about! I wish Buddha Hall would open and swallow me up. I drop my head, hiding my face. I'd like to die!

"...Krishna Prem wrote a letter to me, saying that he remembers that in many past lives he has been related to Divyananda, with whom he is in love. In the past life, he was the mother and Divyananda was the son. And he could not fulfil all the motherly duties in that life, so that's why he is in love with Divyananda now."

I am not *in* love with him, I want to shout. I love him, but I am not in love with him! God, I wish he'd stop. Everyone's laughing and I feel such an ass. I just wish he'd stop.

"But now, it seems that the debts are paid," he goes on mercilessly, "and Divyananda is hurting me in many ways, so should I finish the relationship?

"I sent him a message: Go and talk to Teertha. He was very much hurt. Naturally. He was talking about such big things..."

Despite myself, I'm laughing as hard as everyone else. Boy, is he ever taking the piss at me this morning!

"Deep down he must have waited for this," Osho continues. "Rather than saying anything about his great experience, I told him to go to Teertha and talk. That must have hurt him deeply, because I am not directly answering him, I am sending him to Teertha. And who is this Teertha anyway? Krishna Prem being sent to Teertha? Krishna Prem is as highly evolved as Teertha—so why? Or maybe he is even higher or holier. Why? Why to Teertha?

"For two days he lived in great despair. Now, such a small thing and he could not detect it. It took forty-eight hours for him to detect it. Then he understood: this is just a shock to my ego. And then immediately, in that understanding, all despair disappeared. In that understanding, just that moment, all darkness was gone and he was light, happy and back to his natural being again. But it took him forty-eight hours to detect it.

"Now there is no need. Krishna Prem, you need not go to Teertha. Now I will find something else!"[15]

"Something Else"

It's as if the day has been declared Krishna Prem Day in the commune. I am hugged and kissed and showered in love and laughter to the point where, at nightfall, I retreat to my room gratefully, uncertain, had the day gone on any longer, if I could have taken any more.

Lying in bed, I wonder what that "something else" will be. But after a bit, I drop thinking about it—trying to second-guess my Master's a total waste of time. I find myself pondering the situation with Divy. I'm not concerned with debts any more. That's all over. But, watching the sleeping form on the other side of the room, I know I'm still attached to him. And I know I want to be free.

In the middle of the night I am suddenly aware that I am dreaming, an incredibly sexual dream. The sensation is odd. I am asleep, and I am aware that I am asleep. I am dreaming, and I am aware that I am dreaming. And the awareness comes at the moment my body, in the dream, begins the climb towards orgasm.

But in the dream I am a woman! Where my male genitals should be, there is nothing external. There is just a fire, a burning, a heat. And somehow I know the orgasm building in me is female, a woman's. It's unlike anything I've ever known, yet I recognize it. It's total, complete, mad, ecstatic; it's all over my body. As it peaks, the explosion milliseconds away, I am suddenly afraid. I don't want this. And like a swimmer struggling to the surface from the ocean depths, I fight to awaken, to break the dream. But I am too late. There's nothing I can do to stop the ejaculation.

I open my eyes. And I am rocked to my foundations. From the centre of my belly, rising from my navel, is a thin, silver cord. My uncomprehending eyes follow it across the room to Divy's stomach, where it ends.

---

15. *The Book of Wisdom*

At dawn I write to Osho once again: "I have to be free!"

Lacking the strength to face another device, I don't go to Laxmi's room after discourse for the answer. I simply can't; I'm too freaked out. In the middle of the morning Arup calls me to the office. "Laxmi had to go to Bombay," she tells me. "She showed your note to Osho. He says to come to darshan the day after tomorrow and he'll cut the cord."

The rest of the day there's a new relaxation in me—soon this will all be over; soon I'll be free. Divy and I talk and it's suddenly fine again. He'd felt I wanted to curb his freedom; now he sees it's not the case.

Just before darshan Mukta drops by. She has a friend arriving from Europe this evening. "She'll be at the Blue Diamond about eight," Mukta says. "I'll be in darshan. Would you call her and tell her I'll come by the hotel about nine?"

As I leave my room at eight for the telephone at the reception desk in Krishna House, I hear a voice. It's been a long time, but I recognize it. "Now you're going to meet the woman you've been waiting for," it says.

I just keep walking, trying not to think, trying not to interfere in any way.

To my own surprise, I am quite calm. I make the call for Mukta and replace the receiver in the cradle. I turn to go. Outside Krishna House, standing on the steps, is a woman, watching me through the glass door. Our eyes meet. "That's her," the voice says.

My own voice sounds stunned when it reaches my ears: "Vasumati?"

Vasumati?

I hadn't bargained on this. I'd known a woman was coming, but never for a second had I thought it might be her. But it is. There is no question whatsoever. Looking at her, I know.

My world stopped the moment our eyes met. It was as if I'd fallen through a rent in time and space, dropping into a dimension where everything around me had halted abruptly, frozen in mid-stream, as if in a sudden shower of ice. Nothing existed but the look that flowed between us, strong and compelling, like the current of a great river.

And it had been the same for her: I read it on her face. She stood on the steps of Krishna House, utterly still and unmoving, her gaze meeting mine. And in that look, something forged between us.

I know I have to call her. "Krishna Prem, you need not go to Teertha," Osho had said the other morning, "now I will find something else." And it's Vasumati. We're being given to each other, devices to help each other grow. I know I have to call her. But I can't. My throat is dry and the words won't come. At last, I manage to raise one hand and beckon to her. Slowly, she starts up the stairs, her eyes never leaving mine. I hold the door for her. She steps inside and, without a word, follows me across the reception area into the press office.

For a while we just sit. Neither of us quite knows what to say, what to do. There's a question in her eyes, as if she's trying to understand what's going on, and I know I have to say something, that the opening move is up to me, but for the moment all I want to do is look at her, at this woman I'm to be with.

How I could ever have thought her fat makes me laugh. She's strikingly beautiful—one soft, luscious curve after another. And there's an aura of raw femaleness about her that both excites and scares me. This isn't going to be an easy liaison: I see tempestuous seas stretching out before me. But let's get on with it. "Osho's answer to your question about relationship the other day was very moving," I say, diving straight in. I know I can't tell her about the voice. At least not yet.

"It finished the one I was in," she chuckles ironically, relaxing a little now that the door's been opened.

I hadn't known she'd been involved with someone. But no matter. It's absolutely right she's free now. And I, for the first time in ages, feel ready for a relationship with someone.

I stand and hold out my hand. "Come on. Let's go to my room and I'll make us some coffee."

Again, neither of us knows what to do next. With her sitting on Divy's mattress and me across the room on mine, we look at each other, both poised on the brink of something new. Then everything stops again. And for what seems a lifetime, nothing stirs.

Suddenly, on all fours, she begins to move across the room towards me. Gently, almost tentatively, she lays her head on my chest. There is no need for words after all. The silence says all.

Finally she breaks the spell. "I've got to go, Krishna," she tells me reluctantly. "I'm in a group, I've got to get back." In the stillness that follows I detect a question.

"What are you doing tomorrow night?" I ask, replying to what she's left unsaid.

"I'll be in darshan," she says. "Every once in a while Osho's been calling me, using me as a medium. Today, Arup told me I'm to go regularly, once a week. Tomorrow's my first night. But afterwards," she adds, "I'm not doing anything. I'm completely free."

"Then I'll pick you up at Lao Tzu gate."

I need no signal to tell me darshan is over. Like a swelling billow heading for shore, I can almost see the wave of love rolling towards me down the tree-lined footpath that leads from Chuang Tzu auditorium. One and two at a time, and then in small clusters, I watch the sannyasins approach the gate, slowly, noiselessly, as if loath to leave his presence for the milling world of the commune beyond. Each and every face is aglow, shining out of some inner place—and when Vasumati appears, her step suddenly springing at the sight of me, I'm blown away by the beauty radiating from her.

Whatever it may mean to be a medium, it's obvious she's been flying. Her feet barely touch the ground as we make our way through the crowd towards the street. She chirps incessantly all the way to the Blue Diamond, as thrilled with her first night as a medium as a fledgling that's just flown solo, just tested its wings. It's not that I'm preoccupied, but I hardly hear anything she's saying. Walking with her, hand in hand, I'm amazed at the absolute rightness of being with her, of having her beside me. And I'm remembering something that happened with Laxmi in the morning.

As had become my daily habit, I'd been waiting in her room when she'd come from her post-discourse get-together with Osho.

Apart from actually being with him in Buddha Hall, it had become my favourite time of day. It was as if she carried a bit of him with her, a bit she shared generously and lovingly with Sheela and Arup and me, with those of us who met with her in her room before heading for our offices.

This morning we'd been alone. She'd spoken to me about some press matters at first and then, to my surprise, had suddenly brought up the thing I'd written to Osho about—the silver cord I'd seen running from my navel to Divy's a few nights back. "You are coming tomorrow for come-close darshan?" she'd asked. "Good," she'd said when I'd nodded. "He said to tell you cord is already cut. But come-close darshan will happen anyway."

I was a little taken aback. The whole purpose of this come-close darshan, I was told, was to sever the cord. And now he told her it had already been cut? At first I was confused, but then the penny had dropped. I'd cut it myself. When I made the move towards Vasumati, I'd somehow done it myself. Had I not listened to the voice, had I not acted on it immediately, without thinking, I'd still be bound to Divy and Osho would have to cut me free. But I am free now. Walking along with this delicious, vital woman beside me, I feel it intensely. No ties bind me. I'm free. Free for something totally new.

I want to hear all about darshan. I refill Vasumati's glass with beer. "What's it like, this medium-thing?"

She shushes me instantly. "You mustn't ask about that," she admonishes, glancing around to see if I've been overheard. I understand. Whatever role she and the other mediums are playing in the Master's drama is between them and him. It's personal, private.

"But," she adds dramatically, leaning confidentially towards me like a neighbourhood yenta about to impart a particularly tasty bit of gossip, "something quite incredible did happen!" She pauses for effect. "Tonight Osho said he was beginning a new phase of his work, and that from tomorrow night the whole commune would be in darkness during these darshans so everyone could participate. He said he'd been going to wait for the new commune, but had decided to start right now."

"I heard something about it," I say. "I was in Laxmi's room this morning when Haridas and the electricians were trying to figure out how they're going to plunge the entire commune into blackness in a split second. Anyway," I add, "I'll be in darshan tomorrow night anyway. He's giving me a come-close darshan."

"Really?" she asks, her brows lifting. "Osho called you?"

I remind her of the discourse where Osho spoke of my being Divy's mother in a past life. And then I tell her what happened afterwards, about the cord and about Osho's saying he'd cut it for me. For some reason I don't mention his message that it's already been cut. Nor do I say anything about her part in it.

"This cord-thing is really weird," she says thoughtfully. "I'd like to be there, to see what he's going to do. But I'm only supposed to go as a medium once a week."

Leaning back in her chair, she falls silent. For a few moments she says nothing. She simply looks at me, scrutinizing me, as if she's trying to figure me out.

"A silver cord running from your navel to his!" she says at last, shaking her head in complete incomprehension. "You're a strange man, Krishna Prem."

Then she says, gathering her shawl about her shoulders, "Let's get out of here."

On the way back to the commune the air between us is charged with a sense of expectancy that makes conversation impossible. As if on their own, as if guided by something else, our feet keep on moving, taking us past the gate to a darkened wall where we sit, facing each other. And then, so suddenly I can hardly believe it's happening, she is in my lap. This total embrace is so absolutely, utterly right and perfect, it takes my breath away.

A New Darshan Begins

It's been a while since I've been to darshan. And it's changed. Around

Osho's chair the set-up is the same but off to the right now sit the mediums and a group of musicians. Obviously, music is to play a part in this new phase as well.

The mediums intrigue me, and, I imagine, everyone else. Vasumati had burst into my office during the afternoon to tell me she'd just seen Vivek and had been told to come to darshan every night. "He's chosen five regular mediums," she'd said, almost beside herself, "and he'll try others out and add new ones from time to time." Teertha's consort Maneesha, the Australian editor of the darshan diaries, had also been included. Vivek, of course, would be medium-number-one.

Although it's changed physically, the format of darshan is pretty much the same. As usual, Osho gives sannyas first, explaining the meaning of each new name and suggesting what groups are needed. Then, as before, he talks to sannyasins who've just returned to Pune and to those going back to their homes in the West. Afterwards, he chats with a few ashramites who've come with personal problems and does a quick check with the group leaders present to find out how things are going. But no matter what he says this evening, I find it almost impossible to concentrate. I'm fidgety, on edge, hardly able to wait to see what he's going to do to me. He said the cord has already been cut, but still, my curiosity is overwhelming. I've heard virtually nothing about these come-close darshans; they're too new for much talk to have hit the commune grapevine. I know he touches people and uses the mediums as channels of some sort—but that's it.

"Krishna Prem," I hear Mukta call at long last.

On my way towards him, I catch Vasumati's eye. She flashes me a huge, reassuring grin. It must be blatantly apparent how nervous I am.

As I approach him, Osho indicates the space on the floor in front of his chair. I sit, cross-legged. He looks down at me for a moment and then lifts his gaze to include everyone. "Now," he says, "before we work, a few things for the mediums and for the others too." With a wave of his hand he summons the mediums, arranging them wordlessly in a semi-circle behind me. My mind races in circles, like a squirrel in a cage. What's going to happen? What's he going to have all these women do to me? I start to shake inside. I begin to wonder if I'm going to faint. But when I look up at him, at the love on his face, I relax again. Whatever's about to happen, it's suddenly okay.

He leans back in his chair and begins to speak. "The word 'energy' is not yet rightly understood," he says. "It is one of the incomprehensibles. Physics talks about energy, metaphysics talks about energy, but nobody defines it. It is indefinable; it is as indefinable as God. In fact, it is a new name for God.

"What we are doing here," he continues, with a sweeping gesture that embraces me, the mediums, the musicians, the entire assembly, "is creating a harmony of energy in which a few windows which have remained closed for you can become open—a few doors which have remained shut for you can be helped to be opened. If the energy is in harmony, if your energy is in a state of dance, the key suddenly fits the lock. And the key fits in the lock only at a certain state of harmony, never before it.

"And when you are really moving, swaying, dancing," he says, his hands undulating softly, like leaves in a gentle breeze, "when you are not holding yourself back in any way; when you are offering yourself totally, you will feel, you will hear the key moving in the lock—the lock opening. You will hear the *click*. And that click, once heard, can never be forgotten. Then your life starts taking a new colour. After that click you are never the same: you *cannot* be the same. That click is very important.

"And that is the purpose of these close-ups."

He pauses for a moment. "The society," he continues after a bit, "tries in every possible way to move your energy to the left hemisphere of your brain. It is locked there; it is hung-up there. And the left hemisphere of the brain is the most mundane, utilitarian—the marketplace. It calculates, it argues; it is cunning, clever, competitive, violent, male. Hundred per cent energy is locked in the left hemisphere. Fifty per cent of it has to move to the right hemisphere—that's what we are really trying to do. Only fifty per cent of it has to move. Then the balance arises, and the harmony settles, and you will hear the click and the opening of the door and the unlocking of the lock."

All at once I recall the darshan years before when he'd hit me on the left temple—three sharp blows. I'd been with Devika then and the next day a door had opened, a door that had shut on women when my mother had died. Is this what he's talking about, I wonder? Have I already experienced it and lost it? But even if I have, this isn't the time to think about it. He has more to tell us and I don't want to miss a word.

"Darkness is helpful to move the energy from the left hemisphere to the right," he's saying. "That's why you cannot sleep in light. It is difficult to sleep in light. You need darkness, because sleep is part of the right hemisphere. That's why you are afraid in the dark—because the left hemisphere thinks of darkness as the enemy.

"It is for this change that I tell you to close your eyes—because with open eyes the left hemisphere functions. You are looking extrovertly; you are looking at the world, at objects. With closed eyes a change becomes possible: the right hemisphere starts functioning. Hence all the meditators down the ages have been sitting with closed eyes.

"*Women* know the secret," he says emphatically, indicating the mediums behind me with an arch of his eyebrows. "If you hug a woman, if you kiss a woman, she closes her eyes. She immediately moves to the right hemisphere—because love is part of the right hemisphere just as logic is part of the left hemisphere.

"Music helps. Music, poetry, sculpture—all arts belong to the right hemisphere. Hence," he adds, turning towards Chaitanya Hari and his group, "the musicians are here to help you. And if you start swaying, an inner dance of energy starts happening. And if you lose yourself and become part of the flood it becomes easier, because the ego, the separation, that 'I am separate from others' is, again, engrained in the left hemisphere.

"Whenever you lose yourself with somebody—two lovers melting into each other—immediately the left hemisphere is no more the master. In orgasmic states the right hemisphere predominates, becomes the master...

"These close-ups are an effort to move the energy from the left to the right. But all depends on you. If you allow it can happen. If you are in a let-go, it can happen. It cannot be forced on you. If you are ready to receive, then great mutation is possible.

"And I am not telling you that hundred per cent energy has to move, because that will be again a state of lopsidedness. Only fifty per cent energy and a balance arises. And balance is beauty, and balance is music, and balance is truth, and balance is godliness."

I chuckle quietly to myself. Balance. He couldn't have found a better word to make me ready to receive. To a Libra, balance is the magic word.

"So while you are here with me," he says, his voice suddenly rising, "dissolve in the totality. Don't keep yourself separate. Don't be an observer. Become a *participant*. And you can participate only if your eyes are closed. If you keep your eyes open you are not a participant, you are an observer. You remain in the wrong side of your brain—the wrong side for this context, for this space, for this energy.

"And don't sit, holding yourself. Sway! Be like a small, innocent child, dancing in the wind, under the sun, or in the rains with the trees. Forget that you are human beings. Think of yourself as trees or birds or animals. Forget your egos. Just *be*!

"And this is something that can be understood only when it happens to you. It is happening to many people; I would like it to happen to many more. Slowly, slowly, you all have to become my mediums—because we have to turn on the whole world! We have to create such a great energy field that whosoever enters it is turned on just by entering. Just by entering inside the gate he will feel as if he has taken LSD! He has to become stoned!

"This is just the beginning of a great experiment," he adds over the laughter. "I am just preparing the ground. Contribute to it with your totality.

"Good," he says in conclusion, the word sending the mediums scurrying back to their places and triggering a knot of panic in the pit of my stomach. Even if I wanted one, there's no escape. He fixes me with a look that makes me feel suddenly raw and naked and totally, utterly exposed. There's no smile on his face, no twinkle in his eye. His voice reveals nothing either. "Come close to me," he says straightforwardly.

He signals to Vivek to position herself on the floor to his right, just in front of Vishnu. "Face Vivek," he instructs. I turn in her direction. Over her shoulder I can see Vishnu, Mukta, Vasumati, the other mediums, the musicians—everyone watching me intently. "Raise the arms," he says. Vivek lifts hers as well. Our palms touch lightly. She smiles at me, green eyes crinkling, all liquid and light.

"Savita," he calls. It's the English editor whose mum first brought Bernard Levin to our attention. She's placed behind me, on her knees, her hands resting lightly on my shoulders.

Next: "Vasumati." Immediately, I wonder if he knows. But there's no sign, he's totally intent on setting the stage for whatever's about to happen. He tells Vasumati to be behind Savita and to encircle us with one arm. I feel her hand on my chest, over my heart. She wiggles her fingers in an almost imperceptible tickle, in a lover's secret hello.

Out of the corner of one eye, just before I close them, I see Osho raise his hand towards the musicians. The second the lights go out the music begins, loud and throbbing—the sitar, the tamboura and the tablas wild and insistent, already at a peak. Vivek begins to move slowly, her torso swaying gently, her hands tracing circles in the air. I follow, keeping contact with her palms. For the first few moments I'm uncertain what to do, but it suddenly occurs to me that we're dancing, simply dancing. We may be cross-legged on the floor, but still we're dancing. I let go into it, swaying with her, meeting her hand to hand.

And then, from deep inside, a new energy begins to rise. Hot and shivery, it bubbles up, like a percolator rushing towards the boil. In the blackness I can hear Vivek giggling—soft, throaty gurgles of delight—and from Vasumati, high, cascading peals of laughter. Behind me, Savita is rigid, unmoving.

As Vivek starts to sway faster and faster, my whole body begins to tremble from the heat. It's like a raging fever. It tears upwards and, strangely, settles in my hands. They feel as if they're about to burst into flame. Sweat streams down my arms into the sleeves of my robe.

Suddenly the lights are on again and Osho's hand is on my head, his thumb pressing into the centre of my forehead, forcing my head back against Savita's breast. On my chest, Vasumati's hand burns like a brand.

And my eyelids go mad again—exactly as they'd done in Chuang Tzu during the Tantra series when I'd heard him speak on intelligence becoming meditation. And down the flapping tunnel of my vision I see Osho's other hand on Vivek's head. It's as if he's pouring himself into me through her. I try to shut my eyes, as he's said to, but they simply won't obey. The fluttering continues, uncontrollable, until he lifts his hand from me and the music stops, as abruptly as it began.

My body crumbles forward, drained, exhausted. At last I manage to turn to him, my hands meeting in namaste. But instead of the gentleness I'd expected, I find the look he's giving me surprisingly stern. "The problem is dissolved," he says in matter-of-fact dismissal. "Don't come to me with it again."[16]

That very night I remember Vasumati.

Lying beside her after she'd drifted into sleep I felt a remarkable and inexplicable intimacy with her. It was strange; it made no sense, but I felt as if I'd shared a bed with this woman for forty years. I knew exactly what it had been like for my grandfather to sleep night after night, for four decades, with my grandmother at his side. And then the vision had come—the farmhouse kitchen, the woman bending over the wooden table, scrubbing it clean. Vasumati. Brittany. The north of France. And the love! The whole room had been filled with it. There'd been love in the curve of her back, in the motion of her arm as she worked. And then, with an undisputable clarity, I'd known. With that particular quality of knowing that came at times such as this, I'd known that we'd been husband and wife before, and that there, in France, whenever it was, we'd gone as deeply into love as a man and woman could go—without the guidance of a Master.

16. Source: Unpublished Darshan Diary

And now there's now. And now there's Osho.

Laxmi Comes Calling

I don't sleep for long. Almost before I realize it, I am sitting bolt upright in the bed. "Laxmi's been here!" I blurt, even before my eyes are open. When I do open them, it's to see Vasumati, wide-eyed and frightened.

Her voice is thin and scared. "How do you know?"

"I don't know, but I *know* Laxmi's been here. I'm right, aren't I?"

She nods, her eyes filling with tears.

"At first I thought I was dreaming," she begins, "but then I realized that I wasn't asleep, that I was actually awake. And Laxmi was in the room. Not really, not in her body, but Laxmi was in the room."

"What did she do?" I ask.

"Nothing," she answers, "she just said my name. And then she said, 'I've come to tell you that above all the work comes first. You are a medium and he is a vehicle and you mustn't let your personal relationship interfere with the work. The work comes first.' Then she said it again: 'The work comes first.' And then she said, 'Never let your personal ambitions interfere with the work.'"

"Out travelling last night, little mother?" I ask, poking my head into Laxmi's room the following morning. I can't get a word out of her. All she does is laugh uproariously.

Vasumati fares a bit better. By lunch she'd calmed down sufficiently to face Laxmi. "She was alone in her office," she tells me while we eat, "so I just looked in."

"Did you say anything to her?"

"Sure I did!" she answers defiantly. "I said, 'The next time you're out visiting at night, maybe you could announce yourself first.'"

"And?"

"She laughed. Then she said, 'If you got the message, Vasumati, there won't be a next time.'"

"That's it?"

"That's it." She frowns slightly. "You don't find any of this that weird, do you, Krishna?"

"Not really," I admit. "I don't understand any of it, at least not with my mind. But I know I feel Osho's hand in it." It's time now; I tell her about the voice and about the memory of having been with her before.

She's quiet for a few moments, as if she's weighing something. "I don't get *any* of this," she says after a while, "but there's one thing I guess I should tell you too."

"And what's that?"

"You know the discourse where he talked about you and Divy? When he spoke about sending you to Teertha?"

I chuckle wryly. "How could I forget?"

"Well, at the end, when he said there was no need to go to Teertha, that now he'd find something else..." She stops for a moment and simply looks at me, her gaze clear, direct, open. "I was very calm with it, and nothing moved inside," she says tenderly, reaching for my hand, "but I knew that the 'something else' would be me."

Commitment and Suffocation

Back home after another excursion with the press office to Bombay, I'm told by a friend that Vasumati had a little thing with a guy while I'd been away. I don't get it: she'd seemed genuinely happy to see me. By the end of our second night together, when she still hasn't said anything, I tell her what I've heard and that I'm not interested in a relationship with someone who's moving around.

I don't wait for her reaction. I just walk away. And it's the last I see of her for a few days.

During this period, when I'm not at work, most of my time's spent looking at my jealousy, at my possessiveness. And I'm surprised. I really believed I'd purged it with Rani and with Devika. Obviously, I haven't. It's as strong as ever, perhaps even more so.

And then there's the voice. "That's her," it had said. More than the jealousy, it's the voice that haunts me. I know I've no claim on Vasumati, no right to ask for exclusiveness, for fidelity—but something tells me nothing significant will happen between us unless there's a commitment. It's all a muddle and I don't know what to do. So I wait.

Getting ready for my third night on my own, I'm in the midst of putting up my net when, all of a sudden, I hear the voice again. "Go to her," it says. Without a thought I drop the net, throw on a robe and head for Jesus House roof. Climbing the stairs, my heart is pounding. I have no idea what I'm going to find. She may be alone, she may be with someone. But I have to follow the voice.

"Vasumati?" I call softly, pulling the curtain aside. "Are you there?"

After an interminable silence, there's a "Yes" that's almost a sigh. I slip under the net and into the warmth of her. Then we talk.

She tells me about everything that's happened for her and then says, that sexually she hadn't been fulfilled recently.

In the moment of silence that follows her declaration, I go through a million trips. I feel bad, inadequate, impotent, angry, ashamed, insulted—but she's cradling me with such love I drop my reactiveness and open to her, ready to hear. We talk about what happens for each of us sexually. No woman's ever been this honest and direct with me before.

"Let me tell you something, Vasumati," I say. "When I was with Rani I realized I knew nothing whatsoever about women, that whatever I'd been told wasn't true, that I'd simply been programmed by other sleepy people. I remember realizing that what I had to do was watch, observe, and learn about women from my own experience. Now I see I have to do the same with sex.

"I was always told that bed is the man's territory, that there's a proscribed way to do things, a certain expected performance, a standard to be met. You're the first woman who's ever told me the truth. I see now what men are told women want isn't the case at all.

"What I've just seen is that bed is the *woman's* territory—not the man's at all. I see that it's up to the woman to set the rhythm. From now on, in bed, I surrender to you. I've been making love to you out of my head, not with my body. From now on, I'll just kick my head out of bed."

Sexually it gets better. In every other way it gets worse. I'd gotten the commitment I'd wanted; I hadn't realized it would involve suffocation as well. I find myself withdrawing from her, pulling away. It's the clinging. It's driving me mad.

Wherever we go, whenever we're together, I feel as if the talons of a frantic eagle are digging into my flesh, trapping me, claiming me: "Mine! Mine!" And yet I love this woman. Something happens with her at night of a depth and richness I've never known before. But during the day, I'm fast coming to the point where I can't stand her.

We talk about the clinging and she promises to stop. Her resolve lasts a day or so. Then the hook's into me again. The third time we talk it over I'm very disturbed, really shaky. I love this woman, but this obsessive, paranoid, constant clutching at me is destroying something valuable, something I don't want to lose. I don't know how to handle it.

"Always give people three chances," Laxmi once said to me, talking about dealing with the press office staff. "The first time someone makes a mistake, point it out to them gently—maybe with a joke. The second time, be loving but a little firm. The third time it happens, be very strict, no-nonsense. The fourth time," she'd said, clapping her hands loudly, "finished!"

On the subject of clinging, Vasumati and I have already used up the first three.

The fourth comes one morning in Buddha Hall. When the discourse is finished and Osho is gone, I stand to leave. Vasumati reaches out to haul me back, her fingers curled like claws. The look on my face draws her eyes to her own hands. She pulls them back sharply, shocked at what she's seen. I say nothing. Slowly, we walk from Buddha Hall together, neither of us speaking. I can tell she's aware it's happened once too often.

My entire day is spent in the pits. Somewhere deep inside I know, without the slightest doubt, that something of incredible worth is going to happen with this woman. But we've come to an impasse I simply don't know how to cross. And with the same quality of knowing that I felt when we first came together, I see that this clinging has to go before we can move into the next act of our drama together. I feel utterly helpless and terribly, terribly sad.

I know we're not finished. I love this woman. But I don't know what to do. And then the voice comes. "Tell her it's finished," it says.

I know we're not finished. With all my heart I know it. But I obey the voice that brought her to me.

She begins to cry. I turn abruptly and walk away. I can't let her see I'm crying too.

Chapter Eight: 1980

POWER TO THE WOMEN

Essentially, the commune is now run by women. Except for shipping, security, carpentry and the press office, all the departments have women at the helm. Even male domains like plumbing and electricity have been invaded, their former overlords reduced to technical advisors—which means they still do the work, but now it's under the orders of a female administrator. Not an easy place to be a man, the Osho commune.

As to why, Osho himself made it clear. In one discourse, he said that women primarily function from a space of intuition, whereas men act out of intellect. He wanted the place run by the heart, he said, not by the head. Reluctantly, I conceded the point. If men were running the show, I had to admit, we would function more like West Point cadets.

So far, I've been pretty much bypassed, not interfered with, left alone to watch my buddies getting the chop. For the most part, in press office affairs, I've been dealing directly with Osho, via Laxmi, or with Laxmi herself. And we've grown: the staff's over twenty now. We've just had two great new additions—Lalit, a wild young Canadian photographer, and Vadan, a lanky Libra from New York. Vadan has joined Madhura and me in dealing with journalists. And he's good at it: he's light and funny and has a terrific mouth. Everything's going fine. Madhura gets the Indians, I take the English and the Yanks and the French, and Vadan, thanks to a *STERN* cover-girl wife and a few years sculpting in Sicily, is handling the Germans and the Italians with ease. Everything's running smoothly.

But one afternoon, when Laxmi summons Lalit and me, I sense trouble. Flanking the two empty chairs reserved for us are Chandana, who heads the darkroom, and a buxom blonde I've never seen before. Waving us into our seats, Laxmi introduces her as Tara.

Never one to mince anything, Laxmi gets straight to the point. "Lalit," she says eyeballing him with the force of a laser, "now you no more work for a man."

She tosses her head in my direction. "Now you join darkroom and work for Chandana."

His face goes white. He manages a couple of stammering attempts at speech before Laxmi butts in. "Lalit," she says, "Laxmi loves you and your work is good. And Laxmi wants you to understand. This is not a punishment; this is for your growth. Still you will take press office pictures, but now, when Krishna Prem needs photos, he will tell Chandana and she will send you."

"But why?" he sputters. I appreciate his confusion. None of this makes any sense to me either.

"Because," she says straightforwardly, "for your growth, you have to surrender to a woman. Now you surrender to Chandana."

He swings around in consternation, facing Chandana. She's gone all soft and gooey, like a mother who's just adopted a son. From the look on his face, I can tell he wants to punch her out. "But Laxmi..." he pleads, turning back.

"Look, Lalit, listen carefully and Laxmi will try to explain. We are all here with Osho to dissolve our egos, to become one with existence. Existence is feminine. It is passive, receptive, receiving, like a woman; it is not hard and aggressive, like a man.

"For a man to dissolve into existence, he has to surrender to the feminine principle. But if you say to a man, 'Surrender to the feminine principle,' what he will do? It is too much for him: existence is too vast. So we have to start somewhere. And we start where we are, on the gross level. We start with the first step—Lalit, you surrender to Chandana."

The subject is closed. Now it's my turn. "Krishna Prem," she says, "Laxmi is not pleased with way press office is being run. Mangala is not right person for this work, so give her other job to do. From now on, Tara will administer office. You give directions and Tara will see that the work happens."

As we stand to leave, Tara flashes me a toothy smile. I don't return it. I'm fighting an urge to shove those big white teeth down her throat.

"Screw the feminine principle," Vadan mutters from the floor of my room, his feet propped solidly against the door, as if to keep any infringing females out. Slurping Ness-coffee and sucking on bidis, we're indulging in our favourite sport of late: bad-mouthing women.

It's rough all over. At the office, Tara is driving the pair of us round the bend. She'd worked in Washington on a political campaign before coming to Pune and, no matter how I try, I can't get it into her head that Osho isn't running for president. She's so gung-ho it makes me want to puke. Our present positions—Vadan supine on the floor and me prostrate on the bed—pretty much illustrate our approach to labour these days. Tara is about as passive and receptive as Genghis Khan. "And," Vadan adds with a snarl, "about as effective as a fart in the wind."

Personally, it's not much better. Around the time Vasumati and I separated, Vadan's wife had vacated their nuptial bed for the hut and arms of a German commune guard. He, on the rebound, had tried the French, while I'd gone from one princess to another, from the Jewish-African variety to an Austrian who'd married into one of Europe's defunct royal houses. For a while it had been fun—nightly carousals at Lalit's flat, careening motorcycle rides into the hills, skinny-dipping under the stars—but the novelty paled quickly.

I had to admit I wasn't really with the Austrian girl, that I was more not-with-Vasumati than anything else. And then there'd been no point any more. For Vadan either. "At least," he moans, "you've got your voice to tell you when you can go back!"

"Do I?" I wonder morosely. "These days I'm not so sure."

"Shut up," he says, pointing towards the window where a shape had suddenly appeared. "It's one of them."

It's Mangala. "Can I come in?" she asks, pushing vainly on the door.

"No," Vadan answers, planting his feet even more firmly against it. "You're a woman."

Muttering something inaudible, she disappears from view. Suddenly, under the door, a newspaper clipping appears. Vadan reaches languidly for it and raises it slowly to eye level. He's bolt upright in seconds. "That asshole!" he shouts, flinging it in my direction. It's Harry Schindler's Associated Press article. And it's horrendous. If he were here I'd stand him next to Tara and slug them both in the teeth.

He's clever, Harry Schindler; I have to give him that. The article's slanted and distorted—but he's covered his ass beautifully. He's included Osho's assurances that what occurred in Jonestown could never happen here, but then managed to negate them with snide innuendos and provocative counter-questions. He's painted a picture of authoritarianism and mindless slavery in an atmosphere of sex and violence, totally ignoring anything nice he saw. It's one of the best hatchet jobs I've ever seen. And there's nothing to be done. "He's a smart cookie," Vadan agrees. "You can't sue a reporter for the things he doesn't write."

I'd rather liked Harry Schindler; I'd been open and honest with him—and look at the result! I get so down I finally write to Osho. Basically, I trust people, I tell him. By nature, I say, I'm not a suspicious person. Do I have to become suspicious of the journalists who come? I want to know. Do I have to change my approach? Do I have to become guarded, secretive?

"He said to tell you," Laxmi informs me the next day, "that it makes no difference what they write. He said no journalist will ever comprehend what's happening here. He said for you to just keep trusting everyone, and let them write whatsoever they want."

I see my focus has been wrong. I've been invested. I've been wanting journalists to understand and have been upset when they haven't. My expectations suddenly seem ridiculous. After years with Osho, my own understanding of him, of his vision, of what he's doing here, just begins to scratch the surface—and I've been expecting outsiders to get it? They come for a day or so—attend a discourse, watch the meditations, tour the workshops and chat with us a bit and I've been expecting them to understand?

I think of Osho and the discourses. Every morning, year after year, he comes out and talks to us, sharing his experience, pouring his love. If *he* were invested in whether we get it or not, he'd have given up ages ago!

Dealing with the press, the gestalt changes. I concern myself with my own brand of pouring. Openly, unabashedly, filled with love for my Master and a new trust in existence, I just start telling it how it is—and if they understand or not is completely irrelevant. And something beautiful begins to happen for me. That feeling of inner emptiness returns. I haven't felt it since the days at the typewriter on Staveley Road, where I watched *I* step aside and saw, through me, words manifesting on the page. Now it's happening with speaking. Talking to the press, it's not *me* who's talking. Somehow, from some other source, the words are coming, flowing through me. I feel like Krishna on the flute, singing existence's song. I get a little cocky.

But it's not for long.

Inner Work

In the next morning's discourse Osho replies to a question that Pratima, the young Australian who runs the commune's publications department has sent in.

I have an old connection with Pratima. We'd been together at Kailash and it had been there, watching her cross the fields one afternoon, that I remembered her. It had been her walk. Pratima treaded tentatively—still does—as if, at any moment, the ground could give from under her feet. Watching her that day, I suddenly recalled an aged, cowled nun in the garden of a cloister—the cautious, halting steps exactly the same. And that I'd been there with her, From then on, she was no longer Pratima to me. From then on, she became "Old Lady".

But another odd thing with the Old Lady, who's all of twenty-six, is that whenever Osho had said anything to her, there had always been something in it for me. Time and time again I'd seen it—so, that morning in discourse, when, after reading a question, I'd heard him begin his reply with "Yoga Pratima", I'd paid close attention.

"Osho," the Old Lady had written, "five years ago I had a dream in which you looked at me and said very sternly, 'Why don't you go away?' Now, whenever I am in front of you and at other times also, I feel *me* so strongly. I wish I would go away."

"Yoga Pratima," he'd begun, "you are just holding to something which is no more there. You are clinging to a shadow; you are just clinging to a memory. And that is the case of many of my sannyasins. Their egos are gone. Just the traces, footprints, past memories are there. And they go on clinging to those past memories, thinking these are their egos.

"It takes time to recognize the fact that 'I am no more'..."

Coming out of the discourse, I was convinced he'd been speaking of me as well. "And that is the case of many of my sannyasins," he'd said. "Their egos are gone,"[17] he said. Remembering how it had been with journalists of late—the sense of emptiness, the feeling of being a vehicle—I was sure he'd meant me too. I was very pleased with myself. As he said, there are shadows—but shadows are insubstantial, I told myself, not worth much bother.

Had I been a little less puffed-up I might have saved myself some hassles. Had I looked into my shadows, I might have noticed Sheela lurking there.

Tara hadn't worked out, and informing me it was strictly an interim arrangement, Laxmi reinstated Mangala. Then, hitting the road on her never-ending search for land for the new commune, she told me to deal with Sheela in her absence. It's a disaster. As far as I'm concerned, Sheela hasn't a clue how the press office functions, and it's driving me bonkers, having to explain the most fundamental procedures over and over again, day after day. I know my business and I just want to

17. *The Guest*

get on with it. But Sheela's not having any of it. Laxmi's told her to get involved and, by God, she's going to. Every encounter ends in an argument, the pair of us yelling and screaming, at each other's throats like a couple of alley cats.

Laxmi summons me to the office on her return. "This conflict between you and Sheela has to be resolved," she tells me sternly. "This office administers commune activities and this office has to be one. Laxmi, Sheela and Arup are one—and you have to merge into this oneness too, Krishna Prem.

"Tonight, Laxmi wants both of you to do something. Laxmi wants you, Krishna Prem, to ponder this situation with Sheela. And Laxmi wants you," she says, turning towards Sheela, "to do same. Tomorrow morning, after discourse, both of you come to Laxmi's room and let Laxmi know what problems are there."

I approach the evening of self-examination with the kind of single-mindedness I'd always given, in the past, to the meditation techniques. Nothing that goes on in the commune escapes Osho's attention, and I'm certain Laxmi's told him of the quarrels with Sheela. Through Laxmi, he's asking me to resolve things. And he wants it done tonight. I set out, determined to walk the streets of Koregaon Park until the answer comes.

It's not Sheela I have to look at, it's me. I've been throwing the whole blame for our altercations on her shoulders, and it's just not on. Up and down the darkened streets I go, reviewing what happens each time we come face to face. For a good half hour, my mind chews over and over on when-Sheela-does-this-I-feel-like-this and when-Sheela-does-that-I-feel-like-that. And then, in a sudden flash, it dawns on me. The only bridge, the only common thread, is *I!*

With the rush of journalists lately, there's been so much talking about Osho, so much the feeling of being a vehicle for him—and so little sense of me—that I'd really begun to think I had gone. And his answer in this morning's discourse had been the clincher. But I've been kidding myself. The I is still there. And what Sheela does is bring it out, calling it sharply to my attention. She's so trapped in her own ego, in her own self-importance, she mirrors my ego like no one else. No wonder I've resented her.

Walking back to the commune, it's clear what I have to say to Sheela tomorrow morning. I have to thank her. I am a sannyasin, above all.

When the discourse is finally over the next morning and we're both sitting in front of Laxmi, I spill it all out, sparing myself nothing.

"And you, Sheela?" Laxmi asks softly when I finish.

"I took a good look last night, like you asked," she says matter-of-factly, "and I don't have anything against Krishna Prem." She begins to laugh. "I do like to push his buttons, though," she admits.

And the conflict drops. But in the period that follows, I begin to see that what's actually dropping away for me is my male insistence that things be done in a certain sequential, logical way. I've recognized something about the commune and the way it's being run, and surrendered to that.

Laxmi and Sheela are involved in the implementation of Osho's vision on a larger scale, and the press office is just a tiny cog in a greater wheel. I begin to accept their directions without question, without argument, trusting that this is how he wants it, that this is how his work gets done.

This brings a kind of peace with it. And inside, for the first time in ages, it's really quiet. I guess the feminine principle's not so bad after all.

Reconnecting with Vasumati

Vasumati and I begin to see each other again—not as lovers, just as friends. Every once in a while we connect casually, usually ending up sitting on the bridge that spans the stream behind the commune.

And then, one evening, the voice comes at last. It's the twelfth of May, a full-moon night, and I'm getting into bed when it rings loud and clear in my head. "Now," it says. "Go to her." Within minutes, still half-clothed, I'm on my way to her room.

We reconnect and talk for a while and then she props herself up on one elbow and looks at me intently. "It may sound strange to you, but I've seen what my attraction to you is. It's the attraction to silence."

"Silence? Me!"

"I'm blown away by the silence in you." And she laughs. "You are such a blabber-mouth, but inside you're so silent."

For both of us it's a fresh new beginning. And we're together almost every night. I collect her from darshan and we walk through Koregaon Park, thrilled to be together again. But still, I find myself reluctant to commit myself totally, to say a complete and final okay. I take the occasional night off with the boys, but I always seem to come back to her.

One evening I go to a party by myself. It's mostly couples and I find myself missing her, wishing she'd come, seeing I'm not enjoying myself much without her. Looking away from the party, I lean back in my chair and turn upwards, towards the stars. Suddenly, it's as if my heart's about to burst. "What am I doing here?" I ask. "Who am I trying to kid? I love that woman! And if I'm going to be with her, I have to be with her totally!"

Down the street towards the commune I tear, running as fast as I can, my heart pounding with excitement. Throwing open the door to her room, I pounce on her. "I love you, Vasumati!" I shout. "I love you. I love you!" I bellow over and over again. "And I surrender!"

The Anti-Sannyas Aggression Escalates

We like each other immediately. She's quick and efficient, needs things explained once—and she's been married to a Libra for twenty years. "I saw your interview on the Whicker show in London," Leela tells me in her clipped South African accent over morning chai in the press office, "and I *knew* we'd work together one day." I like her even more. We're going to get along just fine. She's an old esoteric too.

Laxmi's timing in finding the right successor to the Mangala-Tara-Mangala dynasty couldn't have been better. The press office is utterly swamped these days. We seem to be the hottest news in India.

The spark that had really set things hopping had been our loud and widely publicized protestation over a scandal involving the Pune visa police. Kendra, blonde, beautiful and fifteen, had gone for a routine first-visa extension and had been told by a CID Inspector he'd give it to her in exchange for one thousand rupees and a night at the Blue Diamond. Frightened, she went straight to Laxmi. And with Kendra's cooperation, the Anti-Corruption boys were secreted in the suite's bathroom with a tape recorder. But to my surprise, the bust had acted more as an invitation than a warning. As each day passes, more and more sannyasins show up with bruises, broken noses, cut lips and welts from sticks and bicycle chains. Sannyasin-bashing from speeding scooters is, once again, Pune's favourite sport.

I love India and am shocked by all of this. I can understand Morarji's antagonism and the politicians' fear, but this hatefulness, this awful, ugly aggression... It goes against everything I've ever felt about this country and her people. I put my feelings to Osho.

"Krishna Prem," he replies in discourse, "the people who come to India from the West come with certain ideas they have derived from books like the *Vedas,* the *Upanishads,* the *Dhammapada,* the Gita, the teachings of Ramakrishna, Ramana and Krishnamurti. But the real India is very different. Yes, there have been many buddhas here, but these can be counted on one's fingers. And it is because of these enlightened ones that India became famous. But this light belonged to the individual Masters; it has nothing to do with the huge mass of this country. Their glory India has taken for granted. This is wrong: the people of India cannot claim it as their own existential experience. Hence the Westerner, when he comes to know the real India, is troubled. The same anguish has arisen in your mind...

"You have come to me in search of truth and so this price will have to be paid...

"Many times I think of leaving this country. But there will be other difficulties. There, it may not be possible for me to stay even for one day because what I am saying is hard for any society to tolerate. They cannot expel me from this country, but I can be driven out of another country any time... And so you will have to move with me any number of times. And in such circumstances, the buddhafield will never come into being. That is why I am concerned that a place should be found where we can be by ourselves among the hills...

"Please put up with the hypocritical Indian culture for some time more. Do so intelligently and with understanding. Put up with these attacks with clubs and chains for some time more. Maybe you can utilize all this for your growth: the barbarism which exists all around you is the real state of man...

"I am aware of your difficulties and pained by them," he says, his tone suddenly tender. "They bring tears to my eyes. Yet nothing can be done. Wait a little more."

He moves on to the next question. But I'm not listening. My attention is elsewhere. Inside, I'm watching a never-ending queue of unsympathetic journalists being paraded before me; I'm hearing myself talking, talking, fruitlessly talking for aeons to come. Permission to build anywhere is still being refused, the situation in Pune is hideous, the whole world is negative—and I've seriously begun to wonder if Osho's beautiful vision is ever going to become a reality. From what he's just said to me I should feel inspired. But I don't. I just feel depressed.

But he isn't letting me wallow. "Osho, why should there be a press office here?" I suddenly hear him read. Someone's asked a question about my baby!

I perk up immediately.

"Why not? I am a modern man," he says. "In fact, a little ahead of my time. I am going to use every possible means to spread the truth: newspapers, video, tape recorders, film, radio, television, satellite transmission, everything.

"Buddha had to go to every village. You didn't ask him, 'Why do you go on walking from one village to another village?' That was a primitive way of spreading the message. For forty-two years he was travelling and travelling: to do that now would be foolish. I can be in my room, and I can fill the whole world with my message...

"The press office creates a question in many people's minds. They think truth need not be declared. It *needs* to be declared! Jesus said to his disciples: 'Go in every direction and shout from the housetops! Only then will people hear, because people are deaf.'

"I will not tell you to go and shout from the housetops. Better means are available. Man has invented great technology. Everybody else is using that technology, but when it is used for truth, questions start arising. If you use it for politics, good; if you use it for evil, perfectly right—but if you use it for God, then questions start arising.

"I am going to use all kinds of media.

"It pays to advertise. And this is not a new thing either. Krishna Prem has been with Moses too. He is an ancient pilgrim; he is not with me for the first time only."

That I'd been with him before I knew. But *Moses!* Whether he's having me on or not, it's the shock I needed. A new wave of energy surges up in me. I feel impassioned, inspired, ready for any challenge.

But he's not finished. Over the loudspeakers comes the sound of shuffling papers. He's looking for a joke. "Moses," he begins, locating it, "standing on the shores of the Red Sea with his press agent, announced, 'I am now going to raise my hand and the sea will part so my people can walk across safely. Then I will lower my hand and the sea will come together again.'

"Elated, Krishna Prem, his press agent, screamed, 'Baby, you pull that one off and I'll get you two full pages in the Old Testament!'

"Enough for today?"[18] he chuckles, standing to leave. Long after he's been driven back to Lao Tzu House, the laughter still fills Buddha Hall.

Clearly and concisely, this morning Osho's laid the challenge of his vision before me. And he's spelled out my role in it. Moses may have been satisfied with two pages—but not him, not this Master. And I remember something he said years ago. "When I die," he'd said, "I don't want anyone in the world to be able to say, 'How come I missed him? How come I never heard of him?'"

18. *The Guest*

Suddenly I feel I've got an awful lot to do.

To my surprise, the focus on me continues—to the point where Buddha Hall explodes into instant laughter at the mere mention of my name. Some of his replies are press office material; others, irrelevant and unusable. I suspect a purpose behind all this sudden attention, but what it is, I haven't a clue.

Then it begins to happen in darshan as well.

The waves Osho had predicted from Germany, Holland and Italy have turned into floods. New people are literally streaming through the gates. And not only from Europe. Looking about, there hardly seems a country, no matter how tiny or obscure, that isn't at least represented. Groups, bodywork, counselling sessions—everything's strained beyond capacity. And in darshan, where a handful once sat with him, there are now hundreds every evening. So, to give commune workers regular access to him, a new system has recently been introduced.

Each department is to go to darshan twice a month, en masse. Department heads are to sit in the front row, joined, on a rotational basis, by the rest of their workers. Energy darshans can be booked once every three months. All we need, Osho had said. More often would be too much.

Four energy darshans was pretty much the evening's limit, but one night, during the press office's fortnightly attendance, after the four had been given, Osho's voice broke in on my silence. "Krishna Prem, come here."

Awkwardly, taken aback, I approach him. It takes a moment to realize he's going to give me an energy darshan. He calls Vivek to be in front of me; one of the new mediums, Krishna Radha, behind. The lights go out and the music begins. I'm dancing with Vivek and falling back into Radha's juiciness and his hand touches me—and then there's nothing. As if I were a dry leaf carried on the wind, his hand on my forehead just blows me away. Two weeks later, it's "Krishna Prem, come here" again. And two weeks after that, it's "Krishna Prem, come here" once more.

I still don't have a clue what's going on. Then the chicken pox hits. I can't really say I'm sorry. Whatever good all this attention from him may be doing me, it's also knocking me on my ass.

The infection comes in the middle of the Hindi series. Suddenly half the youngsters in the commune are covered in tiny red spots. Osho, it appears, has never had chicken pox, and Laxmi declares a general quarantine, sealing our Master in his room in Lao Tzu House. No one who hasn't had the childhood disease goes near the place, she says emphatically. There's no discourse; there's no darshan. But for Vasumati and me, there is something, something we've had precious little of since we've fallen in love—time.

The rains are late this year, and there's oppressiveness in the air. We stroll the streets behind the commune; sometimes we talk, filling in the years apart; sometimes nothing is said at all. And strangely, none of the violence touches us. Except for a few well-aimed stones from a passing car one night, we're left alone.

When the quarantine is over and Osho's ready to come out again, it's announced that instead of resuming the Hindi series, we'll sit in silence with him for ten days, a prelude to a six-month period of discourses on the *Dhammapada,* the Buddhist scriptures. There is to be twenty minutes of music, with gentle humming and swaying, followed by twenty minutes of silence, and then, to complete the hour of satsang, of sitting in silence with the Master, more music, humming and swaying. By the end of the fifth day, I find myself wishing he'd never speak again, that we could always sit with him like this. I'm coming out of Buddha Hall higher, more heartful, than from any discourse.

It's not only the silence that's doing it to me. It's the humming and swaying as well.

From the old Nadabrahma meditation, I knew the secret of humming. If it were the right pitch, if it were begun with full lungs and continued until they were empty, the belly flat against the backbone, my third eye would begin to vibrate like the strings of a tamboura. And as to the swaying, I remembered the Gourishankar meditation with the blue light from the first Pune camp years before. "No more than twelve inches to either side," he'd said. For the past five days I'd been keeping both these things in mind.

On the sixth morning of the satsangs, suddenly I can't hum or sway any more—everything seems to have stopped on its own. With effort, I resume, but it stops again. After the third try, it's apparent something else is happening, so I relax in mid-hum, in mid-sway.

And all at once I recall a discourse at Woodlands in Bombay. He'd been speaking on Lord Vishnu's one hundred and twelve techniques for enlightenment, and one of them had struck me as particularly funny. It had something to do with riding in a bullock cart, with swaying on one's buttocks, with finding the perfect balance and then dropping into it. I remember Osho had said, "Balance is God," and I recall a blackout in my room when my whole body had gone into orgasm—and then my mind simply wouldn't function any more. Then there was nothing but an omnipresent silence and a spreading bliss that, bit by bit, consumed me. And suddenly, sitting in Buddha Hall, swaying, my whole body explodes into orgasm. I'm still quivering with the aftermath of ecstasy long after Osho has gone.

I'm useless at work that day—all I want is for tomorrow morning to come. But when it arrives and I'm back in Buddha Hall, the orgasm won't happen. The waves of ecstasy begin, deep inside, but they won't explode over me; they won't climax. I leave the auditorium frustrated, like a lover who's been unable to climax. Vasumati just laughs at me. "Things like that are gifts," she tells me that night. "You're being greedy. You can't force existence."

That night the weather changes. Lying on our wall behind the commune, Vasumati and I watch the black monsoon clouds rolling in, carried on gusts of chilling winds that whip the feathered branches of the giant Gulmohar trees above us into sudden frenzies. We snuggle into each other for warmth, and then, as quickly as the storm clouds came, they burst. As if from an overturned bucket, the rains pour down in a single, relentless stream. The next morning we both have terrible colds.

Really Sick

For the next month I'm in and out of bed with the regularity of the rains. First it's bronchitis, then amoebas in the liver. I can't seem to get better.

Thank God for Leela. We work together in my room in the mornings, me either racked with coughs or clutching my liver in agony, but at least I don't have to worry about the office.

Things finally take a turn and I book a silent darshan. It seems ages since I've seen Osho and I've been missing him. When the night of the darshan arrives, Vasumati is in bed with a high fever. Not being able to be in darshan is bothering her—out of all proportion, it appears to me. "Why?" I ask.

"Intuition," she replies anxiously. "I don't know what, but something's going to happen."

Sitting in darshan later, I don't know what to expect. He won't call me for an energy darshan, of that I'm certain. Although I'm feeling better, I look terrible, pale and gaunt, with dark circles under my eyes. But I'm wrong. "Krishna Prem, come here," he summons. I stand with effort and go to him.

For the first time he positions me away from the mediums and the musicians, telling me to face Laxmi. He places Vivek behind me. I feel incredibly fragile and a little apprehensive.

The blackness and the swelling music engulf me simultaneously, and inside, I begin to fall, suddenly and swiftly, into a dark and bottomless hole. It's as if death is claiming me. At first I panic. But I trust Osho, and I let go—into this black and terrifying space that's enveloping me.

All at once my arms begin to stiffen, moving straight out from my body. Vivek is behind me as Osho's index finger descends on me, hitting the centre of my forehead. There is nothing gentle in the touch—it is hard and insistent, driving, like a spike. And the voice comes. Over and over again, resounding in my head: "He's crucifying you! He's crucifying you!"

There is no choice—I give up. I let him have his way. And from my dry, parched lips, I hear a distant whisper: "Thy will be done." And then he lets me go.

One halting step after another gets me at last to Vasumati's room. "Krishna," she cries, moving towards me, "what's he done to you?"

I can only shake my head in confusion. I don't know what he's done, but I sense something's finished, that he's going to leave me be for a while.

The next morning I awaken with a raging fever. Once more it's back to bed.

Word must have reached Laxmi, because the next morning I open my eyes to find her and Arup standing in my room. "Someone will come for you this afternoon," she says. "You go see Dr. Sardesai, Osho's physician."

Two days later, the verdict comes: pneumonia, hidden deep in the right lung. Laxmi wants to hospitalize me, Sardesai informs me, but he's convinced her it isn't necessary. Loading me with prescriptions, he tells me she's found a room in the commune where I can get well. "Don't worry," he reassures me. "It's not that serious, it's just that it's been there a long time. A month in bed and you'll be fine."

A month! A month is a lifetime.

Divy's awaiting me when the car brings me back to the commune. "Come with me," he says. "Ramesh is in America and they're putting you up in his room. Laxmi called me in and asked if I'd take care of you, bring you your food. I said sure. But no visitors. Not even Vasumati. Okay?"

"What choice do I have?" I ask with resignation. I suddenly feel very weak and frail and exhausted. "I just want to get into bed."

A couple of hours later, Vasumati's standing in the door. She's upset, but relieved at the same time. "At least now we know what's wrong," she says, smoothing my brow. "And now you'll get better."

"There is also something I want to tell you. Vivek called me a little while ago and gave me a message from Osho. He said you couldn't have visitors for at least three weeks and that I could either take care of you or come to darshan as a medium."

I don't even need to hear her decision. "If you had chosen me over darshan," I whisper into her ear, "I'd have been really angry with you, and a little disappointed. One thing I've always known about us is that ours is a sannyas-relationship,that our being together is, for both of us, part of our paths."

I hold her for a moment, for the last time in a while.

One long and final look at the doorway, and then she's gone. And I'm alone.

Lying there, I know I've been wrong. After that crucifixion-darshan I'd figured Osho was going to let up on me for a while. "Not yet," I murmur into my pillow. "He's not quite finished with me yet."

Never before has my body been incapable of obeying me. For the first week, except for faltering trips to the bathroom, I never leave the bed. I watch the chair in the centre of the room like a faraway goal, waiting for the day I'll have the strength to reach it. Apart from the cleaners, Divy's visits with food and the love-notes from Vasumati, I'm left utterly alone. The discourse tapes come each morning, but I rarely hear one through. I'm constantly nodding off. I had no idea just how ill and exhausted my body really was.

Mid-way through the second week I can manage to get to the chair. But I get trapped there: it seems to take ages before I gather enough energy to make it back to the bed. Wrapped in a blanket, I sit for hours, watching the rain, listening to the muted sounds of the commune. Occasionally someone stops by the window, to ask how I am, but ten seconds of conversation leave me drained, drenched in sweat. I take to sitting in the dark, the curtains drawn.

Reading between the lines of her letters, it's obvious the separation is hard on Vasumati. The messages are bright and cheerful, filled with news and gossip, but I sense that the time after darshan is particularly lonely for her. I've accepted that we can't be together and, in a way, I'm grateful. I've nothing to give right now. I need all my energy for me.

One night, the first of my fourth week in isolation, the door suddenly flies open and Vasumati's standing there. It's a shock. It's as if a whirlwind has burst into the room. She seems so strong, almost aggressive, and I feel so fragile and delicate.

Talking is difficult. I've hardly spoken in weeks. I let her know by my touch that I'm happy to see her. She wants to stay and I somehow can't refuse her.

Waking the next morning, I'm weak and exhausted again. The following day I'm as ill as I was almost a month ago. And angry. Justified or not, I find myself blaming her for this relapse. I'm angry at her selfishness, angry that she couldn't wait, angry that she couldn't see or care how sick I was. Alone in this room, everything had been going so well, and this woman barges in, demanding satisfaction! I'm like ice that night. I'm hard and cold, and I just tell her that I want to be left alone. Going to the bathroom later, I see her shoes outside another guy's door, next to mine. Let her have her little revenge, I think. But it's not going to work. I can be selfish too.

Osho's Father Dies

A few nights later, my door suddenly bursts open once again. I look up, expecting Vasumati, but it's one of the girls from the front office.

"Everyone's to go to Buddha Hall right away," she informs me. "Osho's father just died."

Osho's mother and father had been living in the commune for some time, occupying, with assorted relatives in true Indian fashion, the ground floor of Francis House, the guest cottage of the private mansion Jesus House had once been. Neither of them spoke English, and they had little contact with the Western sannyasins but their tiny house was always a hive of activity, the sound of kirtan pouring from the door after every morning's discourse. Though we couldn't really talk to them, everyone loved them—Mataji, the mother, short and round in her bright orange sari, and Dadaji, the father, bald and stocky, resembling Osho, always poking about, his walking stick curiously jabbing here and there, asking questions through an interpreter, wanting to know about everything going on.

About his mother, Osho spoke rarely, but he talked often in the discourses about Dadaji. He painted a picture of a simple yet extraordinary man, incredibly loving and unwaveringly supportive of the idiosyncrasies of his strange and different son.

He'd fallen ill a short while back, his heart failing, and he'd been in and out of Jehangir Hospital several times. When Divy had told me Osho had gone to see him one evening, I had an inkling his condition must be grave.

Now he's dead.

Buddha Hall is jammed to capacity: some people sitting, as if for discourse; others dancing and singing: "Welcome to the holy fire, welcome to the holy flame." On the dais, covered in marigolds, is Dadaji's body. Beside him, Mataji kneels, weeping. Married as children, they've been inseparable for decades. I'm reminded of my grandmother's grief when my grandfather was no longer there, suddenly gone after forty-nine years.

Awaiting Osho, a wreath of leaves in her hand, Mukta stands at the bottom of the steps leading to the platform. Her eyes are swollen. She and Dadaji had been close—a friendship beyond words.

Through the swell of music I hear the car approach and turn to see Osho arrive. He looks as he does for discourse: glowing and radiant, his hands folded in namaste. He mounts the podium and, accepting the wreath from Mukta, lays it on his father's heart. He lays his hand on Dadaji's head for a moment, a gesture of loving farewell. Standing, he blesses his mother—and then he's gone.

Members of the family lift the stretcher from the dais and lay it gently on the floor, bringing ropes to secure it for the procession to the burning ghat.

I'm suddenly exhausted again. I can't take any more.

A Devastating Darshan

Except for that brief moment in Buddha Hall with Dadaji's body, it's been a good ten weeks since I've seen Osho, so a day or so out of bed I arrange to go to darshan. Sitting there, suddenly I hear "Krishna Prem, come here."

In the darkness, there's nothing but movement—arms dancing, hair flying, squeals of ecstatic delight as Osho's touch moves from one person to another. When he touches me I begin to cry, tears gushing down my cheeks. He begins to caress me, smoothing my brow like a mother easing a troubled child. The crying turns to sobbing, and my hands reach out to him, as if I'm offering myself. I feel his hand leave my head and suddenly he's holding my hands in his, gently, delicately, with the tenderness of a lover.

When it's all over I lie in a heap against the wall, crying and crying until the cleaner taps my shoulder softly and whispers that everyone's gone, that I should go too.

The next morning I pay a call on Laxmi, just to let her know I'll soon be back at work. "The body is well?" she asks.

"Better, Laxmi. Still a bit weak, but better."

"Good news," she says. Then she mentions last night's darshan. "It was beautiful the way he held the hands," she says. "And this morning too, he spoke of Krishna Prem to Laxmi."

"Really?" I ask, moved and flattered.

"Yes," she continues, looking me straight in the eye. "He said, 'One word gets Krishna Prem, and that word is "Laxmi". Now he's vulnerable. Now you get him.'"

The floor disappears from under my feet.

She returns to her papers. "Just so you know."

Laxmi, the perfect vehicle, takes our Master at his word. She's on my case with a vengeance. No matter what I say, she explodes into anger, criticizing, finding fault, telling me I'm negative, that I'm not surrendered, that I don't really love Osho. When I'm not being berated, I'm off somewhere in tears. I know what she'd been told, but what I'm supposed to get from this escapes me totally.

Smoking. She's on and on about smoking. She must bring it up ten times a day. I'd quit with the pneumonia and hadn't picked it up again—and according to her, everything's wrong with me because I dropped bidis.

"It's good smoking stopped," she barks at me one morning, "but this negative attitude cannot be allowed in the office. Laxmi is the first to admit it's good this negativity is coming out at last, but office is not the place. You think it over. Laxmi's suggestion is a break—guarding maybe—some work where there's no need to deal with people. Three months or so and then we see. You think about it."

"Laxmi, I don't *feel* negative. I don't know what you're on about!"

"See!" she shouts. "Exactly what Laxmi means!"

I don't get it and I write to Osho: "Laxmi is berating me constantly. Every time I leave her office I burst into tears. I don't understand what's happening."

The next afternoon, in the answer box: "See Laxmi." With a sinking feeling in my stomach, I enter the lion's den once more.

She looks up from her papers. "He says it has nothing to do with Laxmi. He says to start smoking again." Everyone laughs but me. I'd heard him ridicule smoking in discourse dozens of times—and now he's telling me to start again! Okay, I think. If that's what he says, okay. I wonder if Divy's left any bidis lying around the room. As I prepare to leave she thrusts a book into the air. "This is for you," she says, her gaze still fixed on the letters on her desk.

It's a copy of my last Indian-English effort, *The Long and the Short and the All,* fresh off Motilal Barnarsidass' New Delhi presses. I open the book and there, on the frontispiece, I read, "To Krishna Prem, with love," signed with Osho's flourish. Underneath he's penned the date: "10.10.79". It's my forty-first birthday. I feel tears welling up inside and I beat a hasty retreat. I'm damned if I'm going to let that woman see me cry. Glancing back I see her trying to contain a smile. She's really enjoying this. She loves this cat-and-mouse game! Behind me I hear laughter—hers, Sheela's, Arup's. It makes me boil.

But the bidi! It's the most amazing thing. Two drags and my whole inner gestalt changes—I feel light, almost happy again. Could she have been right? I wonder. Well, even if she is, I tell myself, I'll never let her know.

The morning after a horrendous birthday dinner at the Blue Diamond, Laxmi summons me to her office. "Osho wants commune run by women," is her opening line. I'm immediately convinced I'm getting the axe. "He wants women to administer and organize," she says icily, "not the *ugly* male mind." I could slap her for that one. "So now, in press office, Leela will administer. You guide, tell her what needs doing, and then you stay out of the way. All you are to do is blabber to journalists. With Vadan. Is that clear?"

"Abundantly." My tone is as cold as hers.

Leela panics at first. Ever since the success of the Bombay exhibition, Laxmi had been looking for something else, and when a group of former actors had approached her with the idea of staging *A Midsummer Night's Dream* in Bombay, she jumped at the idea. She had a nose for publicity any Hollywood press agent would give his left nostril for, and the newly formed Osho Theatre Group was right up her alley. "What a great way to cut my teeth!" Leela wails. "I don't know *anything* about theatrical publicity."

"I spent a couple of years in the theatre after university," I tell her. "I'll show you what to do. But that's all I can do apparently—show."

"Don't remind me."

It's a mess in the press office. We lost Madhura to the play, as well as Subhuti. This left an avalanche of work I'm not allowed to do. And the women in the office, willing though they are, know as much about mounting a publicity campaign as I know about menstruation. Every evening I go home in rage and frustration. "Dump it somewhere else," Divy says cryptically. There isn't anywhere else. I take my bidis to bed and seethe.

All Laxmi does these days is bitch. We're trying to put together a press kit, prepare photos and biographies, design a program, write ads, print tickets, invite the press—with me guiding, of course, and doing absolutely nothing else—and all she does is complain. Day after day. "This isn't good enough. This is rotten. This is insulting to the good name of Foundation. Why did we do it this way? Why didn't we do it that way? Do it over again!" Leela's in tears half the time. And the fact that I'm supposed to let the women do things and not interfere spares me nothing. Every hour on the hour I'm told, "Laxmi wants you." I go into her office, sit in front of her, and listen to her scream. It's like having a cannon go off in my face.

On top of it all, Osho's playing with me as well. Talking about old angers waiting for a chance to surface one morning, he brings me up. "This is happening to Krishna Prem," he says. "Just a few weeks ago, Laxmi was after him: 'Stop smoking!' He was smoking too much. And finally he stopped; with great will he forced himself. Since that time he has not been in good shape. He became ill. For weeks he remained ill, weak. Now he has come out of his illness. He had to take many medicines and treatments. Now he gets angry at any slight excuse, or no excuse."

What's he on about? This is all bullshit! What about the pneumonia?

My mind's a chaos. I don't get any of this at all.

"Just the other day he asked me, 'Osho, what should I do?'" he continues.

"I said, 'Smoke! And don't listen to Laxmi again!'"[19]

Don't listen to Laxmi! God, I'm confused. I do not understand! Divy does. And he thinks the whole thing is a hoot. "I've never known you to take so long to get a point," he laughs. "Osho's just teasing you. Look. He gives you a birthday present and talks about you in discourse, just to show how much he loves you. And on the other hand he's using Laxmi to show you something."

---

19. *The Dhammapada: The Way of the Buddha, Vol. 7*

"But what?" I shout in exasperation.

"*That* you have to get for yourself," he replies simply. "But look at it this way. Your big mistake is that you *listen* to Laxmi, to what she says. I never listen to her: the woman's loony. It's just energy. When I'm in front of her I get energy from her. She could be talking Chinese for all I care. She just gives me energy and I use it." I don't know what he's talking about.

That afternoon Pratima tries. "Having a rough time with Laxmi, huh? Let me tell you a story," she says. "Once Yatri took in this book design to show her. I walked by the office and saw the pair of them in there, screaming at each other. I went in. She was telling Yatri what he'd done was garbage and to do it again. He was yelling back at her, telling her she had no taste, all sorts of things. I grabbed him by the collar and pulled him out of there. A half hour later, I went back in myself, laid the same layout on her desk—untouched, unchanged. 'Beautiful,' she said. 'Send it to the printer.' Get the point?"

"God, Old Lady, I wish I did."

"I don't know how else to tell you," she laughs, hugging me tenderly. "You're a hard nut to crack. But Laxmi will do it, no matter how long it takes."

"Krishna Prem, Laxmi wants you," I hear from her office window.

"Laxmi," I begin, wishing for a little warmth from her, but getting nothing but a cold, emotionless stare. "On the list of people going to the play in Bombay there's no photographer. We need some really good colour slides, especially if we're taking the play to New Delhi later. Indian magazines need colour at least eight weeks in advance."

"Fine," she says, returning to her papers. "Veetmoha can do it."

"Veetmoha!" I scarcely believe my ears. "Veetmoha's your *driver!*"

"Veetmoha is a good photographer," she replies, in a tone that precludes further discussion. "He took beautiful pictures in Kutch."

I know the photos she's talking about. He'd stood in front of the castle and clicked the camera. I need professional photos. And she's giving me Veetmoha!

Back in my office the faintest of lights begins to dawn. For the first few moments, I'd sat at my desk, my mind short-circuited, as if the plug had been pulled, like when I mentioned the BBC to Morarji Desai. Suddenly it had all become so ridiculous, I started to laugh. And with the laughter came the first inkling of awareness. Laxmi's showing me, I realize, my insistence on logic, on the male way, on following A with B and C right through to Z. She's trying to shake me out of this pattern.

I begin to watch what's happening and, sure enough, whenever I present her with something logical, sequential, she throws something illogical at me, blowing my fuses time and time again. And I begin to understand what Divy and the Old Lady tried to tell me.

She must notice the change and it's obvious she's communicated it to Osho. "He says to tell you that now you have to become a woman," she announces one morning. My mind can't absorb the message, but something inside, albeit vague and distant, somehow understands.

Observing her, I see she operates solely out of intuition. No wonder she drives men mad. And I start making a conscious effort to do the same, allowing decisions to surface from my heart and not from my head. And I begin to feel more comfortable, easier with myself. If this is what he means by becoming a woman, it's not so bad.

But in the office there's virtually nothing for me to do. Leela has everything under control. There aren't many journalists these days, so I take to my room, trucking out my old portable typewriter and start to write. I see, after a bit, I've the beginnings of a book. Yet there's no sanction for what I'm doing; I'm just filling time. My situation, it seems to me, needs review. I write to Osho. "Beloved Osho," I say, "a couple of years ago you asked me to begin a press office, and that's been done. Now there's a machine that functions very well, and I feel quite redundant. Am I hanging on to something where I'm not needed? Is it time for me to move on to something else?"

"He asked Laxmi what put this into Krishna Prem's mind," she says the next morning. "Laxmi told him it's probably because of Leela. He says you're still head of the press office." It's pointless getting into it. I just go back to my room. "Call me if you need me," I tell Leela on the way.

But Laxmi's not finished with me yet. Every day she calls me. Still, nothing's ever right. Fed up with her tirades, I yell back one morning: "Why do you always have to shout and scream!"

"This is Laxmi's way," she replies at top volume. "If you deserve it, take it; if you don't, just laugh."

But I don't find it funny at all. And when she and Veetmoha leave for Bombay, I breathe a delicious sigh of relief. It's wonderful not to be yelled at. But when, sitting on my bed smoking a bidi one morning, I see Veetmoha wrapped in a towel and heading for the showers, I know Laxmi's back and my mind turns to sheer panic. I can't take any more of this. I write to Osho again, leaving the note on Laxmi's bedside table when she's out of her room.

The morning passes in terror. From across the hall I see her enter her office. I sit in mine, terrified she's going to summon me. Suddenly I remember something Osho had said in Bombay: "Whenever you come up against something you fear, jump into it. And the fear will automatically disappear." So, like a moth drawn to a flame, I head for her office. We have some work to do together and we just get on with it, my note to Osho unmentioned. It's incredibly quiet between us, for the first time in ages. Her eyes are on me, keen and penetrating, but my focus is on the fear, bubbling up inside. We're both aware something apart from the work is going on, but nothing is said. I love this woman, I confess to myself, but I'm frightened of her.

Back in my own office, the fear suddenly goes. I can literally feel it leaving me, like in the Pink Panther cartoons, when all the colour drains away. And then everything is clear. It isn't Laxmi I've been fearing, it's this new space in me, it's Osho's challenge to move into the unknown. Become a woman, he'd said. Drop this insistence on logic and begin to live and function from a deeper place, from intuition, from the heart. Surrender to the feminine principle. And he'd used Laxmi to help me. The fear becomes gratitude.

And this thing with the press office. Again, I'd been utterly male. I'd seen Leela as an invader, a usurper, taking my territory away. But nothing's been taken—I've been given a *gift!* I've been released from the mundane, day-to-day details of administration and been given the space to become Osho's vehicle, talking to journalists, beginning to write a book.

When I collect my answer in mid-afternoon and find another "See Laxmi" I just can't. I feel such a fool, bothering Osho with all this nonsense. I can't go to Laxmi; I don't even want to know what Osho said. The rest of the day I make myself very scarce.

Towards the end of the afternoon a lady from the BBC's *Everyman* series calls me. She's in Pune on another assignment and would like me to join her for dinner. When the time comes and I'm heading for the rickshaw stand, I suddenly turn back down the drive. I can't leave this way. I have to see Laxmi before I go.

She's in her room, working with Arup. She looks up as I walk in. "Come for answer finally?" she asks.

"No, Laxmi. I don't even want to know what Osho said. There's no need. It's taken a long time, but I get the point. I've just come to thank you."

"Thank Laxmi? For what?"

"For helping me smash my dependence on the male mind. For showing me that logic is a tool, something to be used. For showing me how to function out of intuition. For lots of things."

"Well!" she whistles, her mouth forming a big round O. "Well, well. Krishna Prem is becoming a woman!"

"Never mind that," I say, embarrassed. "And thank you for Leela. At first I saw it all as taking something from me; now I see it as a gift."

"No need for thank you," she smiles. The game's over. We're friends again. "Laxmi enjoyed," she adds with a twinkle.

"I didn't," I confess. "But now I'm starting to."

"Okay, swamiji. Laxmi and Arup have work. Enjoy the dinner with lady from BBC."

Chapter Nine: 1980

VASUMATI'S PARENTS

Vasumati's mother and father are waiting for us in the dining room of the Blue Diamond—positioned together on one side of the booth, to afford a better view of their eldest daughter and her new man.

I like them immediately. And I see where Vasumati's inherited her looks: her mother's quite beautiful. She's fine-featured and bright-eyed, with soft auburn hair loosely framing an open and expressive face. "I enjoyed you on that television program, that *Whicker's World,*" she says right away. Her voice is light and musical; the accent, cultured, incredibly British. Her father, burly, grizzled and red-faced from the African sun, slouches in the corner, taking me in with clear, evaluating eyes. He reaches for my hand. "When are you going to make my daughter an honest woman?" he asks crustily.

"Daddy!"

"Why shouldn't I ask?" he shrugs, unperturbed. "It's a straight question." We look at each other for a moment, man to man, and then we both begin to laugh. We like each other. "Let's order," he says, calling the waiter with a cursory wave. "How's the curry here, Krishna?" he asks. "I like hot Indian food. None of that bland touristy muck for me!"

As the dinner progresses, her mother, a lady of seemingly inexhaustible energy, wants to know "absolutely everything" about the commune—what there is to see, what there is to do, how she can get involved. She wants information, but Dr. Jewish wants answers. He wants to know about Osho, about sannyas, about being with a

Master. He's right up my alley and I love talking to him. He's sharp and intelligent and asks good questions. And what's even more refreshing, he listens to the answers.

Over the next several days they seem to enjoy their time. Her dad's easy. He spends most of his day at the Blue Diamond pool, wading through a copy of *My Way: The Way of the White Clouds,* my solution to his endless store of questions. Esther, though, is at the commune constantly. Everyone loves her.

When we meet up with them at the coffee shop there are more questions.Esther, Morris and I do most of the talking. Vasumati's quiet, appraising. Over our second cup of tea, her mother turns to her. "Could you explain just what it is you do in these groups you're leading?"

"Let's see," Vasumati considers and closes her eyes for a moment, as if waiting for the words to come. The three of us are silent. The floor is absolutely hers.

"I work on people's energy," she begins. Her tone is clear and confident. "And the work is to do with creating an atmosphere," she continues, relaxing, warming to the subject. "When someone is saying yes, when they're open, when they're prepared to move with their energy, that creates a climate. And that climate is akin to a buddhafield, to the kind of thing Osho is working on with us. The group is like a mini-buddhafield, and the whole emphasis is on sharing your energy, on giving what you have, on putting it into a common pool. That's what's happening in the commune, in Osho's buddhafield—the individual personality is dissolving in a pool of energy. The group is the same thing.

"So what we do, firstly," she says, "is work with the body energy—opening the body, helping them move. Like dancing. That creates energy. And another thing that creates energy is bringing them into contact with each other.

"Often people just say yes and it happens, but sometimes we'll be sitting around and I can see that for several people it's just not happening, they're feeling closed, separate, isolated and afraid. I look for the place where someone is holding back or holding on. Maybe there's something going on he or she hasn't said. Even if he's saying something negative, the minute the negative charge is released he becomes positive and he can relax and fall back into the pool of energy. He's not holding back any more. Do you understand?

"And what happens when that energy is released is that people start to get exhilarated—because there's so much energy in the room, and it's concentrated. It's not leaking; it's not going anywhere; it's just becoming more and more intense.

"Now, mom, don't be shocked," she adds with a laugh, "but other times people are holding onto their sex energy," she says, expelling the words emphatically. "Well, the moment they can be encouraged to simply feel that energy, to let it be there, the release of that contraction enables more energy to be put into the room, into the group. The more energy that's available, the higher you get. And, ultimately, you get more and more blissful, more and more ecstatic."

"Do they do it sometimes in the groups?" her mother asks tentatively. "Sex, I mean?"

"Sometimes," Vasumati replies directly.

"Oh," her mother replies flatly. "I see."

"Do you?" her father asks.

"What?"

"You know. There. In the group."

"You mean sex?" Her eyes widen in horror. "Daddy, I'm the group *leader!* Besides," she laughs, reaching across for my hand, "I love my sweetness."

"Go on," her mother encourages. "This is fascinating."

"Okay, what we come to now is the reason people hold back. They hold back because there are certain energies they judge as not being appropriate, acceptable or good. Anger, for example. There's a great taboo against anger. People are afraid of their anger; they feel they shouldn't be angry, so when that energy comes up they're afraid of it and they repress it. And the energy in the whole room feels depressed, heavy. But the minute they can be shown, as Osho says, that all energy is divine, that all energy can be transformed, that very anger can become love. Then they see that the effect of anger held back is more damaging than anger released. They see that once it's exposed, seen, it can be purified, transformed.

"Sometimes a person who's released all that stuff can move directly into meditation. The energy just turns back inside and he becomes very silent and very blissful.

"Often when that energy's released it wants to move into sex, that's its natural flow, and if it happens, it happens; we don't push either way. And then, after that, is love. When people's anger is released, their sex is open, flowing—whether it's actually physical or not is irrelevant; what's important is that the energy's there, present and available, the next thing is love. People just open; they just trust. They fall into their most natural space—into love, awareness, celebration, meditation."

The next evening at the Blue Diamond coffee shop they want to know about darshan. They've seen photos of the energy darshans in Sannyas magazine and, understandably, are intrigued—and, we suspect, a bit disturbed. In many of the pictures of Osho using the mediums, Vasumati figures prominently. She's almost always there, up front. And in a variety of postures—kneeling behind someone, her arms raised as if in supplication, her head thrown back in abandon. In some of the photos, Osho's focused totally on her, his finger boring into her forehead; in others, he's bridging her with someone else. I suggest she take them to darshan to let them see it for themselves. Dealing with the press, I know how impossible attempts to explain the phenomenon of Osho's energy work can be; the experience is utterly subjective. So far, she hasn't wanted to take them. "They'll just freak," she says whenever the subject arises. "They'll freak and I'll be uptight. If there's no other way, I'll do it. But I really don't want to."

Tonight, though, darshan has to be dealt with. After last night's eloquent openness about her work in groups, there's no way her being a medium can be ignored. When the topic's raised, it's obvious to me Vasumati needs a little time to muster her thoughts, to find an angle that'll afford them some kind of comprehension. I come to her rescue, explaining how darshan is structured and what happens there. I also tell them about the evening Osho had surrounded me with the mediums and had talked about the energy work, about his effort to move energy from one hemisphere of the brain to another. They're polite and attentive. Both have scientific backgrounds—Morris is a doctor and Esther's a speech therapist—but they want something more specific: they want to know about "this medium thing" Vasumati's into every night. She gestures helplessly: "I don't know what to tell you."

I dive in once again. I tell them about stepping aside, about letting God manifest, relating it to the symbol of Krishna playing on his flute. I tell them how it's happened to me, through writing, through speaking to journalists.

"It happened on that *Whicker's World* interview you saw," I say.

Madhura's sudden arrival closes the subject of darshan for the evening. "Laxmi was looking for you," she tells me, sliding into the booth beside Vasumati. "I told her you were probably here, with Vasumati and her parents. She said to tell you to come see her in the morning, right after discourse."

"What's up?"

"Well, I don't know whether I should say anything or not," she grins, "but you know me. It looks like we're moving to Saswad. Laxmi's said to hell with Morarji and the Maharashtra Government and their permissions. It seems we're just going to move in, rather like squatting. Anyway, guess who has tons of work?"

"You, me, Leela, Vadan, Subhuti. As usual."

"You got it," she laughs. "Journalists from Bombay, an inauguration ceremony, six thousand sannyasins to be bussed out to Saswad—the whole shooting match!"

"When?"

"Osho's birthday. December 11."

"Jesus! That soon?"

"You know Laxmi, Krishna. You're just lucky it's not tomorrow."

"Morris," I say, turning to Vasumati's father, "I know you're a teetotaller, but how about buying a pair of hard-working press agents a couple of bottles of beer?"

"Sure," he replies, signalling for the waiter.

Indira Gandhi Returns to Power

To a country beleaguered by more than two years of regressive, repressive rule, of leadership by Morarji Desai and his bungling, bickering pack of old fogies, the re-election of Indira Gandhi with an absolute majority is a ray of hope. All over India people explode into celebration. In New Delhi, hundreds of thousands descend on 12 Willingdon Crescent, garlands and sweets and coconuts carried in tribute, cheering, calling "Mataji! Mataji!" begging her to show herself. The papers are filled with pictures of her, smiling and radiant in victory. There's a new promise in the air.

And nowhere is the sense of jubilation more prevalent than in Pune. It's odd to watch foreigners hurrah a political upset in a nation where we're all tourists, but for us, Indira's return to power signals an end to harassment, to violence, to police indifference, to visa problems, to film embargoes. And for Laxmi it means the very real possibility of land for a new commune.

Despite the fact we'd played it to the hilt, I never quite believed in Saswad. On Osho's birthday, when six thousand of us and assorted journalists had stomped the rock-strewn hills, no matter how hard I tried to accept it as the site for our new city, I simply couldn't. Something had been off. Madhura had felt it too.

"An absolute non-event," she remarked cryptically when the day had finally drawn to a close. Now, watching Laxmi's wheels turning, I'm more convinced than ever we'll be returning Saswad to the grazing sheep. Had Morarji won, we might have shifted there. Something, after all, is better than nothing. But Indira's back. And Laxmi, it's obvious, has bigger things in mind.

"When are you going to New Delhi to see her?" I ask.

"Soon, soon," she replies. "First, let her settle in. Let her cabinet happen. Then Laxmi will go."

I might have known. She sends me first. For some reason that eludes me, she decides to hold a press conference in New Delhi to announce the inauguration of our new city at Saswad. I still don't believe we're ever going to move there. My unvoiced suspicion is that she simply wants to test attitudes in the capital, to see what the general climate is in relation to Osho, to us, to the establishment of our new commune, wherever it might be.

A week later, sitting in her suite at the Oberoi in Delhi, we agree the press conference doesn't even deserve a post-mortem. "What to say about negativity?" Laxmi shrugs. "Negativity is negativity." But she's undaunted. She's banking on Indira's support. I just hope she's not kidding herself. After the drive from Pune to Delhi, my own optimism is pretty shaky.

The back seat laden with press kits, slide carousels and video equipment, Veetmoha and I had set out at six in the morning in the commune's air-conditioned Mercedes. The night before I'd said goodbye to Esther and Morris, who would be gone on my return.

The ride through Maharashtra had been dismal, through one filthy village of hovels after another. Everywhere men and women and naked children squatted listlessly in the dust, the euphoria of Indira's return as short-lived as the ragged Congress Party victory posters that hung in shreds from the sun-bleached, rain-stained walls. And in between these clusters of hopeless humanity, we drove through mile upon mile of empty, unused land. I thought of our six jammed acres in Pune. "There's so much land," I said to Veetmoha. "You'd think they'd be happy to sell some of it, to make it productive."

"Those people in that village we just passed?" he replied, gesturing over his shoulder. "That's India. Poor and starving; chained to their past and their gods. Sometimes I think the new commune will happen, but mostly I don't. Whenever I'm out in India and I see what it's really like, I can't see how they'll ever let us do something new, especially something that's going to remind them how awful their own lives are."

"Even Indira?"

He nodded, pulling out to pass a slow-moving lorry. "Even Indira. I'd never let Laxmi hear me say this, but I don't think Indira's going to risk supporting us. We're too hot an item. I've been with Laxmi on some of these meetings with politicians. I think some of them would genuinely like to help us, but their hands are tied. Votes. It all comes down to votes."

We sleep in Ahmedabad, at a local sannyasin's house, and start north again, heading towards Mount Abu where I attended my first camp with Osho six years before. And, driving through Gujarat, I understood why Laxmi kept insisting on this particular state. Gujarat is lush and rich and prosperous: the land well-irrigated and productive; the people healthy and smiling and well-fed. After the squalor of Maharashtra, I am very impressed. But when we cross into Rajasthan, there is real poverty again. The roads are pitted, untended; the farms, sparse and lean. Even the camels that pull the Rajasthani carts seemed sullen and morose in comparison with the high-stepping dromedaries that bounce along the roads of Gujarat.

We arrive in Delhi after midnight and sleep at the centre in suburban Safdarjang. In the morning, we collect Laxmi at the airport and move into the Oberoi. The press conference is scheduled for four that afternoon.

The basic problem is that Mrs Gandhi is out of town and Delhi's better journalists, including most of the foreign correspondents, have followed suit. What we end up with is a gaggle of aggressive hecklers who do their best to give Laxmi a hard time. But she gives tit for tat. I'd seldom seen her so fiery—she lets them have it straight in the teeth. For once I kept my big mouth shut. When I witnessed that familiar tremor run through her body just before we began I knew Osho had things in hand and all I had to do was watch. I found myself wondering whether our nice-guy days with the press were over. "We can't be so rigid, swamiji," Laxmi says afterwards in the suite. "Whatever the situation, the correct response. Today fire was needed—and he gave." She looks at me closely. "You saw?"

"I saw."

"Good. Then something positive did happen: Krishna Prem witnessed our Master's mystery once again." She jumps to her feet, clapping her hands. "Come on, children," she says to Veetmoha and to me. "This is not right time for Delhi. Laxmi will come back when Indira is here. Let's go home."

It's two in the morning when the bottle-green Mercedes pulls through the front gate. I shower in seconds and head for Vasumati's room.

Bernard Levin Returns

It's good to see Bernard Levin again; it's been almost a year. "You both look wonderful," he says as Vasumati and I join him in the Blue Diamond coffee shop. "This past year has been good to you."

A few weeks back I'd received a letter saying he was coming. The strike was over and *The Times* was on the stands again. His articles on the commune had been ready for months. On the way home, after covering the opening of Sydney's new Opera House, he said he'd stop by—"just to refresh my impressions".

I'm dying to ask what Britain's most esteemed journalist has written about us, but I can't. It just isn't done. He asks after Osho, Laxmi, friends he'd made here. The conversation is light and friendly. I'm sitting on my question. He must pick up on it: he finally rescues me.

"After I returned from Pune last year," he says, "I received a letter from one of my readers, from a lady whose daughter is here. She was concerned about her. She'd heard I'd been to the commune and wanted to know my impressions. I sent her copies of the three articles I'd written, telling her they were for-her-eyes-only, since they hadn't been published yet. She returned them within the week, saying that although she'd read me for years and respected my opinion, she felt I had been far too kind."

I betray nothing but interest, yet inside I'm whooping with glee that, at last, something positive about us is going to appear in a major paper. The news is too good to keep until morning. Leaving Vasumati to wait for me at Lao Tzu gate, I drop in on Laxmi to tell her what Bernard had said. She tells me to invite him to tea the next morning.

Her first question is about Peter Jenkins of *The Guardian*. "What happened with your friend who came with you last year?" she asks. "Osho answered his question so beautifully, but nothing has come in his paper. His writing never happened?"

"That's an interesting little story," Bernard chuckles. "Jenkins was as impressed as I was when we were here. I know he was: we talked about it at length before he left.

"When I returned to London I was curious to see what he'd written before writing myself, so I went to the library to check back issues of *The Guardian*. Nothing. So I telephoned him. He said he hadn't written anything as yet, but was planning to do so in the very near future. I wrote my own articles and filed them away for resurrection when *The Times'* strike was over, and for the next week or so I checked *The Guardian*, but saw nothing. Eventually, I just forgot about it.

"Some time later I was invited to a party," he continues. "Jenkins was there with his wife. I overheard snatches of conversation, including a few references to Pune, and then I understood. What had happened was that Jenkins had returned to England, all gung-ho, ready to write about what he'd seen and felt, prepared to champion you people as it were, and his wife and friends had laughed at him, telling him he'd been sucked in by some Indian guru and that he'd look a proper fool if he wrote in your favour. He became scared. And so he didn't write."

His eyes suddenly flash at the memory. "I don't know whether it was the two champagne cocktails or not," he laughs, "but I suddenly became angry and just couldn't let him get away with it. I strode across the room, grabbed him by the lapels and let him have it. 'Jenkins,' I said. 'You're a bloody coward!'"

"What did he do?" I ask.

"Nothing," Bernard replies. "He simply looked at me in shock. That sort of thing is not my style at all, you know. He didn't move or react or anything—I suppose because I'd been right. And that was that. So," he concludes wryly, "don't expect anything from Peter Jenkins to appear in *The Guardian*."

He leaves for Bombay that afternoon. I'm sorry to see him go. But not nearly as sorry as I am a week later. After seven days with William Rittold* of *Der Spiegel* and Heike*, the ice-maiden he'd espoused, I miss Bernard Levin like a long-lost lover.

Childishness

Since the beginnings of the press office, German journalists had been the bane of my existence. I'd been nice and I'd been nasty; I'd been accommodating and I'd been insulting, but I'd never been able to get through. It's as if they came to Pune armoured in Krupp steel, minds made up in advance, programmed to find fault, probing and condemning, like inquisitors from the SS. They'd come from all levels of German journalism, from the sleazy Joseph Kammer of *Bild-Zeitung* to the respected Conrad Zander of *STERN*, but they'd all been the same. After a couple of days, I'd find myself fighting the recurring urge to kick them up their tight Prussian asses. But William Rittold is the worst by far. Satyananda, our former *STERN* reporter, tells me Rittold's one of Germany's top writers, a deep thinker, a man with a reputation for insight and understanding, an expert in matters of psychology and religion. I think he's a first-class prick. When Satyananda had introduced us it had been instant dislike.

The Gestapo-style questions are one thing—I'm used to being under a barrage of negative fire—but the utter childishness of Rittold and his wife drives me round the twist. It's the pre-discourse sniffing, the checking for odours that aggravate Osho's allergies, that brings out the nasty, rebellious child in each of them.

Day after day they are refused entry to discourse. And day after day they complain. Fed up with explaining about the fragility of Osho's body again and again, I confront them one morning. I tell them either to make sure they don't smell of perfume or just to forget about discourse totally. I let them know, in no uncertain terms, that the rule isn't going to be waived for them, no matter how important they may feel they are. Faced with it, Heike finally admits she's been doing it on purpose, dousing herself with scent before trying to get into discourse—"just to see what would happen". I've nothing to say and turn to him. He's been even worse than her, insisting he has been using our scentless soap and shampoo, arguing at the gate, demanding entry. With a look of proud disdain he reaches into his pocket and extracts a handkerchief drenched in cologne. "Why?" I ask.

"To protest this practice of sniffing people."

"What have you come here for?" I ask flatly. "To make an issue of the way we live or to report on what you've seen?"

"To report," he admits, his tone suddenly sheepish.

"Then why don't you just do that and stop behaving like a child!" I walk out of the office. I don't trust myself to spend another minute with them right now.

Everyone they meet feels the same. They keep asking us to arrange interviews, to show them this or that, but whenever they show up they're late or they've lost interest. William finally stops coming altogether. He sits by the Blue Diamond pool, reading Satyananda's book about the commune, the recently published *Ganz Entspannt im Hier und Jetzt.*

"I don't believe your husband!" I tell Heike one afternoon. "The commune is five minutes away and he sits at the Blue Diamond *reading* about it!"

She fixes me with that icy Teutonic stare. "William's a very deep man," she informs me caustically. "You, of course, wouldn't understand him."

When he *does* drop in again, I let go with something I've been holding back for ages in dealing with the German press—the good old Führer, the celebrated Austrian corporal, Adolph himself. Rittold hates it, but I couldn't care less. Hitler surfaces in almost every sentence I speak.

Of all the nationalities attracted to Osho, it's the Germans who've come in the greatest numbers—so many, actually, that the German government and press were becoming concerned. To me it made perfect sense. How much further could young Germans go in the other direction than from Hitler to Osho? "You brought them up in hate," I tell Rittold. "And now you wonder why they turn to someone who shows them how to live in love? For a man of your reputed insight it should be blatantly obvious."

It may be mean of me, but I keep on hammering. I know there's no way he's going to write anything positive, so I figure I've nothing to lose. "You German journalists are just like the Indian ones," I say. "The Indians keep coming here and criticizing Osho, saying he's trying to destroy five thousand years of culture and tradition. I ask why they want to preserve it. The country's held together by rope and bamboo. Why would anyone want to keep it like it is? It makes them angry: they don't want to hear the truth.

"And to me, you German journalists are the same. You're freaked out that so many of your young people are leaving Germany and coming here, and you come to find fault with us instead of looking in your own back yard, instead of seeing that there must be something wrong in Germany if they want to leave. Ever thought of that?"

He has no answer. I get nothing but a steely stare and, that very afternoon, the news that they're leaving. My goodbye resounds with relief.

The afternoon they go, Satyananda wants to talk to me. "I don't want to deal with journalists any more," he says. "I'm happy to translate, to write a second book, anything. I just don't want to deal with journalists. It's a total waste of energy. They just don't get it."

I commiserate. But I also tell him he's missing the point. "It's not whether they get it or not that's important. It's what happens to *you*." He's not convinced.

"Just think about Osho, Satyananda. Every morning he talks to us for two hours. If he were constantly worried about whether we're getting it or not, he'd have given up years ago. He's not goal-oriented. He'd like us to get it, of course, but if we get it, we get it; if we don't, we don't. He just keeps on pouring, sharing his experience. You have to adopt the same attitude in relation to journalists." The look he gives me over his glasses is still sceptical.

"What happens to me when I talk to journalists is that sometimes I step aside and an energy comes through me. That's what's important to me—that ability to set *me* aside and let existence flow through me. In whatever way it wants. With Bernard Levin, love was the right way—and that was what came. With the Rittolds, it was totally different. They needed slamming; they needed some of their own nastiness to be thrown back at them. I wasn't mean on purpose. That was what was happening. And I just allowed it.

"If you can get out of the way and allow whatever wants to come through you to do so, they get something—whether they can admit it or not—and you get something. The Rittolds had a look in the mirror; I got the experience of being a vehicle. That's what's important. And do you think whether his article in *Der Spiegel* is negative or positive is really going to stop the young Germans from coming here?"

"No," he admits with a wry laugh.

"So there's no problem. Just have a good time with them. If you are out of the way, what comes has to be right on. Just be available, a vehicle, and leave the rest to Osho."

Deceit

Vadan and I are alone in the press office, perusing the papers, when one of the receptionists ushers in a blond, thick-set Englishman in his mid-thirties. With an overly hearty handshake, he introduces himself as Christopher Hitchens[20] here on behalf of the BBC. "Actually," he says, "I write for *The New Statesman*, but Tony Isaacs has asked me to script a show on you for *The World About Us*."

For the next hour or so, Vadan and I fill him in on the commune and its activities, explaining how each and every aspect relates to Osho's work. By tea-time, I notice one of his hands is shaking. "Are you unwell?" I ask. "Is there something I can get for you?"

He's obviously embarrassed by my observation, but need overcomes nervousness and, fortified by a deep breath, he lets it out.

20. Hitchens' "fanciful version" of this visit is reported in Chapter 14 of his book *God is Not Great*

"I have a little confession to make," he says. "What I really need is a drink."

Boy, I think to myself, is this a winner! Vadan and I carefully avoid each other's eyes; if our gazes meet we're sure to laugh. "Apart from the bar at the Blue Diamond," I offer, trying to sound sympathetic and understanding, "I doubt if you'll find a bottle of scotch for miles."

"Some in my room at the hotel," he mutters with a sheepish grin. "So if you chaps don't mind, I'll toddle off now and come back tomorrow." He holds up the literature we've given him. "Enough homework to keep me busy until then."

The next day we wait for him, but he doesn't show. He doesn't come the following day either. By the third afternoon it's apparent he isn't coming back at all. "Jesus," Vadan mutters sarcastically, "if that guy's going to write a television script about us, it's really going to be great!"

"What he writes doesn't worry me as much as that bit he dropped about Veet Artho selling the BBC some of his footage," I reply. That mock encounter group Laxmi had set up for Veet Artho and his German crew to film is still, for me, one of her major booboos.

The subject's been unbroachable ever since and so, since she's in Delhi, I take my concern to one of her secretaries.

"I'll get onto the BBC and tell them Veet Artho's broken his contract with us—which he has, the schmuck—and let them know he's got no right to sell them anything, that the film legally belongs to us," she says. "Don't worry. I'll handle it."

I wish I knew how to handle my situation. Except for Bernard Levin and a few Indians like Bachi Karkaria, I've been faced, for the last couple of years, with an unending parade of total journalistic assholes, of phoneys and liars and manipulating cheats. And somehow the combination of Rittold and Hitchens is the straw that, I feel, is about to break my back.

Something's About to Transpire

A while back the format of darshan had changed: except for when he was giving sannyas, Osho had stopped speaking. Actually, the initiative had come from us, rather than from Osho. More and more people, when asking for darshan, were indicating they had nothing to say to Osho but just wanted to sit with him in silence for a few moments. In response, he began the "blessings darshan". In pairs, sannyasins would kneel before him for the laying of one of those magic thumbs on the third eye. In the energy darshans he used the mediums as before, but in the new blessings darshans he set them dancing.

At the first press office darshan after an ineffectual Hindi fanatic tried to hurl a knife at Osho during discourse, an odd number of sannyasins had booked blessings darshans and at the end, to fill the empty space, Osho calls me forward.

The next morning, en route as usual to Laxmi's room, I see Vasumati talking to Vivek. I hang in the background, curious. Walking towards me, she looks perplexed. "Vivek just said the strangest thing to me," she says. "'You know what you asked me about a month or so ago,' she said. 'Well it looks like it might happen after all.' Then she walked off."

"It could be about a place where we can be together," I suggest.

There's an odd grin on Laxmi's face when I enter her room. We talk about work for a bit—she's not at all satisfied with the Maharashtra prosecutor's handling of the assassination attempt case—and then she asks me to come to her office at one-twenty. There's something she wants to discuss.

"One-twenty!" I laugh. The idea of Laxmi being that specific about time breaks me up. "One-twenty? Laxmi, you don't even know what *year* this is."

"True, swamiji," she admits with a chuckle. "But one-twenty it is."

I'm sitting before her on the dot. She gets straight to the point. "Do you want to live with Vasumati?" she asks.

"I never really thought about *living* together," I tell her honestly. "But it is difficult for us to find a room in this commune to be alone together."

"Fine," she says. "Let Laxmi know this afternoon."

I find myself wondering if living together is the right step for me, for her, for us. And when talking it over with Vasumati it becomes obvious that neither of us is able to reach a decision. "Why don't we toss it back to Osho?" I suggest.

Back in my room, Vasumati peering over my shoulder, I compose a letter to Osho. A few moments later we're handing it to Laxmi. A smile plays across her lips as she reads it. "Laxmi will show this to him tonight," she says.

The answer comes the following day, after discourse. "He says to tell you it's better not to live together," she informs me. "Otherwise, he says you'll ruin it."

But the problem of a place where we can be together still isn't resolved. As I mention it to Laxmi, I've a sudden inspiration. "What about Eckhart roof?" I suggest. Eckhart Village is the original servants quarters for Jesus House. I like Eckhart—a series of small, cosy rooms around a plant-filled courtyard—and on the flat roof, sleeping huts, respites from the night-time heat.

"There's one empty spot up there, big enough for a bed. Could we build a sleeping hut up there?"

"Why not?" she smiles. "It's fine with Laxmi."

Before going to the office, I climb the bamboo ladder to Eckhart roof and stake our claim like a prospector about to pan for gold. I leave signs: "Reserved for Vasumati and Krishna Prem". Existence *does* take care of us!

Essentially, a bed is what it is—a big, wide, comfortable double bed. Raised off the roof and covered with an A-frame, it's tucked away in a corner, shaded by the branches of a giant Gulmohar. There's a brand new lime green mosquito net and split-bamboo roller-blinds all the way around. It's the perfect love-nest. All we need to buy is a waterproof tarpaulin. The monsoon's not very far away.

And plants. After a few expeditions to Empress Gardens, the hut's surrounded—ferns and palms and willowy grasses for Vasumati; every variety of begonia I can find for me.

Despite Osho's admonition that we not live together, it's pretty well what we find ourselves doing. Every night after darshan, we head straight for our bed, lying around together, talking, drinking coffee, making love. Our own rooms become closets, places where we keep our clothes. Even after Osho reminds us in one morning's discourse, nothing changes—we still sleep together each and every night.

He'd been speaking of himself as a mirror, saying how difficult it is for people to face. "But *you* can understand it," he'd said, "you who are here, who are with me. You can understand this fact: I am just a mirror... Anything wrong, and the mirror is bound to show it to you. The mirror is not at fault. If your face is looking sad the mirror will show it. Don't destroy the mirror.

"That's what the poor man was doing here who threw the knife to kill me," he continued. "He could not tolerate the mirror. He had listened to me for only three, four days, but he became so agitated because what I was saying showed his fanaticism, showed his Hindu chauvinistic attitude, and it became intolerable for him.

"Psychologists say that if every person in the world decides to be absolutely authentic and true for twenty-four hours—just for twenty-four hours the whole world decides: 'We will not be polite and we will not tell lies and we will not be formal; we will simply say the truth as it is, as it appears to us'—then there will no longer be any friendship in the world: no more husbands, no more wives, no more lovers. All will be finished!

"That's why to my sannyasins I always suggest that if you want to continue your relationship with somebody it is best not to live together, because if you start living together, how long can you be polite? How long can you be formal? Sooner or later the truth starts surfacing."

I'd known, then and there, that he was going to talk about us. And sure enough! "Just a few days ago," he said, "Vasumati wanted to live with Krishna Prem. Their relationship has lasted for almost one and a half years. It is such a long, long time in this commune—almost impossible!" Everyone had laughed, except Vasumati. Sitting beside me, she cringed. I knew what she was thinking. She hadn't asked if we could *live* together.

"Almost impossible—for the simple reason that they are not living together so they meet only once in a while. They cannot even meet every day because Vasumati is sharing a room with other people,

Krishna Prem is sharing with somebody else. So only once in a while, when they can manage some privacy, they can meet—only for a few hours per week, twice or thrice a week." Now it was my turn to wonder. Where did he get this twice-or-thrice-a-week bit?

"So it remains a love affair: it has not yet become a marriage. Otherwise it would have finished long ago!

"But when she wanted I had Vivek—Vivek came to me and said 'Vasumati wants to live with Krishna Prem'—I said, 'That's what every woman wants and that's how every woman destroys the relationship.' And the man cannot say no because if he says no it is immediately finished. But I said, 'If she wants to, then we will manage it in some way.'" Poor Vasumati. I felt her beside me, wishing the floor would open and swallow her up.

"There was one opportunity," he continued. "I inquired of Krishna Prem. He proved to be really wise. He wrote a letter. He said to me, 'Osho, *you* decide, because I don't know what is right. My desires say be together, but I am an unconscious person—I don't know what will happen out of it. I can't see very far into the future, but you can, so you decide.'

"So I decided that they live separately."[21]

"No matter what Osho says," Vasumati tells me later, "I feel fine with things the way they are right now. I don't see any problem and I don't want to manufacture one."

"I'm fine too," I say. Somewhere in the back of my mind the fact that our Master never speaks lightly or casually niggles at me. But I shove the thought aside. I'm happy with things. "If there are any consequences," I say, "we'll deal with them when they come."

Of late, Vasumati seems preoccupied, a bit distant and withdrawn. I ask what's going on. She feels stuck, she tells me, like she's in a marriage.

"There's no excitement, no uncertainty any more," she complains. "I think I preferred it when we didn't have our own place. And I feel dead."

---

21. *Tao: The Golden gate, Vol. 1*

She feels dead and I feel pissed. All I've heard for months has been grumbling about not having a place, and now that we have one, she's still not satisfied.

The next thing I know I'm back in the ward at the health centre. Amoebic dysentery. When Vasumati comes to see me after darshan, I hardly have the energy to talk. My body's totally drained—from the high fever, from the non-stop shits, from the constant sweating. She sits beside me for a while, saying nothing, and then kisses me goodnight. I'm too ill to be any sort of company.

In the morning I awaken to the sight of Vasumati sitting by my bed. She looks disturbed, distracted. Before I can say anything, even good morning, she blurts it out: "Krishna, I made love to somebody else last night."

It's as if I've just been slapped in the face. I stare at her in shock. I can't believe my ears. "Where?" I manage at last. I already know the answer, but somehow I've got to ask.

She looks down at her hands. She can't meet my eyes. "In our bed," she whispers.

I'm sick and in the hospital. How could she? I turn towards the wall, away from her.

No day has ever been this long. Or this lonely. I'd seen this relationship as sacred, as Osho-given, as being beyond all the sordid little events that plague ordinary ones. But it's no different after all. And the realization makes my heart ache. By mid-afternoon the ward's suffocating me. I just have to get out. Fever or not, I put on my clothes and head outside. Right now, I need to walk. And I need a bidi.

On the street I suddenly feel someone rushing at me from behind, but before I can turn I am crushed in an embrace. It's Vasumati. "Come on," I say, taking her hand. "Let's sit down and talk."

"Me first," she says, taking a deep breath. "The minute we started to live together; the minute we moved onto the roof together—routine and habit—I started to feel trapped. There was something beautiful about not having a place that was ours because we could never become a couple. And the minute we became a couple, a relationship, something in me started to die."

"Why didn't you say something?"

"I tried, but you wouldn't listen. You kept saying it was all in my mind. I just couldn't get through to you."

"Then what about last night?"

She looks me straight in the eye. "I didn't plan it." Her voice is direct, no-nonsense. "Don't think for a second I planned it. I know what I was doing. It might not have been fair to him, but I was using him: it was just a way of moving my energy. Whenever I've felt stuck like this in the past, it's always worked. It was the only way I knew to move my energy again.

"He left and I slept alone. But when I woke in the morning I felt awful. As soon as I could I came up to the ward. You looked so happy to see me, and when I told you, there was such pain on your face I wanted to die. But I had to tell you. There was nothing else I could do." Her voice drops. "That's all I have to say. You?"

"I don't know how just or unjust any of this is," I begin, "but I'm going to let it out." And I do—a tirade of rage and hurt.

"I fall into a pattern very easily, Vasumati. And I resist change. A great part of me wants everything to be safe and secure, unchanging. But, at the same time, when change comes I can flow with it, enjoying the new space. But I still resist it at first. When we lived together, it even used to freak me out if Divy rearranged the furniture. That's how much I resist change." She laughs, hugging me. "So, there's something in the stability of relationship that appeals to me. It's easy and it's comfortable. But this shows me that I need to put effort into our relationship to keep it alive."

"In any other relationship I've ever been in," she says, "whenever I found myself going dead, I would go out and be with someone else. And it would change things for me. But with you it doesn't work—I've seen that. But one thing it has done is shake us up, made us take a good look at things. And I'm glad it happened, just for that."

"Me too," I admit, grinning at last.

"From now on, Krishna," she says, her voice determined, "I'm not going to let things come to the point where I have to break out like this. I talked to Divy this morning, and he said something to me about you. 'One thing about Krishna Prem is that he has a great respect and admiration for the truth. You need never be afraid to tell him the truth.'"

"That's true."

"So here it is," she says, holding her arms out to me. "The truth. I love you. And no matter how much of an old stick-in-the-mud you are, I'm going to keep this relationship juicy." I love her feistiness; I love it that she won't take my crap.

That night, when one of the nurses brings the tape of the morning's discourse for the ward patients, the first question makes me laugh. "Can a woman really drive a man crazy?"

"It depends on the man," Osho begins. "If he is wise he becomes a hen-pecked husband; if he is not so wise, then there is no other way than to be crazy...

"Nothing is wrong with the woman," he continues. "She is not deliberately trying to drive you crazy. Their minds just function in a totally different way. In fact, that is their attraction: their polarities function like a magnetic field. The more different a woman is, the more she will attract you...

"A living relationship between a man and a woman is bound to be a little bit crazy. Man cannot drive the woman crazy because his argument, his way of thinking, is logical. The woman's way of thinking is illogical, but that is her way; that's how she's made. She functions instinctively at the lowest and intuitively at the highest. Man functions intellectually at the lowest and intelligently at the highest. The way of instinct and intuition is the way of illogic. Logic cannot drive the illogical person crazy; if anything is going to happen it is going to happen to the logical mind...

"She never tries to understand *you,*" he says. "The illogical functioning of the psyche is not interested in understanding; it simply reaches the conclusions without any procedures—it *jumps* to the conclusions. And the miracle is that the woman is almost always right and you are almost always wrong! That drives you crazy! And you have been functioning so logically, mathematically, step by step: still your conclusion is not right…" I can feel a wry smile forming. This I learned the hard way. Laxmi saw to that.

His tone suddenly changes. Good, I think, here comes the advice. "Rejoice in her! Rejoice in her differences; rejoice in her different approach towards life. Rejoice that she is not a man but a woman… When you are with your woman, put your mind aside. Become more existential and less intellectual. Love her, dance with her, sing with her, but don't try to argue with her… The moment she says anything, say, 'Right! Absolutely right! That's what *I* was thinking!'

"Be a little more meditative. In fact, meditation has been discovered as a defence. It is not the discovery of women, remember. Many people have asked me, 'Why have women not discovered meditation?' Why should they discover it? They have no reason to discover it: it is man's discovery. Surrounded by his meditative energy he is protected. Nobody, not even a woman, can drive him crazy!"[22]

A Picture of My Mother

I haven't spent time with Mukta the Greek in ages. Divy says she's coming up after darshan tonight and that she's been asking how I am. I think I'll hang out with them a bit.

During the course of the evening Divy's looking for something in one of the drawers when he suddenly starts to laugh. "Here, Mukta," he says. "Look at this. It's Krishna Prem's mother."

"My God!" Mukta hoots. "It's Vasumati! Amazing! Have you shown this to Osho?" she asks.

"No."

"Oh, you must! It'll give him a good laugh. You must send it in to him!"

The next morning I do. Clipped to the photo I enclose a note: "Beloved Osho, you know how you're always saying that a woman looks for her father in a man and that a man looks for his mother in a woman? Well, I showed this photo of my mother to Mukta and she said you'd enjoy it, so…"

---

22. *Zen: The Special Transmission*

"You will fall in love many times," Osho says in discourse a day or so later, "but every time you will feel frustrated for the simple reason that deep down the cells of your mother are projecting a chemistry in which you can be fulfilled only if you can find a replica of your mother in your beloved..." I know what's coming. Vasumati doesn't. She has no idea I sent the photo in.

I watch her, waiting for his next words. "Just a few days ago," he continues, "Vivek brought me a picture of Krishna Prem's mother." Vasumati snaps to sudden, wide-eyed attention. I start to laugh. "It was amazing!" he says. "The mother looks exactly like Vasumati. *Exactly* like Vasumati! The nose, the face. And Krishna Prem has been gay... Suddenly, seeing Vasumati... he has fallen in love... And he was not even consciously aware of his mother's existence because the mother died very early. I think he was only two months old or something when the mother died, so he does not remember. But the chemistry remembers. Each cell has its own memory... He has found something similar..."[23]

Vasumati looks pensive. "Does it bother you when he talks about you having been gay in the past?" she asks.

"Not at all. It's as if he's talking about someone else. I just can't relate to it any more."

"Nor can I," she laughs. "We've been lovers a couple of years now. I know your energy. The idea makes me laugh. I've never come across a man whose energy is more un-gay!"

"When he talked about it this morning," I admit, "it kind of took me aback, especially when he mentioned my mother. I always thought I'd become gay because she died, but some time ago I saw that, really, it had nothing to do with her, it had to do with my father."

"How so?"

"You know how they say a chick fixates on the first being it sees after hatching from the egg? And from then on, whatever that was—a duck, a goose, a dog—that's its mother and it will follow it around no

23. *Gudia Spirituale*

matter what. I reckon it's the same for babies. Usually it's the mother, but mine died and it was my father.

"I always found it odd, but the first thing I would notice in a man was his chest, and it was his chest that would form the basis of an attraction. Then, one day, I remembered my father telling me that I had whooping cough when he brought me home from the hospital after my mother's death. There was no mother, so he used to walk me up and down at night, trying to get me to sleep—holding me against his chest. The day I saw that consciously, all attraction to men just dropped away."

"And that was it? It was that simple?" She takes my hand in hers. "I'm just curious. I get a lot of gay men in groups and individual sessions."

"It was a little more complex," I explain. "Without a mother, I transferred all my emotional needs to my father. But he couldn't give me much. His whole number was so uptight-Christian—men don't do this, men don't do that, very hold-it-all-in. Yet there was this need in me. When I grew up the only men who would give it to me were gay. There was a price—my body—but I didn't care, as long as I was drunk enough. Afterwards, I would be with a woman for a while but that was so complicated—I had major abandonment issues with women, as you can understand—that I would go back to getting drunk and being with a man.

"I always knew there was *something* available from men, something they weren't giving or couldn't give," I say, "and it wasn't until I came to Osho that I found it. You know how the men are here—they hug each other, kiss each other on the cheek, but there's nothing sexual to it. Here, the men are real, authentic with each other. They love each other, like brothers, and they display their affections with ease. You know how Vadan and I are with each other. Could you imagine me and Vadan in bed?" I laugh at the utter ridiculousness of the idea.

She grimaces. "It's easier for women, I guess," she says. "It's quite natural for women to be affectionate with each other."

"And it's natural for men too. It's just that, out there in the world, men won't let themselves be natural."

Chapter Ten: 1981

WOOING INDIRA

There are a couple of quick trips to Delhi. I fly up to address a luncheon meeting of the Thursday Club of Diplomats and, a week or so later, return with a commune fashion-and-music extravaganza that's been booked into the Taj Mahal Hotel. While the rest of the troupe lolls about the pool, Laxmi and I tour the available theatres, finally settling on the government-owned Mavalankar Auditorium for two nights in October. We're going to wow the capital with *A Midsummer Night's Dream* and the theatre group's latest Shakespearean effort, *Twelfth Night*. By then, Laxmi figures, things in the government will be back to normal.

Delhi is in turmoil. The shock of Sanjay Gandhi's death in his private plane has pretty much put government machinery on hold. Although Laxmi feels for Mrs Gandhi and Sanjay's widow Maneka, her major focus is seeing Osho's work happen. And, before everything ground to a halt, she'd apparently been making progress.

Subhuti has been working with her in Delhi, and just before I leave Pune to talk to the diplomats, he fills me in. "The first time we met Indira, Laxmi presented her with a list of our grievances. They spoke in Hindi, but later Laxmi told me she'd said, 'Your things are being taken care of. It will take time, but it will all happen.' After the Morarji years, Laxmi was thrilled.

"And," he continued, "things did start happening after that: visas started being granted, mail stopped being censored, that sort of thing." He shakes his head in admiration. "I'm always amazed at her energy. She's tireless. You know how slowly the machinery grinds in India—but she's dauntless.

"No matter in what area she's working, the first thing she does is make what we need clear to Indira. Then she goes to the ministers of the various departments and does the same. And she keeps on going, all down the line—from joint secretaries and additional secretaries to the clerks in the office. I must have seen her slide show on the commune ten thousand times. She'll show it to anyone who'll take the time to watch it. One night," he said, laughing at the memory, "we went to this minister's house to show it. He wasn't home when we arrived, and by the time he got there Laxmi was showing it to the servants.

"Anyway," he concluded, "things are happening. The two big issues are land, of course, and getting the Foundation recognized in a big way. She says if the Foundation can be granted national status as an important trust it will really help in establishing avenues for Osho's message to spread in India. Indira keeps saying yes to Laxmi. But then, all politicians say yes. Sometimes in Delhi I get the feeling I'm on a bicycle, pedalling like crazy but getting nowhere. But you know Laxmi's tenacity and optimism. She hangs in, plugging away.

"October, swamiji," Laxmi says as the lot of us leave the Taj for the Delhi railway station. Standing in the midst of cases of clothes and musical instruments, the determination in her voice makes her sound ten feet tall. "October! Then Indiraji will give Laxmi the big yes—the yes to everything. Of that, Laxmi's convinced!"

I hope she's right. God, how I hope she's right.

Good with Vasumati, Awful with Work

All the way home my thoughts are ahead of me, with Vasumati. I can't wait to see her. But the thrill of my homecoming is short-lived. The second morning I awaken in a terrible mood. I haven't been this depressed in ages. But it has nothing to do with Vasumati, it's work.

"It's the routine," I tell her when she asks what's wrong. "It's the bloody routine I hate. In Delhi I was really blissful—and it was such a surprise, feeling like that, I couldn't help but notice it. I was doing exactly the kind of work I like—arranging interviews, talking to editors, getting press coverage, that sort of thing.

"By the time we got there," I say, "the Taj publicity people had done nothing for the fashion show. I took over and the next morning we had photos on the front pages of three of Delhi's five major papers. I was out in the field, working on my own—and I loved it!

"I was *so* flowing, Vasumati! And it was incredible with Laxmi. No matter where I was, I knew when she wanted me. I'd call and she would say she had just been thinking about me. There was this magical sense of oneness with her, with the work. But now that I'm back, that feeling of blissfulness is gone. There's the office and the decisions and letters to dictate—letters about copyrights and all that crap, and I hate it. I felt like I was flying in Delhi. Here, I just feel trapped."

"Why don't you write to Osho about it?"

I shake my head. "I'll just hang in and wait. Part of me knows that when it's time for things to change, Osho will step in. All I can do is keep on going, stay patient, and do my best not to let the routine get me down."

I've got to do something to liven things up; the press office is as dull as Morarji Desai's personality. Checking the papers, I see the country's plagued with riots again, that soldiers have even shot a few civilians in Ahmedabad, so I decide to send a question in to Osho. "Who knows?" I say to Leela. "Maybe he'll say something interesting, something to put the Foundation back into the papers."

I underestimated my Master. He gives us headlines.

"My own suggestion to Indira Gandhi is: Impose a stricter Emergency than before, and for fifteen years hold no elections in this country... For fifteen years this country needs no democracy; it has not that much intelligence.

"India has lived for two thousand years in slavery," he adds. "If it has freedom it does not know how to cope with it. In these fifteen years, try forcibly to teach this country how to live independently. Nobody has taught this country how to live independently."[24]

---

24. *Theologica Mystica*

For the next few days I am deluged with irate Indian reporters. Osho has lit a fire under them. They shout and yell at me, but I make no attempt to mollify their anger.

"You miss the point," I say. "Osho is saying India needs a government tailored to India's needs, and that these fifteen years should be spent in developing a system that's right for India. What you've got here is an English-style government, a relic from the Raj. Nehru and all the other leaders who've run India since Independence were trained in England. Mahatma Gandhi too. And what they did was bring a system that worked in England to India. It doesn't work here. India's India; it's not England." It's like talking to a herd of buffaloes. Their precious democracy's been threatened and they're really pissed off. They can't get to Osho so they take it out on me.

And then Osho tosses out another bombshell. He advocates a benevolent dictatorship under Indira, the imposition of compulsory birth control and abolition of the law against euthanasia for old people who want to die. Everyone knows India's killing herself with over-population, but no one wants to face it. Very few papers print our news release. Osho's words are too hot to touch.

When Laxmi calls from Delhi I ask if she's given copies of the discourse tapes to Mrs Gandhi. She has. "And?" I ask. "What did Indira have to say?"

"Nothing," she replies, "not a word has been mentioned. When a Master hits a disciple, it's one thing," she says, "but when a living buddha gives an entire country a stick like this one, swamiji, it takes some time to absorb such a shock. No one has ever spoken to India like Osho has, Krishna Prem. No one."

"Do you think what he's said will affect things? Like land for the new commune?"

"One can't say. All Laxmi knows is that he is the Master and he knows what he's doing. Laxmi never tries to understand; Laxmi is just his instrument. If India cannot accept his love and his compassion, it is India's loss. For over twenty years he has been trying to show India the way. But we are a foolish people, filled with pride. Whether Indira will listen or not, Laxmi can't say. Only time will tell."

The Delhi press reaction to the plays is lukewarm. "So what!" Laxmi snorts, tossing the clippings onto the coffee table in the Taj suite. "Government came! Ministers, secretaries, clerks, ambassadors came. Gandhi family came. Even the Great Lady herself had little peek! Who bothers what these press people say?

"Laxmi wants land," she says emphatically. "Laxmi wants to create more talk, more interest, so that many ears are reached. The Great Lady's ear is open, and Laxmi wants to make certain that the voices that whisper in it have positive things to say. Land for new commune *has* to happen! And Delhi is the key."

Indira had seemed open when she'd dropped by the craft exhibition we mounted in the Mavalankar lobby. Nothing of Osho's advice to her had been mentioned, but she seemed open, friendly and interested. She excused herself from attending the plays—the period of mourning for Sanjay wasn't over—but Laxmi made sure she saw part of a final rehearsal. All in all, Laxmi's pleased. And when a call comes from the PM's house, inviting the cast for a visit with Mrs Gandhi before we leave for Pune, she's delighted. "Laxmi knew," she shouts triumphantly. "Laxmi knew she enjoyed!"

The next morning, dressed in our best, the lot of us, en route to the station, had toddled off to the Prime Minister's residence at 1 Safdarjang Road. Past scores of waiting Indians who had come to petition Indira for this or that, we were ushered into a covered marquee set up on the main lawn of the PM's compound.

After a few moments Mrs Gandhi appeared. She seemed ill at ease; there were more awkward silences than anything else. She apologized for missing the plays, explaining, once again, that she was still in mourning for her son. She chatted about her daily routine, about the challenge of governing the country and about her illustrious father, Jawaharlal Nehru. But nothing of any significance was said—not by her, not by us. There was no reference to our need for land, no mention of the assassination attempt on Osho by the Hindu fanatic in Pune or his acquittal by the local court—nothing.

For me, the whole thing had been a disappointing waste of time. Laxmi, with her usual undaunted optimism, had been pleased. Apart from the fact Mrs Gandhi acknowledged us by an official invitation to her residence, I didn't see that anything had been accomplished. "I get the feeling I'm on a bicycle," Subhuti had said to me, "pedalling like crazy but getting nowhere." Leaving 1 Safdarjang Road, I feel exactly the same. I can't pin it on anything, but there's an undeniably bad taste in my mouth. All I want is to get on the train and head home.

Osho Asks if I'm Happy

The next afternoon Arup, who's been going in to see Osho about commune work while Laxmi and Sheela are away, summons me to the office. "Osho asked me about you this morning," she says.

"Really?" My curiosity is piqued. "What did he ask you about? What did he want to know?"

"He asked me if I thought you were happy."

Happy? Am I happy? Over the next few days I ask myself that question time and time again. And I see that I'm not really happy. But I don't write to Osho. There had been something in Arup's tone that indicated Osho was just planting a seed, making me take a look at myself. But one morning he *does* want a reply. "He wants to know if you're happy," Arup tells me. "He said to tell you if you're not happy in your work it can be changed."

I'm at a loss for words.

"It's been obvious for a while that you're not terribly happy," she continues. "You get into moods. And these moods affect other people. From what I hear a lot of people in the press office are afraid of you, and this isn't how he wants the departments run. So," she adds matter-of-factly, "what should I tell him?"

"Give me a minute," I say, closing my eyes. I feel a bit ashamed, a little ridiculous, but I have to admit she's right. "It's true," I say after a moment. "I'm not happy in my work any more. And I know what it is—it's frustration with the routine and with the constant negativity. Apart from Bernard Levin and a few Indians, the negativity is overwhelming and it's really getting me down.

"I know myself well enough to be aware that when I get angry or into moods it's because my energy's frustrated. Sometimes it's sexual energy that's got nowhere to go. But this time it's not. This time it's my creative energy that's frustrated. There's nothing creative about trying to deal with negativity all the time.

"You know," I continue, "I've been doing this same kind of work for almost twenty years. And there's nothing new in it, no challenge. It's like driving a car on the freeway: you press down on the accelerator and that's it. Every once in a while you may move the steering wheel an inch or so this way or that, but that's about it. Running the press office has become like that for me. And I'm sorry if people are afraid of me..."

"You *can* get pretty dark at times," she laughs. "But tell me, do you have any idea what you'd like to do?"

I can't be specific and I tell her so. "But there is a certain space that happens to me, Arup," I say. "It's a space I love, a space that fulfills me, and it only happens in a couple of ways. It happens when a good journalist comes, someone interesting and intelligent.

"It happens the second a camera points at me. It's strange, but with a camera it's instantaneous. I just disappear—talking happens, but I can't claim it. Inside, there's this delicious silence. It's the sense of being a vehicle, a hollow bamboo—like Krishna and his flute.

"And the other time is when I'm writing. The words just come out of that silence and manifest on the page. I love the knitting together of words, the creativity that involves—and the silence.

"Those are the times I'm happiest, the times I'm most fulfilled."

Her smile is soft and loving. "I'll tell him tonight," she says, gathering her papers.

That night I barely close my eyes. I waver between exhilaration at the prospect of something new and creative, and terror at the possibility he might do a number on me and send me somewhere horrid, like the kitchens. "Will you stop!" Vasumati shakes me in exasperation. "He's not going to do anything like *that* to you!"

An exhausted wreck walks into Arup's office the next morning. "You look terrible," she laughs. "Couldn't sleep?"

"Never mind. Just tell me what he said!"

"I talked to him last night and told him what you'd said. First of all, he asked me in what press office areas I thought you were indispensable. I told him my feelings and this is what he said. He says you should stay on as head of the press office, but you just guide Leela. Go in, mornings, guide her, give her the benefit of your experience—and you can spend the rest of the day in your room, writing a book about your experience here in Pune.

"And a couple of other things," Arup continues with a smile. "He says you should contribute ideas, that you should help the writers and be available to deal with important journalists; just the important ones. The rest of the time is yours, for the book. Nice, isn't it?"

"Nice!" I hug her hard. "Arup, it's far fucking out! Tell him I love him and tell him thank you!"

"I'll tell him tonight," she promises. "But I'll polish the language a bit. He can use that word in discourses, but I doubt I could ever say it to his face."

My Father Dies

Vasumati's parents are back and have invited us to spend a week with them at the Race View Hotel in Mahabaleshwar, a hill-station some three hours' drive from Pune. The only thing missing at the Race View is the British. Now it's affluent Indians, mostly Parsis from Bombay, instead of English officers and their ladies, but nothing else has changed. It's still separate tables with cut-flowers and stand-up menu cards announcing the five-course lunches and dinners for the week. It's still French service from waiters uniformed in faded white, cuffs and collars frayed from years of washing.

At the far end of the dining room is the lounge—ratty sofas, dog-eared novels, well-thumbed magazines, a bridge table without cards and a peeling upright piano that's irrevocably out of tune.

After the close confines of the commune, our rooms are the ultimate in luxury. There's space; there's actually room to move around. We've an enormous bedroom with a four-poster bed, a dressing room and a gigantic bath. Esther and Morris's suite adjoins ours, and we share a common terrace that overlooks the distant hills. Rock-beds, thick with flowers, dot the grounds and everywhere, potted and hanging, are begonias of a variety and profusion I've never seen before. And orchids. Carried by the winds from one moss-laden branch to another, they are everywhere I look, their leggy roots entwined around the tall and willowy trees.

The rest, the crisp air, the good food, and just being able to be together without the pressures of life in the commune, is an incredible gift for both of us. We're meeting each other again, finding new places, new spaces. And with Esther and Morris, we're becoming very close friends.

At tea-time one afternoon, I find myself writing a letter to my stepmother and another to my half-brother. On the tray, wedged between the white tea-cozy and the screen protecting the plate of meringues from the flies, is a letter from Leela. Included with it is a telegram from my brother telling me my father is dead.

Vasumati and her parents are concerned for me, but there's no need—I feel surprisingly untouched by the news of my father's death. He and I died to each other long ago.

"Come on, lovie," Vasumati says after a bit. "Just come for a walk with me. I want you to talk to me about your father." She lays a warm sweater across my shoulders and guides me towards the door. "In all this time together you've hardly mentioned him. Come on."

She leads me to a flat rock on the side of a nearby hill, sits me down and wraps her arms around me. "Talk," she orders.

"Vasumati, there's nothing to say. We weren't even close."

"Talk!"

"But about what?"

"Just talk to me about him. I know you: it's affected you. I want you to let this out. Anger, bitterness, love, whatever—just let it out!"

It's Vasumati the group leader, but maybe she's right. "Actually," I begin, "there wasn't much of a relationship between us for me to mourn. I think he used to wonder how he ever fathered a child like me—we were so different."

"Even as a child?"

"I was told we were close when I was a baby. Poor man, it must have been hard for him. He and my mother had only been married two years when I was born and two months later, she was dead. He was twenty-seven; she was twenty-four. And there was this two-month-old son." Talking about it, I'm beginning to see Vasumati's wisdom. I'd thought I'd purged it all long ago, but there's still emotion around it all.

"Just keep talking."

"Well, on her death-bed, my mother apparently said to her sister Isabel, 'Take care of my baby,' and, afterwards I gather, there was a kind of conflict between her and my father—over me. I don't know whether it was out of love for me or out of that terrible sense of duty that plagued him all his life, but he married her. When I was about eight she got pregnant and went into the hospital to give birth. I remember my father coming to my grandmother's house where they parked me while Isabel was in hospital to tell me that both she and the baby had died. He sat on the edge of my bed and cried. I cried too, but I didn't really understand. And, a few days later something happened that gave me nightmares until I was twenty."

"What?"

"In the afternoon this great-aunt of mine came and dressed me up. She told me we were going to see Isabel. I was really excited. We went to my other grandmother's house and I remember running in to find her lying in this box in the middle of the front parlor. I was only a kid; I thought she was asleep. I went over and touched her." I shudder at the memory. "Have you ever touched an embalmed corpse?" I ask.

"No," she answers softly, taking my hand in hers. "No, I haven't."

"It's quite something, Vasumati. Quite something indeed. Anyway, after that, my father redid our house and my grandparents—my two mothers' parents—moved in. The house was full of laughter for the first time. They were each other's best friends. But when I was about nine, my father started bringing this other lady around. And then they got married. My grandparents left. I asked my father if I could go with them, but he wouldn't have it."

"And how was your new stepmother?"

"Nice, really. For a long time I resented her and wanted her to go away, but she was patient and understanding with me and we eventually became friends. I never thought of her as my mother, but I liked her."

"And how was she with your father?"

"She thought the sun rose and set on him. And then my half-brother was born and for the first time, after all that trying, he had a complete family unit.

"But with him and me it got progressively worse. He was good to me, materially, always buying me things, but he couldn't give of himself. And he was incredibly strict. He had this rigid code he lived by, and whenever I broke it, he punished me."

"Physically?"

"At times, but when he did I usually deserved it. And it wasn't any big deal: I was always a tough little fucker. The hardest thing for me was his insistence that I had to do all the things he hadn't been able to in his life. The fact that none of them interested me was irrelevant. He seemed to look on me as a possession, like a car he'd bought and paid for and expected a certain performance from. This went on until I was fourteen."

"What happened then?"

"I was in high school, and one Friday night there was this party I wanted to go to. I told my father I'd probably be home late. 'You'll be home at nine o'clock,' he said. I tried to reason with him, but he wouldn't listen—he just went into the living room and sat down with a newspaper. I followed him, trying to get through, but it was as if I didn't exist.

"Finally, after sitting there talking at this newspaper, I got angry. You know the kind of anger that turns to white heat and then this amazing clarity follows?" She nods. "Well, I stood up, walked across the room and shredded the newspaper down the centre. The look on his face was quite something, as he sat there looking at me with amazement and a strip of newspaper in each hand. I said, 'I'm going out and I'll be back when I'm back!'

"'You're not leaving this house!' he yelled. I couldn't believe it: he threw himself across the front door like an Italian housewife. Somehow I knew we'd come to a crunch, and that if I didn't stand up for myself and take my freedom now, I'd never get it, I'd always be his possession. My coolness and detachment quite surprised me. I walked out into the kitchen and found one of his hunting knives. I came back and held it to his throat.

"Whenever we fought it always ended up with him driving me to the local jail and parking in front. 'You either go in there,' he would say, 'or you come home and obey me.'

"Standing there at the front door, with his hunting knife in my hand, and knowing full well I could never hurt him physically, I called his bluff. 'This prison or another prison,' I said. 'A prison is a prison; get out of my way or I'll shove this knife into your throat.'"

"Krishna!" Vasumati clutches her own throat in disbelief. "You?"

"It was a terrible way to have to take my freedom, I know. But I'd had years of him; it was enough. Anyway, for the first time in my life, he looked at me, directly into my eyes. For the longest while, it seemed, he just stood there and looked at me. And the bluff worked. He had never seen me so angry or so determined. And he stepped aside. There were no more problems after that. Actually, I think from then on, he was frightened of me."

"And how was it afterwards?"

"In a way, the game continued. But I wasn't a mindless pawn any more. I let him push me into university, but when I decided to drop out he was surprisingly understanding. And when I did well in work, he was proud of me—although he could never tell me directly; it was always via my stepmother. But when I dropped my company and split from Montreal, he just couldn't compute it. I think he just gave up on me. And my being with Osho was totally beyond his comprehension."

"Did you see him after you took sannyas?"

"Once. I went there for a weekend. As I walked in the door I heard him mutter 'Beads' under his breath and my stepmother shushed him—and that was that. Here I was in red, with a beard and the mala, back after a year and a half in India—and it was as if none of it existed. I talked to him on the phone a couple of times afterwards, but I never saw him again."

I stand. It's enough. I've never known the father-son relationship—and I never will. I mourned it throughout my entire childhood. I would have loved for us to have been friends, but it wasn't possible.

It's over. There's no bitterness, nothing. There's just a gratitude that, somehow, what happened between us helped push me towards Osho. And there's a wish for him. I hope that one day, in some life, a Master will find him and help him realize his reality and fulfill his potential as well. He wasn't a bad man, my father. Like us all, he was a product of his conditioning. But unlike me, he was too locked into that conditioning by fear to even wonder if, perhaps, there might be another, better way.

An Attack on Osho

The next evening, at dinner, I notice an Indian man at one of the tables. There's something familiar about him, but I can't place the face. I shrug it off, figuring he's probably a Bombay reporter I've met at some point.

We're on the fifth course, the dry crackers and the bland buffalo-milk cheese, when I hear a "May I join you?" at my elbow. It's him. "My name," he says, offering his hand, "is Vimal Anand*."

The penny drops. As I introduce, his history comes back to me. He's one of India's biggest film directors and, for a long time, had been a sannyasin. Then, suddenly, he dropped sannyas and turned vindictively negative, filling the papers and movie magazines with anti-Osho interviews.

For a while the conversation is primarily about cinema. But, listening to Vimal's urbane, witty chatter, I sense an undercurrent of something else, of something to do with Osho. I know he hasn't invited himself to join us because we're all so cute. And there isn't long to wait. "You have an old mala," he observes at last. "How long have you been with Osho?"

"Since late seventy-three."

He flashes me a cross between a smile and a sneer. "That's rather a long time to remain with a fake guru," he says. From Esther and Morris comes a joint gasp.

"And who are *you* to judge?" I ask coolly, not at all perturbed. Actually, I have a feeling I'm going to enjoy this.

For the next half hour, the four of us sit and listen to him rant against Osho. His voice gets louder and louder, to the point where the entire dining room is focused on our table. His gripe is that he surrendered totally to Osho for five years and didn't get enlightened; therefore, Osho's a fake. Vasumati and I start to laugh—it's as if he's talking about a business deal. Again and again he declares that Osho no longer matters in his life. But it's obvious that there's still lots of energy for Osho. Finally, we've had enough of this and Vasumati and I excuse ourselves. He can discuss with Esther and Morris or keep bad-rapping Osho. It's suddenly immaterial to me.

"Krishna Prem!" someone calls from Jesus House garden below a couple of days after we've returned to Pune. Poking my head out I see one of the gardeners, standing at the bottom of the stairs. "I went to the Hindi discourse this morning," he shouts up with a grin. "I don't know what he was saying, but I kept hearing: Krishna Prem, Vasumati, Mahabaleshwar. He said it again and again."

I know what Osho was talking about. When we returned from Mahabaleshwar I told Vinod, our sannyasin film star, about the meeting with Vimal Anand. They'd been good buddies at one time. And, at Vinod's insistence, I sent the story in to Osho. At lunch, Keerti, one of the Indian editors, hands me a translation.

"Only yesterday I received a letter from Krishna Prem," Osho said. "Krishna Prem had been to Mahabaleshwar for a week; there he happened to see Vimal Anand in a hotel. Vimal Anand told Krishna Prem that he had broken away from me completely, that he had no relationship with me any more, but he talked about me alone for two full hours. Then Krishna Prem said, 'What kind of separation is this? You did not talk so much about him when you were with him; now you talk much more. And yet you say that you have severed all your connections with him!'"

I laugh. I love how Osho dramatizes things to make a point. "This thing is a little beyond understanding," I read on. "The pendulum of the clock has swung from one extreme to the other.

"In the course of his talk, Vimal Anand said that for five years he lived with me, totally surrendered—he had surrendered his all—yet he did not attain enlightenment. That is why he left me and, also, dropped sannyas.

"It is something worth considering: how can a person retreat after making a *total* surrender? He must have withheld something—some space to withdraw. He must have saved a portion of the bridge; he did not destroy his whole bridge with the world, so that he might retreat at some stage. This sort of surrender cannot be total. It cannot be total, because withdrawal is not possible after total surrender. How can one withdraw? Because there remains no one to withdraw. How can one return after being drowned in the ocean completely?

"Secondly, this surrender was not total if there was a desire, a longing to attain enlightenment through it. If there was a calculation on his part that if, even after five years of surrender, he did not have enlightenment, then the surrender was not total at all. As if five years were a long time!

"The truth is that the desire for enlightenment is in itself a great impediment on the way to enlightenment. Every desire is an impediment, desire to attain anything is greed; it is ego. What can I do? What can anyone do? You have to attain, but if the poison of desire is there in you, you cannot attain enlightenment. It can be attained in a moment—but surrender has to be absolute, total.

"And two things are essential to surrender. One, that it should be without a cause, a motive. If there is a motive, then there is no surrender. There must not be any desire, any greed, any motive attached to your surrender...

"Love is without cause, without motive. And surrender is nothing but fulfilment of love. It must be without cause. If there is a cause to it, it is no surrender; it is mere deception. It is deceiving oneself, and none else.

"And the desire for enlightenment is an ego-trip. Enlightenment is not an achievement: it is a gift. He alone receives this gift who surrenders silently, unconditionally. He alone attains who surrenders himself completely, totally...

"Vimal Anand's greedy mind could not understand this thing. He tried to convince them that they must care for enlightenment, that it is most essential to attain it.

"It has been a deep longing with the Indians. People renounce wealth and power, but they strive to find God and enlightenment. The striving remains: only its objects change. But it is the same desire, the same greed, the same ambition; it does not make any difference.

"Vimal Anand could not understand when Krishna Prem and Vasumati laughed and said they were blissful and did not bother about enlightenment. They also said that their sannyas was without a purpose.

"When sannyas is without a purpose, then alone one's surrender is total. Then there is no way to retreat. When there is no desire, failure is not possible. If you do not seek, the question of defeat does not arise.

"Surrender is this way... I am worried about the Indian mind. Even when it takes to sannyas, it clings to the same old desire for freedom and enlightenment. The Indian mind is too much greedy. It is obsessed with the desire for heaven. This greed of his has spoiled his life in this world and is going to spoil his other world also. It is much better to have greed for this world—you may achieve something concrete here."[25]

25. From the Hindi series *Peevat Ramras Lagi Khumari*, as yet not translated into English

"Then he went on to something else," Keerti said. "But he really got the Indians this morning," he laughed. "Telling them that two Westerners knew about surrender and we didn't. It was a good slap for the Indian ego. You know how superior we think we are in matters of religion!"

"God," Vasumati laughs when I show her the translation that evening. "Are we *that* surrendered?"

"Maybe we are. All I know is that I'm with Osho for the whole ride, that I passed the point of no return a long time ago. And he's right about the desire for enlightenment too. It's not something I ever think about any more. It's like I'm on a train going to Delhi. I know we're going to get there; I'm just enjoying the ride."

Writing

With the major part of my day spent writing, my mood has improved a hundredfold. Perched above the garden in my pine-sheltered aerie, I tap away, hour after hour, reliving Bombay, Lonavla, Mount Abu, Kailash, the early years with Osho. I'm even enjoying the time in the office with Leela. To my surprise, my mind is hardly involved at all. There's a deep silence inside, and the words seem to pop forth, almost audibly, from the centre of my chest. All I have to do is put them onto the page. I love the feeling: it's rich and tremendously rewarding.

More and more, I begin to sense Osho's presence. Laxmi's told me he said he wanted this book done, and it's as if he's here with me, in my room. The day it hits me is the morning I suddenly realize I've given no thought whatsoever to the structure of the book. I've never written anything but PR stuff, I have no novelist's craft, yet it's happening. And *I notice* the structure's there, available to me, like a presence in the atmosphere—and all I have to do is plug in. It's him. My mind tells me I'm nuts, but my heart knows it's him.

And it seems to be progressing well. Evenings, I give what I've written to Vasumati, the toughest critic I know. She lies on Divy's bed, reading, murmuring little cooing sounds of approval as she goes through the pages.

We're very fine together these days, her and me. There's not much sex energy, but the heart connection is exquisite. We lie together more than romp, basking in each other's glow—hers from darshan, mine from the silence out of which the book is growing.

The Tiresome Spectre of 'Other Men'

Vasumati and I were lying in bed one night when, in the middle of the conversation, I heard those two terrible words: "other men". It had been a casual reference, without any substance or intent implied, but it had set me spinning. "Look," I said, "I know there's nothing going on with you and anyone else, but I'm so sick and tired of freaking out every time I hear those two words that I'm just going to go into it and see if I can burn it out."

For the next day or so, I fried. Every time I saw her with another man, I imagined them in bed and watched what surfaced in me. And I began to see it wasn't so much a question of jealousy or possessiveness, but rather an old fear of abandonment that went all the way back to my mother's death.

Waking the next morning, the first thing I do is write a question to Osho, taking it immediately to Krishna House and dropping it into the question box. On the way back to my room, I find myself wondering what that was all about. And I know he's going to answer it. It's as if he's got something he wants to say about this whole thing—and he's going to do it through me.

Sure enough, in the very next discourse, I hear my name. "Krishna Prem has asked me," he says. "Osho, I look around and I don't see any ecstatic men, including me, but I see ecstatic women. Why is it so difficult for men to let themselves go?"

Many heads turn in my direction, including Vasumati's. She looks surprised; I hadn't mentioned writing the question. But how could I? I didn't feel as if it were my question at all.

"It is simple," Osho begins. "All the religions have been created by men; there is not a single religion which has been created by women. And why did men create all these religions? And all these religions have been repressive—repressive particularly because of sex.

"A few things have to be understood," he says. "Man is afraid deep down of sex, because as far as sex is concerned he is far weaker than the woman. The woman is capable of having *multiple* orgasms; man is not capable of that.

"Hence all the societies, particularly the so-called civilized societies, have destroyed the very possibility of women knowing—even *knowing*—that they are orgasmic. It is only just within these last twenty, thirty years that it has been discovered that the woman not only has the orgasmic capacity, she also has the capacity of multiple orgasms. But man must have known from the very beginning that no single man can satisfy a woman if she has the multiple-orgasmic capacity. Man can only have one orgasm; with one orgasm he is finished. And the woman is still on the way, may not even have started!" Buddha Hall is in an uproar of laughter, but I discern a notable absence of male hilarity.

"The second trouble is: she is slow, and she is slow for a basic reason. Her sexuality is not local; her sexuality is total. Her whole body has a sexual quality. Man's sexuality is local, it is genital; woman's sexuality is not local, it is not focused: it is diffused; it is all over her body. So unless she can go into a sexual dance while making love she will not be able to have an orgasm. But if she goes into a sexual dance while making love—shrieks, screams, sings, shouts, says 'Alleluia!'—the man will become so much afraid. Because whatsoever she will be saying will be gibberish; it will not make any sense. It will be sensuous but not sensible! She will be speaking a divine language; it will be just coming." At this, there are peals of high-pitched laughter—but not a basso to be heard.

"Even *she* will be surprised what is coming up," he continues. "What is she saying? And why? For what? It has nothing to do with expressing any particular thing: she is just so excited, ecstatic. Her whole being is in a dance; she is in a temporary state of madness. And this can freak out the man—the poor fellow may even forget about his own orgasm! He may become concerned about the neighbours and the police and the fire brigade and whatnot!" God, he's so bang on! I remember nights feeling just exactly that. Vasumati had made so much noise I *had* been freaked out, expecting the guards at any second.

"Krishna Prem," he says, "in my community, in my commune, it is going to be difficult for men..." As if it isn't already! "The women will be ecstatic because for the first time they have a chance to be as orgasmic as possible, and men are going to be constantly afraid. And you can see them: always walking, tail between their legs, afraid, watching here and there. Any woman can jump and catch hold of them. Where are you going, Krishna Prem?" he shouts above the laughter.

And then he calls my name again, loudly, quieting Buddha Hall. "Krishna Prem, you can be ecstatic only if you forget about sex." From Vasumati, a "No!" escapes, her arms suddenly encircling me. "I am the only ecstatic man around here!" he says. "If you remain sexual, you cannot be ecstatic; you will be continuously drained out, walking dead, dull. You can be ecstatic only if you go beyond sex. The old way was: repress the woman. That is ugly. Why repress the woman? That is not right; that is not human. Let the woman be expressive, but if you feel that sex is a drain on you, a drag on you—and soon one feels it—then you go beyond it. But don't be repressive, just transcend. Transcendence comes by itself, slowly, slowly. It takes a little time to understand, to see the point.

"Women will also get tired, but they will take a little longer time. They are slow; they are not so efficient, so quick. First men will transcend, and the women will go on helping men to transcend, because new men will be coming and they have to help them. When they have helped many then they will start thinking, 'How long am I going to help others? It is time I should be enlightened myself!'

"In my commune this is going to be the way: men can be ecstatic only when they have transcended sex; women will have a far better time. They will be ecstatic while they are in sex and they will be ecstatic when they have transcended sex. My commune is going to be matriarchal. And you can see it: the whole show is run by women! I trust women more because they are going to be ecstatic *all* the way. Man will be ecstatic only at the very end of the journey; he can be trusted only after that. Women can be trusted. I trust *ecstasy!* I trust blissfulness!

"And why did man start this repressive business?" he asks. "First it was to save his ego; second, it was to keep control and possession of the woman, to reduce the woman to property. And then he has the great intellectuality. The women are emotional, they are heart people; men are head people. They are intellectual, so they rationalize their repressiveness. They made much fuss about repression; they started making so much noise that they even made women feel guilty—that something is wrong if they are happy in their sexual life. In fact, happiness itself became a sin. To remain sad and serious becomes a necessary condition for being respectable, for being known as a saint and a sage."

He leans towards the microphone, laughing. "Enough for today?"[26]

It sure is enough, Osho. It's more than enough. Most of my male friends would like to throttle me—all of our egos have had a pretty good deflating this morning. I wish I'd never sent in the question. I wish I'd just torn it up.

Being a Darshan Medium Finishes for Vasumati

Of late, after darshan, Vasumati's been taking a little time for herself, but tonight, moments after it's over, she's in my room. Something's going on: she's still wearing her medium-dress and cape. She lies on Divy's bed, staring abstractedly out the window. "It's finished, you know," she says quietly.

"What is?" I ask with a surge of instant panic.

Her voice is flat, emotionless: "Darshan."

"What are you talking about?"

In the half-light she turns towards me. "I don't know, Krishna, but I do know." She pauses, gathering herself together with an apparent effort. "You know how Osho's been adding mediums in darshan, trying out new women? Well, there was a new one tonight. And the

26. *The Wild Geese and the Water*

moment I saw her I knew she would replace me. It's finished. I know it's finished."

For two and a half years she's been a medium, beside Osho every night, and I've long since learned to bow to her hunches. I take her in my arms; there's nothing I can say.

The next day I'm getting ready to shower before lunch when I hear her familiar step on the stairs. There are tears streaming down her cheeks. It's happened; I can tell. "There was a message for me to see Vivek," she sobs, "but she was really beautiful with me. Really straight. She said, 'He says it will be good if you don't come to darshan every night any more.'" The memory pains. "I asked her if there was anything wrong. She said no, just something about needing space to train new mediums."

I leave her pretty much to herself over the next few days. She needs time to absorb what's happened between her and her Master.

A couple of days later Vasumati comes rushing to my room with the news she's going on a six-week tour of Europe—London, Hamburg, Munich, Zurich, the south of France. She's to leave mid-July. "All sorts of group leaders are going," she says excitedly. "And there's a big event in London this month. It's changing, Krishna," she grins. "We seem to be moving out into the world. And I love it. I'm going to miss you, but it's only six weeks. I love the idea of something new, of a challenge, of being able to do my own thing for a while." She searches my face. "You don't mind, do you?"

"Not at all, sweetheart," I assure her. "I'm happy for you. You'll have a great time—and six weeks ain't forever." I haul her onto the bed. "Come on, let's enjoy the time we have left."

"Krishna!" she laughs, resisting. "It's almost four months away!"

"Doesn't matter! It'll be here before you know it."

But she's already somewhere else. She's not in London or Hamburg or Munich, but down MG Road with Ramul, her toothless tailor. "Let's see," she mutters as I try to kiss her. "London's grey and cloudy in July, so I'm going to need a few warm things. I've never been to Germany in the summer." She suddenly laughs and, cooing female apologies into my ear, we get into what I've been wanting ever since she came with the news.

My Back Goes Out

Now that Vasumati's not in darshan, now that Osho's not thumbing her third eye every night and pulling her energy upwards, we begin to make love a lot again. It's like it was in the beginning—playful, joyous, full of laughter. It's better than ever between us. We find ourselves moving to depths we've never known before.

Making love the night before the Enlightenment Day celebration I find myself disappearing, dissolving, when all at once I'm snapped back to reality—I remember she's fertile. The sudden realization panics me, tenses me, but I ignore the tiny pain in the small of my back.

The next morning I head for the office, ready to deal with the journalists attending the celebration, but when I sit down with Leela to chat about the day, my back is really hurting and I'm feeling nauseous. "I've got to lie down for a bit," I say.

By the time I'm back in my room I know the celebration's going to happen without me. The pain is excruciating. I don't know what has happened to my body, but I'm in agony. I can't manoeuvre the stairs; I don't know what to do. I lie, hurting, hoping someone will come.

"Krishna!" I hear Vasumati calling from below. "I saw Leela," she says as she mounts the steps. "What's going on?" Reaching the doorway she sees something's wrong at a glance. "You were fine this morning. What's happened?"

"I don't know," I reply through gritted teeth. "It's in my back. Can you get someone? I've never felt pain like this in my life."

Moments later she's back with one of the bodyworkers. He tries a few manipulations, but nothing works. Later that day another bodyworker tries, and the next morning, one of the doctors from the health centre, but there's no relief. That evening I look up to see a familiar shock of carrot-red hair. It's Vishnu, the Scottish osteopath. "Arup heard you'd hurt your back," he says. "She asked me to come and have a look."

"Have I thrown my pelvis out again, like at Kailash?" I ask after his examination.

"Nope. You've slipped a lumbar disc." He positions me for a manipulation. "Let's put it back." There's a loud click. And the disc is in. "Now," he says, "for the next week you stay in bed, flat on your back, with a folded towel under you for support. Get someone to bring your food and only use the stairs for the bathroom. I'll look in on you in a day or so."

"How long will this take to heal?"

"Six to eight weeks."

"Six to eight weeks!" I can't believe my ears. "It's like a death sentence!"

"And you'd better tell Vasumati not to expect any love-making from you for a while," he adds with a wink.

"For six to eight weeks?"

"No," he grins, "not that long. But nothing for a week or so. And when you do make love," he says, "do it gently. Otherwise, you'll throw it out again."

When Vasumati finally comes I can tell she's upset with me. I know the look. "Out with it," I say.

"Have you done this to yourself?" she asks, not mincing words.

"What do you mean?"

"You know exactly what I mean," she says. "The night before this happened was the most incredible love-making we've ever had. Have you done this to yourself?"

"I don't know, Vasumati," I say. "If I have done this to myself—to avoid the edge, to avoid disappearing—then it's at such an unconscious level I'm not in touch with it at all."

Cunning Sheela Mounts a Coup d'Etat

After so many years, it's almost impossible to believe. He warned us for years, but my mind can hardly absorb that the day has come.

Leela appears in my room to tell me Sheela has called a meeting of all department heads. Although there is no reason to, I feel odd. But, still, I never expected this.

Sheela delivers the bomb directly: "Osho is going into semi-retirement. He says that now we are ready, and now he is entering the final and ultimate phase of his work. Beginning May first, he will come out intermittently—not every day; just when he feels to—and sit with us in silence. He's not going to speak any more.

"And he's not going to give darshan any more either," she adds. "Swami Anand Teertha will give sannyas, blessings and energy darshans to Westerners, and Ma Yoga Laxmi will do the same for Indians. I'll be in charge of the commune."

Walking back to my room I find myself recalling the ten days of sitting in silence with Osho the year before. So much had ended of late—my involvement in the press office, my daily visits with Laxmi, Vasumati's being a medium. And so much has begun too—my book, Vasumati's European tour, new vistas in our relationship. And now this—my Master's final and ultimate phase. I feel no nostalgia. I'm not too thrilled with the idea of Sheela running things: I don't trust that woman for a second. She's addicted to power and will do anything to get it.

And when I run into my old friend Pratima, what she tells me makes me angry. She tells me how, in Laxmi's absence, Sheela managed to usurp the reins of power for herself.

"She was very cunning," the Old Lady explains. "I've found out she told Osho that the sannyasins were very unhappy with the way Laxmi was running things, and that many of the department heads felt that she—Sheela—was more modern, more in touch with the world and would do a better job."

"You're kidding," I say. I found the level of betrayal hard to imagine, let alone swallow.

"Apparently he told her to bring him letters from the department heads to support her statement. And that she did. She went to all her friends that run departments and got them to write letters. But you'll notice she didn't approach department heads like you or me, people she knows love Laxmi and would be loyal to her.

"I've heard that when he read the letters he said 'Okay' and told Sheela she could take over Laxmi's job."

I'm shocked and saddened by what I've heard. And it would have been nice had Sheela been courageous enough to tell us the truth. "Not a good omen," I mutter to myself, "for a new beginning."

Back in the Hospital

As well as walking daily on uneven ground, Vishnu also told me I should swim. I couldn't afford the monthly membership at the Blue Diamond pool, so, one afternoon, despite the fact it's at the other end of Pune and involves a rickshaw ride, I agree to give Swimquip a try. The pool is hideous. It's a raised tank, crawling with Indian families, and there's so much chlorine in the black water it's like jumping into a vat of disinfectant. I know I'll never go there again. Miraculously, a friend who's renting a house with a pool offers me its use whenever I need it.

That evening, bored with eating from a metal tiffin in my room, I decide my back is well enough to join Vasumati and the rest of the commune at dinner in Mariam canteen. Halfway through the meal my back begins to hurt but I ignore it: I'm sick of being an invalid. But the next day I wish I'd listened to my body. I'm back in the ward, the disc out again, still shaking from the torture of a ten-minute epidural injection straight up the spine.

The following week is the absolute pits. Vasumati is fine. She's loving, caring, supportive—and surprisingly patient. But I'm in hell. It's a week of massage and traction, of manipulations and injections—and utter rage and frustration with existence. Trapped. I feel totally, inescapably trapped—in this mound of flesh that refuses to remain healthy, that, after all these years in India, just seems to be falling apart. But no matter how I rail at life, nothing changes. At last the anger and the tears subside. All I can do is cooperate with the doctors and wait to heal.

Suddenly I hear someone call my name. It's one of the nurses. "I have a message for you from Osho," she says. "He sent you a tape recorder and a microphone. He says that while you can't sit at your typewriter, you should tape your book."

Whether the grin on my face means anything to her or not, I can't tell. My smile is an outward manifestation of what's happening in my heart.

At eighty-two, James Cyriax is still built like a bull. And the resemblance to Alfred Hitchcock is uncanny—the same veined, bulbous nose and tiny piercing eyes, the same big belly and jiggly jowls. "The expert," one of the physiotherapists tells me as she massages my back. "He's written volumes on traction and manipulations. And he developed the epidural injection." My body tightens at the memory: I'm not so sure I want him to touch me after all. But the doctors aren't certain my disc is totally in place, and while Cyriax is in Pune to treat Osho's back he's agreed to look at me and a few others.

His arrival at the commune had come as a surprise. Until then, the gravity of Osho's condition hadn't quite registered. We'd heard that a couple of our own bodyworkers had been called in to try to unpinch the sciatic nerve troubling him and that they'd been unsuccessful. But a top specialist from London! None of us had any idea things were that bad.

By the end of the second day and the eighth manipulation, my compassion for my Master is unbounded. I've been tossed and turned, crunched and cracked, ground through a wringer. But the disc is in. I'd heard it snap back into place. I can't imagine *anyone,* not even the world's best, doing this to Osho. His body's too fragile, too frail. But whatever transpired between him and Cyriax remains undiscussed and unrevealed. We're all going to have to wait until May first to see.

The New York State Thruway Revisited

May first. Satsang. High and sweet, resonating like the quivering strings of a sitar, I hear the song of Taru from Buddha Hall. Buddham Sharanam Gachchhami, she chants. Even in English, the words of our new litany are deeply moving: "I go to the feet of the Awakened One." And then, resounding throughout the commune, comes the response—Buddham Sharanam Gachchhami—thousands of voices lifting, ringing, and then, softly, falling into stillness as heads bow low to touch the floor in surrender to our own buddha.

Sangham Sharanam Gachchhami: "I go to the feet of the commune of the Awakened One."

Dhammam Sharanam Gachchhami: "I go to the feet of the ultimate truth of the Awakened One."

At first, lying in my room, I want desperately to be there, to be in the auditorium, in my Master's presence, with the rest of the community. But I still can't sit. I'm up to sitting ten painful minutes three times a day, and a cross-legged hour in Buddha Hall is out of the question. Everyone has been waiting for the satsangs to begin for so long I knew they'd be crowded, and I wrote Osho, saying I would have to lie down. I hated the idea of dragging cushions with me, but I hadn't wanted to miss him either. "Stay in your room and feel the energy within," he replied.

And it's exquisite. Faintly, in the distance, I can hear the sounds of muted music and readings from *The Prophet,* but my attention is, as Osho had suggested, on the energy within. Everything falls silent inside, and then, out of the silence, bliss begins to bubble, building bit by bit until, at last, every cell explodes into orgasm—and my arms, vibrating in delight, lift in supplication and invitation. As a woman opens to receive her lover, my heart, my body, my energy is suddenly available to existence, to God. I feel his breath on me. And we are intimates, him and me. Like a leaf dropping from a tree, I give myself to him—in trust, in surrender. Buddham Sharanam Gachchhami.

Everyone's skittish these days. There's a feeling of impermanency in the air, as if nothing can be taken for granted, as if our very world might disappear tomorrow. And the atmosphere at the satsangs is strange, Vasumati tells me. Everyone's tense, anxious, wondering if this could be the morning he simply doesn't come any more. "When we hear the car," she says, "there's this huge, communal sigh of relief."

Osho's health seems to be deteriorating rapidly. Whatever success James Cyriax had with me, he didn't have it with my Master. Vasumati and Divy bring home stories of his difficulty standing and sitting, of him bumping into his chair, of his needing help to get back to the car.

The next morning, while everyone else is in Buddha Hall with Osho, I lay on my bed as usual, floating on the music from Buddha

Hall. And then, abruptly, I was gone, disappearing once again into the pool of silence I first encountered on the New York State Thruway all those years before. My next awareness is of standing outside on the balcony of my room, overlooking Jesus House garden, laughter bubbling up from my belly. "This is *it*!" I hear my voice shouting. "This is it! I've been searching for lives and lives, and *this* is it!" Tears of laughter blurr my vision; everything looks different. There's a new aliveness everywhere—in the green of the trees and the grass, in the reds and yellows of the flowers. Everything is sharper, more vibrant, literally pulsing with the juices of life.

And the more I laugh, the more and more ridiculous looking for what is becomes. "How can I search for what's already here?" I hear myself ask. "How can I look for my self when I already am?" Then, just as suddenly, I am back on the bed. But the man who lay here now is different from the one who sprung to his feet and cried and laughed in relief and wonder out there on the balcony.

When I tell Vasumati, she insists I write to Osho. But I don't want to bother him—and with what? Everything is fine. I've had another glimpse of the silence at my core and that's more than enough.

"I feel good, I feel happy, I'm getting healthier," I tell her. "And things are good with you. And I feel as if I've found what I've been looking for all these years—and the most ridiculous thing is that it's always been there, right in front of my nose."

"And do you still have that sense that something new is coming for you?"

"I don't know. Whatever's on the way is on the way. And something tells me I don't have to wait very long."

It comes that afternoon.

Just before tea I look up from my taping to see my friend and group leader Prasad standing in the doorway; behind him, crowded onto the tiny balcony, are three men and a woman. I've never seen any of them before. "May we come in?" Prasad asks. "We'd like to talk to you about something."

He introduces Indivar, centre leader of the Satprakash centre in Sydney. The other men are Viren, Indivar's assistant, and Lionel, his financial backer. The lady is Garimo, a former Canberra journalist. They're planning a major festival in Sydney in September, Prasad tells me, at the Opera House, "like the March Event in London". They want my ideas on publicity.

The next thing I know I've been invited to handle the publicity myself, it's been cleared with the office, and I've agreed to fly to Sydney with Prasad on the twenty-second of July.

"My schedule's just been confirmed," Vasumati says when she brings me dinner. "I leave Pune on the twelfth."

"That's only ten days before me."

She hasn't a clue what I'm talking about. "What do you mean? Where are *you* going?"

"To Sydney."

"Australia?"

"Australia. For the event at the new Opera House."

"Oh, Krishna!" she squeals. "I'm *so* glad! I hated the idea of leaving you here. And when we're back, we can lie around and tell each other stories."

"Laxmi wants you!" I can hardly believe my ears. It's been so long since I've heard that familiar summons—she's been in Delhi for the past four months. I rush to the office, but by the time I arrive she's preparing to see Osho. "Come tomorrow, swamiji," she says. "Laxmi has much to tell you."

The next afternoon I decide to go for my swim before seeing her. I paddle around the pool for a while when, all of a sudden, I have to get back to the commune as quickly as possible. Somewhere in the back of my mind old visions are trying to surface—old pictures from Bombay and Mount Abu and Kailash—as if they're being brought out for a final look, like snaps in an ancient, dusty album. Something's going on. I have to get back.

Vasumati's standing inside the gate, as if she's been waiting for me. Her eyes are wet with tears. "He's gone," she says softly, taking my hand. "They just drove him out the front gate. The word is he's being taken to America for medical treatment.

"It's over, Krishna," she cries. "Pune is finished."

Silently, I pull her to me. Somehow, at the pool, I already knew.

And it's fine. I remember that banner above his chair at the meditation camp in Mount Abu. "Surrender and I will transform you," it read.

I accepted his invitation, his challenge to surrender. And he kept his word. I'm a totally different man from the one who walked through the commune gate seven years ago. And this new man is ready for whatever life brings, for whatever adventure is next to unfold.

Epilogue: 2007

In order not to leave you, the reader, hanging in the unknown, I should add that most of us who lived in the Pune commune went off to America, to manifest and live out a dream Osho had—and I first encountered in one of those old Hindi translations I rewrote—to build a city that would show the world that people could live in love and harmony with each other. Like the Kailash experiment many years earlier, that's what it turned out to be: a dream. I watched Sheela build it and I watched Sheela destroy it out of a lust for power laced with paranoia and a vision of herself as a modern-day maharani of an empire in the high desert of Oregon. And it's something for which she still accepts no responsibility.

Out of love for Osho, an amazing city was created, but since he was in silence and essentially unavailable to us—we could write to him but few of us believed the letters made it past Sheela—it had no beating heart. Sheela ruled by fear and coercion, with a coterie of selfish, hard-hearted, power-hungry women enforcing a single rule: submit in silence or leave. The religious quality which permeated Pune was completely absent, and this was incredibly painful for me. But, like my friends Pratima, Divy and Vadan, I survived. It was a stunning lesson in how power corrupts, in the heights of psychosis to which a deluded and deranged ego can rise, and how, like night follows day, chickens always come home to roost. Sheela ended up in prison and now runs an old folks' home near Basel in Switzerland.

Enough said. I have neither the urge nor the interest to dwell any further on the Oregon experiment. Readers who are interested are directed to an excellent and informative book by Pulitzer Prize-winning American journalist Frances FitzGerald, *Cities on a Hill.* It is a truly amazing story of incredible accomplishment fueled by our collective love for this one remarkable man.

My relationship with Vasumati, by the way, also ended among the stunted trees and sage brush and mud pits of what, for me, was the ugliest landscape I had ever seen. Following a pregnancy while we were in California and her decision to abort, the relationship was beyond redemption. In Oregon, she chose the momentary thrills of casual sex over love and commitment, and with a mix of sadness at a lost potential and relief at freeing myself from a burden that wasn't mine, I stepped out of her life and let her go.

Divy and I are the closest of friends to this day.

There were a couple of relationships in the years that followed, but I never stopped looking for that special one. In January 1993, on a six-month sojourn in Pune, where Osho eventually returned and many of us visited for extended periods of time, and where, since his death in 1990, the commune has continued to thrive as an international meditation resort, I met her—"the one". Ma Dhyan Sourabh, the fragrance of meditation. After living in Switzerland, where she had been raised, for a year and a bit, we married and moved to Australia.

We're still here.

Fast Forward to Now

The real test of the totality of my surrender has now arrived. I am in the process of dying. And it's clear now to me that this surrender, this final let-go into the unknown is where what we call life has always been heading. If we look deeply into each moment of living, there is always a tiny surrender involved: letting the present moment go before diving into the new one existence is presenting. Looking back, from this vantage point, it seems that all of my life has been a preparation for this moment I am about to face.

Several years ago, a close friend, Yuthika, died of cancer. When I heard she was ill, and that the cancer was inoperable, I telephoned her.

At one point during the conversation I asked if she were afraid. "There's fear around managing the pain," she replied. "But the strangest thing is this underlying sense of excitement that I'm about to embark on the last great adventure." I now understand exactly what she meant. I, also, am excited.

Recently, I had a heart attack—after vacuuming the house. I soon found myself in an ambulance with Sourabh on the way to the nearest hospital and handed over to a loving and light-hearted emergency crew. As a nurse cut my sweat-soaked T-shirt from me with a pair of scissors—"I love doing this," she said—one of the male nurses read the ambulance report and announced to the room, "See, this is proof men aren't meant to vacuum!" Everyone laughed, me included—and this lightness somehow set the tone for everything else that has followed. I can't take any of what's happening that seriously. My situation is what it is. Dying is as ordinary as living. And surrender is the key.

It was in the hospital after the heart attack, and the subsequent installation of a stent, that cancer was discovered. There were metastases in the liver—thanks, in part I imagine, to the ameobas who regularly lodged themselves in my liver during the years in India—and in the lungs. I was also told there was a primary tumour somewhere else, but wherever it was the combination was incurable.

And so I said okay, it's obviously time to go, so let's do it with grace, gratitude and acceptance; in other words, in surrender. I said no to chemotherapy and other treatments that weren't going to make any difference and let Sourabh bring me home.

The first few days after deciding that surrender was the only intelligent course on offer, I found myself wondering if I really were as surrendered as I thought I was. I looked into all the nooks and corners as closely as I could and came to the conclusion that, yes, this surrender is total. I've had a good life, filled with love and laughter and with the gift of Osho and his wonderful people, and I could find nothing undone or incomplete. There just simply isn't any reason to hang around any longer.

I have been through—totally—relationships (with men *and* women, as one friend pointed out), as well as marriage, the husband-as-provider role, and satisfying work that allowed me to earn a good living through my creativity. There is no incomplete karma to work out. There's nothing I wanted to do that I haven't done. It became abundantly clear that, like "marriage", my life on this planet has also run its course and now all that remains is Yuthika's "last great adventure".

Recently, a friend wrote to me asking if, now that I'm about to vacate this body, this biodegradable vehicle with its hidden use-by date, if I have any advice about preparing for this moment that we're all going to face? Yes, I do, as a matter of fact. Not a lot, however. There are just four things.

Separation

First, if you give any credence whatsoever to the Christian lie of separation, deal with it and dispel it as quickly as you can. In my view, it is the biggest crime, among many, that the institution of Christianity has perpetrated on a fear-ridden mankind. It's the ugliest kind of politics disguised as religion.

Right now in the Blue Mountains outside Sydney where we live, it's autumn. The leaves are turning red and yellow and falling to the ground like snow. Whatever analogy works to give you a glimpse of the underlying oneness of existence, use it. When we speak of a "tree" we include everything—the trunk, the branches, the hundreds and thousands of individual leaves that form the tree's canopy. Each of us is a leaf on life's tree, a wave in life's ocean—whatever metaphor speaks to you. Each of us is an individual, unique leaf and, at the same time, inexorably bound together, an indispensable part of "tree".

I cannot conceive of anything more childish than the notion of a creator, of a fantasy father in a fantasy heaven. And the fact that billions of people buy this nonsense paints a frightening picture of the average level of intelligence and awareness of those who populate this world.

In whatever way you can find to deal with the lie of separation, I urge you to do so without delay. My friend Vadan rang from New York the other day, and at one point during the conversation he said, "I've never said this to you before, but I always felt that you and I are the same person."

I know what he meant. In Pune, one always knew what the other was thinking, or the view the other would have on a particular subject. We would laugh uproariously at the same silly things and a love beyond words flowed between us like a tributary connecting two powerful rivers. There were just no differences.

"And whenever Osho would talk about all of us being one, I understood," he added. "Because you and I are the same person." Whatever works.

Dispelling the childish nonsense that we are separate from existence creates a foundation for surrender. And, as Osho said many times and I have tried to communicate in this book, for a seeker surrender is the master key.

Surrender

If you can realize experientially that there is no separation between you and existence, that the illusion of separation only exists on the surface, then surrender becomes an act of intelligence. How can the part fight with the whole? It's a no-win scenario; it's a recipe for defeat.

I first discovered the power of surrender by accident, so to speak, in that car crash on the New York State Thruway almost forty years ago. When I realized there was no Great Hand going to descend from the sky and scoop me aloft to safety, I surrendered to the inevitable—and that surrender was an act of intelligence, of accepting the reality I faced. That simple act of surrender propelled me straight to my centre, to the pool of fecund silence out of which form arises and that is, in effect, the oneness that lies beyond the mind. You can feel it whenever you're doing something creative. Pay close attention, and you will feel the words or the music or the brush strokes arising out of the silence at your core.

When I say surrender is an act of intelligence, I'm also pointing towards the unintelligence—and inevitable defeat—of the part fighting with the whole. For example, imagine one spoke of a wheel wanting to go in one direction when the wheel is heading in another. Not possible, is it? It's simply intelligent to understand that the part cannot dictate to the whole, so why even bother trying? No one gets hurt but you.

This is the understanding contained in what Osho said to me in October of 1974: "If you let it, Krishna Prem, existence will take care of you in the same way it takes care of the birds and the trees and the flowers." Had he never said anything else to me in all the years that followed, this would have been sufficient teaching for a lifetime.

Let existence take care of you. Don't bring the mind into everything; don't think everything to death. Look around you and see that existence is beneficent. And practice surrender, letting-go, saying yes to life; however you envision it. Give your surrender muscle a good workout each and every day. Because where I am now is coming to everyone. And don't kid yourself by thinking that when the moment of death comes you'll be able to surrender so why worry about it now. Life doesn't work like that. Do you want to miss the culmination of your life in fear and fight and denial? There's a saying, "Death is the greatest orgasm of them all. That's why life saves it for the end."

Surrender is the master key to living a flowing life in tune with your inner world and the world around you. It's also the secret to dying, to releasing your consciousness, to letting your drop dissolve in the ocean of which it has always been a part. More metaphor, but what to do? Language is of the mind and the mind has limitations.

Clean Up Your Messes

What I'm talking about here is karma, about cleaning up past messes and learning not to create new messes as we go along.

There's an expression here in Australia, land of the boomerang: What goes around, comes around. And in that saying lies the essence of karma. The energy that drives existence travels in circles, and a circle begun is a circle begging for completion. Karma is a consequence of incomplete action. Paying the piper may be instantaneous; it may take lives—but you can be sure that whatever you put out will come back to revisit or to haunt you. It's also prudent to learn not to create new karma as you go along.

In this life, one of the major messes I had to clean up was with Divy, with a child I'd abandoned in an earlier incarnation in Spain. It took ten years and now the slate is totally clean. I learned something valuable from that—to make sure I complete everything I start, that every interaction with others is finished before I move on to the next. Now, as I face death, I can honestly say there isn't any karma to complete; there are no messes to clean up. There may well be people who have incomplete issues with me, but that has nothing to do with me. Your past karma and the karma you create as you live your life is your issue and yours alone. Blame is one of the biggest traps to avoid in dealing with karma. Blame is simply a childish avoidance of responsibility for one's own actions.

Totality

I remember at age fourteen lying in bed planning what I would do with my life once I got away from the confines of Campbellton, New Brunswick, and promising myself, "The day I die, I don't want to be able to say, 'Why didn't I ever…?'" That became a guiding principle of my life.

Now, as I prepare to vacate this body in which I've resided as a tenant for so many years, there is nothing I didn't do that I wanted to do, nowhere I didn't go that I wanted to go, nothing I didn't experience that I wanted to experience. I've had a full, rich and interesting life, filled with love and laughter and great adventure. I've taken risks—and sometimes, inadvertently, stepped on some toes—but I'm going with no regrets, with no feeling that there's anything I've missed. It feels good; life feels complete.

I trace it all back to that promise I made myself at age fourteen. And that's it. Those are my four things.

With love from me—however you knew me, as Jack Allanach or as Krishna Prem.

Glossary of Hindi Terms

Acharya	Teacher in religious matters
Ashram	Spiritual community headed by a religious leader or mystic
Barfi	Indian sweet made from condensed milk and sugar
Bas	Enough
Betel	Leaves of a vine used to wrap nuts; chewed as a stimulant and breath freshener
Bhajan	Devotional song
Bidi	Small hand-rolled cigarettes manufactured in India
Bodhisattva	Enlightened being
Brahmin	Class of educated Hindi scholars
Chai	Spiced milk tea
Chai lao	Bring tea
Chappati	Thin unleavened flatbread
Chikki	A traditional sweet made from groundnuts and jaggery
Chillum	Pipe
Chowks	A place where paths intersect
Darshan	Sanskrit word meaning "sight". One can "receive darshana" of the deity in the temple, or from a great saintly person, such as a guru.
Dhal	Indian lental dish
Dhamma	The Truth taught by the Buddha
Dhobi	Person doing laundry for households
Dhoti	Traditional loincloth worn by Hindu men
Dwij	Twice born
Ek	One

Feni	Liquor made in Goa from cashew apple
Ghat	Steps near a river where bodies are cremated
Gopis	Girls unconditionally devoted to Krishna
Gurkha	People from northern India of Mongolian origin, who were thought to be naturally warlike
Jaggery	Unrefined sugar
Jain	Follower of ancient religion in India prescribing a path of non-violence
Khadi	Hand-spun and hand-woven cloth
Karma	Eastern religious concept of law and effect
Kirtan	Chanting of hymns or mantras
Kohl	Traditional mascara worn by women in India and the Middle East
Kundalini	Here: Osho Meditation Technique
Ladoo	Indian sweet
Lakh	Unit number of 100,000
Lhassa Apso	Tibetan breed of dogs
Lingam	Male organ of generation (Phallus)
Lunghi	Wrap-around cloth worn as a skirt by men and women
Maharajah	Sanskrit for "great king"
Maharani	Wife of maharajah or woman ruling in her own right
Mala	String of prayer beads worn by disciples around the neck
Mandala	Here: Osho Meditation Technique
Maya	Illusion
Memsahib	Term of respect for a female white European in colonial India
Munis	Jain monks
Nadhabrahma	Osho Meditation Technique based on the Tibetan healing method of humming
Namaste	Respectful greeting, often with folded hands, acknowledging the other's inherent divinity
Nataraj	Osho Meditation Technique involving dance
Neem	Evergreen tree with medicinal properties
Paise	Indian coin

Paan	Betel leaf chewed with areca nut, as a palate cleanser and a breath freshener
Pakora	Fried savory snack
Panwallah	Seller of paan
Parsi	Member of the Zoroastrian community
Prasad	Gift of the divine. Food graced by god or a guru
Purdah	Muslim and Hindu practice of women covering their bodies and face
Ranns	Seasonally marshy, saline clay deserts located in Gujarat
Rupees	Indian currency
Sadhu	Hindu ascetic dedicated to liberation through meditation or yoga
Sahib	Term of respect for a white European in colonial India
Samosa	Fried pastry shell with savory filling
Sannyasin	Renunciate, seeker, saffron-robed monk, disciple of a guru
Satsang	Sitting in the presence of a Master, or in the presence of Truth
Shaktipat	Energy of a Master which may trigger energy in people, producing involuntary physical and emotional responses
Swami	One who devotes his time to the direct experience of spiritual realization
Suji	Indian semolina porridge
Sutra	A distinct type of literary composition
Tabla	Percussion instrument
Thali	A selection of different dishes
Tola	Unit of mass, approximately 11.4 grams
Tonga	A light horse-drawn two-wheeled vehicle
Tanka	Painted or embroidered Buddhist banner
Towers of Silence	Structure used by Zoroastrians for exposure of their dead
Tratak	Osho Meditation technique of gazing
Upanishads	Hindu scriptures constituting the core teachings of Vedanta
Vedanta	Philosophical tradition concerned with self-realization
Wallah	A person concerned or involved with a specified thing or business